Effectively Managing
Nonprofit Organizations

Edited by
Richard L. Edwards
John A. Yankey

NASW PRESS
National Association of Social Workers
Washington, DC

Elvira Craig de Silva, DSW, *President*
Elizabeth J. Clark, PhD, ACSW, MPH, *Executive Director*

Cheryl Y. Bradley, *Publisher*
Schandale Kornegay, *Publications Manager*
Marcia D. Roman, *Managing Editor, Books*
Crystal McDonald, *Marketing Manager*
DeQuendre Bertrand, *Project Manager*
Chris Davis, *Copyeditor*
Bernice Eisen, *Indexer*

Cover design by Debra Naylor, Naylor Design, Inc., Washington, DC
Interior design by Cynthia Stock, Electronic Quill, Silver Spring, MD

© 2006 by the NASW Press

Library of Congress Cataloging-in-Publication Data

Effectively managing nonprofit organizations / edited by Richard L. Edwards, John A. Yankey.
　　　p.　cm.
　"Revision and expansion of two earlier books, Skills for effective human services management (Edwards & Yankey, 1991) and Skills for effective management of nonprofit organizations (Edwards, Yankey & Altpeter, 1998)"—Introd.
　Includes bibliographical references and index.
　ISBN 0-87101-369-X
　1. Human services—Management. 2. Human services—United States—Management. 3. Nonprofit organizations—Management. 4. Nonprofit organizations—United States—Management. I. Edwards, Richard L. II. Yankey, John A. III. Skills for effective human services management. IV. Skills for effective management of nonprofit organizations.
　HV41.E344 2006
　658'.048—dc22

　　　　　　　　　　　　　　　　　　　　　　　　2006000671

Printed in the United States of America

We are delighted to dedicate this book to our grandchildren:
Tyler Edwards, Drew and Mattox Flatt,
and *Joshua, Matthew,* and *Alex Lakota*
and
Jennifer, Jordan, Jacob, Jillian,
Jaron, Jessica, and *Janelle Yankey.*

They bring so much joy to our lives.

We hope they and others of their generation grow to adulthood
in a world marked by civility, peace, and social justice.

R.L.E. and J.A.Y.

Contents

Contents

Acknowledgments

In every edited book project, many individuals contribute to the final product. We first thank the authors of the individual chapters. Their efforts were critical to making this book possible. We also thank individuals at NASW Press who have been involved in various editions of this book, in particular Cheryl Bradley, Schandale Kornegay, and DeQuendre Bertrand. Without their efforts overseeing the coordinating and editing processes, the book would not have been possible. Special thanks goes to Chris Davis, who was responsible for copyediting.

Others who deserve special thanks include Mark Litzler, who contributed the cartoons included in the book and Professors Robert Quinn and John Rohrbaugh, who originally conceived of the competing-values approach to organizational and leadership effectiveness, which serves as the organizing framework for this book. We also thank Ann Cham for her work in helping us get the manuscript in final form.

We want to thank our other mentors, academic colleagues, and leaders of nonprofit and business organizations who have taught us so many valuable lessons about managing effectively. For our managerial strengths and successes, we give them full credit; for our shortcomings, we take full responsibility. And, we especially thank the thousands of students who have provided us with unending opportunities to learn with and from them, opportunities for which we shall be eternally grateful.

—*R.L.E. and J.A.Y.*

Introduction

If there is one constant in nonprofit management today, it is the need to deal with change. Contributing to this environment are changing conditions, such as increased demands for services provided by nonprofits; evolving service technologies; and reduced government appropriations for human services, the arts, and the humanities. However, also contributing to this environment are developments in management in the for-profit arena.

In the early 1980s, traditional approaches to American management began to be questioned. The characteristics of successful businesses and managers were identified, and questions were raised about whether management education programs were adequately preparing leaders for the realities of contemporary management. A major business school curriculum study (Porter & McKibbin, 1988) suggested that management education programs needed to place greater emphasis on human skills. Quinn, Faerman, Thompson, and McGrath (1990) noted that:

> What is now available in management education is necessary but insufficient. All . . . modern organizations, as never before, and even at the lowest levels, are in need of competent managerial leaders. They want technical ability but they also want more. They want people who can survive and help organizations prosper in a world of constant change and intense competition. This means both technical competence and interpersonal excellence. (p. v)

Numerous books have been written about what makes for excellence, high productivity, and overall success (for example, Blake, Mouton, & Allen, 1987;

Kanter, 1983; Lawler, 1986; Ouchi, 1981; Peters & Waterman, 1982). The management of nonprofit organizations is influenced greatly by what is happening in the for-profit or business sector. Today in for-profit organizations there is increasing stress on excellence, leadership, and accountability, as well as on human relations skills. Nonprofit managers must identify and acquire the technical, human relations, and conceptual skills and the various competencies needed to successfully lead nonprofit organizations in the years ahead.

Nonprofit managers often experience some difficulty using texts and training materials that were developed for the for-profit sector. This book addresses the particular needs of nonprofit managers. The content is aimed primarily at mid- and upper-level managers who can benefit from it directly as they strive daily to attain excellence, as well as indirectly as they help those they supervise do a better job of managing. Although this book is directed mostly to managers, it also will be useful to students who are studying nonprofit or public management.

ORGANIZING FRAMEWORK

The organizing framework for this book is a metatheoretical model of organizational and managerial effectiveness called the "competing values framework" (Edwards, 1987, 1990; Edwards, Faerman, & McGrath, 1986; Edwards & Yankey, 1991; Faerman, Quinn, & Thompson, 1987; Quinn, 1984, 1988; Quinn et al., 1990; Quinn & Rohrbaugh, 1981, 1983). This model, which is described more fully in Chapter 1, serves to integrate four contrasting sets of management skills: boundary-spanning, human relations, coordinating, and directing. Each set has two inherent roles that managers must play to be successful in that particular sphere of organizational activity. The eight roles are those of broker, innovator, mentor, facilitator, monitor, coordinator, producer, and director.

The competing values framework helps explicate that managers must function in a world of competing values in which their daily activities usually do not represent a choice between something "good" and something "bad." Rather, most choices that managers must make are between two or more "goods" or values. As used in this book, the competing values framework helps managers consider the complexity and multiplicity of their roles within their organizations and stresses that the performance of a management role is rarely an either-or situation.

The first section of the book provides overviews of the competing values framework. The remaining chapters are organized into five sections. The first four sections relate to the four major sets of skills and the eight managerial roles identified in the competing values framework. The final section deals with the issue of leadership skills needed to manage in turbulent times, under conditions of financial uncertainty and changing organizational missions. Also included is an appendix that contains Web sites that may be of interest to nonprofit managers.

The validity and importance of the eight roles have been demonstrated in several empirical studies. One study (Quinn, Denison, & Hooijberg, 1989) of more than 700 managers revealed that the measures of the eight roles met standard validity tests and that the roles appear in the four indicated quadrants. Another study (Pauchant, Nilles, Sawy, & Mohrman, 1989) involving more than 900 managers also found support for the eight roles and indicated that of 36 possible roles, these eight were considered the most important ones to be performed by managers. Still another study (Quinn, 1988) found that managers who did not perform these eight roles well were considered ineffective, whereas those who did perform these roles well were considered very effective.

LEARNING APPROACH

This book is designed to be used in a number of ways. It can be used as an individualized learning tool, as a primary text for management-training programs or academic courses, or as a supplement to other texts. The chapters are organized in a way that facilitates the development of competencies needed to perform the various managerial roles identified in the book. The structure of the chapters represents a variation of a learning model developed by Whetten and Cameron (1984), which involves assessment, learning, analysis, practice, and application. The first chapter includes an assessment instrument that enables readers to gain insight into their relative strengths and weaknesses in relation to the eight management roles. Each chapter contains a narrative section that provides information about particular topics and one or more skills—application exercises that provide opportunities to apply the material to realistic job situations.

This book is a revision and expansion of two earlier books, *Skills for Effective Human Services Management* (Edwards & Yankey, 1991) and *Skills for Effective Management of Nonprofit Organizations* (Edwards, Yankey, & Altpeter, 1998). The topics addressed in the earlier versions and the present edition were identified as a result of the editors' experiences as hands-on managers, consultants, trainers, and educators. The array of topics covers many competencies that are not typically found in a single management book but that are vitally important in the real world of nonprofit management. The authors are a diverse group in terms of gender, race, and ethnicity, and they bring a wealth of real-world management experience.

Finally, the editors believe that effective management requires, in addition to a wide range of technical and human relations skills, a healthy sense of humor. Thus, a number of cartoons have been included in the book.

REFERENCES

Blake, R., Mouton, J., & Allen, R. (1987). *Spectacular teamwork: How to develop the leadership skills for team success*. New York: John Wiley & Sons.

Edwards, R. L. (1987). The competing values approach as an integrating framework for the management curriculum. *Administration in Social Work, 11*(1), 1–13.

Edwards, R. L. (1990). Organizational effectiveness. In L. Ginsberg (Ed.), *Encyclopedia of social work* (18th ed., 1990 Supplement, pp. 244–255). Silver Spring, MD: NASW Press.

Edwards, R. L., Faerman, S. K., & McGrath, M. K. (1986). The competing values approach to organizational effectiveness: A tool for agency administrators. *Administration in Social Work, 10*(4), 1–14.

Edwards, R. L., & Yankey, J. A. (1991). *Skills for effective human services management*. Washington, DC: NASW Press.

Edwards, R. L., Yankey, J. A., & Altpeter, M. A. (1998). *Skills for effective management of nonprofit organizations*. Washington, DC: NASW Press.

Faerman, S. K., Quinn, K. E., & Thompson, M. P. (1987). Bridging management practice and theory. *Public Administration Review, 47*(3), 311–319.

Kanter, K. M. (1983). The *change masters: Innovation for productivity in the American corporation*. New York: Simon & Schuster.

Lawler, E. E., III. (1986). *High-involvement management: Participative strategies for improving organizational performance*. San Francisco: Jossey-Bass.

Ouchi, W. C. (1981). *Theory Z: How American business can meet the Japanese challenge*. Reading, MA: Addison-Wesley.

Pauchant, T. C., Nilles, J., Sawy, O. E., & Mohrman, A. M. (1989). *Toward a paradoxical theory of organizational effectiveness: An empirical study of the competing values model* (Working Paper). Quebec City, Canada: Laval University, Department of Administrative Sciences.

Peters, T. J., & Waterman, K. H., Jr. (1982). *In search of excellence*. New York: Harper & Row.

Porter, L. W., & McKibbin. (1988). *Management education and development: Drift or thrust into the 21st century?* New York: McGraw-Hill.

Quinn, R. E. (1984). Applying the competing values approach to leadership: Toward an integrative framework. In J. C. Hunt, D. Hosking, C. Schriescheim, & K. Stewart (Eds.), *Leaders and managers: International perspectives on managerial behavior and leadership*. Elmsford, NY: Pergamon Press.

Quinn, R. E. (1988). *Beyond rational management: Mastering the paradoxes and competing demands of high performance*. San Francisco: Jossey-Bass.

Quinn, R. E., Denison, D., & Hooijberg, R. (1989). *An empirical assessment of the competing values leadership instrument* (Working Paper). Ann Arbor: University of Michigan, School of Business.

Quinn, R. E., Faerman, S. K., Thompson, M. P., & McGrath, M. K. (1990). *Becoming a master manager: A competency framework*. New York: John Wiley & Sons.

Introduction

Quinn, R. E., & Rohrbaugh, J. A. (1981). A competing values approach to organizational effectiveness. *Public Productivity Review*, *5*, 122–140.

Quinn, R. E., & Rohrbaugh, J. A. (1983). A spatial model of effectiveness criteria: Toward a competing values approach to organizational analysis. *Management Science*, *29*(3), 363–377.

Whetten, D. A., & Cameron, K. S. (1984). *Developing management skills*. Glenview, IL: Scott, Foresman.

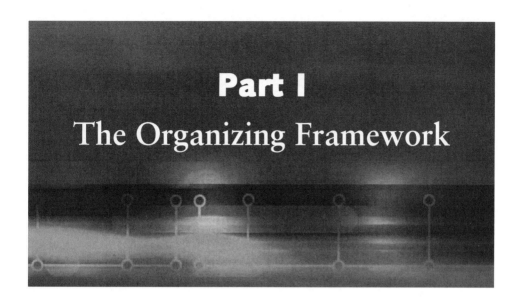

Part I
The Organizing Framework

The organizing theme for this book is an approach to organizational and leadership effectiveness known as the "competing values framework." In the first chapter, Richard L. Edwards and David M. Austin provide an overview of the roles that managers must perform, comparing and contrasting the roles of managers in the for-profit, public, and nonprofit sectors. They then identify three broad types of skills that managers must have, suggesting that the desired mix of these skills will vary depending on the level that a manager occupies in the organizational hierarchy. Next, they discuss the competing values framework, which organizes the roles that managers must play within four distinct sets of skills. Eight specific roles, two related to each of the skills sets, are discussed. They also discuss the concept of leadership. The chapter concludes with a self-assessment instrument that enables individuals to develop a graphic profile of their strengths and weaknesses in relation to each of the eight managerial roles. The graphic profile can help managers identify areas of content in this book that may be particularly useful in helping them build skills in areas that need strengthening.

Managing Effectively in an Environment of Competing Values

Richard L. Edwards and David M. Austin

We live in an era in which organizational life is characterized by shifting priorities, changing patterns in the allocation of resources, and competing demands. Nonprofit managers often must function in an environment of heightened demands for our organizations' services, higher expectations for accountability, and increased competition for funding, all the while being buffeted by change. Indeed, it seems that the only constant in management today is change.

Contemporary managers must be equipped with a broad range of knowledge, skills, and abilities to perform in a competent, effective manner. Beginning with a comparison of the executive management role within for-profit, public-sector, and nonprofit organizational contexts, this chapter provides an overview of how managers can be effective in an ever-changing environment of competing demands and values. The chapter then provides an overview of managerial skills needed at different levels of the organizational hierarchy, explains a multidimensional model of organizational and management performance, and considers the nature of managerial decision making.

EXECUTIVE MANAGEMENT ROLE

The role that top-level managers in nonprofit organizations must perform is similar to and yet distinct from the roles performed by their counterparts in for-profit and public organizations (Austin, 1989). In the for-profit corporate sector, the simplest version of the role of chief executive officer (CEO) combines policy making and implementation. In the corporate or industry model, the CEO serves as a member of the corporation's board of directors as well as its senior administrator. The ultimate measure of the effectiveness of the executive's performance is the level of financial return to the shareholders. In the public administration model, the traditional role of the CEO has been the implementation of policy but not its formulation. Elected legislative bodies make policy for public-sector managers to carry out (Wilson, 1978). Several measures can show effectiveness, including the consistency of implementation with legislative intent, continuity of the government organization, and break-even financial management—that is, operating within the limits of available financial resources (Austin, 1989).

In the nonprofit sector, the CEO has traditionally been called the "executive director," but some nonprofits now use titles that have been more characteristic of the for-profit sector, such as "president" or "chief executive officer." However, regardless of the title, the nonprofit manager's role is shaped, in part, by organizational characteristics that nonprofit organizations share with other types of formal organizations (Austin, 1988). Nonprofit managers, like their counterparts in the for-profit world, are becoming active participants in the formation as well as in the implementation, of policy. It is often the top-level manager, or CEO, who brings most policy issues and recommendations to the nonprofit organization's policy board, which may be called the "board of trustees" or "board of directors."

Like their counterparts in the world of public administration, nonprofit managers are concerned with such issues as the extent to which implementation efforts are congruent with policy, the ongoing health of their organizations, and break-even fiscal performance. Also, like their public administration counterparts, nonprofit managers have no direct personal economic stake in their organizations' financial performance. Their salaries do not increase in proportion to the size of their organizations' budgets, nor do they get year-end bonuses that are based on financial performance.

Despite these similarities, the role of the nonprofit manager also differs from the roles of the for-profit corporate executive and the traditional public administrator and, in many ways, is more complex (Austin, 1983). Perhaps the most significant difference is the criteria used to determine success. In the nonprofit sector, the most important measure for judging the manager's performance is the quality of the services provided by the organization (Patti, 1987).

MANAGERIAL SKILLS IN THE ORGANIZATIONAL HIERARCHY

Successful nonprofit managers must be prepared to be interactive, adaptive, and able to formulate contingency plans that take into account the operational characteristics of the particular organization and its environmental context. Managers must be proactive. However, the typical nonprofit manager is invariably confronted by a series of competing values or demands that are likely to pull him or her in many directions at once. This situation was captured in part by Perlmutter (1990), who pointed out that "not only is it necessary to keep the shop running smoothly and efficiently today to meet current needs, but it is also necessary to have a vision of and anticipate what is possible and necessary for tomorrow" (p. 5). Thus, successful nonprofit managers must be skilled at both tactical and strategic management.

Managerial performance within any type of organization occurs in a context of organizational change (Cooke, Reid, & Edwards, 1997; Edwards, Cooke, & Reid, 1996). Like human beings, organizations are not static but go through a variety of phases and life cycles. Hence, different stages in the organizational life cycle may require a manager to use different types of skills (Quinn & Cameron, 1983). Likewise, organizations that perform similar work but exist in different types of environments may require a different mix of managerial skills. For example, arts organizations may target different client groups and compete for different resources than do human services or grassroots advocacy organizations; these differences affect which management styles and skills are needed. Individuals also may shape the specific elements of their managerial positions in different ways on the basis of their personalities, training, and experience, as well as their perceptions of the needs of their organizations at a given point in time.

Furthermore, the level of the management position within the organizational hierarchy often shapes the skills are needed (Figure 1.1). According to Katz (1974), management skills may be categorized broadly as (1) technical, (2) interpersonal and human relations, and (3) decision-making and conceptual skills.

In entry-level managerial positions, technical skills tend to be very important. However, the relative importance of technical skills tends to diminish as managers move up the organizational structure. At upper-management levels, the need for decision-making and conceptual skills increases in importance. For top-level managers, conceptual skills are essential, but the nature of their jobs does not require the use of technical skills to the same extent as do lower-level managerial positions. On the other hand, interpersonal and human relations skills are equally important for managers at all levels of the organizational hierarchy (Katz, 1974; Whetten & Cameron, 1984).

In nonprofit organizations, individuals who are competent direct-service practitioners in human services or health organizations are sometimes promoted to supervisory or entry-level managerial positions. They may perform effectively in their new roles because their positions require good technical and interpersonal skills. As these individuals gradually move up the managerial hierarchy into positions that require greater conceptual skills, they may continue to be successful. However, they also may begin to display deficiencies and become unsuccessful and ineffective, thereby fulfilling the so-called "Peter Principle" of being promoted

---

FIGURE 1.1
MANAGEMENT SKILLS REQUIRED AT DIFFERENT LEVELS

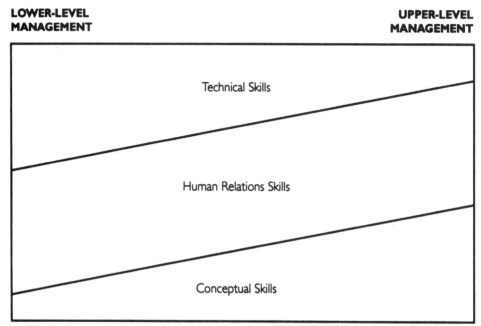

SOURCE: D. Whetten, K. Cameron, A. Shriberg, & C. Lloyd, *Developing management skills*, 3rd edition, Instructor's manual & transparency masters (transparency no. 8). © 1995 Addison Wesley Longman. Reprinted by permission of Addison Wesley Longman.

---

to positions that are beyond their level of competence (Peter & Hull, 1969). Thus, as one moves up the organizational management hierarchy, one must attain the additional competencies necessary to be effective. Success at one level in an organization will not necessarily guarantee success at a higher level.

Competing Values Framework

There is no one best style of management performance. However, there is an inclusive, multidimensional model of organizational and management performance, called the "competing values approach" (Quinn, 1984, 1988), which can help one understand the criteria that are used to judge the effectiveness of organizations and the various roles that managers perform (Edwards, Faerman, & McGrath, 1986).

The competing values model is an analytic framework built around two dimensions representing competing orientations or values in the organizational context (Figure 1.2). These dimensions are (1) flexibility versus control and (2) internal

FIGURE 1.2
COMPETING VALUES FRAMEWORK: EFFECTIVENESS

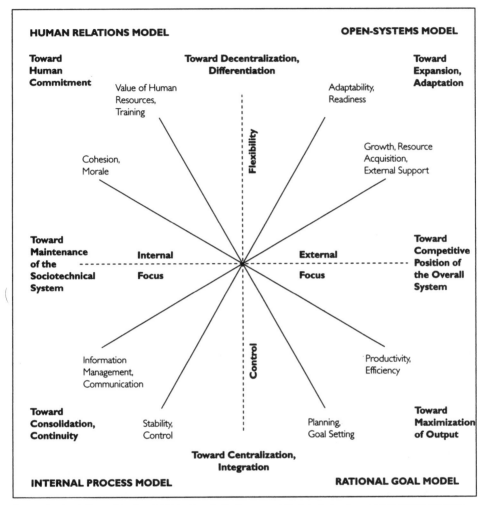

SOURCE: Reprinted with permission from R. E. Quinn, *Beyond rational management: Mastering the paradoxes and competing demands of high performance.* Copyright © 1988 Jossey-Bass, Inc., Publishers. All rights reserved.

versus external. The combination of these two dimensions distinguishes four sectors of organizational activity, each of which embodies distinctive criteria of organizational effectiveness (Edwards, 1987, 1990; Quinn & Rohrbaugh, 1981, 1983). In combination, the four sectors identified in the model deal with two major criteria for assessing organizational outcomes: (1) the quality of services provided and (2) the continuity of the organization (Austin, 1989).

For an organization to perform well with respect to the various criteria of effectiveness, managers must use these different and sometimes conflicting sets of skills:

- Boundary-spanning skills,
- Human relations skills,
- Coordinating skills, and
- Directing skills.

Of course, no single managerial position involves an equal emphasis on all four of these sectors. In any given organization, the top-level manager may be involved primarily in activities that require the use of certain types of skills, whereas other people who are part of the executive component, or management team, may carry major responsibilities for activities in other sectors that require other types of skills. Yet, the CEO or top-level manager bears ultimate responsibility for the effectiveness of the organization's performance in all four sectors. Some of the key concepts associated with each sector of organizational performance and the relevant managerial roles are summarized in Figure 1.3.

Boundary-Spanning Skills

Each quadrant depicted in Figure 1.3 relates to a different set of skills, and each set of skills includes managerial traits, behaviors, and patterns of influence inherent within it. To perform roles depicted in the upper-right quadrant, managers will be called on to use boundary-spanning skills. Because nonprofit organizations are highly dependent on their environments, a manager will constantly be involved in activities that cross the formal boundaries of the organization. These activities include obtaining financial resources, establishing and maintaining the organization's legitimacy, adapting organizational programs in response to environmental changes, managing external requirements for reporting and accountability, negotiating formal and informal interorganizational agreements, participating in action coalitions, lobbying, dealing with public relations and media issues, and positioning the organization to take advantage of new opportunities or withstand external threats.

In the competing values model, this sector is defined by the flexibility and external dimensions. That is, a manager performing the roles in this sector will need to be adaptable and flexible, because he or she will be participating in activities that involve dealing with individuals and organizations that are not under his or her direct control and that are external to the formal boundaries of the organization.

Quinn (1984, 1988) identified two managerial roles that are relevant to this sector: (1) the innovator and (2) the broker. To effectively perform the role of

FIGURE 1.3
COMPETING VALUES FRAMEWORK: LEADERSHIP ROLES

HUMAN RELATIONS SKILLS   **BOUNDARY-SPANNING SKILLS**

Toward   **Toward a Responsive,**   **Toward**
Human   **Open Style**   **an Inventive,**
Commitment   **Risk-Taking**
                Mentor Role   *Innovator Role*   **Style**
                Caring, Empathetic   Creative, Clever
                (Shows Consideration)   (Envisions Change)

                                                            Broker Role
          Facilitator Role   Resource Oriented
          Process Oriented   Politically Astute
          (Facilitates Interaction)   (Acquires Resources)

                          Flexibility

Toward a   **Toward a**
Cooperative,   **Longer Time Horizons**   **External Focus**   **Dynamic,**
Team-   -   **Competitive**
Oriented   **Internal Focus**   **Shorter Time Horizons** **Style**
Style

                          Control

                Monitor Role   *Producer Role*
                Technically Expert   Task Oriented
                (Collects Information)   Work Focused
                                                  (Initiates Action)

Toward   **Toward**
Consolidation,   *Coordinator Role*   *Director Role*   **Maximization**
Continuity   Dependable, Reliable   Decisive, Directive   **of Output**
                     (Maintains Structure)   (Provides Structure)

                     Toward a Structured,
                        Formal Style

COORDINATING SKILLS   **DIRECTING SKILLS**

innovator, managers need to be creative and clever. These traits require having good conceptual skills and constantly being on the lookout for unusual opportunities. The behavior associated with the performance of this role is directed toward envisioning and facilitating change. Hence, to perform this role well the manager must be the type of individual who seeks new opportunities, encourages and considers new ideas, and is tolerant of ambiguity and risk.

To perform the role of broker effectively, managers must be resource oriented and politically astute. These traits require being aware of and sensitive to external conditions, especially those related to the organization's legitimacy, influence, and acquisition of resources. The behavior associated with the performance of the broker role is directed toward acquiring resources, so managers also must be skilled in developing interpersonal contacts, monitoring the organization's environment, amassing power and influence, maintaining the external image of the organization, and obtaining resources (Quinn, 1984, 1988). Nonprofit managers also must be skilled in fundraising (Edwards, Benefield, Edwards, & Yankey, 1997) and adept at navigating the political arena (Gummer & Edwards, 1995).

The boundary-spanning-skills sector involves the political or open-system dimension of organizational performance that is least subject to technical skills and computerization. A manager functioning in this sector will need political or negotiating skills and an understanding of the nature of power relationships in the task environment in which those management skills are practiced. Boundary-spanning skills also may require a manager to perform short-term contingency decision making, in contrast to the systematic and long-term participatory internal decision-making processes that may be important in the mobilization and motivation of human resources, This sector of activity is perhaps the least likely to be fully delegated to other members of the executive management team. However, it also may be the sector that policymakers, such as volunteers who serve on the organization's board, define as their particular area of activity and in which explicit limits may be placed on the scope of the manager's activities.

The effectiveness of the process of contingency decision making, or strategic adaptation, whether carried out by policy makers, the manager, or both, may be severely constrained by considerations involving other sectors in which policy makers and managers perform. For example, successful "opportunity-seizing" initiatives involving responses to short-term funding opportunities, such as responding to various requests for funding proposals, may be inconsistent with the organization's overall goals, may require substantial expenditures for the development of new technical production procedures, and may disrupt the cohesiveness and morale of the staff.

Human Relations Skills

The second major sector of executive responsibility, shown in the upper-left quadrant of Figure 1.3, involves the use of human relations skills. In performing the roles in this sector, managers are responsible for ensuring that the organization has a competent workforce. Because many of the services provided by nonprofit organizations are produced and delivered through person-to-person interactions, these generally are what are called "labor-intensive organizations." As a consequence, human relations activities constitute a particularly important component in the life of such organizations.

In the competing values model, this sector is defined by the internal and flexibility dimensions. Managers will be dealing with individuals and groups who are internal to the organization and who, as autonomous individuals or groups with the skills required to produce services, represent decentralized centers of authority and influence that often managers cannot directly control. Quinn (1984, 1988) identified two specific managerial roles in this sector: (1) the mentor and (2) the facilitator.

In the role of the mentor, managers need to be caring and empathic. Those who possess these traits tend to view organizational members as valued resources and are alert to members' individual problems and needs. They operate in a manner that is perceived as fair and objective. Managers also must be skilled listeners and try to facilitate the development of individuals (Quinn, 1984, 1988). Behavior is directed toward showing concern about and support for staff members.

To be an effective group facilitator, managers need to be process oriented, diplomatic, and tactful. They must have excellent interpersonal skills and be good at facilitating interaction among individuals and groups in the workplace. Managers also should be adept at fostering cohesion, building consensus, and bringing about compromises. The ultimate aim is to foster a cooperative, team-oriented style that permeates the organization.

In performing the roles of mentor and facilitator, the manager's goal is to secure, retain, and motivate a qualified, competent, and committed work force. The human resources—in other words, the people of the organization—should have the knowledge, skills, and abilities to perform their jobs effectively. However, achieving the goal of a well-qualified, competent, team-oriented work force is not easy, because the staff often includes members of one or more professions as well as a variety of volunteers who are involved both in the delivery of services and policymaking. In addition, the work force often is diverse, including men and women as well as people from a variety of racial and ethnic groups. Furthermore, service users may be a critical element in mobilizing and motivating staff.

Because of the composition and the competing needs and interests of the human resources component of the organization, managers must be concerned with the organizational culture, which includes symbols and traditions, and the definition of organizational values, which together may be significantly related to staff motivation (Austin, 1989).

Coordinating Skills

The lower-left quadrant of Figure 1.3 identifies the coordinating-skills sector, which is defined by the internal and control dimensions. Quinn (1984, 1988) identified the roles of the monitor and the coordinator in this sector. The activities related to this sector are focused primarily on matters that are internal to the organization and that are involved in maintaining the organizational structure. The technical areas in this sector include budgeting and fiscal controls, scheduling procedures, information and communication systems, personnel administration systems, technical training programs, reporting systems, evaluation and quality control measures, and management of technical equipment and physical facilities (Austin, 1989).

To perform the role of monitor effectively, managers must be technically competent and well prepared. These traits suggest that the manager needs to be well informed and knowledgeable about the work of the people in the organization and have a high degree technical expertise. The manager's role is directed toward collecting and distributing information that is necessary for the smooth functioning of the organization as well as for the orderly flow of work. To perform well in the role of coordinator, the manager must be dependable and reliable. Those who have such traits are likely to be consistent, predictable people who seek continuity and equilibrium in their work units (Quinn, 1984, 1988). The focus should be on maintaining structure, organizational stability, and work flow and using managerial skills in scheduling, coordinating, problem solving, and ensuring that rules and standards are understood and met. This also is the sector of organizational life in which systematic and rational procedures often have their widest application (Austin, 1989).

Because nonprofit organizations are typically so labor intensive, the systematic organization of personnel activities and monitoring of service production activities assume great importance and become major elements in the managerial or executive position. In a small organization, it may be possible for the manager to carry out many of these tasks directly. However, in larger organizations, these types of managerial tasks, especially personnel administration, financial management, and the maintenance of computing systems, most likely involve technical staff specialists and sometimes entire staffing units.

The use of computers in all kinds of organizations, including nonprofits, has become widespread. It is in the coordinating-skills sector that computers are particularly valuable, because the activities involved often represent structured decision-making choices among known alternatives. For example, issues such as the impact of different combinations of direct salary and fringe benefits on staff compensation; the effects of different combinations of staff work schedules; and the patterns of service use by clients, procedures for handling organizational funds, and the tracking of clients or patrons all lend themselves to the use of computers. These activities and others like them are areas in which consistent, centrally controlled decisions seem to be highly correlated with efficiency and effectiveness.

Directing Skills

The lower-right quadrant of Figure 1.3 identifies directing skills. This sector is defined by the external and control dimensions. Thus, the focus in this sector tends to be on activities that are external to the organization and that are relatively structured and formalized. In the management roles in this sector, managers will be dealing with the interface between the products or output of the organization and its external environment. The technical activities involved include both tactical and strategic planning, goal setting, and activity monitoring. Quinn (1984, 1988) identified the roles of the producer and the director in this sector.

The point of managerial activity in this sector is the goal-oriented process, which is aimed at improving the organization's efficiency and effectiveness as well as enhancing its relative position within its environment. This sector involves activities in which the manager plays a pivotal role, such as the improvement of productivity and goal setting (Austin, 1989).

In performing the role of director effectively, managers must be decisive and comfortable in guiding the work of others. Those who have these traits tend to be conclusive individuals who can plan work appropriately and provide direction. Activities include setting goals and objectives, clarifying roles, monitoring progress, providing feedback, and establishing clear expectations (Quinn, 1984, 1988). In using directing skills, managers need to know how to stimulate individual and collective achievement. Thus, they must be comfortable with the use of authority and skilled at delegation, planning, and goal-setting technologies (Faerman, Quinn, & Thompson, 1987).

To perform the role of producer well, managers must be task oriented and work focused. Those who exhibit these traits tend to be action-oriented individuals who are highly generative. Managers must be the kind of individual who is willing to invest large amounts of energy and who derives a great deal of satisfaction from productive work. Efforts will be directed at stimulating the performance of staff members.

Because nonprofit organizations are established to accomplish particular societal objectives, the process of defining goals is essential. Nonprofit organizations are dependent, to a great extent, on their external environments. Managers must be cognizant of environmental developments and trends, including those that affect the organization's users or clients, financial and personnel resources, technology and, ultimately, legitimacy in political terms. Furthermore, organizational continuity assumes relatively great importance for nonprofit organizations, because the costs involved in setting up such an organization and the goodwill represented in its legitimation by the community cannot be turned into financial resources that can be used for other purposes (Austin, 1989).

When confronted by the often-difficult choices that are inherent in the competing values environment of nonprofit management, managers can use the organization's mission as a kind of litmus test for decisions. That is, consider how a particular decision will help or hinder the organization to achieve its mission. Thus, a manager should view the organization's mission as a kind of North Star that can guide him or her through the wilderness of competing values and demands.

Those who occupy a managerial position must possess and use many types of skills and must perform many roles. The demands of these roles may shift over time as the organization moves through different phases in its life cycle. In small organizations, the top-level manager role may encompass many skills and roles, whereas in larger organizations, the top-level manager may delegate certain roles to others on the management team.

NATURE OF MANAGERIAL DECISION MAKING

Because organizational life is characterized by an environment of competing values, managerial decision-making requirements are complex. The choices that confront managers daily are rarely choices between something that is good and something that is bad. If this were the case, the job of manager would be relatively easy. Instead, management most often involves choosing between two or more things that are positive or valued. This type of choice makes the job much more difficult. For example, a manager may be confronted with shrinking resources and thus not be able to hire additional staff or provide opportunities for staff development. At the same time, he or she may be confronted with a growing demand for services from clients. Because the size of the workforce cannot be enlarged, the increased demand for services may cause the manager to take steps to increase the caseloads of the existing staff. Such an approach may result in greater efficiency, that is, more clients seen without an increase in staff. However, the approach also may have a negative impact on the morale of the staff, which could lead to increased stress, burnout, and turnover. Thus, the organization may lose some of its experienced staff, which may result in added expenses for recruiting, hiring, and orienting new staff. There also is likely to be some loss related to the time it takes new staff to become fully productive.

Understanding that managers are likely to experience pulls from many directions may help to identify the possible consequences of decisions and enable the manager to take appropriate steps to minimize negative consequences. Viewing organizations from the competing values perspective can help managers assess particular areas of strength. No one individual will be equally adept at performing all the roles identified in Figure 1.3. Managers who are secure about their abilities are likely to surround themselves with subordinates whose strengths

"Faced with the two of you, I'm forced to ask, 'Who's holier-than-thou?'"

complement their own, whereas managers who are less secure tend to surround themselves with individuals whose strengths mirror their own (but who may not be as strong, so they are less threatening). This latter situation often results in the organization's needs being inadequately addressed.

A nonprofit manager must possess a range of knowledge, skills, and abilities and must perform many roles, more or less simultaneously. The particular balance of technical, interpersonal and human relations, and conceptual and decision-making skills required will vary depending on a manager's position within the managerial structure and the organization's needs at any given point in time. Each category of skills involves the performance of different managerial roles, which are related to different criteria of organizational effectiveness and which create an environment of competing values. In this environment, managerial choices most often represent a trade-off between two or more values, or "goods," rather than a choice between something that is good versus something that is bad. By understanding the multiple role demands and competing values of the job, managers may be better able to guide the organization toward effective performance.

Leadership

There often is some confusion about the concepts of management and leadership and some debate about whether one can be an effective manager without being a competent leader. It is our belief that effective managers exhibit leadership qualities. One certainly can exhibit leadership without being in a management position. However, we believe that one cannot be a successful nonprofit manager without being a good leader.

Bennis (1999) suggested that managers are people who do things right, while leaders are people who do the right thing. Bennis (1999) identified the following characteristics of successful leaders:

- *Technical competence:* business literacy and grasp of one's field;
- *Conceptual skill:* a facility for abstract or strategic thinking;
- *Track record:* a history of achieving results;
- *People skills:* an ability to communicate, motivate, and delegate;
- *Taste:* an ability to identify and cultivate talent;
- *Judgment:* making difficult decisions in a short time frame with imperfect data; and
- *Character:* the qualities that define who we are.

The importance of character as a quality of leadership cannot be overstated. Nonprofit mangers have a responsibility to lead by example. They must be highly ethical individuals who follow codes of ethics of their own professions and must ensure that their employees follow their professional codes of ethics. "Research at Harvard University indicates that 85 percent of a leader's performance depends on personal character. Likewise, the work of Daniel Goleman makes clear that leadership success or failure is usually due to 'qualities of the heart'" (Bennis, 1999).

Leadership is a process of influencing people to meet organizational goals and objectives. Chapman (2001) suggested that leadership is first about behavior and second about skills. He indicated that "good leaders are followed chiefly because people trust and respect them, rather than the skills they possess. To Chapman, leadership differs from management in the sense that the latter places more reliance on planning, organizational, and communications skills. He acknowledged that leadership relies on management skills as well but suggested that leadership relies more "on qualities such as integrity, honesty, humility, courage, commitment, sincerity, passion, confidence, positivity, wisdom, determination, compassion, and sensitivity."

Jack Welch, a respected business leader and writer, proposed several fundamental leadership principles (as cited in Chapman, 2001):

- There is only one way—the straight way; it sets the tone of the organization.
- Be open to the best of what everyone, everywhere, has to offer; transfer learning across the organization.

- Get the right people in the right jobs; this is more important than developing a strategy.
- An informal atmosphere is a competitive advantage.
- Make sure that everybody counts and that everyone knows that he or she counts.
- Legitimate self-confidence is a winner; the true test of self-confidence is the courage to be open.
- Business has to be fun; celebrations energize an organization.
- Never underestimate the other guy.
- Understand where real value is added, and put your best people there.
- Know when to meddle and when to let go; this is pure instinct.

As a leader, your main priority is to get the job done, whatever the job is. To this end, leaders create effective, productive teams and enable them to be successful. To accomplish this, leaders need to:

- Be clear about their objectives and have a plan for how to achieve them;
- Work at building a team committed to achieving the objectives; and
- Invest in helping all team members give their best efforts.

Leaders must know themselves, that is they need to know their own strengths and weaknesses so they can build the best team around themselves. Rudolph Giuliani, former mayor of New York City, in his book *Leadership* (2002), identified several principles of leadership. Among these are the following:

- First things first organize around a purpose (leaders must be able to prioritize and keep in mind the purpose of their activity);
- Everyone's accountable, all of the time (leaders need to hold people accountable);
- Surround yourself with great people (leaders need to create effective teams by getting the best people for the job);
- Develop and communicate strong beliefs (leaders need to be clear about their vision and be able to communicate it);
- Weddings discretionary, funerals mandatory (leaders need to tend to the personal needs of their people); and
- Study, read, learn independently (leaders need to engage in personal development and self-renewal).

Because a key element of leadership is being able to influence others, human relations skills are critical to success as a leader. Covey (1990) identified what he called the seven habits of highly effective people. In our view, managers who want to be effective leaders will do well to read Covey's books (1990, 2004) and should give serious consideration to learning and practicing the following habits identified by Covey, as summarized by Chapman (2001):

- Habit 1—Be proactive. People need to be able to control their own environment and not to let it control them.
- Habit 2—Begin with the end in mind. People need to figure out where they want to be, clarifying their personal vision and mission.
- Habit 3—Put first things first. People need to be able to organize and implement tasks and activities in such a way that their actions will actually lead to where they want to be.
- Habit 4—Think win–win. People need to remember that any achievements that organizations—and individuals—make will largely be dependent on the cooperative efforts of many. Thus, people need to adopt the attitude of finding solutions that enable all parties to win rather than have some folks in the organization come out winners while others come out losers.
- Habit 5—Seek first to understand and then to be understood. People need to be concerned about communication, but particularly that they need to become skilled at listening. As Covey (1990) said, we need to diagnose before we prescribe.
- Habit 6—Synergize. People need to attempt to see the potential value in everyone's contributions, remembering the principle that the whole is greater than the sum of its parts.
- Habit 7—Sharpen the saw. People need to develop the habit of self-renewal, and everyone needs to constantly be concerned about taking care of their spiritual, mental, physical, and social or emotional needs if they are to be successful managers and leaders.

In their research on leaders, which has extended more than 30 years, Kouzes and Posner (2003) have identified five "best practices" of the leadership experience, which they call the "Five Practices of Exemplary Leadership." These practices, which bring together many of the leadership characteristics and practices identified by Bennis (1999), Chapman (2001), Covey (1990), Giuliani (2002), and Welch & Byrne (2002) include the following:

- Model the way—You must believe in something, stand up for your beliefs, express your personal values, and set an example;
- Inspire a shared vision—You must envision the future, have a desire to make things happen, want to create something better;
- Challenge the process—You must search for opportunities to innovate, grow, improve, and encourage people to experiment and take risks and create a climate in which people learn from mistakes and failures as well as successes;

- Enable others to act—You must foster collaboration, build trust, strengthen others by giving away some of your power through trusting others and giving them more discretion and authority; and
- Encourage the heart—You must encourage your people to carry on, finding genuine ways to uplift their spirits, recognizing their contributions, and celebrating individual and team values and victories to create a spirit of community.

Managing an organization can be difficult, given that one is working in an environment of competing values, often being pulled in many directions and required to play different roles and have so many types of skills. However, the experience also can be extremely gratifying when one remembers that organizations are made up of individuals who, if treated with respect and dignity, can produce great things even when resources are limited.

SKILLS-ASSESSMENT EXERCISE

The following instrument will enable managers to develop a profile of how they rate on each of the managerial roles identified in the competing values framework.

First, please complete the Competing Values Management Practices Survey and then transfer your ratings to the Computational Worksheet for Self-Assessment. Place the score or rating you give each item on the survey next to the number of that item on the worksheet. Note that where the symbol (R) appears on the worksheet, you should reverse your score; thus, if you rated the item 1 you will reverse your score and record it as 7, 2 becomes 6, and 3 becomes 5. If your rating was 4, then place 4 on the worksheet. Next, total your scores in each category and then divide the total by the number of items in that category. This sum will give you a score to enter on the Competing Values Skills-Assessment Leadership Role Profile. When transferring your scores to the role profile, place a dot at the point on the spoke that reflects your score for that role, keeping in mind that the center of the figure is 0, and the hash mark farthest from the center is 7. When you have entered your scores on all eight spokes of the diagram, draw lines to connect them. The result will be a profile that will help you identify your areas of relative strength as well as those in which you may not be as strong. This information may be useful to you as you review other chapters in this book.

COMPETING VALUES MANAGEMENT PRACTICES SURVEY

Listed below are some statements that describe managerial practices. Indicate how often you engage in the behaviors, using the scale below to respond to each statement. Please place a number from 1 to 7 in the space beside each question.

Almost Never   1 2 3 4 5 6 7   Almost Always

As a manager; how often do you

_____ 1. Come up with inventive ideas.

_____ 2. Exert upward influence in the organization.

_____ 3. Ignore the need to achieve unit goals.

_____ 4. Continually clarify the unit's purpose.

_____ 5. Search for innovations and potential improvements.

_____ 6. Make the unit's role very clear.

_____ 7. Maintain tight logistical control.

_____ 8. Keep track of what goes on inside the unit.

_____ 9. Develop consensual resolution of openly expressed differences.

_____ 10. Listen to the personal problems of subordinates.

_____ 11. Maintain a highly coordinated, well-organized unit.

_____ 12. Hold open discussions of conflicting opinions in groups.

_____ 13. Push the unit to meet objectives.

_____ 14. Surface key differences among group members, then work participatively to resolve them.

_____ 15. Monitor compliance with the rules.

_____ 16. Treat each individual in a sensitive, caring way.

COMPETING VALUES MANAGEMENT PRACTICES SURVEY (continued)

_____ 17. Experiment with new concepts and procedures.

_____ 18. Show empathy and concern in dealing with subordinates.

_____ 19. Seek to improve the work group's technical capacity.

_____ 20. Get access to people at higher levels.

_____ 21. Encourage participative decision making in the group.

_____ 22. Compare records, reports, and so on to detect discrepancies.

_____ 23. Solve scheduling problems in the unit.

_____ 24. Get the unit to meet expected goals.

_____ 25. Do problem solving in creative, clear ways.

_____ 26. Anticipate workflow problems; avoid crises.

_____ 27. Check for errors and mistakes.

_____ 28. Persuasively sell new ideas to higher-ups.

_____ 29. See that the unit delivers on stated goals.

_____ 30. Facilitate consensus building in the work unit.

_____ 31. Clarify the unit's priorities and direction.

_____ 32. Show concern for the needs of subordinates.

_____ 33. Maintain a "results" orientation in the unit.

_____ 34. Influence decisions made at higher levels.

_____ 35. Regularly clarify the objectives of the unit.

_____ 36. Bring a sense of order and coordination into the unit.

COMPUTATIONAL WORKSHEET FOR SELF-ASSESSMENT

Facilitator

9 _____
12 _____
14 _____
21 _____
30 _____
    Total _____ ÷ 5 = _____

Innovator

1 _____
5 _____
17 _____
25 _____
    Total _____ ÷ 4 = _____

Producer

3 _____ (R)
13 _____
19 _____
29 _____
33 _____
    Total _____ ÷ 5 = _____

Coordinator

7 _____
11 _____
23 _____
26 _____
36 _____
    Total _____ ÷ 5 = _____

Mentor

10 _____
16 _____
18 _____
32 _____
    Total _____ ÷ 4 = _____

Broker

2 _____
20 _____
28 _____
34 _____
    Total _____ ÷ 4 = _____

Director

4 _____
6 _____
24 _____
31 _____
35 _____
    Total _____ ÷ 5 = _____

Monitor

8 _____
15 _____
22 _____
27 _____
    Total _____ ÷ 4 = _____

COMPETING VALUES SKILLS-ASSESSMENT LEADERSHIP ROLE PROFILE

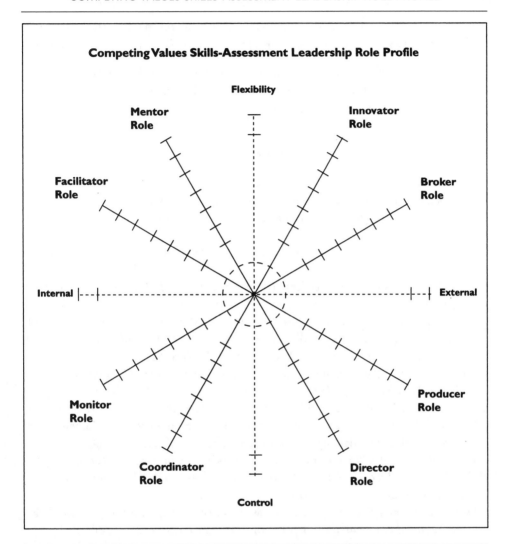

DISCUSSION QUESTIONS

The following questions may assist managers in developing managerial skills:

1. What is your reaction to the personal skills profile revealed on the role profile diagram? Do the results meet your expectations? Were there any surprises?

2. On the basis of your profile, what areas of managerial skills appear to be the highest priority for further development? What strategies can you use to assist you in developing your skills?

REFERENCES

Austin, D. M. (1983). Administrative practice in human services: Future directions for curriculum development. *Journal of Applied Behavioral Science, 19,* 143–151.

Austin, D. M. (1988). *The political economy of human service programs.* Greenwich, CT: JAI Press.

Austin, D. M. (1989). The human service executive. *Administration in Social Work, 13*(3/4), 13–36.

Bennis, W. (1999, Spring). The leadership advantage. *Leader to Leader,* p. 18–23.

Chapman, A. (2001, February 3). http://www.businessballs.com

Cooke, P. W., Reid, P. N., & Edwards, R. L. (1997). Management: New developments and directions. In R. L. Edwards (Ed.-in-Chief), *Encyclopedia of social work* (19th ed., 1997 Suppl., pp. 229–242). Washington, DC: NASW Press.

Covey, S. R. (1990). *The 7 habits of highly effective people: Powerful lessons in personal change.* New York: Free Press.

Covey, S. R. (2004). *The 8th habit: From effectiveness to greatness.* New York: Free Press.

Edwards, R. L. (1987). The competing values approach as an integrating framework for the management curriculum. *Administration in Social Work, 11*(1), 1–13.

Edwards, R. L. (1990). Organizational effectiveness. In L. Ginsberg et al. (Eds.), *Encyclopedia of social work* (18th ed., 1990 Suppl., pp. 244–255). Silver Spring, MD: National Association of Social Workers.

Edwards, R. L., Benefield, E.A. S., Edwards, J. A., & Yankey, J. A. (1997). *Building a strong foundation: Fundraising for nonprofits.* Washington, DC: NASW Press.

Edwards, R. L., Cooke, P. W., & Reid, P. N. (1996). Social work management in an era of diminishing federal responsibility. *Social Work, 41,* 46–79.

Edwards, R. L., Faerman, S. R., & McGrath, M. R. (1986). The competing values approach to organizational effectiveness: A tool for agency administrators. *Administration in Social Work, 10*(4), 1–14.

Faerman, S. R., Quinn, R. E., & Thompson, M. P. (1987). Bridging management practice and theory: New York State's public service training program. *Public Administration Review, 47,* 311–319.

Giuliani, R. W. (2002). *Leadership.* New York: Miramax Books.

Managing Effectively in an Environment of Competing Values

Gummer, B., & Edwards, R. L. (1995). The politics of human services administration. In L. Ginsberg & P. R. Keys (Eds.), *New management in human services* (pp. 57–71). Washington, DC: NASW Press.

Katz, R. L. (1974). Skills of an effective administrator. *Harvard Business Review, 51,* 90–102.

Kouzes, J. M., & Posner, B. Z. (2003). *The leadership challenge workbook.* San Francisco: Jossey-Bass.

Patti, R. J. (1987). Managing for service effectiveness in social welfare: Toward a performance model. *Administration in Social Work, 11*(3/4), 25–37.

Perlmutter, F. D. (1990). *Changing hats: From social work practice to administration.* Silver Spring, MD: National Association of Social Workers.

Peter, L., & Hull, R. (1969). *The Peter Principle: Why things go wrong.* New York: William Morrow.

Quinn, R. E. (1984). Applying the competing values approach to leadership: Toward an integrative framework. In J. G. Hunt, D. Hosking, C. Schreisheim, & R. Stewart (Eds.), *Leaders and managers: International perspectives on managerial behavior and leadership* (pp. 10–27). Elmsford, NY: Pergamon Press.

Quinn, R. E. (1988). *Beyond rational management: Mastering the paradoxes and competing demands of high performance.* San Francisco: Jossey-Bass.

Quinn, R. E., & Cameron, K. S. (1983). Organizational life cycles and shifting criteria of effectiveness: Some preliminary evidence. *Management Science, 29,* 33–51.

Quinn, R. E., & Rohrbaugh, J. A. (1981): A competing values approach to organizational effectiveness. *Public Productivity Review, 5,* 122–140.

Quinn, R. E., & Rohrbaugh, J. A. (1983). A spatial model of effectiveness criteria: Toward a competing values approach to organizational analysis. *Management Science, 29,* 363–377.

Welch, J., & Byrne, J. A. (2002). *Jack: Straight from the gut.* New York: Warner Books.

Whetten, D. A., & Cameron, K. S. (1984). *Developing management skills.* Glenview, IL: Scott, Foresman.

Wilson, W. (1978). The study of administration. In J. M. Shafritz & A. C. Hyde (Eds.), *Classics of public administration* (pp. 3–17). Oak Park, IL: Moore.

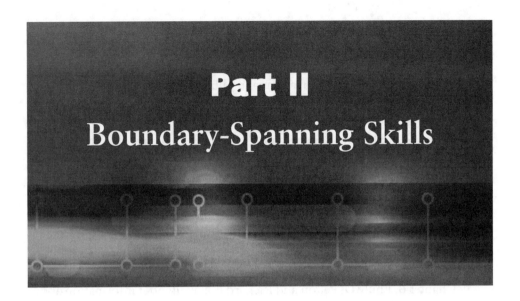

Part II
Boundary-Spanning Skills

Managerial boundary-spanning skills encompass two major roles—innovator and broker. Competencies for the innovator role include creative thinking and living with and managing change. Competencies for the broker role include building and maintaining a power base, negotiating agreement and commitment, and presenting ideas. The chapters in this section are related to these roles and competencies in terms of the challenges confronting nonprofit managers.

In Chapter 2, Douglas C. Eadie discusses the changing environment confronting managers and underscores the need for developing competencies related to creatively leading and managing innovation. He identifies the characteristics of an effective change leadership and management process and cautions against trying to deal with change through a "quick-fix" approach. Instead, Eadie recommends that managers focus on building in themselves and their organizations the capacity to lead, innovate, and implement. He stresses the importance of strategic planning and management to better position organizations to deal with their ever-changing environments.

In Chapter 3, Christine E. Henry focuses on the proposal-writing skills required of nonprofit managers in effectively performing the broker role. She provides an overview of different types of foundations, suggesting ways that nonprofit managers can learn about funding opportunities. Henry also identifies the components typically included in funding proposals and provides some guidance about writing such proposals.

In Chapter 4, Elizabeth A. S. Benefield and Richard L. Edwards point out that nonprofit managers are spending increasingly large amounts of time in fundraising activities. They urge managers to plan, develop, and implement broad-based, multifaceted fund-raising strategies. Benefield and Edwards provide information about a range of activities, including annual giving and major gift work based on sound prospect research, planning, cultivation, and public relations efforts.

In Chapter 5, Todd Cohen provides some valuable tips for developing mass media relationships, which are critical for favorably positioning nonprofit organizations in the public eye. Recognizing the difficult challenge that the development of positive media relationships presents for nonprofit managers, Cohen urges that nonprofit managers develop a media strategy for their organizations and provides concrete suggestions for doing so. He also provides helpful information about writing news releases and getting an organization's story in print or on the air. In addition, Cohen provides tips on handling interviews, setting up press conferences, and dealing with crises. He concludes with a discussion of marketing the organization.

In Chapter 6, Emily D. Pelton and Richard E. Baznik offer information about dealing with the legislative and executive branches of government to secure resources and favorable policy decisions. The competencies involved in building and maintaining power bases are considered, as well as the importance of nonprofit managers' ability to present ideas, negotiate agreement and commitment, and be creative in their approach to solving problems.

Building the Capacity to Lead Innovation

Douglas C. Eadie

Change is nothing new in the world. Indeed, life and change go naturally together, and history is replete with tales of humans struggling to cope with powerful forces beyond their control. But nobody questions that these are uniquely challenging times for all of us, including economic development professionals. O'Toole (1995) observed in *Leading Change* that "there is reason to believe that in fact the depth of the alterations experienced today is more profound than ever before" (p. xii). And in *Riding the Waves of Change,* Morgan (1988) described change these days as "a sea . . . that can twist and turn with all the power of the ocean" and as having a "degree of flux that often challenges the fundamental assumptions on which organizations and their managers have learned to operate" (p. 1).

Without doubt, the world around us is not only changing at a dizzying speed, but change also is growing in both complexity and magnitude. No wonder many of us are occasionally tempted to remove ourselves from the race altogether, retreating to our own private Walden Pond. The nonprofit and public sectors are no more immune from the impact of the sweeping changes swirling around us than the business sector. Phenomenal technological change—in communications,

Note: A modified version of this chapter was originally published in 1997 as "Building the Capacity for Innovation." In D. C. Eadie (Ed.), *Changing by design: A practical approach to innovation in nonprofit organizations* (pp. 20–38). San Francisco: Jossey-Bass. Revised and reprinted with the permission of Jossey-Bass Publishers.

information processing, medicine, and many other areas—has generated new products, new businesses, and new tools for managing.

The increasingly global economy has steadily eroded the capacity of individual nations, states, and communities to manage and develop their own economies in isolation. Inexorable federal government downsizing since the mid-1970s has forced public and nonprofit professionals to explore new revenue streams and to sharpen entrepreneurial skills (Edwards, Cooke, & Reid, 1996). Corporate downsizing, along with the two-career family, has radically reduced the amount of volunteer time to serve on nonprofit boards, committees, and task forces. The list goes on and on, a familiar litany to everyone involved in leading and managing nonprofit organizations.

In a calm and stable world blessed with a high degree of predictability, being a board member, chief executive officer, or manager of a nonprofit organization would be a tough enough job. But in today's topsy-turvy world, the task of leading organizations can seem overwhelming at times. One thing is dramatically clear: The only viable response to the change going on around us and our organizations is to take command of our own individual and organizational innovation and to guide and direct that innovation to capitalize on opportunities to grow and to counter threats to well-being. Merely standing pat, or circling the wagons for a battle, would be a disastrous course.

The fact that the only sensible course in today's world is to lead and manage innovation creatively is not news to the great majority of nonprofit leaders, particularly chief executives. Indeed, the term "change management" has nearly achieved buzzword status. What is news, however, is the rapidly accumulating knowledge about leading innovation and the more powerful innovation management tools that have been developed and tested recently. For one thing, we have become more knowledgeable about the very natural, deep-seated resistance of most human beings to change, regardless of what they might say about thriving on change. We now know that the beloved traditional model of chief executive leadership—the broad shoulders, macho rhetoric ("The buck stops here!"), administrative focus, and control fetish—does not suffice in a world that is always challenging and frequently threatening—a world that demands flexibility, creativity, and the expansion of human capability.

Fortunately, a new chief executive model has emerged that consists of key skills and attributes for successfully leading in tumultuous times. We have learned a considerable amount about ways to build a positive, productive, and close partnership between the board and the chief executive, which is indispensable for successful change leadership. We also have learned ways to move beyond the traditional control bias of planning and to make planning a more powerful innovation engine for economic development organizations.

TRAVELING THE CHANGE PATH

Three tall barriers stand in the way of a nonprofit undertaking the journey of self-determined, consciously directed innovation:

1. Failure to see the need to change,
2. Fear of changing, and
3. The relentless grind of day-to-day operations.

Readers who have embarked on their own personal growth journey know how daunting these challenges can be. Changing one's own life can be a monumental task; moving a whole organization in new directions is more so. Well-traveled paths may offer little in the way of excitement, but at least they feel comfortable and far safer than meandering around unknown terrain, where who knows what terrors await. Doggedly working toward the never-seen bottom of the constantly filling in-basket day after day may feel productive and virtuous, but it leaves little time and energy to pick up signals from the wider world that change is needed, much less to begin to plot a new journey.

So as individuals and as organizations we often wait for major crises—a heart attack, a separation or divorce, a precipitous drop in membership or revenue, an anticipated budget deficit, an exposé in the local press that threatens a stellar reputation—to jolt us out of our complacency and force us to embark in new directions. Fortunately, even major crises, while inevitably painful and costly, are seldom fatal, and as goads to needed action they can be seen as blessings, albeit often well disguised. Crises do not force most nonprofits to close up shop, turn off the lights, and lock the doors. There are second chances: Lessons can be learned and put to good use in the future, budgets can be balanced eventually, and good reputations can be restored. However, the cost of waiting for a crisis to spur action can be appallingly high in dollars, in pain and suffering, in eroded public credibility, in the consumption of precious energy, and in declining internal morale. Indeed, being anticipatory and proactive is cost-effectiveness at its most powerful.

For example, concerned by the sea of gray heads at every concert, a symphony business manager and board might take action—such as giving concerts in various neighborhoods, initiating a children's concert series, and direct-mail marketing to new audiences—to deal with what appears to be an ominous trend before many empty seats show up in the hall. Fearing stagnant sales, a health product sales association might take the initiative by redefining its basic markets and aggressively seeking merger opportunities with other associations in the field. Any alert and aggressive organization can decide, before the crisis hits, to take a leading role in its own change.

But in doing so, the board, chief executive, and management team should understand that the journey of self-determined and guided change is seldom smooth, and failure is not uncommon in the world of large-scale organizational change. As De Pree (1989) pointed out, "Anything truly creative results in change, and if there is one thing a well-run bureaucracy or institution or major corporation finds difficult to handle, it is change"(p. 33). No matter how capable, courageous, and disciplined its people, an organization can fail in managing change for one or more of several important reasons: weak board and chief executive leadership; absence of a clear strategic framework; an unsystematic, skewed approach to change; a quick-fix mentality; uncreative thinking and narrowly circumscribed strategy formulation; unrealistic implementation planning; inadequate implementation management; and staff resistance. The approach to leading and managing change that is described in this chapter is intended to deal with all of these major spoilers that have limited the effectiveness of nonprofit efforts to lead and manage change in the past.

EFFECTIVE CHANGE LEADERSHIP AND MANAGEMENT PROCESS

Nonprofit board members, chief executives, and managers who are committed to taking command of their own organizational innovation and change should insist that, as a result of using a particular change process, their organizations are able to put their resources to the best feasible use in capitalizing on environmental opportunities and in coping with environmental threats.

Clear, Detailed Strategic Framework

Strategic framework means the values that the nonprofit most cherishes and that comprise its most important do's and don'ts; its vision for the future in terms of what it aspires to be and the role it aspires to play; and its mission in terms of its services and products, its customers and clients, and its key roles and functions. Without a well-defined framework addressing overall purposes, aspirations, and boundaries, organizational change will not, by definition, have any rhyme or reason, and it will be just as apt to produce bad results as good. The values that govern a nonprofit's change should serve as an ethical framework and, as such, should include the small number of what O'Toole (1995) called the "moral absolutes," which include "only a few moral principles based on natural law. Though most of the major issues in social life are subjective and relative, not all are. There are, in short, some moral absolutes that are not contingent on circumstances" (p. 105).

Rational Priorities

Rational priorities are the change initiatives that an organization should tackle first things first in terms of organizational opportunities and needs. Only so much time, money, and energy can be devoted to changing things in an organization while also continuing to manage day-to-day operations, so careful selection of targets is imperative if resources are not to be frittered away on lesser matters while problems threaten organizational existence or one-time opportunities are lost forever.

Humane Expectations

Implementing change, whether personal or organizational, is taxing enough without adding to the pain by making unrealistic demands on the people who must translate change targets into practice. A humane approach will take into account both the feelings and the capabilities of an organization's employees and will never demand the impossible. On the other hand, the adage "no pain, no gain" applies in any serious change process, and so no participant should expect a pain-free experience.

Comprehensive and Balanced Approach

As much attention should be given to the what of change—its content—as to the how—its implementation. All of the forms that change can take should be comprehensively considered in determining exactly what change should be undertaken in any given year. There is outward-looking change, such as in revenue sources, customers and clients, and stakeholder relationships, and there is more internally focused change, such as in planning and management systems. The creative challenge is to choose the mix that best meets an organization's needs in the context of the changing world around it (Tichy, 1983).

Creative and Innovative Responses

Creativity is at the heart of innovation, which is basically the process of bringing the new into being. In a complex, rapidly changing world, merely projecting conventional wisdom into the future would be a high-risk course of action. Being creative means to see what has not yet occurred, to envision responses that are not being made, and to have a more open and questioning process so that practical innovations will yield important benefits (Boden, 1991; Csikszentmihalyi, 1996; Gardner, 1993).

Realistic Expectations

Shooting high and falling short is a surefire recipe for disappointment, lost credibility, frayed tempers, cynicism, and even organizational chaos when the failure is dramatic enough. The point is to implement fully the changes that have been planned and to do so on time, within budget, and without unnecessary pain and suffering (Eadie, 1996).

Self-Sustainable Process

Any process for leading and managing change will ultimately prove too expensive if a nonprofit board, chief executive, and management team cannot use it on an ongoing basis without endless consulting assistance. And only if it becomes one of the nonprofit's mainline planning and management processes can it yield a powerful return on the investment of time and energy.

QUICK FIXES

Trying to figure out what is happening in a rambunctious world that at times defies understanding and attempting to fashion initiatives for organizational change that will make sense in that environment are part of a complex process that flies in the face of an apparent widespread appetite for quick-fix solutions and low-cost panaceas. The more complex and ambitious the changes being attempted, the less the likelihood of immediate, visible results, and so patience and the willingness to bear costs for some time before reaping benefits are requisites for successful change leadership. Unfortunately, they often are in short supply, especially when things are not going smoothly.

Over the years, many nonprofits have lurched from one half-understood and inadequately implemented management innovation to another, inevitably finding the fault in the innovation rather than in their taste for the costless and painless solution. Management by objectives, program budgeting, strategic planning, participatory management, total quality—these all have been tried and abandoned when the costs became clear, the pain was felt, and immediate results failed to materialize.

The instant gratification approach to change not only fails to achieve the desired affects, but it also misuses and abuses the people in an organization while damaging morale. For example, a task force was preparing for a two-day strategic planning retreat. The specific assignment for this group of smart, hardworking managers was to assess internal capabilities, and one of the issues they focused on was how to assess the agency's experience in managing change and how to convey that assessment to the assembled management team at the retreat.

The day of the retreat, the room rocked with laughter when the slide the task force had designed appeared on the screen. The slide depicted a graveyard crowded

"Welcome aboard, and I think I speak for all of us when I say that we expect fresh, different, and innovative ideas from you. . . . Not just more of the same old thing, right guys?"

with stones. Each stone named a management innovation that had been attempted and abandoned and stated its years on this earth. The average life span was 18 months. The next slide analyzed the reasons for so many premature deaths among such a large population of innovation projects and estimated the hours and dollars wasted over the years. It did not take long for sadness, then anger, to replace humor, as the assembled managers thought about the better uses to which their time and money might have been put (Kemp, Funk, & Eadie, 1993).

BEYOND QUICK FIXES: THE THREE-CAPACITY APPROACH

Three broad organizational capacities are essential for successful nonprofit leadership and management of change:

1. The capacity to lead,
2. The capacity to innovate, and
3. The capacity to implement.

These closely related and mutually reinforcing capacities are a kind of internal infrastructure that supports the efforts of boards, chief executives, and management teams to determine and direct their organizations' change.

Capacity to Lead

The pre-eminent leadership team of a nonprofit consists of its chief executive and its governing board, and the success of a nonprofit's change efforts depend heavily on how well the respective leadership roles are played and on how effectively the two parties work together (Carver, 1990; Eadie, 1994; Houle, 1989). A nonprofit's chief executive is without question the prime mover in any large-scale organizational change effort (Bennis, 1989; Gardner, 1990). No other person in the organization is in a better position to make or break the change process. No one else possesses comparable authority, influence, and resources (not even the board, contrary to theory). No other person's words and actions are listened to and observed as closely. And experience has taught that unless the chief executive has a deep understanding of the process of change and is strongly committed to developing his or her organization's capacity to change, little important change is likely to take place.

Chief executives can promote self-determined and managed change by articulating a clear vision that inspires employees; by building a culture that is change friendly; by ensuring that planning and management systems promote and support change; and by ensuring that the resources, primarily money and time, required to implement change initiatives are committed. Boards can be a precious resource in the change leadership and management process, basically by contributing knowledge and experience to the process of creating a nonprofit's strategic framework—its values, vision, and mission—by helping generate financial and political resources and by supporting the chief executive in carrying out change.

All too often, this top leadership team does not function well (Carver, 1990; Eadie, 1993, 1994). Many nonprofit boards play only the most perfunctory role in blessing vision and mission statements prepared by staff or in signing off on plans that have already been written, edited, and bound. Such boards, involved only at the end of the planning process, naturally feel little ownership of planned change initiatives or accountability for the successful implementation of change. As a passive audience, they have the luxury of sitting back with crossed arms to judge the chief executive and staff, and they cannot be depended on to back the chief executive when the going gets rough.

There are plenty of boards at the other end of the spectrum, too, that can become the enemy of planned change by dabbling in details that are obviously operational and having an ego investment in current operations. For example, membership organizations that are heavily volunteer driven, such as civic clubs, often treat board service as the top rung of the volunteer "career ladder." Having worked their way up the ladder by rolling up their sleeves and getting their hands dirty with the details of running programs, these volunteers-become-board-members can become wedded to these programs and be quite resistant to changing them. Board members with strong emotional attachments to particular organizational methodologies also can become enemies of creative change. For example, recovering-alcoholic members on the board of a chemical dependency treatment center would not allow any alternatives to the Alcoholics Anonymous 12-Step approach to be considered because of their passionate commitment to a treatment process that had literally, in their minds, saved their lives.

Many nonprofit chief executives are ill prepared technically and emotionally to provide strong, creative leadership for a change process that actively involves both board and staff members. They have frequently ascended the professional ladder by demonstrating technical and programmatic virtuosity in specific programs or functions, but these skills do not provide a comprehensive picture of the organization they now lead. In addition, the very competitiveness, drive, decisiveness, and rat-a-tat style that got them where they are now poorly equips them to lead a creative change process.

Perhaps the most serious professional limitation among nonprofit chief executives is a strong need to be in control, which can stifle openness, limit organizational creativity, overly constrain planning, and impede meaningful involvement and partnership. Argyris (1993) wrote about "espoused theory" and "theory in practice," observing that it is not uncommon to find a person espousing one theory while contradicting it in practice, without recognizing the inconsistency. Some chief executives may preach participatory management while at the same time, with apparent unconscious motivation, employing the Louis XIV–style of participatory management—I pronounce, you listen and obey.

It is unrealistic to expect that every chief executive, no matter how smart and competent, can grow psychologically to the extent required to lead the change process effectively. Years of training in traditional management, with its control orientation, mitigate against easy transformation. One very bright and capable chief executive was handed an evaluation that his board had just completed. Every technical category was marked A+. He was judged top-notch over the entire management spectrum, from planning and budgeting to financial management and supervision of staff. But the evaluation concluded with the recommendation that he seek other employment because his clear need to be right in every instance, his combativeness in proving his points, and his defensiveness when challenged made him too difficult to work with. Despite advice and encouragement to deal with an obvious character problem that was deep seated, he was not able to rehabilitate himself. Not long after this incident, he lost his job, and eventually two others for basically the same reason, and he has now left the field of nonprofit management.

Another example involves the struggles of the managing director of a nonprofit theater. She was bright, talented, committed to artistic quality, and incredibly hardworking, but her deep-seated need to be in command was so strong that, despite her publicly announced and apparently sincere intent to involve the board and staff creatively in setting directions, she could not relinquish control enough to allow meaningful partnerships to develop. As a consequence, the one-woman show was perpetuated, and the theater's slow and steady decline continued.

A new model of chief executive leadership that is suited to the demands of leading and managing change in turbulent times is emerging. This model sees the job as being far more than the boss at whose desk the proverbial buck stops, the program expert who understands the operational dynamics and cannot be snowed by his or her managers, or the technocrat who makes sure the support systems run. The chief executive as effective change leader must be a visionary, not only capable of thinking of the organization in terms of long-run purposes and ends, he or she also must be strongly committed to a collaborative approach to fashioning the vision that creatively draws on the knowledge, expertise, and experience of board and staff members. In this new model, the chief executive must also be an architect and designer, eschewing the old-time command approach to leadership. He or she concentrates on design, putting together all of the complex pieces of the organizational puzzle: board and management team roles, systems such as strategic planning and performance management, programs to enhance individual creative capacity, and more. Only through conscious organizational design can a modern chief executive ensure that creativity is transformed into innovation, that systems are compatible and integrated, and that one or more of the quick-fix solutions being peddled these days is not bought. The chief executive also must play the role of facilitator and coach, helping board and staff members perform their respective functions more effectively and grow in capability. This requires that the chief executive not only be supportive of capability-building efforts but also that he or she teach by doing rather than by preaching, by visibly engaging in growth strategies even though this will pierce the shield of chief executive infallibility. The chief executive also must be an active partner with his or her board, welcoming its substantive contribution and creative involvement and being committed to developing the board's leadership capacity. This means embracing a nontraditional model board leadership that sees the board as both a precious asset that needs, for the sake of the organization, to be fully utilized and as a company within the nonprofit corporation that generates essential products.

This type of new leadership is secure, nondefensive, and open. It welcomes and encourages wide-ranging questions and new ideas, even if they challenge official positions.

Chief executives who aspire to build their organization's capacity to lead and manage change must be courageous in two major respects. First, they must develop their own creative capacity, which means taking what mythologist Joseph Campbell (1968) called the interior "hero's journey" themselves, looking inward and becoming more self-aware by venturing into the subconscious sphere of the mind. Chief executives cannot lead the innovation process effectively without this deeply personal, psychological exploration of their creative capacity. Second, they must be willing to promote the psychological growth of their employees, being "lead psychologists" in the face of almost certain skepticism and even opposition. Talking about the self and the subconscious does not follow traditional macho management rhetoric, and the chief executive who dares to lead in creative capacity building must steel himself or herself against accusations of flakiness or even dementia from traditionalists.

A new approach to board leadership that goes well beyond the traditional board-as-passive-audience also is being successfully tested around the United States (Eadie, 1994). In active partnership with the chief executive, the board of the future will function as a kind of business within the nonprofit corporation, guided by a clear leadership mission and focused on producing bottom-line outcomes for the nonprofit. For example, an activist nonprofit board might hold a retreat with the chief executive and management team every year to revisit the vision and mission statements, identify new issues facing the organization (opportunities as well as challenges), and reach agreement on major change initiatives for the coming year.

The board of the future will be accountable for the quality of its membership and for its performance, setting detailed performance standards and regularly monitoring board operations. The board's precise leadership roles and responsibilities will be a matter of ongoing discussion, guided by the needs and circumstances of the nonprofit at any given phase of its development. The division of labor between the board and chief executive will go beyond the old-fashioned policy—administration dichotomy. For example, a small young organization may want its board to play a hands-on role in securing the financial resources to fund growth by making telephone calls to donors and visiting foundations. A more removed stance, involving monitoring rather than doing, may make sense when the nonprofit is securely established and revenue streams are secure.

Capacity to Innovate

The second critical capacity in successful leadership is innovation. The concepts and techniques comprising what is popularly known as "change management" are for the most part aimed at deciding how to implement change, with lots of attention to securing the buy-in of participants who must do much of the work of changing. Deciding how to implement change is, however, distinctly subordinate to the fundamental question that ultimately determines success or failure: What will the content of the change be? Determining the *what* of change, rather than merely the *how to*, inevitably leads a nonprofit into the realm of innovation, which is the process of putting something new into practice, whether a service, product, relationship, or management system. In a complex, rapidly changing environment, systematic innovation is a survival tool rather than a luxury, and the greater the complexity and faster the external change, the more pressing the need for innovation.

Innovation means going beyond the tried and true and transcending conventional wisdom in responding to challenges. Innovative solutions are not conveyed in slogans or on bumper stickers. Being innovative requires openness, careful listening, and learning; it means recognizing complexities and subtle distinctions and taking them into account when fashioning effective solutions. Being innovative means seeing through the shell game of no-cost solutions to complex challenges and having the courage to bear the costs.

Innovation is a challenging process; innovative solutions to complex problems can be difficult to explain and sell to the man and woman on the street who elect our public officials and more or less provide the resources to implement solutions. Simplicity can be seductive; sound bites, if not ultimately nourishing, are easily chewed; stereotypes save time and demons are fun to hate.

But no matter how stiff the challenge, true innovative leadership demands more than appeasing anger and pandering to an appetite for no-cost, no-brainer solutions. It means asking second, third, and even fourth questions and seeing beyond the immediate outcomes. Innovative nonprofits do not merely train unemployed people for jobs that do not exist or will quickly become outmoded or place their clients in minimum-wage jobs with no future merely to meet the immediate performance standards of the U.S. Department of Labor. Nor do they buy into the notion that the complex issue of violent crime can be solved through three-strikes-and-you're-out sentencing or filling jails to capacity. They know enough to distrust gut reactions and simplistic solutions.

The innovation capacity consists of two major subcapacities: (1) creativity, which generates the ideas, the possibilities for change, and (2) planning, which selects from possibilities and eventually translates them into concrete change projects or initiatives that can then be implemented. They are an inseparable team. Lots of creativity without a well-developed planning capacity is a recipe for unrealized potential, frustration, and little important change. A well-developed planning process run by people with little opportunity to build or express their creative capacity will severely limit the possibilities for innovative action.

CREATIVITY. Think innovation, and creativity comes immediately to mind; the two concepts go hand in hand. Although they are frequently treated as the same thing, it makes sense to view creativity as the capacity that undergirds and enriches the innovation process. Creativity is the supplier of the newness that the innovation process translates into practice. An ill-defined concept having as much mystery as science about it, creativity involves seeing in the mind patterns that have not been seen before. It means going beyond the tried and true and transcending conventional wisdom in thinking about possible responses to environmental challenges. Creativity is the capacity to generate mental possibilities which, through innovation, are put into practice in the real world (Boden, 1991; Csikszentmihalyi, 1996; Gardner, 1993).

Developing the creative capacity that is at the heart of a nonprofit's capability to innovate is a matter of developing the creative capacity of the individual human beings comprising the organization. Individuals, not the systems that support decision making, are more or less creative, and no planning process, no matter how sophisticated its design, can fully compensate for inadequate individual capability.

PLANNING. Planning, especially of the strategic variety, can be the innovation machine that transforms creative ideas into practical innovations in a nonprofit organization; therefore, it is potentially one of the pre-eminent drivers of nonprofit change. Unfortunately, since the 1970s, strategic planning has earned a reputation for generating more paper than action (see Chapter 17 for a more comprehensive discussion of planning). This is by no means a bum rap. In actual practice, if not in theory, strategic or long-range planning has tended to be focused on control rather than innovation, basically taking what an organization is already doing and merely projecting it forward three, five, or more years into the future. Of course, because the wider world refuses to oblige us by remaining static or by changing in a nice, neat fashion, such mammoth globs of paper have quickly become outdated and have routinely ended up on dusty shelves, seldom if ever consulted (Bryson, 1995; Eadie, 1993).

It may have been professional planners, with their penchant for order, who created the three-, five-, and 10-year planning cycles. These surely correspond to no natural cycle in human affairs, nor have they ever delivered the world they promised. If the benefits of formal planning have been scant, the costs have been high. For one thing, the illusion of control that bloated documents can create has lulled many nonprofits into a false sense of being secure and in control of their destinies, thereby actually making them more vulnerable than if they had never done formal planning. For another, the time spent writing, editing, printing, and binding such formal plans might have been better spent gathering information on environmental trends and conditions and focusing on specific change targets. In addition, going through the planning motions for no useful purpose has bred understandable cynicism among managers, making it more difficult to build support for serious planning.

Just because strategic planning has been misused as a tool does not mean that it cannot produce powerful results. In reaction to traditional wheel-spinning in pursuit of the illusion of control, serious planning reforms have revitalized the process since the mid-1980s. Indeed, a significant new variation on the strategic planning theme, typically known as "strategic management," has been successfully tested in hundreds of organizations, including several nonprofits (Bryson, 1995; Eadie, 1994, 1997; Mintzberg, 1994).

A strategic management process that is seriously applied results in the identification of "change challenges"—strategic issues in the form of opportunities to move closer to an organization's vision or barriers blocking progress toward the vision, the selection of the challenges or issues to be addressed now, and the development of change initiatives to address the selected issues. Taken together, the change initiatives at any given time comprise a kind of organizational change portfolio or agenda, which must be managed separately from day-to-day operations if it is not to be overwhelmed.

The annual process of operational planning and budget preparation also can be a source of systematic organizational innovation, although on a smaller scale than in strategic management and within established boundaries. Because operational planning is by its nature control focused and is a long-surviving, hearty tool without much glamour, its innovative potential has received less attention than it deserves.

Capacity to Implement

The third critical task in successful leadership is implementation. The gap between intent and practice, between plans and action, is frequently not successfully bridged. The following case demonstrates this gap.

The two days could not have gone better for the board and staff of the Center for Family Services. Millhaven was a superb facility, offering spacious, well-equipped conference rooms, a sylvan setting, and numerous recreational opportunities. The facilitator did a great job of steering the group through a complex process of visioning, assessing external conditions and trends, and identifying several issues that appeared to deserve closer attention. The group narrowed the issues down to four that everyone agreed should be explored in greater detail in the coming weeks and turned into concrete change strategies: (1) an expected cut of 30 percent in the next year's United Way subsidy; (2) a proposed merger with the Children's Services Agency; (3) the need for an aggressive financial development program; and (4) eroding board enthusiasm, as evidenced by several resignations and the cancellation of two board meetings for failure to attract a quorum. Loud applause greeted the chair's closing comments, the meeting ended on a high note, and everyone drove home anticipating the positive changes on the horizon.

Days, weeks, and months went by. Copiers and faxes spewed out paper, staff were up to their eyeballs with just getting through the day-to-day operations without major mishaps, board members occasionally asked about follow-up from the retreat, which was well on its way to becoming a hazy memory. Things went along pretty much as usual. Fortunately, some last-minute lobbying resulted in a smaller-than-expected cut in the United Way allocation, and so only a couple of positions had to be eliminated. Filling three board vacancies made achieving quorums easier, but enthusiasm was still lacking.

This downbeat scenario probably sounds depressingly familiar because examples of breakdown between verbal intentions and actual practice are everywhere around us. Planned change is frequently not implemented for three major reasons: (1) unrealistic implementation planning, (2) inadequate implementation structure and process, and (3) a milieu that is unfriendly to change (Dalziel & Schoonover, 1988; Kanter, 1989; Tichy, 1983).

Through detailed implementation planning, an organization determines for each change initiative or project precisely what steps must be taken to carry out the initiative, who is accountable for seeing that each step is accomplished, the timetable that will be followed, and the resources required to implement the plan. A truly realistic plan will pay close attention to the required resources, looking not just at the obvious cost in dollars but also looking at staff skills that may have to be upgraded to ensure full implementation. For example, there may be no point in moving forward with an image-building strategy if a part-time person is not hired to handle media relations.

Change initiatives or projects easily can be overwhelmed by the press of day-to-day events. A change structure and implementation process that is kept separate from the daily management process can provide the protection, nurturing, and oversight required to keep change initiatives alive and well. Many organizations have created special change programs, with a steering committee composed of management team members who meet regularly for the sole purpose of overseeing the implementation of change initiatives or projects, a team member serving as the coordinator of change projects and as the quality control officer, and staff task forces accountable for seeing to the many details involved in implementing the projects. Everyone involved wears only the "change hat" when participating in the program, which is kept well away from normal operations. So, for example, change matters never become the last item on a crowded Monday morning staff meeting agenda.

A nonprofit's internal milieu is another factor with substantial influence on the implementation of change. An organization's milieu is in large measure its culture. Schein (1985) defined *culture* as a "pattern of basic assumptions—invented, discovered, or developed by a given group as it learns to cope with its problems of external adaptation and internal integration—that has worked well enough to be considered valid and, therefore, to be taught to new members as the correct way to perceive, think, and feel in relation to those problems" (p. 9). The organizational milieu also consists of the current climate, including the feelings and attitudes of the staff. Obviously, an organization lurching from one crisis to another over a period of weeks or months, with a fatigued, nervous staff, will have a harder time concentrating on the implementation of change than one with a more secure and peaceful climate. Furthermore, a staff that has been negatively affected on several occasions by abrupt, seemingly irrational changes of course by the chief executive is likely to hold back both commitment and energy when asked to participate in a change process.

CHANGING TO GET READY FOR CHANGE

Developing the essential capacities to lead, innovate, and implement, thereby building a foundation for continuous self-generated and guided change, will in itself involve organizational change. Therefore, most nonprofits will be well advised to tackle capacity building early on, even while concurrently responding to change signals from the external world by fashioning new strategic directions, programs, and services. This will require virtuoso juggling among a plethora of competing values, because while a nonprofit works on capacity building to enhance its capability to respond to the changing world, it will have no choice but to respond to specific external opportunities or threats when the stakes are high enough.

In a practical example, in a recent management team meeting a nonprofit nursing home without a contemporary strategic management process has taken note of growing consumer demand for one-stop retirement living, or continuum of care, that offers a full range of accommodations and services without having to leave a core campus. As they live longer and healthier lives, senior citizens want to begin at one end of the spectrum with truly independent living in detached cottages and then move through a range of living styles until they arrive at skilled-nursing care in a traditional long-term-care setting at the other end of the spectrum. The strength of the demand dictates that the organization begin to explore strategies for expansion from its current traditional home to a wider range of facilities and services. At the same time, the team has decided that it must take a more systematic approach to identifying and acting on strategic issues in the future, so it also has decided to create a task force to design a new strategic management process for this purpose.

It would not be feasible to ignore the changing outside world while focusing exclusively on building the internal change leadership and management infrastructure. The key is to create an overall change agenda or portfolio that balances the need to respond to external events with the internal capacity-building need, making sure that first things are put first. For example, strengthening the leadership of a board that is not fully involved in setting strategic directions but that is not malfunctioning in any important way would obviously take second place to dealing with the imminent loss of a grant supplying one-third of the budget. However, a board that is upset about its role and mad enough to consider firing the chief executive would merit concerted attention before considering possible diversification options as part of a long-term growth strategy.

A nonprofit's board, chief executive, and management team must work together closely to keep the change agenda or portfolio balanced from year to year, ensuring that it responds effectively to external challenges and opportunities while continuously strengthening the essential capabilities on which effective change leadership and management depend. Their choice of change initiatives should be based on a realistic assessment of what is at stake for their organization in dealing with particular initiatives, and their responsibility is to create a mix of initiatives that promises the greatest benefit possible, including loss reduction, at an affordable cost.

SKILLS APPLICATION EXERCISE

- Describe the overall experience of your organization, or of an organization you are familiar with, or of your own personal experience in leading and managing innovation. What change initiatives or planned innovations have been implemented? What change initiatives have fallen by the wayside? Why do you think these have not been successful?
- Assess the strengths and weaknesses of the chief executive's leadership of change in your organization, or in an organization you are familiar with, or your own personal leadership of change in your life. What skills and attributes need to be strengthened to lead change more effectively?
- Assess the strengths and weaknesses of your board's leadership of change or of a board you are familiar with. What aspects of the board's leadership process and structure might need to be strengthened to enhance its change leadership?
- Does the planning process in your organization, or an organization you know, or your own personal planning actually produce practical change initiatives consciously aimed at significant innovation? If not, why not? What features of the planning process need to be changed, and how?
- What is the experience of your organization, or an organization you know, or your own personal experience in implementing change initiatives? What might you do in terms of implementation structure and process to strengthen the implementation process?

REFERENCES

Argyris, C. (1993). *Knowledge for action: A guide to overcoming barriers to organizational change.* San Francisco: Jossey-Bass.

Bennis, W. (1989). *Why leaders can't lead: The unconscious conspiracy continues.* San Francisco: Jossey-Bass.

Boden, M. A. (1991). *The creative mind: Myths and mechanisms.* New York: Basic Books.

Bryson, J. M. (1995). *Strategic planning for public and nonprofit organizations: A guide to strengthening and sustaining organizational achievement.* San Francisco: Jossey-Bass.

Campbell, J. (1968). *The hero with a thousand faces* (2nd ed.). Princeton, NJ: Princeton University Press.

Carver, J. (1990). *Boards that make a difference: A new design for leadership in nonprofit and public organizations.* San Francisco: Jossey-Bass.

Csikszentmihalyi, M. (1996). *Creativity: Flow and the psychology of discovery and invention.* New York: HarperCollins.

Dalziel, M. M., & Schoonover, S. C. (1988). *Changing ways: A practical tool for implementing change within organizations.* New York: AMACOM.

De Pree, M. (1989). *Leadership is an art.* New York: Dell.

Eadie, D. C. (1993). *Beyond strategic planning: How to involve nonprofit boards in growth and change.* Washington, DC: National Center for Nonprofit Boards.

Eadie, D. C. (1994). *Boards that work: A practical guide for building effective association boards.* Washington, DC: American Society of Association Executives.

Eadie, D. C. (1996). *Leading and managing strategic change.* In J. L. Perry (Ed.), *Handbook of public administration* (2nd ed., pp. 499–510). San Francisco: Jossey-Bass.

Eadie, D. C. (1997). *Meeting the change challenge.* Washington, DC: American Society of Association Executives.

Edwards, R. L., Cooke, P. W., & Reid, P. N. (1996). Social work management in an era of diminishing federal responsibility. *Social Work, 41,* 468–479.

Gardner, H. (1993). *Creating minds.* New York: Basic Books.

Gardner, J. (1990). *On leadership.* New York: Free Press.

Houle, C. O. (1989). *Governing boards: Their nature and nurture.* San Francisco: Jossey-Bass.

Kanter, R. M. (1989). *When giants learn to dance.* New York: Simon & Schuster.

Kemp, E. J., Funk, R. J., & Eadie, D. C. (1993). Change in chewable bites: Applying strategic management at EEOC. *Public Administration Review, 53,* 129–134.

Mintzberg, H. (1994, January/February).The rise and fall of strategic planning. *Harvard Business Review,* p. 102–114.

Morgan, G. (1988). *Riding the waves of change.* San Francisco: Jossey-Bass.

O'Toole, J. (1995). *Leading change. Overcoming the ideology of comfort and the tyranny of custom.* San Francisco: Jossey-Bass.

Schein, E. H. (1985). *Organizational culture and leadership.* San Francisco: Jossey-Bass.

Tichy, N. M. (1983). *Managing strategic change.* New York: John Wiley & Sons.

Writing Winning Proposals

Christine E. Henry

As described in Chapter 1, nonprofit managers must be skilled at performing the broker role and must be engaged in acquiring resources and relating effectively to the organization's external environment. Managers will need good boundary-spanning skills to serve as the interface between the organization and others in its environment. Managers also will need to be knowledgeable about funding sources and adept at preparing funding proposals. This chapter provides information about how to identify potential funding sources and how to develop effective proposals to secure foundation and government funding.

The challenge confronting managers is that the competition for dollars and recognition is fierce, particularly as the pressure grows to fill in gaps left by cuts in government funding. The ability to meet these challenges involves constant attention to social trends and the demands for organizational and client service and also the ability to work together with government and business to meet changing needs. A successful nonprofit organization must have a healthy mix of funding sources. A fundraising strategy that includes government funds, direct-mail solicitation, foundation grants, individual major gifts, earned income, and special events is most successful in the long run (Edwards, Benefield, Edwards, & Yankey, 1997).

The economy of the United States generally includes the government, business, and nonprofit sectors. There are now more than 1.5 million nonprofit organizations in the United States, and the number grows daily (Independent Sector, 2001). Indeed, 6 percent of all organizations in the country are nonprofit. The sector itself quickly is coming into its own as a viable field of teaching, research, and application for academicians, practitioners, and policymakers. The sector is recognized as a social, economic, and political influence on the way Americans work, learn, serve others, and enjoy leisure time. It is a significant source of employment, as 1 in 12 Americans works in nonprofit organizations. Although the majority of nonprofits have annual revenues of less than $500,000, the annual revenues of nonprofits exceed $670 billion. As a group they spend more than $340 billion each year (Independent Sector, 2001). Management expert Peter Drucker has referred to the nonprofit sector as America's largest employer—the combined labor pool of paid staff and volunteers in the United States amounts to more than 90 million people each year (Independent Sector, 2001).

Only about 12 percent of the revenue from private sources to nonprofits is from foundations. The vast majority of private funds come from individuals, either from direct gifts or bequests (Carlson, 1995). Nevertheless, grants from foundations are an important part of a nonprofit's funding plan. More than 50,000 foundations in the United States make annual grants to nonprofit organizations totaling more than $12 billion (Independent Sector, 2001). Foundations play a powerful role in soliciting support (through challenge and matching grants), encouraging new initiatives, furthering causes, servicing trends, and shaping evaluations.

DEVELOPING THE CONCEPT

The first thing to do before investigating foundations or submitting a proposal is to be absolutely clear about the organization's mission, qualifying status, and specific purpose for the proposal. Develop the who, what, why, where, when, and how of the proposal, whether it be to support general operations or to fund a special project. The following questions will help clarify and develop the proposal:

- Are the organization's mission and purpose clear? Does the project truly support its mission, or is the idea being tailored to a funder's interests?
- Does the organization have its nonprofit tax designation from the Internal Revenue Service (IRS), or does it have a qualified agency that can serve as its fiscal agent?
- Have the need and population that the organization intends to address been assessed carefully, taking into account other agencies or programs that offer similar services? How is the proposal unique? What gap does it fill?
- Does the organization have a concrete plan that addresses a need that is important to society?
- Can the organization provide measurable goals and objectives and a reasonable time frame?

- Is the organization capable of implementing the project?
- Has the organization carefully developed the financial components and made plans for continued funding?

Put the answers to these questions into written form to serve as a rough draft for the proposal. This first step of clarifying the purpose also will help focus the investigation on those foundations that are well matched to the organization's interests. Most foundations are relatively clear about what they want to fund. For example, some foundations fund only mental health or environmental projects, whereas others are interested in scholarships or the arts. Many have geographic restrictions, and some do not respond to unsolicited proposals. They may specify that they do not contribute to general operations, respond to annual appeals, or fund capital projects.

INVESTIGATING THE POSSIBILITIES

Between 80 and 95 percent of all proposals are declined (Golden, 1997). The reasons for rejection include limited foundation dollars, a proposal that is outside of a foundation's guidelines, an unclear project, costs that are too high, or an idea that is not compelling. The chances of a proposal being funded are increased significantly if the organization has carefully researched the types of foundations and their interest areas, guidelines, and limitations. Foundation representatives spend a great deal of time and effort acquiring new information about their areas of interest and learning about the needs in their communities. They often gather at conferences and forums to discuss ways to meet community needs through targeted funding and collaborative measures. Some foundation representatives get very involved in the projects that they fund.

Foundations usually publish their interest areas and funding guidelines in an annual report, grant guidelines, or an application form, all of which can be obtained on their Web site (if they have one) or through a letter or telephone call to the foundation. These publications are very specific about the format, deadlines, and limitations the grant seeker should follow in submitting a proposal. It is important for an organization to obtain this information and do its homework about a foundation's areas of interest and its limitations before submitting a proposal. A preliminary letter of inquiry, an email, or a telephone call (the guidelines often say which) is the best way to get a feel for a possible match.

Also, pay attention to the differences from foundation to foundation, and personalize the proposal as much as possible. Developing relationships with foundation representatives is important, especially if the foundation gives operating support to the same organizations over a long period. The foundation is primarily interested in the scope and general application of a project and in how it advances the foundation's philanthropic interests (Brewer, Achilles, & Fuhriman, 1995).

TYPES OF FOUNDATIONS

There are many kinds of foundations. *Independent* or *family foundations*, referred to as "private foundations" by the IRS, are established by individuals or families and are usually funded through inherited wealth or wealth accumulated through a business activity. Many of these foundations are established through a substantial bequest on the death of the founder, who may have left specific instructions about what program areas the foundation will fund. Foundation funds may later be augmented by contributions from other family members. Family members often become very involved in the awarding of grants, although the majority of the foundation's giving is consistent with the interests of the original donor. Some of these foundations are quite large and powerful, employ several executives and program officers, and wield a good deal of influence in their areas of interest. Some examples are the Charles Stuart Mott Foundation (microenterprise and low-income entrepreneurship), the Ewing Marion Kauffman Foundation (public policy), and the Annie E. Casey Foundation (children and youth). Most foundations, however, are small, and the grants they make are handled by trustees, lawyers, or family members.

Corporate foundations are funded by major national and international corporations such as Sony, Kellogg, and Ford, as well as smaller local corporations. Their annual contributions vary with the company's profits. The foundation executive is usually a company employee who may have other responsibilities in public or community relations. Corporate giving is strongly linked to the company's business interests. Grants and contributions are given to nonprofits that are within the geographic interests of the company operations, to community organizations in which company employees are actively involved, or to program areas that are consistent with company products. For example, computer companies tend to give to nonprofits that request funds for projects that use computers, and companies that produce children's products tend to support programs for children. Often corporate foundations will be more interested in in-kind contributions such as furniture, equipment, publicity, technical assistance, or employee volunteers rather than cash awards.

Requests to corporate foundations often need not be as lengthy and detailed as other foundation proposals; often a letter may suffice. Although there are corporate giving directories, many corporations do not publish their giving programs. Telephone calls to corporations and talking with staff at other nonprofits that have received corporate support is the best way to gather information.

Community foundations, such as the Cleveland Foundation, the New York Community Trust, and the Community Foundation for Southeastern Michigan, are funded by contributions from numerous individuals and families in a given community. They limit their grants to nonprofits within a narrowly defined geographic area such as a city or region. Although grants are approved by the foundation board or its distribution committee, many donors retain a degree of discretion over grants made from the funds they contribute. Large community foundations may employ several professional staff, including specialists in various areas, and may be leaders in developing giving patterns in their communities.

Operating foundations are private foundations that use their resources to conduct research on a specific topic or to provide a direct service. The Smith Foundation for Restorative Neurology, the Mariton Wildlife Sanctuary and Wilderness Trust, the Breckenridge Aviation Museum, and the World Peace Fund are operating foundations. Although some are listed in foundation directories, they do not make grants to the general nonprofit community.

Most individual, family, and community foundations invest the contributions that they receive from donors and use only the interest or earnings as the primary source of grant dollars. Whether the earnings are high or low, however, these foundations are required by law to give away a minimum of 5 percent of their assets annually to charitable organizations.

The range of categories that foundations may fund includes capital support, general operations, endowments, scholarships, matching or challenge grants, program support, research, start-up funds, bridge funding to ease cash-flow problems, technical assistance, emergency funding, and program-related investments.

GOVERNMENT SOURCES

Government agencies whose primary purpose is to make grants are funded by public contributions, generally through annual legislative appropriations. Examples are the National Science Foundation, the U.S. Department of Housing and Urban Development, the National Endowment for the Arts, and the U.S. Department of Health and Human Services (HHS). Typically, these agencies are professionally managed and take some of their direction from advisory boards. Government agencies at local, state, and regional levels also operate ad hoc grant programs as mandated by current legislation. For instance, some grants are targeted to issues such as job development related to welfare reform or child support enforcement initiatives.

Federal agencies regularly issue requests for proposals that call for specific program ideas and contain detailed guidelines regarding proposal preparation. In 2004, the government established a comprehensive Web site, www.grants.gov, that allows organizations to electronically find and apply for the more than 900 grant programs offered by the 26 federal grant-making agencies. The site guides users through the entire process.

Federal grants usually are given in the form of special project funds and often go to a state agency to be distributed to nonprofits within that state. For example, the HHS has special project funds for AIDS prevention that are given to state governments, which in turn award them to local organizations that seek funding to perform services (Carlson, 1995).

There also is federal block grant money that is given to cities to distribute to nonprofits for capital projects and programs considered to be of major significance to the welfare of the community, such as the rehabilitation of neglected urban housing or commercial areas or the development of inner-city recreation sites. Information about this type of grant may be obtained through the mayor's office from the person who deals with Community Development Block Grants.

Government grant funds are declining, but some funds are still available. Learn which government agencies might be interested in the organization's program and what their application requirements and deadlines are. Get to know the influential people in the government agencies, and stay in close contact with them. The application process may be detailed and lengthy and may entail site visits and presentations to the decision makers to justify the need for the funds. Many government agencies use score sheets and assign points to different components of the proposal. Request a copy to refer to as the organization develops its proposal.

RESEARCHING FOUNDATIONS AND CORPORATE FUNDERS

Parallel to the national database of federal funders, the Foundation Center is the pre-eminent source of information on foundation and corporate funders. The center's electronic database, print directories, foundation annual reports, guidelines, and many other resources are available in a national collection located in New York City and Washington, DC, and in regional collections in Atlanta, Cleveland, and San Francisco. The center also has local collections in 190 community libraries throughout the United States. Free orientation and proposal-writing programs are available at the national and regional Foundation Center libraries, and center staff members often visit local collections to conduct these programs. All Foundation Center collections have written materials that outline the research process and suggest places to start.

The Foundation Center's major publications and computer services are the *Foundation Directory, Foundation Grants Index, Foundation Center National Data Book*, Comsearch printout, and Sourcebook profiles. Individual directories list foundations by type, location, geographic focus, fields of interest, type of support, recipient type, total assets, total giving, and so on.

The Foundation Center's database covers 40,000 U.S. foundations and corporate givers; includes descriptions of nearly 200,000 grants; and lists more than 180,000 trustees, officers, and donors. Information also is available through direct online search engines. The Foundation Center maintains a Web site, www.fdncenter.org, which is a gateway to a wide range of philanthropic information services.

Information on foundations, including newer and smaller ones, can be obtained also through GuideStar's Philanthropic Research Inc. at www.guidestar.org. This comprehensive site allows users to access information on the operations and finances of nonprofit organizations as well as to retrieve data services, salary searches, performance reports, and links to IRS information.

WRITING THE PROPOSAL

After the organization has specified the purpose of its proposal and identified which government agency or foundation to apply to, determine who will actually write the proposal. This is a time-consuming process that should be considered as important as the design and implementation of the project. For may grant seekers, the proposal is the only opportunity to educate the funder about their organization and proposed projects. Thus, the proposal must generate a positive overall organizational image (Geever & McNeill, 1997). The proposal need not be slick, but it must convey all the important ideas in a clear, concise, and compelling manner. The proposal must answer six basic questions: who, what, why, where, when, and how (Frost, 1993).

When deciding whether to have a staff member, volunteer, or consultant write the proposal, ask to see writing samples. The writer should spend a great deal of time talking with those close to the project and developing the form, style, and content of the document. Often the foundation representative who receives the proposal must condense it into a brief summary format for the other board or committee members. Hence, the key ideas should appear in the very beginning of the proposal and should be expressed briefly, positively, and in simple but compelling language.

Some foundations ask that proposals follow their guidelines in the order that they are written. Typical components of proposals are the cover letter, executive summary, organizational overview, project description, budget, post-project plans, and appendixes.

Cover Letter

Addressed to a specific person at the foundation or government agency, the cover letter should identify the organization, briefly describe the project, reference the connection between the proposed project and the funding entity's interests, state the amount requested, designate a contact person in the organization, and express gratitude for the opportunity to present the proposal. The letter should welcome a visit from or meeting with the grant maker. It should be signed by the board president, which indicates the board's involvement and support, and the executive director. The cover letter should be no longer than one page.

Executive Summary

The first page of the proposal is the most important section of the entire document, because it specifies the importance of the proposed project. The opening of the proposal serves as a sales presentation to convince readers that the project is worthy of the government agency's or foundation's support (Geever & McNeill, 1997). It is not unusual for a proposal to be rejected because the grant maker lacked interest in this summary. To capture readers' attention, the summary should include a brief description of the problem or need, the proposed solutions, the overall goals for the proposed project, the funds that have already committed to the project by the organization and what additional funding is needed, and a brief reference to how the project furthers the organization's mission. It is helpful to write the executive summary last.

Organizational Overview

This section introduces the organization to the funder; it should include when, why, and how the organization was started; the mission statement, purpose, goals, and guiding philosophy; significant historical events; current activities; accomplishments and impact; description of the organization's constituency; funding sources; board, staff, and volunteer makeup; notable accreditations and affiliations; and plans for the future. Include important facts, but do not overload the organizational description with unnecessary details about its structure and philosophy. Focus on the organization's credibility in the area in which it seeks support. If other organizations are involved, provide evidence of their credibility as well as their support of the proposed project.

Project Description

The project description is the heart of the proposal. It should provide the details that flesh out the summary statements made in the beginning of the proposal. The project description should answer several questions: What is the need or problem to be addressed, and how was this need determined? What target population will benefit from this project—how many people, and in what way? What are the specific goals and objectives? What methods (activities, procedures) will be used to implement the project? How will progress be measured, evaluated, and reported? What is the project's time frame? Who is responsible for implementation, and what are his or her qualifications? Will other organizations be involved? Is the project clearly related to the purpose and the goals of the organization? Does the project have reasonable dimensions?

Each topic should be addressed individually and completely, but as briefly as possible. The description of each topic should flow logically into the next, and explanations and rationales for choosing certain approaches should be presented. Describe what the organization will do in terms of specific ways that it will serve clients or constituents rather than discussing broadly conceptualized problems and needs. Although some foundations and government agencies specify page lengths for this part of the proposal, this section is usually not more than six to eight pages.

Budget

A good budget is a plan of action and a powerful tool for exercising managerial control. The proposal should include a project budget as well as the most current audited financial statements of the organization itself. Different funders require different degrees of detail in the budget. Government agencies require extensive detail and often provide forms and instructions. Foundations and corporations are less structured but require a clear and complete budget. A good budget and budget narrative will relate directly to the objectives and activities of the project and will be consistent with the proposal narrative. For example, if a specific staff or staff positions are named in the project description as having a role in the proposed activities, and the organization is seeking at least part or whole support for their salaries, then these names and positions should be listed in the personnel section of the budget. Similarly, if the organization names a product such as agency brochures as a proposed materials development for which it is seeking funding, then the budget should clearly name and reflect the costs of producing such brochures.

There are two broad categories of expenses: direct and indirect. *Direct costs* are expenses related to salaries, rent, utilities, telephone, equipment, printing, supplies, postage, insurance, and travel. *Indirect costs,* also known as "overhead," reflect an organization's administrative costs to operate several funded projects. Typical indirect costs include the cost of operating and maintaining buildings, grounds, and equipment; depreciation; and general and departmental administrative salaries and expenses. Sometimes indirect costs are calculated as a percentage of the total organizational direct costs, of the personnel costs, or of the salary and wage items alone (Geever & McNeill, 1997). Some foundations do not fund indirect costs, or they cap the indirect percentage rate. Determine if the foundation to which the organization is applying has a policy about including

"You know, I think we had that grant request approved right up to the point when she counted the zeros on the funding amount."

indirect costs. A revenue statement, if requested, should list anticipated or committed grant funds; income from fees, publications, and services; and earned interest and income from fundraising activities.

Post-Project Plans

A concluding paragraph or two should summarize the future of the project, outline follow-up activities, and discuss ways that the organization plans to acquire future funding. Briefly reiterate what the organization wants to do and why it is important. This also is the organization's last chance to make its appeal (Geever & McNeill, 1997).

Appendixes

The appendixes serve as a reference section and should include information not already presented in other parts of the proposal, such as the operating budget and other financial information; the list of board members; the organization's IRS tax exemption letter; the organization's annual report; news articles about the organization and its accomplishments or the problem it hopes to work on; and letters of support.

Packaging the Proposal

Different funders have different requirements for packaging the proposal: Some ask for multiple copies, whereas others ask for only one. Customize each proposal. Do not bother with binding or fancy folders, as these are usually removed. If possible, send the proposal so that it arrives at the funder's office at least several days before the final deadline to allow time for any necessary follow-up on either end. If the proposal is not there by the submission deadline, it will not be considered.

Follow-Up

If the proposal is funded, send a personalized thank-you letter. Often, at the same time the organization receives the written notice of award announcement, the funder will include the reporting requirements. Some funders require periodic progress reports and budget statements in addition to final activity and expense reports. Be sure to comply with these requirements. Even if the reporting requirements are minimal, it is important to keep the funder informally updated about the project's activities and progress. If the proposal is declined, send a note thanking the funder for reviewing the proposal. Call at another time to find out why the proposal was not accepted.

COMMENTS FROM THE FIELD

Following are some thoughts and ideas from funders and grant seekers who have a great deal of experience in soliciting funds through proposals.

From the Funders

- Do your homework. Every funder is different. One success does not lead to others. The main reason that proposals are declined is because they do not fit the guidelines.
- Do not assume that the reader knows your field, but do not go on and on about what is common knowledge.
- Relate your idea to current and important theories in your field or in some area of human behavior relating to motivation, communication, or change.

- Initiate innovation. Suggest a creative funding package or idea, or initiate a collaboration.
- Make a proposal brief; easy to read; free of jargon; and written in a positive, energetic style. It should not sound desperate or preachy. Write with excitement, eagerness, and confidence about the organization and the project.
- Know that foundations view their grants as investments and expect good returns on them.
- Know that the real test of a project's success is a reduction of the need that precipitated the project (Brewer et al., 1995).
- Know that the most critical issues in funding relationships are trust and credibility.

From the Grant Seekers

- The foundation culture varies in different communities. In some areas funders are very competitive, and in others there is a great deal of collaboration. Find out where the sensitivities are, especially on the corporate side.
- Many foundations are not receptive to helping or even calling back. Larger, staffed foundations were the most accessible and responsive.
- Some grants came easy; others might have come easier if we had done more homework. Personal contact made a big difference in the positive responses.
- Government grants are tough; it is easier to get renewals than to get new funding.
- Expect to modify the proposal for each potential funder based on that funder's interests and guidelines.
- It will show in your proposal if you are fudging the activity just to fit the foundation's wants and likes. Do not get caught up in the latest funding fads.
- Foundations have a lot of influence. They often are the only evaluators of how an organization or project is doing.
- Securing grants combines many skills. You have to be resource oriented, clever, politically astute, and creative and also a negotiator, risk taker, and good presenter.
- New books and articles about grant seeking are coming out constantly; stay on top of the latest resources and trends.

SKILLS APPLICATION EXERCISE

Each funder has priorities, restrictions, and guidelines that govern its grant making. Using the funder's specific criteria, review a proposal that has been submitted to a private foundation, a corporate giving program, or a government agency. Copies or samples of proposals can be found in library materials about grant writing. Grant seekers may be willing to share "old" proposals. Based on the information provided by the proposal, answer the following questions:

1. *Screening and eligibility.* Has the organization provided IRS and basic financial information? Does the executive summary allow you to determine the proposal's eligibility for consideration? Does the request meet the foundation's requirements and interests?

2. *Organization strength.* Is this a credible organization in the program area for which it is seeking funds? What are its mission, professional standing, and track record? Who is served? Are there similar services in the same area? Is there community support? What are the distinctive merits of the organization?

3. *People.* Do key personnel have the qualifications to undertake the proposed project? Who provides the vision and leadership of the organization? Does the board composition reflect an appropriate diversity of skills and backgrounds?

4. *Financial condition.* How does the organization finance day-to-day operations? Is there a broad base of support? Does the project budget match the narrative? Does it seem reasonable?

5. *Problem or need to be addressed.* Has an important issue of workable dimensions been presented? Have data been given to substantiate the problem? Have the people who will be affected been involved in the needs-assessment and solution process?

6. *Program objectives.* What will the proposed funding accomplish? Are the objectives clear, realistic, and measurable? Do they relate to the need? How does the project compare to similar programs?

7. *Methods.* Are the plans sufficiently detailed? Is it evident how much the methods will bring about the expected results? Is the timetable realistic? Is there adequate and capable staff to carry out the project?

8. *Evaluation.* Is there a procedure to measure, evaluate, and report the project's progress? For new, pilot, or model projects, are there plans to share the results and findings with funders and other organizations?

9. *Future funding.* What other funding sources have been identified? If the project is to continue beyond the grant period, is there a plan for ongoing financial support?

10. *Language and form.* Is the proposal clear and logically presented? Are assumptions and facts supported? Have you avoided jargon and verbiage?

REFERENCES

Brewer. E. W., Achilles, C. M., & Fuhriman, J. R. (1995). *Finding funding* (2nd ed.). Thousand Oaks, CA: Corwin Press.

Carlson, M. (1995). *Winning grants step by step*. San Francisco: Jossey-Bass.

Edwards, R. L., Benefield, E.A.S., Edwards, J. A., & Yankey, J. A. (1997). *Building a strong foundation: Fundraising for nonprofits*. Washington, DC: NASW Press.

Frost, G. J. (1993). *Winning grant proposals*. Rockville, MD: Fund Raising Institute.

Geever, J. C., & McNeill, P. (1997). *Guide to proposal writing*. Washington, DC: Foundation Center.

Golden, S. L. (1997). *Secrets of successful grantsmanship: A guerilla guide to raising money*. San Francisco: Jossey-Bass.

Independent Sector. (2001). *Giving and volunteering in the United States, 2001*. Available at http://www.independentsector.org

The author acknowledges and thanks the following foundation and nonprofit professionals for sharing their comments and insights into the proposal-writing process: K. C. Bergman, nonprofit consultant, Cleveland, Ohio; Carol Zett, grants manager, Kelvin and Eleanor Smith Foundation, Cleveland; Kelly Sweeney McShane, executive director, Hannah House, Washington, DC; William J. O'Neill, Jr., and members of the Grantmaking Committee, William J. and Dorothy K. O'Neill Foundation, Cleveland.

Developing a Sustainable Fundraising Program

Elizabeth A. S. Benefield
and Richard L. Edwards

A major function of nonprofit managers, particularly those who occupy chief executive officer (CEO) positions, is securing resources for their organizations (see Chapter 1). Nonprofit managers must be prepared to spend a significant portion of time fundraising. And the higher their position in the managerial hierarchy, the more managers will need to devote increasingly larger portions of their time to the business of raising money.

The next several decades promise challenges as well as opportunities for nonprofit organizations. Perhaps like no other time in history, the landscape of philanthropy is changing. Many new trends and forces are requiring nonprofits to consider new and creative ways to raise funds. Most significantly, new technologies are enabling new ways to give.

An enormous surge in e-philanthropy activities and online giving demonstrates how quickly Americans are changing how they conduct charitable activities. According to *The Chronicle of Philanthropy's* sixth annual survey of online fundraising activity (Wallace, 2005), online donations soared in 2004, with many nonprofits receiving twice as much in donations as they did in 2003. More than 174 organizations received $163.3 million in electronic gifts (Wallace, 2005). Attributed in part to the impact of recent global disasters, such as the 2005 Asian tsunami that prompted an unprecedented number of online donations, Americans are showing increased comfort with going to their computers for information about and access to charitable opportunities.

Although most experts watching the surge in giving following catastrophic events or global natural disasters share concern that local and domestic charities could be hurt, most also believe that new giving patterns ultimately will benefit all charities (Hall, 2005). Growing numbers of nonprofit organizations are exploring Web-based communication and giving tools, and many are creating new partnerships with companies that provide full service online giving technical assistance and support. There also is considerable "landscape noise" around entrepreneurial activities that directly link the financial service industry with charitable organizations that are recipients of philanthropic gifts.

Other trends and social forces are affecting the way that nonprofits seek charitable dollars. The blurring of the traditional public–private sectors and emergence of a fourth sector and public benefit economy will create new partnership opportunities to link the missions of nonprofit organizations and profit-making companies. A buzzword in the 1980s, *corporate social responsibility* (CSR), is again on the rise although in new forms, pushed forward by the success and progressive thinking of such models and product lines as Newman's Own, Merck & Co., and Stonyfield Farm (Business for Social Responsibility, 2005). The discovery of widespread corporate corruption, such as in the cases of WorldCom and Enron, is forcing for-profit companies to consider seriously the public perception of their charitable cultures and activities. In fact, U.S. companies gave at historic levels in response to the recent domestic and global disasters of September 11 and the tsunami (Stock, 2005).

Finally, shifting demographics, such as the aging of Baby Boomers into retirement, increasing involvement of women and members of racial and ethnic minority groups in charitable giving, an enormous transfer of generational wealth, and changing wealth status of some minority populations also are affecting the philanthropic landscape (Nichols, 2004). The African American community is seeing the development of "giving circles," a high-touch method of fundraising that engages potential donors in thinking about and giving collectively. Operating much like investment clubs, and often meeting over potluck dinners in people's homes, small groups of participants establish minimum member giving levels and then research and vote on charitable recipients (Jonsson, 2004).

Boston College's Center on Wealth and Philanthropy has reported that charitable giving by African Americans increased 5 percent each year from 1992 to 2001 (Havens & Schervish, 2004). A 2003 study by *The Chronicle of Philanthropy* also found that race plays a powerful role in giving patterns. When comparing whether people who live in high-cost regions such as New York or San Francisco are as generous as those who live in low-cost towns such Angleton, Texas, or Rexburg, Iowa, it was found that race was an important factor. "In counties and cities with above-average numbers of blacks who make $50,000 or more, giving rates tend to be higher than those dominated by whites of similar income levels (Anft & Lipman, 2003). Religion plays an important role, and the church is an essential part of African American giving. *The Chronicle of*

Philanthropy study also found that married couples of all races and single women—especially single mothers—are far more generous than are single men.

Government support for many kinds of nonprofit activities continues a decline that began in the late 1990s, as the federal government seeks to shift more responsibilities to the states. Federal and state governments are being confronted with major budget deficits that are likely to result in reductions in various government-provided services at all levels. As a result, there are likely to be increased demands for services by many nonprofit human services organizations. This is resulting in increased use of purchase-of-service contracts for the provision of certain kinds of programs and services by nonprofit organizations (Edwards, Cooke, & Reid, 1996). Because of the changing nature of government funding initiatives, many nonprofit organizations have learned that it is a risky business to become too dependent on public funding. Thus, it is prudent for nonprofit organizations to give significant attention to generating financial support from private, nongovernment sources.

However, over the past decade there has been significant growth in the number and assets of foundations and, specifically, community foundations. The number of U.S. foundations now exceeds 66,000 (Foundation Center, 2005). Despite slight declines in 2002 and 2003, foundation giving more than doubled between 1997 and 2004. Examples in growth of community foundations are abundant. One case, which is not at all atypical, is the Triangle Community Foundation located in Research Triangle Park, North Carolina. Founded in 1983 with an initial fund of $3,000, its assets grew by 2005 to $96 million, with an additional $112 million in known bequests and trusts. The number of donor-driven funds with the Triangle Community Foundation has grown to more 550 ("St. John Stepping Down," 2005). Another example is the Oregon Community Foundation in Portland, which in 2004 received its largest gift ever, a $32 million bequest from an individual. Created in 1973, this foundation now manages more than 1,000 funds and has assets totaling more that $652 million (http://www.ocf1.org). The growth of community foundations perhaps reflects donors' desire to make a meaningful community impact with their giving and a willingness to consider new methods to carry out their wishes.

To thrive in this changing environment, nonprofit organizations and managers must take bold and creative steps to ensure that their planning, management, and fundraising activities are keeping step with the times (Nichols, 2004). No longer can a nonprofit organization rely on one or two funding sources for its operational needs. The key to long-term financial stability is development of a sustaining and diverse funding base that includes individual, foundation, government, and corporate funders. Furthermore, fundraising programs should be multifaceted and include annual fund and major gift solicitations based on sound prospect research, planned giving activities, and a strong marketing and public relations component. The most successful nonprofits in the years ahead will be those best able to adjust to a global philanthropic environment that increasingly is made up of expanding opportunities and players and driven by new technologies.

For an organization to be effective at fundraising, it cannot rely solely on the goodwill of donors. In today's changing and competitive environment, an organization must earn the support of donors by clearly and assertively demonstrating the value of its products or services. An organization must then create ample giving opportunities that take advantage of new global thinking and technologies. This requires that managers approach fundraising in a strategic way that uses the management techniques of analysis, planning, and execution (Firstenberg, 1996).

Nonprofit leaders need not be discouraged or fearful about the challenges of becoming a successful fundraiser. Giving patterns over several decades show that philanthropy is alive and well. In 2004, private sector giving to nonprofits reached $248.52 billion (Kaplan, 2005). Contributions from individuals totaled $187.9 billion, making up more than three-quarters of the total amount given. Another $19.9 billion was given by individuals through bequests. Foundations followed with gifts totaling $28.8 billion, while corporations gave $12 billion (Kaplan, 2005). As has been historically true, an analysis of recent giving trends points to the need to focus fundraising efforts on the cultivation of individual more than corporate or foundation donors, and demographic shifts show that wealth holders increasingly are female and members of racial and ethnic minority groups (Panas, 1996). Therefore, to maximize chance for success, an organization should pursue fundraising strategies that emphasize the cultivation of individual donors and pay particular attention to the needs and interests of nontraditional donors. This approach will enhance its chances for success and place it ahead of many of its peer organizations.

For those who have little experience in fundraising, it may be helpful to keep in mind that fundraising is largely an art rather than a science. And, although no specific formula will work for all nonprofits, this chapter addresses some time-tested strategies and tools that can help managers get started. In addition, the chapter considers the multiple components and strategies that make up a good fundraising program, including prospect research and tracking, annual fund activities, and major gift cultivation. Issues to consider when launching a major campaign, such as internal and external readiness, also are considered.

FUNDRAISING FUNDAMENTALS

Many nonprofit organizations lack the experience, expertise, and resources to build or fund an effective and comprehensive fundraising program. Most lack the financial capital needed to launch new or to sustain tried-and-true efforts. Consequently, uninformed or piecemeal efforts to raise funds are commonplace and often result in poor financial returns. At worst, such efforts cause loss of revenues and organizational credibility. Failed fundraising attempts can be devastating to organizational morale and cause nearly irreversible damage.

Fundraising for nonprofits must be approached in a planned, strategic manner that places long-term benefit over short-term gain. It is best viewed as a multifaceted process that should result in building a solid and lasting foundation for the organization. A successful fundraising program will not only generate significant revenues, it also will increase the organization's visibility and credibility and enhance broad-based community support for its cause.

A key goal of any good fundraising program is to identify and cultivate a diverse network of government, individual, foundation, and corporate donors (Edwards, Benefield, Edwards, & Yankey, 1997; Seltzer, 1987). Gone is the era when nonprofits could rely on one or two funders to sustain operations or meet funding objectives. Additionally, many nonprofits make the mistake of relying on a single strategy—such as a direct-mail appeal or special event—to meet their funding needs. Successful fundraising requires that multiple activities take place within each 12-month period, ideally including both annual giving activities and major gift work. At the same time an organization identifies and retains a base of donors who make annual gifts, it must engage in the cultivation of major gifts tailored to the unique characteristics of diverse donor groups.

Finally, organizations must recognize the important role that a strong public relations program can play in enhancing their fundraising success (Harrison, 1991). A focused, strategic, and multifaceted approach to spreading the word about the importance and success of an organization's products or services can dramatically enhance its fundraising activities. A good fundraising program will maintain a strong base of annual donors through timely and frequent asks, steadily increase the giving level of annual donors, regularly bring in new donors from diverse donor groups, support active and highly personal cultivation of major gift donors, and promote a positive public image of the organization.

Figure 4.1 captures, in a simple way, the essence of fundraising. An organization must identify prospective donors who have the capacity to give; find ways to motivate them to give to the organization or cause; and then provide them with an opportunity to give, that is, an organization needs to ask them in an appropriate manner to contribute.

Success in fundraising requires time, persistence, and the capacity to juggle both internal and external demands. It also requires that organizations make a tangible and multiyear commitment of staff and funding resources to adequately support fundraising activities. Balancing the needs and interests of donors with those of a nonprofit is not easy and requires the involvement of top staff and volunteer leadership. Every organization is unique in the amount of time and resources that it can allocate to raise funds. Because many if not most nonprofits

---

FIGURE 4.1
DONOR GIVING TRIANGLE

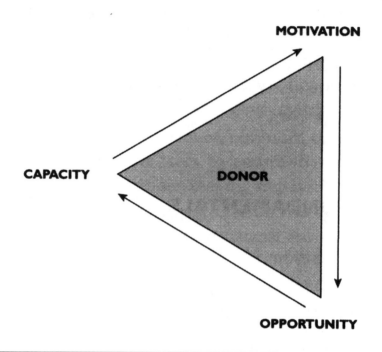

do not have the resources to hire a professional fundraiser, the chief executive officer (CEO) and other senior managers often must assume the fundraising role in addition to their other management responsibilities. Although this arrangement works well for some organizations, for others it creates an environment of competing values, roles, tasks, and time demands.

Whether a nonprofit allocates a percentage of a staff person's time to raise money or hires a full- or part-time development professional, the key to successful fundraising is that a clear commitment of resources is made. Although fundraising activities may heavily depend on volunteers, it is essential that staff time be clearly allocated for this purpose. Volunteers, particularly board members, are often eager to help with fundraising but understandably may lack important knowledge and skills. It is critical, therefore, for an organization to designate a point person who at all times has the big picture in mind, can readily respond to volunteers' concerns and questions, and can promptly provide material and other types of support.

Fundraising success requires a commitment to the highest level of integrity and professionalism. The National Society of Fundraising Executives (http://www.nsfre.org) and the National Charities Information Bureau (http://www.give.org) have established sets of ethical guidelines for fundraising. These organizations also offer valuable guidelines to nonprofit organizations on everything from internal Revenue Service requirements for appropriate gift acknowledgments to the ethical rights of donors. They provide tips to prospective donors about issues to consider as they contemplate making a gift (see the list of organizations at the end of this chapter).

STRATEGIES FOR SUCCESS

Many nonprofits still seek to meet their funding needs by using a single fundraising strategy. This often takes the shape of a direct-mail appeal; a membership drive; or an annual special event, such as a black tie gala, golf outing, or benefit concert. Nonprofits often believe that simply doing more of the same, for example, sending mail appeals to more prospects or bolstering the invitation list to an annual event, will result in increased revenues. It is true that success breeds success, and the establishment of regular and predictable giving opportunities will likely produce an increase in donors and funds over time. However, it is highly unlikely that a single fundraising strategy will enable a nonprofit organization to make significant progress over time in generating support.

Worse, reliance on a single strategy may place an organization in an extremely vulnerable financial position. The funding problems encountered by United Way of America and its affiliates after the scandal involving William Aramony, its former CEO, demonstrate that public sentiment and support for an organization or cause can literally change overnight (Dundjerski, 1995; also see Chapter 21). An unforeseen weather occurrence can wipe out an evening gala after months of work; an economic downturn can dramatically affect a year-end funding appeal; or, as experienced with the events of September 11, the Asian tsunami, and Hurricane Katrina, funds that an organization was counting on can suddenly be diverted to another cause.

It is helpful to think of fundraising as a multifaceted process that involves engaging in numerous activities simultaneously. Minimally, these activities include annual fund appeals, major gift cultivation, and planned giving efforts. The way that these components fit together is analogous to a bicycle. Annual fund appeals are like the front wheel of the bike, whereas major gift cultivation is like the rear wheel. Planned giving strategies, although not addressed in this chapter, are increasingly important to fundraising programs. Using the bicycle analogy, planned giving may be thought of as the training wheels. Fundraising programs will succeed, or the bike will move smoothly ahead, only if organizations simultaneously engage in all three efforts and if all the wheels are turning in the same direction at the same time. Too often, nonprofits rely on one "wheel" to meet funding objectives or use strategies that serve only to increase the size or speed of a single wheel. History has repeatedly shown that this practice does not work in the long run.

To complete the picture, add to this analogy the practice of good prospect research and tracking, perhaps best represented by the frame of the bicycle. Thorough and detailed prospect research and efficient tracking of prospect activities are essential to successful fundraising. Like the bicycle frame, the functions of research and tracking undergird all other activities. Without these functions, nonprofits will lack essential donor information to make thoughtful asks at the donor's giving capacity level, and they will have no system to record important steps (thus leaving no legacy for future efforts), which will diminish their overall fundraising potential.

Fundraising success requires the skills of a master juggler. The practice has little room for shortcuts. With every thoughtful and patient step of planning and execution, a nonprofit is building a strong and lasting foundation of support.

ANNUAL FUND APPEALS AND CREATING A CULTURE OF GIVING

Annual fund activities are the bread and butter of a nonprofit organization's fundraising strategy. Most often taking the form of direct-mail appeals, annual events, telethons, or membership drives, annual appeals should:

- Establish a donor base that produces predictable annual income,
- Provide unrestricted cash support,
- Regularly generate new donors, and
- Encourage the development of a culture of giving.

Annual gifts typically result from a single ask. They generally are relatively small gifts, often ranging between $5 and $50, although sometimes higher, and usually are given as cash. Direct-mail campaigns are by far the most common annual fund appeal method used by nonprofits. Klein (1994) suggested that "direct mail remains the least expensive way an organization can reach the most people with a message they can hold in their hands and examine at their leisure" (p. 58). Response rates and giving levels will vary based on the strength of the association and involvement of the donors with the nonprofit.

Annual fund success will be enhanced by efforts to personalize methods. For example, telethons will typically produce much higher participation and giving rates than will direct mail, and highly personalized appeals targeting an organization's board or key volunteers will likely show an even greater return.

Most households are barraged daily or weekly by direct-mail requests and telephone solicitations. Therefore, creativity and thoughtfulness in approaching donors even for smaller gifts will be appreciated. Above all, personalize the approach as much as possible, carefully assessing the needs and interests of donors, and express genuine appreciation for giving at all levels.

Success in annual fund efforts will be greatly enhanced by an organization's ability to establish a tangible culture of giving. Churches, in particular, do an excellent job of creating such a culture (Klein, 1994). Many factors come into play. Most importantly, churches ask, and they do so regularly and frequently. Individuals are often brought up "passing the plate," a ritual that instills at a very young age the importance of giving. Giving is expected, membership usually goes hand in hand with a financial pledge, and it is highly valued. Churches have long known that good stewardship and accountability for expenditure of charitable dollars are critical to their fundraising success. It should come as no surprise that more than 45 percent of all charitable dollars are given to religious organizations (Kaplan, 2005).

A nonprofit organization can create a culture of giving by heeding such lessons. Donors will tend to give, and give more generously, if they feel part of a culture in which giving is expressly valued, is an important membership expectation, and is rewarded with assurances of worth and accountability. Giving will be encouraged by an organization's credibility and success; donors want to feel that their giving is a sound investment. Gone are the days when giving was thought to be motivated solely by goodwill or charitable intent. Donors typically want to support a credible organization. At the same time, high-level donors claim that they most often give to express a belief in a specific cause or organizational mission, and they clearly express interest in supporting organizations that are financially stable (Panas, 1996). Studies that consider giving motivations have revealed that, although donors continue to demonstrate altruistic intent in their giving, they increasingly value strong staff and board leadership and are concerned with issues of community respect and organizational credibility (Panas, 1996).

A successful annual fund program will not only ensure a nonprofit a strong base of operational support, it also will be the foundation on which to build major gift support for capital and other needs. Annual appeals will help an organization identify potential major donors and pave the way for more intensive involvement between the donor and the organization. One major challenge faced is keeping annual fund support strong while at the same time garnering major gift support.

CULTIVATION OF MAJOR GIFTS

Much has been written (Sturtevant, 1996) about cultivating major gifts and the importance of focusing energy and resources on donors with high giving potential and probability or a high motivation to give to a particular organization or cause. Even in noncampaign periods, securing major gifts is a critical, ongoing component of all good fundraising programs (Goettler, 1996).

Major gift cultivation is best viewed as a series of thoughtful steps that begin with the identification of a potential donor and verification of that donor's giving capacity. This process applies to individual as well as foundation and corporate prospects. To ensure that time and energy are well spent on prospects who have clear giving capacity, fundraising programs must include a strong prospect research component (Edwards et al., 1997). Prospect research can be as simple as seeking direct input from volunteers and board members about the giving habits of their neighbors and peers to using highly sophisticated data software designed to paint a picture of a person's wealth status.

Numerous reference books such as the *Who's Who* series by Marquis and publications such as *The Chronicle of Philanthropy* can be useful. Print resources with extensive information about foundation and corporate prospects are available through the Foundation Center. Based in New York, the Foundation Center has library collections in New York City and Washington, DC, as well as field offices in San Francisco, Cleveland, and Atlanta (see organizations list for address information) and also a Web site (http://www.fdncenter.org). With access to the Internet, managers can gain extensive information from company and foundation Web sites, as well as information from a range of entities that can be useful resources for nonprofits. Companies electronically file annual reports and other financial, employee, and trustee information (Edwards et al., 1997; Heller, 1996). Quick access to this information via the Internet can translate into an enormous time savings for nonprofits.

Managers need not be intimidated by the continuous advancements in prospect research practice and technology. Although commonplace for most higher education fundraising shops, sophisticated prospect research practices are not part of the culture for the majority of nonprofits. Most nonprofits in a noncampaign period can gain sufficient prospect information by following closely local and state charitable news and major business transactions and happenings. Many major newspapers now include regular columns devoted exclusively to local philanthropic activity, and many consulting firms publish state and local giving directories to assist nonprofits. Many states have resource organizations to assist nonprofits, and there are statewide publications that focus on philanthropy. Local foundations also may offer resource libraries to help nonprofits in their fundraising efforts. Most importantly, knowledge about income and asset wealth can often best be gathered through direct contact and involvement with the prospective donor. No generic publication can match the knowledge that can be gained from personal contacts.

"I say we add an NCAA Division I football program."

The relatively simple process of identifying and qualifying wealthy people in the community will not bring about fundraising success. Once the giving capacity of potential donors is established, nonprofits must do the hard work of determining if a potential interest exists and if this interest can be turned into tangible support. This process of turning suspects into viable prospects can in part be accomplished through good prospect research and major gift cultivation.

Successful major gift work requires intensive and highly personal contacts with potential donors over a long time, often over many years. In contrast to unrestricted annual giving, high-level or major giving is usually designated to support a particular need or program and often represents commitments of assets rather than income. At the center of successful major gift work is a well-nurtured relationship that is beneficial to both the donor and the recipient organization. The key to such meaningful relationships is developing and implementing highly personalized cultivation plans. Such plans should include frequent, meaningful opportunities for the prospect to learn about an organization and for the organization to learn about the potential donor. Find out about hobbies and talents, arrange for fun and educational exchanges, and seek advice on their areas of expertise. In major gift cultivation, it is important to consider each meeting with a prospect an opportunity for meaningful cultivation and acknowledgment (Sturtevant, 1996). As part of a cultivation plan, fundraisers might (Edwards et al., 1997)

- Arrange a personal visit from the executive director or board president;
- Send a stewardship report on the impact of past giving;
- Seek advice from the prospect on his or her area of expertise;
- Involve the prospect in cultivating others;
- Honor the prospect with awards and special recognition;
- Send personal congratulations on birthdays, anniversaries, and promotions;
- Seek input on developing the organization's case for support;
- Recruit the prospect to serve in a key role at a special event;
- Invite the prospect to do a workshop for staff on a subject about which he or she has expertise;
- Invite the prospect to serve on the board of trustees or an advisory board or committee;
- Communicate regularly with annual reports, brochures, and speech reprints; and
- Send frequent personal notes about items and events of interest.

It is important to consider cultivation moves as part of a clear plan that has specific goals. In fundraising, one must always have in mind the next step (Wood, 1991). It is often useful to discuss with a prospective donor in advance of a meeting or cultivation move the organization's goal for this contact. It is perfectly acceptable, and often helpful, to say directly that the organization will not be asking for a gift at this time but rather is seeking advice or involvement in another capacity. Donors will appreciate knowing the organization's intentions and will likely be more willing to participate in a multitude of activities. Ideally, cultivation plans will be so carefully constructed that managers and prospects will always know what comes next. Before leaving a visit with a potential donor, discuss what follow-up steps are needed and agree on a clear timeline. Then, as important to a nonprofit organization as the cultivation move itself, the manager must document all donor activities and progress. This step should be part of a consistent and detailed system of prospect tracking.

It is essential that nonprofits establish clear procedures to document all prospect-related activities and contacts. Failure to keep adequate records is a common problem for nonprofits. This can result not only in a poor transfer of knowledge but also in a loss of funds or possibly negative audit reports. Although many software programs exist to manage donor information, most nonprofits can get by with a paper system that uses two simple forms and a good tickler file.

First, use a form that enables the organization to maintain a continually updated record of basic biographical information on each prospect that includes such categories as home and work addresses, telephone numbers, e-mail addresses, family makeup, church affiliation, hobbies and special interests, and community service activities. The form also should include information on the nature of the prospect's association with the organization, information on past giving to the nonprofit and others, estimated income level and known assets, anticipated giving level, a section for such items as preferences on how and when to contact, and important peer relationships. Second, use a form to document actual contacts; the type of contact, who made the contact, what was discussed, the outcome of the contact, and next steps to be taken should all be carefully recorded. Finally, institute a tickler file system for donors' and prospects' birthdays, special occasions, and other significant dates. Of course, also maintain files of all original correspondence received as well as copies of everything sent to prospects or donors. Several prospect tracking and management software programs, such as Giftmaker Pro, for example, are available to assist with these activities.

Remember that it takes time for a nonprofit to become an important giving priority for a prospect. It often is a good strategy to ask potential donors directly what it would take for the organization to become a top charitable priority. Take cues from donors. Like most relationships, much of major gift cultivation is intuitive.

If an organization's cultivation plans are effective, making the major gift ask can be the easy part. It is usually important to ask for a specific amount for a specific program or need. It may be useful to start with a gift range and a couple of program options. However, if donor capacity, giving intent, and interest in the organization is well established, it often is better to ask for a specific amount. The major gift ask is typically done by the staff member or volunteer with the closest relationship to the donor. Often, involvement by a peer or high-level staff or board member is essential, With individual prospects, the solicitation is almost always done face-to-face, with a supplementary written proposal available. Corporate and foundation solicitations will vary widely according to proposal guidelines but more often tend to require written requests or proposals. Because major gifts often come in the form of a pledge that is paid out over a period of years, it is a good idea to prepare a simple pledge letter or letter of intent with a blank space for a signature, gift amount, and payout wishes. If possible, attempt to close the gift during a face-to-face meeting; that is, get the commitment in writing on the day of the solicitation. If this is not possible, a pledge letter sent immediately following the visit may suffice.

What does a manager do when a prospect says no? The best way to handle an objection or an unwillingness to make a commitment is to determine the nature of the problem. Has an appropriate ask level been determined? Is the timing right? Has an appropriate environment in which to make the ask been arranged, or are there distractions? Is the nature of the objection a result of simple misunderstanding? By all means, attempt to get to the root of the objection, and address any issues or problems directly and honestly. The objection may be easily resolved, or the manager will need follow-up steps. Or, the organization may need to settle for a gift amount that is less than hoped. In any case, remember that all gifts at all levels are important, that all prospects and donors should be valued and respected, and that everything an organization does lays the groundwork for the next potential gift.

Two schools of thought exist about closing gifts that are less than what is believed that the donor is capable of giving. One position is that it is important to take small steps, to close gifts early in the cultivation process, and to settle for gift levels that are less than a prospect's capacity. The theory is that giving encourages more giving, and as a result, the prospect will develop a stronger connection with the organization and continue to give and do so at higher levels as she or he increases involvement. The second school of thought is that one cannot leap a canyon by taking baby steps. That is, cultivate, cultivate, cultivate until the prospect is motivated and likely to give at capacity level. This theory requires patience and operates on the belief that smaller-level gifts solicited during the cultivation process may discourage the prospect from ultimately making a much larger one.

A good fundraiser is keenly aware of both scenarios and will tailor solicitation decisions based on the individual characteristics of each potential donor. It often is important to solicit early and lower-level gifts from major prospects to create momentum, encourage others, and cement interest. Giving begets giving, and one will rarely, if ever, diminish the organization's overall fundraising potential by making multiple asks. On the other hand, it is important to always maintain a focus on capacity giving and work to raise the giving sights of prospects by making it clear that the organization is counting on them to be leaders. Strategic and goal-oriented cultivation is essential to instill such a level of commitment and participation.

Good major gift work requires taking appropriate steps to identify potential donors, gathering useful information about giving capacity, establishing that a viable interest in the organization exists, and engaging the prospect in meaningful involvement over time. The process then requires thoughtful and timely solicitation with the goal of long-term potential benefits. This process is the central component to any good and comprehensive fundraising program.

In today's environment, the most successful nonprofit leaders are those who are willing to take risks or "think outside the box." Consider the recent success of Triangle Family Services (TFS), a large human services organization in Raleigh, North Carolina (see Chapter 20). Although TFS boasts a 70-year history of providing community-based mental health and family support services, it is relatively new to private fundraising. Seeking to establish its first-ever base of major gift supporters, TFS embarked on a major effort to cultivate individual and foundation donors, following a strategic plan of identification, research, cultivation, and solicitation. When searching the Web one day for prospective foundation matches for its programs, the organization's development director discovered a small, family-run foundation in Maryland that identified homelessness as one of its priorities. The foundation required a relatively simple application and tended to give a few grants each year that average about $50,000. Further, the foundation did not request or require any personal visits or inquiries. On a whim, TFS submitted a simple, well-written proposal, knowing full-well that, without strategic cultivation, a positive outcome was not likely.

However, to everyone's surprise, a check for $50,000 arrived at TFS within three weeks. Little was requested in terms of accounting or stewardship, but not taking anything for granted, and with hopes of establishing a long-term relationship with the foundation, TFS embarked on a year-long cultivation of the foundation. This ultimately involved inviting key foundation leaders to TFS to meet board members and staff so they could get a close view of what TFS was doing with their money and to participate in setting goals and determining evaluation strategies. In turn, the foundation used TFS as a case study in refining their charitable activities, calling on the expertise of TFS staff to assist them. This relationship led to a second charitable commitment from the foundation of $100,000 that included a unique matching gift component that will leverage significantly more community financial support for TFS. This "diamond-in-the-rough" scenario reminds us that it is always good to keep an open mind to less-conventional funding possibilities.

Major gift work can be as tiring as it is exhilarating and as frustrating as it is rewarding. The dynamic and personal nature of major gift cultivation makes it challenging for even seasoned professionals to set aside personal feelings. For example, it is difficult not to feel personally rejected when a request is declined or to feel personally responsible for unhappiness expressed by a donor with whom one has had a long-term relationship. Because of the intensely personal nature of the donor relationship, sincere and lasting friendships often result. For a fundraiser who has adhered without fail to the highest standards of integrity and professional behavior, this can be major gift work's greatest reward.

LAUNCHING A CAPITAL CAMPAIGN

One of the most important decisions a nonprofit organization will make is whether or not to embark on a major campaign. It seems today that every nonprofit is in the business of planning, executing, or closing a campaign effort. Successful major campaigns can generate significant resources and, in some cases, produce the added benefit of bringing unprecedented attention to an issue or cause. However, do not be fooled by the perception that everyone is doing it and doing it well. Nonprofits often embark on campaigns with little planning or with no hands-on experience or expertise. They fail to recognize the importance of considering many readiness factors that are both internal and external to the organization. Poorly conceived and organized campaign efforts can be devastating to staff and board morale, Worse, they can cause loss of organizational stability and credibility. Campaign planning and execution is tough work and requires special skills and knowledge.

As a first step, consider the extent to which the organization is internally prepared to launch a campaign. Is the current board composition adequate to support a significant campaign effort? Ideally, the board should include members who represent three Ws—wisdom, wealth, and workers. In other words, a board needs wise people, those with some financial resources, and those who are willing to pitch in and do the hard work necessary for successful governance and effective fundraising. The organization is fortunate if it has individuals who embody all three Ws; realistically, more often, the board and volunteer leaders will embody one or two of these characteristics. To increase chances for success, consider the following steps in advance of a major campaign (Edwards et al., 1997):

- Recruit at least one attorney and one accountant to the board to provide guidance on charitable-tax law issues; deferred giving; and the appropriate handling of gifts other than cash, such as securities and property.
- Be sure that the board includes at least one representative from the local business community.
- If possible, recruit at least one "famous" individual to the board (e.g., someone who is highly recognizable and widely esteemed, such as a top-level business executive, local television or radio personality, or athlete).
- Be certain that several "worker bees" are on the board, individuals who are willing to do the hard and sometimes not-so-glamorous work of fundraising, such as making telephone calls and visits, hosting gatherings, and stuffing envelopes.
- If possible, recruit at least a few individuals to the board who have wealth, can identify a peer group of other wealthy individuals whom they would be willing to contact, and who would be willing to go "public" with their giving.
- Include on the board someone connected to the print or broadcast media, such as an editor, news reporter or features writer, television reporter or anchor, or someone strong in public relations.
- Make sure that the composition of the board reflects the community served in terms of gender, race, ethnicity, and socioeconomic status.

A second important step in preparing a nonprofit for a major campaign is to create a leadership structure that extends beyond staff and board. Many organizations form a time-limited fundraising advisory or steering committee. Others organize the board and other volunteer leaders into committees or task forces around specific campaign objectives. For example, one group may be responsible for cultivating and closing leadership gifts and another for the continuing success of annual fund activities. Another may address the publications, public relations, and media needs of the nonprofit during the campaign period. The key to success in developing new leadership structures is recruiting individuals who are knowledgeable about fundraising, are highly committed to the organization and cause, and are willing to work. Also key is establishing clear and highly specific objectives for volunteers. It is important to set volunteers up for success.

A major campaign effort can be strengthened by the short-term involvement of individuals who are considered high-level business and community leaders and are peers to major gift prospects and donors. Do not ask these individuals to be your worker bees. Rather, ask for their guidance and participation in learning about and contacting major gift prospects. Very busy individuals may agree to serve in name only to enhance the nonprofit's credibility and visibility; others may be willing to chair a special event, accompany staff on prospect calls, or sign a solicitation letter. Provide a specified timeline to achieve campaign objectives, and stick to it. Respecting the multitude of demands on such individuals will have enormous payoff. A creative option to involve individuals who wish to support the campaign but cannot commit their time is to formulate a document of endorsement and secure their signatures. This document can be an invaluable addition to a case statement or funding proposal.

Before launching a major campaign, it is essential that staff, volunteers, board members, and other constituents agree about funding needs and strategies. Nothing is more deadly to a campaign than disparate goals and solicitation attempts. Good campaign planning requires that an organization review its mission, take stock of personnel strengths and weaknesses (both staff and volunteer), and clearly determine the community impact of a campaign in terms of service and possible detriments. Major campaigns, like fundraising activities in general, are generally very labor intensive and can lead to staff and volunteer burnout. On the other hand, they can invigorate an organization and dramatically increase community awareness and support. The nonprofit organization will be well positioned to succeed if it begins a fundraising campaign with a healthy internal environment, that is, an environment marked by staff and board cohesion, fundraising knowledge, a clear sense of mission and goals, a clear division of labor, and enthusiasm.

In determining the readiness of an organization to launch a campaign, it also is advisable to assess whether the external environment is likely to be conducive. In examining the external environment, consider the following questions:

- What is the current climate of giving in the community and state?
- What other similar organizations are embarking on major campaigns, and with what success?
- Does the nonprofit represent a hot or cold issue?
- Will the current political and economic environment support or hinder the campaign?
- What is the public image of the organization?
- Has an adequate prospect base been identified and determined to have a sufficient interest level?
- What are the consequences, both internally and externally, if the organization undertakes a fundraising campaign and fails to meet its goals?

Assessing the external environment for successful fundraising can sometimes be difficult, particularly if the nonprofit organization has little or no campaign experience. That is why experts suggest that a strong marketing and public relations program accompany fundraising efforts (Harrison, 1991). Research shows that people respond to issues and not organizations, and that issue-oriented public relations will strengthen fundraising potential. According to Harrison (1991), "Positioning an organization as an authority on an issue, and as an important part of the solution to the problem, can build tremendous credibility for the organization" (p. 22). Increasing an organization's public visibility, its success in attracting positive media coverage, and its capacity to position itself as part of the solution are essential elements in enhancing fundraising success and preparing for a campaign.

GOAL SETTING AND THE CAMPAIGN PROCESS

Setting an ambitious yet realistic goal for a major campaign is an important task. The organization will be much better positioned to determine such a goal if the top-level management staff and board have completed a comprehensive planning process that considers issues of internal and external readiness and establishes clear procedures and personnel structures to cover campaign duties.

Determining a major campaign goal requires some homework. Take a close look at past and current donors, particularly major gift donors, and assess the level of support that is likely to be secured from this group of known supporters. Begin to develop expanded prospect lists using good prospect research strategies, keeping in mind that this list should include a broad base of individual as well as corporate, government, and foundation prospects. It may be helpful to establish a simple rating system that considers both giving capacity and the level of giving that will likely be secured.

The most useful tool in determining a feasible goal is the widely accepted gift pyramid. Based on fundraising's rule of thirds, the gift pyramid suggests that at

FIGURE 4.2
GIVING PYRAMID FOR $50,000 GOAL BASED ON THE RULE OF THIRDS

	GIFT LEVEL	GIFTS NEEDED	PROSPECTS NEEDED[a]	TOTAL DOLLARS
Top Third	5,000	2	6	10,000
	2,500	3	9	7,500
	1,000	5	15	5,000
				22,500
Middle Third	750	9	27	6,750
	500	12	36	6,000
	250	15	45	3,750
				16,500
Bottom Third	100	75	numerous	7,500
	gifts below 100	numerous		3,500
				11,000
			Grand Total	**$50,000**

NOTE: It is generally true that at least one-third of your goal, and in many cases up to one-half, will come from your top 10 to 15 gifts; the second third of your goal will come from the next 25 gifts or so; and the remaining third will come from all other gifts.

[a] The number of prospects needed is based on the widespread belief that about one of three prospects will make a gift at their capacity level if they have been appropriately cultivated and asked.

least one-third of the goal, and often significantly more, will come from an organization's top 10 to 15 gifts; another one-third of the goal will come from the next 25 or so gifts; and the remaining one-third will come from all other gifts. Using the rule of thirds, a gift pyramid with a goal of $50,000 might look something like Figure 4.2.

It has been shown repeatedly that simple numbers reasoning—that is, "if we can just get 100 people to give us $1,000 each"—does not work. Such reasoning actually depresses overall giving by flattening giving levels, and it falsely assumes that a single strategy or ask level will appeal to all donors. The gift pyramid reminds us of the critical importance of directing time and energy at securing leadership gifts. Success in securing the top 10 gifts will likely determine the overall success of a campaign.

Gift pyramids are especially useful for organizations that have no past campaign experience. The exercise of developing a pyramid and identifying and qualifying actual prospects is extremely useful in determining the feasibility of a campaign goal. Gift pyramids also remind us that campaign fundraising should follow a specific sequence of activities. All thoughtfully executed campaigns will begin with a quiet phase that focuses on closing leadership gifts, those in the top third of the pyramid. This is a nonpublic phase that typically helps validate campaign objectives and protects an organization from the embarrassment of failing to meet a publicized goal. As a general rule, it is advisable not to go public with a campaign until the organization has received commitments for 50 percent or more of its goal.

The campaign process should begin with and focus on the cultivation of leadership gifts, and over time it should move toward the closure of lower-level gifts. Experience shows that securing leadership gifts is essential to campaign success. Do that first, and do it well. Success also will depend on the diversity and appropriateness of cultivation and solicitation strategies for all levels of donors, the effectiveness of the organization's staff and volunteers, and the capacity to generate strong public interest and support. Do not sacrifice annual giving activities and fund solicitations during a campaign. The momentum and positive public relations that can be generated from a campaign often have a positive impact on annual giving.

Major, time-limited campaigns can significantly boost resources for a nonprofit, but it is important to keep in mind the necessity to build long-term major gift capacity. Major campaigns can be effective stepping stones to building stronger annual giving programs, and they can help an organization's donors develop fund habits that lead to sustained higher levels of support. Building a strong and lasting foundation of support requires that nonprofit managers place a high priority on long-term benefits that can accrue to an organization from a well-planned, multifaceted fundraising strategy.

SKILLS APPLICATION EXERCISE

- Considering your organization or another nonprofit that you are familiar with, set a goal for a campaign, and then create a gift pyramid related to that goal. How many upper-level donors will you need? Is that goal realistic for your organization at this time?
- Analyze the culture of giving in your organization. How would you create or enhance the organization's culture of giving?
- Develop a cultivation plan for two or three major gift prospects.

REFERENCES

Anft, M., & Lipman, H. (2003, May 1). How Americans give. *The Chronicle of Philanthropy*, p. 6–11.

Business for Social Responsibility. (2005, March 20). *BSR Issue Briefs*. Retrieved, November 29, 2005, from http://www.bsr.org/CSRResources/IssueBrief/cfm? DocumentID=48977)

Dundjerski, M. (1995, September 7). United Way: 1% increase in gifts. *The Chronicle of Philanthropy*, pp. 27–29.

Edwards, R. L., Benefield, E.A.S., Edwards, J. A., & Yankey, J. A. (1997). *Building a strong foundation: Fundraising for nonprofits*. Washington, DC: NASW Press.

Edwards, R. L., Cooke, P. W., & Reid, P. N. (1996). Social work management in an era of diminishing federal responsibility. *Social Work, 41*, 468–479.

Firstenberg, P. B. (1996). *The 21st century nonprofit: Remaking the organization in the post-government era*. New York: Foundation Center.

Foundation Center. (2005). *Foundation yearbook, 2005*. New York: Author.

Goettler, R. H. (1996, April). Announcing the "four Ws" of major gift solicitation. *Fund Raising Management*, pp. 40–43.

Hall, H. (2005, January 20). Charities not involved in relief efforts hope donors will stick with them. *The Chronicle of Philanthropy*, p. 12.

Harrison T. A. (1991, March/April). Six PR trends that will shape your future. *Nonprofit World*, p. 21–23.

Havens, J. J., & Schervish, P. G. (2004). *Wealth transfer estimates for African Americans households*. Boston: Boston College Center on Wealth and Philanthropy.

Heller, J. (1996, June). Get the real story from SEC filings for free. *SmartMoney, 5*(6), 38–40.

Jonsson, P. (2004, December 30). An emerging philanthropic trend: The "giving circle." *Christian Science Monitor*, p. 1.

Kaplan, A. E. (Ed.). (1997). *Giving USA—1996*. New York: American Association of Fundraising Counsel Trust for Philanthropy.

Kaplan, A. E. (Ed.). (2005). *Giving USA—2004*. New York: American Association of Fundraising Counsel Trust for Philanthropy.

Klein, K. (1994). *Fundraising for social change* (3rd ed.). Inverness, CA: Chardon Press.

Nichols, J. E. (2004). Repositioning fundraising in the 21st century. *International Journal of Nonprofit and Voluntary Sector Marketing, 9*, 163–170.

Oregon Community Foundation. (2005). *About OCF*. Retrieved November 27, 2005, from http://www.ocf1.org

Panas, J. (1996, August). The sky is falling: But don't worry, it could be philanthropy raining down. *Contributions*, p. 1, 15–16, 19, 29, 31.

Seltzer, M. (1987). *Securing your organization's future: A complete guide to fundraising strategies*. New York: Foundation Center.

"St. John stepping down as Triangle Community Foundation president." (2005, February 18).

Triangle Business Journal. Retrieved November 29, 2005, from http://www.bizjournals.com/triangle/stories/2005/02/14/daily 43.html

Stock, K. (2005, January 10). Corporations are expected to donate hundreds of millions for relief aid. *Knight Ridder Tribune Business News*, p. 1.

Sturtevant, W. T. (1996, April). The artful journey: Seeking the major gift. *Fund Raising Management*, p. 33.

Wallace, N. (2005, June 9). A surge in online giving. *Chronicle of Philanthropy*, p. 7–12.

Wood, E. W. (1991, June). *The six key concepts of major gift fund-raising. The skill and art of major gift fundraising.* Workshop presented by the Office of Development, University of North Carolina at Chapel Hill.

ORGANIZATIONS

The Chronicle of Philanthropy, 1255 23rd Street, NW, Washington, DC 20037; 800-842-7817; http://www.philanthropy.com

The Foundation Center, 79 Fifth Avenue, New York, NY 10003-3076; 212-620-4230; http://www.fdncenter.org

Marquis Who's Who, Division of Reed Elsevier, 121 Chanlon Road, New Providence, NJ 07974; 800-323-3288; http://wwwmarquiswhoswho.com

National Charities Information Bureau, 19 Union Square W., New York, NY 10003; 800-501-6242; http://www.give.org

National Endowment for the Arts, 1100 Pennsylvania Avenue, NW, Washington, DC 20506; 202-682-5400; http://www.arts.endow.gov

National Society of Fundraising Executives, 1101 King Street, Suite 700, Alexandria, VA 22314; 703-684-0410; http://www.nsfre.org

Cultivating Effective Media Relationships and Marketing

Todd Cohen

Nonprofit managers must relate to both their organization's internal constituency and its external environment. The latter often requires that managers act as brokers, which involves a variety of behaviors (see Chapter 1). These include efforts aimed at acquiring resources, establishing the organization's legitimacy and increasing its influence, and promoting and maintaining its external image. Further, managers may be called on to act as a spokesperson for the organization. As a result, managers may find that they frequently have contact with the media and are involved in a variety of marketing efforts.

The role that the nonprofit sector plays in our communities is one of the best news stories in the United States. It also is one of the least reported. The news media's failure to report on the work of nonprofit organizations reflects two interconnected problems: (1) The media do not understand the nonprofit sector, and (2) nonprofits do not understand the media. The media, however, represent a potentially powerful resource for nonprofit managers in carrying out many responsibilities. And just as managers must master each of those responsibilities and figure out how to balance various roles, they also must develop a strategy for working with the media and then integrate that strategy into the functioning of the organization.

This chapter addresses the importance of the media to nonprofit managers and examines strategies and tactics to improve media understanding and coverage of the role that an organization plays. It also suggests methods for dealing with crises and critical coverage of an organization and explores ways to cultivate better mutual understanding between nonprofits and the media. Finally, the chapter suggests methods to use online resources and market an organization to various constituencies.

WHY MEDIA?

The nonprofit sector is the heart and soul of America. No community could continue to function without the services that nonprofit organizations provide, and no nonprofit could continue to function without the volunteer time and charitable dollars that it receives.

Nonprofits are a big part of the U.S. economy. In the 10 years through 1997, the number of charitable organizations in the country grew at an annual rate of 5.1 percent, more than double the rate of growth among businesses. The United States has 1.2 million charitable organizations whose annual operating expenses account for more than 6 percent of the economy. Paid employees and volunteers working in the sector account for 7.1 percent of the U.S. workforce (Weitzman, Jalandoni, Lampkin, & Pollak, 2002). More than 109 million adults, or 55.5 percent of the population, donate nearly 20 billion hours a year, with the average volunteer spending 3.5 hours a week working for a charity (Weitzman et al., 2002). Charitable giving in the United States grew nearly 5 percent in 2004, to more than $248 billion (Brown, 2005).

Nonprofit managers are being challenged as never before. Government is cutting back on services and spending, leaving nonprofits to do more with less (Cooke, Reid, & Edwards, 1997; Edwards, Cooke, & Reid, 1996). Americans are skeptical about the future in general, and because of the nonprofit scandals in recent years, they are skeptical about giving money to charity.

The media likewise are crucial to America. If the U.S. democracy may be likened to a remarkably complex machine, constructed by millions of citizens and organizations and consisting of gears, pulleys, wheels, and levers, the media are the grease that keeps the mechanism moving. In the same way that the Internal Revenue Code carves out special treatment for nonprofit organizations because of the role that they play in society, the First Amendment to the Constitution recognizes the unique role played by the press. One might reason, then, that nonprofits and the media might find in one another valuable resources. Unfortunately, this generally has not been the case. Few nonprofits understand or make an effort to work with the media. And in the news media—pervaded by cynicism, aggression, and superficiality (Gopnik, 1994)—few mainstream news organizations make even a minimal attempt to report on the work of nonprofits or the nonprofit sector (Cohen, 1996). The media simply do not get it. But that lack of understanding creates opportunities for nonprofit managers.

Faced as they are with shrinking support and rising needs, nonprofits can use all the help they can get, and the media represent a potentially powerful

resource. For nonprofit managers, the media offer a link to a host of constituents—consumers, volunteers, donors, all levels of government, other agencies,
and the public.

Nonprofit managers have a difficult enough time simply doing their jobs.
The media can be a valuable resource, but learning how to work with the media
and then actually doing so poses big challenges. Yet it is in nonprofit managers'
self-interest to work more closely with the media to help reporters and editors
better understand how nonprofit organizations help make communities better
places to live and work.

MEDIA STRATEGY

Every organization should have a communications strategy, and that strategy
should be integrated into an organization's overall strategic plan. Communications is a large topic and includes media, marketing, public relations, and communication with a host of constituencies. Most of what managers do every day is
to communicate— with staff, board members, volunteers, donors, government,
other agencies, the public, and the media. A media strategy simply is one of
many related strategies for communicating. Developing a media strategy need
not involve consultants and a lot of jargon. On the contrary, developing a strategy simply offers an opportunity to think about who to communicate with through
the media, what it to communicate, and how to communicate it most effectively.
In other words, how will getting an organization's message into the media help
further its mission?

A simple exercise for thinking about a media strategy might be to list the key
tasks assigned to each member of the organization and then think about the
news value of the work the staff does. Ask what the organization is doing that
might make a good news story and how getting that story into the media might
help it. Consider everything that the organization does from the perspective of
the media and the possible advantages or disadvantages of getting coverage of a
particular program, action, or policy.

A key issue here, and one not easily resolved, is what makes a good news
story. It is nearly impossible to second-guess reporters or editors on what they
consider news. Their choices about what is newsworthy can reflect a decision-
making process that is bureaucratic or arbitrary, and often both. But a good
guideline is to look at how people are affected by the work an organization does.
How does its work improve the lives of people? That is the news value of an
organization's work.

In developing a media strategy, keep strategic planning simple, practical, and
useful. The goal is not to put a sophisticated statement of policy to a board vote
and then file it away to gather dust; the goal is to develop a sense of why an

organization should want to work with the media and how to tell its story through the media. A media strategy also should define who speaks for the organization and should include a game plan for handling announcements, special events, publications such as annual reports, and crises.

CONNECTING

Dealing with reporters and editors is a lot like dealing with prospective funders. Media coverage can be a valuable resource for an organization, but securing that coverage takes a lot of work. The most fundamental principle to remember when dealing with people in the media is to use common sense. In the same way that one conducts research on a prospect before asking for a big contribution, managers should get to know the news organization and the reporter, editor, or news director that they hope to work with before asking and expecting to get a story published. If targeting a newspaper, for example, study the bylines in the paper. Learn which reporters cover which beats, such as public schools, city hall, and social services. Get to know the type of coverage that the news organization emphasizes. For example, does the local television station emphasize a particular issue, such as children or the environment, in its news coverage and public service promotions?

Larger newspapers have general-assignment reporters who cover many topics. Find out who these reporters are and study the types of stories they do; a general-assignment reporter may be interested in covering an organization either for a single story or on an ongoing series. Smaller newspapers employ fewer reporters than larger papers. It may be easier to get to know the managing editor or city editor of a smaller paper in addition to the reporters. Look beyond the local newspaper. The community may be served by a larger newspaper, and the organization's field of interest also may be covered by a trade publication.

Television and radio news operations typically are short staffed and overworked, and they look for breaking news stories with photo opportunities. It may be tougher to get continuing coverage from television and radio, but they are powerful media, and it is equally important to establish and cultivate relationships with them. Television and radio news stations typically employ only a handful of reporters. The news director or producer is the person to get to know.

Newspapers and television and radio stations, large or small, are always looking for feature stories. These stories offer a human-interest perspective and focus on an individual or group making a difference in the community. When dealing with a newspaper or television station, it helps if the story has a photo opportunity. Pay attention to the kinds of feature stories that the local media run, and then when there is a good story to tell, suggest it to the local news organization.

Cultivating Effective Media Relationships and Marketing

Keep in mind that many newspapers and television stations, as well as several other organizations, produce electronic publications on the Internet. Although these electronic publishers use an often unfamiliar medium, this emerging medium is powerful and attracts more users every day. As with traditional news media, it is to managers' benefit to know and understand the benefits and drawbacks of working with Web-based publications and to use common sense in approaching organizations that publish on the Web.

Making Contact

After getting a handle on the local news organization and the people who write, edit, or produce the news, make contact with a reporter or editor. Depending on the size of the newsroom, who to approach may vary. At a small local newspaper, one may want to approach the editor. At a large city newspaper, one may want to talk to a reporter who covers a specialty beat, such as health or social services.

It is a good idea to make contact before having an item for a news story. But remember that reporters and editors are busy people. They work under the pressure of constant deadlines. For a morning newspaper, and even more so for a television news operation, afternoons are busy and stressful. It might be best for a manager to telephone a reporter or editor in the morning and ask to stop by to introduce himself or herself and drop off some materials. Be prepared to be rebuffed, but also be prepared to be politely assertive; at the least, drop off your materials at the front desk or simply mail them. Remember, the initial goal is to make contact.

Building Relationships

The next step is to establish and cultivate a relationship with a reporter. After making the initial contact and dropping off some materials, try to meet the reporter for lunch or coffee. Do not pick up the tab for the meal or even for a cup of coffee; reporters prefer to pay their own way so they do not feel compromised.

A manager offering an invitation for lunch or coffee should explain that he or she simply would like to share some information about the organization and the issues it faces. If the reporter declines the invitation, offer to stop by the news office for 15 minutes to talk. It is important to keep up the initial contact. Do not be frustrated if the reporter puts you off; they are busy people. Keep an eye on the objective, which is to establish a relationship.

Whether a manager gets a longer face-to-face meeting or not, he or she should offer the organization as a resource on issues that it is involved with. If the reporter is working on a story involving those issues, make it clear that he or she should feel free to call and ask for background or a local angle or quote. If an action in Washington, DC; the state capital; or even locally might, with some background or a quote from your organization, make a good local story, pick up the telephone and call the reporter. Also consider the various partnerships that the organization may be involved in. Collaboration is increasing among nonprofits, and reporters may be interested in the fact that nonprofit, for-profit, and government organizations and agencies are working together. The collaboration may be the hook that attracts the interest of the reporter.

A final suggestion for building relationships: If a reporter does a good job on a story, any story, write a short note to that effect. Reporters get a lot of negative feedback but rarely are told that they have done a good job. It also is important to know that reporters, much like fundraisers, tend to move from job to job. Even after investing a lot of time and effort in getting to know a reporter and building a relationship, managers should be prepared to start all over again with a new reporter.

WRITING A NEWS RELEASE

An organization that has news should be prepared to let the media know about it. The most effective way to do that is through a *news release*—a written statement that summarizes the news and explains its importance. A news release should contain all the information that a reporter needs, as well as the names and telephone numbers of contacts the reporter can call for additional information. In deciding what type of information to include in a news release and how to write it, use common sense. What message does the organization want to send to readers of the newspaper, viewers of the television news, or listeners of the radio news?

Keep in mind the fundamental principle that the value of an organization's news to the newspaper or television or radio station is its impact on people. A good rule in writing a news release is to stick to the facts and avoid hype and overstatement. Good reporters are trained to answer the following questions in their stories: who, what, when, where, why, and how? These questions should be addressed in a news release. Never forget that the purpose in writing a news release is to convince a reporter or an editor to publish a story about the organization. The immediate target of the news release is the reporter or editor, not the ultimate reader. The news organization typically will use a news release as a starting point for preparing its own story; although some smaller news organizations may reprint a news release word for word.

In deciding how to write a news release, think about how to explain the organization's news to a friend or family member. In other words, tell the story in plain words, using a conversational style. Think about who will be reading the story that ultimately gets into the newspaper or on television or radio. Who is the ultimate audience? Who is affected by the news? How are they affected? Why, in other words, is the organization telling its story? Get to the point quickly, emphasizing the main points at the beginning. Use details. If money is involved, say how much. Be precise. Avoid jargon and acronyms. If the release must use a term common to the organization's profession or field, explain it. It is useful to provide some background about the organization and the issues involved in the subject of the news release, but do not get carried away. A full-blown history is not necessary. It also is helpful to gear the release to the types of issues and coverage emphasized by the news organization being targeted. And, where possible, link the release to issues that currently are in the news. Include in the release the names, titles, and telephone numbers (work and home) of individuals whom the reporter can contact for follow-up questions. Include any pertinent e-mail and Web addresses.

Try to keep the news release to a single page, as a one-page release is easy for a reporter or editor to absorb. If the story is important enough to require more space, take another page or two, but remember that reporters and editors may not have time to read the entire news release. The easier and shorter the news release, the better.

At the top of the release, include the words FOR IMMEDIATE RELEASE (in all capital letters), unless you do not want the information printed in advance of an official announcement. In that case, include the words EMBARGOED FOR RELEASE UNTIL [the date of the announcement]. If the news being announced in the release lends itself to a photo or to some type of artwork the newspaper or television station might use, make that clear in the news release. For example, the top of the news release might include the words PHOTO OPPORTUNITY AVAILABLE and then briefly explain what the photo opportunity is. If photos of principals involved in the story are available, call the news organization ahead of time to find out if they want them.

Writing a news release does not have to be complicated. Keep these simple guidelines in mind while writing:

- Assume nothing.
- Do not get fancy; keep it simple.
- Determine who you are writing for.
- Determine why the release is worth writing.
- Connect the dots; explain the relationships in the release involving people, organizations, issues, and causes and effects.
- Tell people what you know in terms they that can understand.
- Keep your perspective on the future, and use the past to put into context what is happening now and what is going to happen.

- Know what to omit; do not quote people just because they sit on the board or have important titles.
- Write for the readers and not for yourself, your bosses, or the board.
- Do not use a $64 word when a simple word will do.
- Think about artwork and how to illustrate the release with photos or information graphics; use imagination.

GETTING INTO PRINT OR ON THE AIR

Once the news release is written, the next goal is to get it published or broadcast. The target of the release is an editor or reporter at a news organization, and a manager will want to make it as easy as possible for that person to do his or her job. Before sending a news release, call the reporter or editor to say that the release is coming and ask how he or she would like to receive it—by mail, fax, e-mail, or hand. After sending the release, follow up by calling to make sure that it was received. If the news release includes the names, titles, telephone numbers, and e-mail addresses of individuals whom the reporter can call for further information, make sure that those individuals will be available if the reporter calls them.

HANDLING INTERVIEWS

An organization that has sought coverage should be prepared to get it. In preparing the organization's media strategy, always be prepared to be interviewed, even if the organization has not issued a news release.

In an interview, the best approach is to be direct, honest, and forthcoming. Be prepared both for the question that the organization most wants a reporter to ask and the question it would least want a reporter to ask. Offer to let the reporter call back with any further questions and to let him or her check facts later. However, do not ask to see a copy of the article before it runs; reporters are reluctant to let sources see articles in advance.

If a reporter calls anyone in the organization without warning, and that person is not prepared to answer, he or she should explain that he or she is not prepared at the moment to answer questions. Ask the reporter what information he or she needs, and then offer to call back as soon as that information is gathered. Ask how soon the reporter needs a response, and be prepared to be told within hours or even minutes. Reporters typically call on deadline and are pressed to get something written right away. Return any call from a reporter as soon as possible and certainly the same day. The last thing anyone should do is stall or stonewall a reporter. Nonprofits do not want to be seen by reporters or their readers as trying to hide something.

HAVING A NEWS CONFERENCE

Although the first impulse when an organization believes that it has news worth reporting might be to schedule a news conference to announce that news, think through whether a news conference truly is the format that will best serve the organization. Reporters tend to look on news conferences as canned events, and they do not like to waste time. If a news release will adequately cover the information that the organization is trying to get to the public, do not call a news conference. But if the organization has a remarkable announcement to make that will have a major impact on many people, then a news conference might be in order. Another factor to consider is whether the key individuals who could answer reporters' questions at a news conference can be pulled together. A news conference should not be used simply to make the announcement seem important or because the board or a boss believes that a news conference best frames the organization's message. When in doubt, call a reporter or two and ask if they believe that a news conference would be appropriate.

If the organization decides to hold a news conference, give the news organizations plenty of notice. Treat the news conference the same as a news release: Call in advance, send a release about the news conference, and then call to make sure that the release arrived.

The format and content of the news conference will require planning. Who will speak and what will he or she say? Prepare a release of the news to be announced at the conference, and give these to the attendees. Include biographical sketches of the speakers as well as background material on the organization and the program or issues involved in the announcement. Whoever speaks or appears at the news conference should be prepared to answer a slew of questions, including those that he or she may not particularly want to answer. Be prepared for tough questions, and be prepared for follow-up questions later by telephone.

DEALING WITH CRISES

When an organization has what is perceived to be bad news, do not try to hide it. It is generally better to make the first move and not to wait for a reporter to discover the problem. By avoiding the natural impulse to hide in the sand like an ostrich, the organization will gain several advantages. First, being forthcoming and honest may raise the organization's credibility with the reporter or deepen the level of trust that the organization has built over time. Second, the organization will avoid a situation in which a reporter uncovers the bad news and then, after having cultivated a relationship with the organization over time, wonders why the manager did not let him or her know it. Finally, the organization may be

"Your crisis management plan should include more than 'four Hail Marys and two Our Fathers.'"

able to get part of its version of the news into the story the reporter writes. Before calling a reporter with bad news, however, do a lot of planning. The media strategy should have a plan for dealing with a crisis, including a checklist of steps to take when a crisis hits. These might include informing and consulting with the board and key staff; deciding how to respond; deciding which board and staff members should speak for the organization; preparing them to answer media questions; preparing news releases and possibly letters to donors, volunteers, supporters, and other key partners; preparing an opinion column or letter to the editor for local publications; and possibly scheduling a news conference. The goal is to engage in damage control by acting reasonably, openly, and responsibly and not waiting passively to be discovered.

No matter how hard an organization tries to avoid crises, some actions are beyond anyone's control. A staff member may embezzle a substantial amount of money, or a major donor may eliminate funding. But for those actions that can be controlled, it is always good to keep in mind a simple exercise: If ever in doubt about the ethics of an action, think about the consequences of that action being reported on the front page of the local newspaper.

DEALING WITH COVERAGE

People can't always get what they want. The organization may get good coverage, but it also may get bad coverage. A particular reporter or news organization may always seem to cast the organization in a negative light. Or, despite the organization's best efforts, it may never get any coverage. What can a manager do? It is generally a good idea to try to meet with the reporter involved and talk about the type or lack of coverage. If the reporter refuses to meet, reported something that the organization believes to be unfair and unreasonable, or unjustly refused to report on the organization, then talk to his or her supervisor or a newspaper's ombudsman.

Another option in the face of bad news is to write a letter to the editor or an opinion column for the editorial page. And if all else fails, the organization can always buy an advertisement and tell its side of the story.

DEALING WITH COMPETITION

Reporters and local news organizations tend to be fiercely competitive. That competitiveness can work to an organization's advantage but, it can also work to an organization's disadvantage. Unless there is a good reason for doing so, do not play favorites among reporters or news organizations. Reporters love to get the story before a competitor. A good guideline is to be evenhanded in the treatment of reporters when there is news to announce.

It also may be the case that one reporter is more receptive to writing stories about the organization and more aggressive about checking with the manager to get information. If such a reporter learns something about the organization before the competition does, think carefully about how to handle the matter. Some organizations might want to issue a news release to all the media at the same time. But doing so would be penalizing the reporter who got the scoop. It is a tough call; the manager should think about how he or she would feel if he or she were the reporter who got the scoop, only to have a source give the story to the competition.

EDUCATING BOARD AND STAFF

Dealing with the media should be an essential part of a manager's job. Yet few boards or agency executives are willing to offer the resources and support needed to develop a comprehensive media strategy. There are steps that can be taken to increase the board's or an executive's awareness of the importance of a media strategy and to secure the resources necessary to put a strategy into effect.

The community probably includes individuals who are savvy about media. They might include a journalism professor at a local college, a public relations professional at a local firm, or a communications director at a local agency. Talk to these professionals about the organization's needs, and invite them to meet with the board or staff. The official purpose of the meeting would be a briefing on media issues; the unofficial agenda would be to raise the awareness of the meeting participants about media issues and cultivate them for support for media initiatives. The cultivation can work on several levels. In addition to cultivating the board, the manager also will be cultivating the community experts for possible involvement with the organization. Those same professionals whom the organization asks to speak to its events also can be resources to seek for advice. If the board or executive cannot supply the money needed to develop and practice a media strategy, look to these local experts to serve as informal advisers to help the organization find creative ways to raise money, secure materials or services, and recruit volunteers.

EDUCATING THE MEDIA

Reporters, editors, news directors, and producers always can learn some new lessons. With a little creativity and diplomacy, managers can help turn the media's lack of awareness about the nonprofit sector to their advantage. One useful strategy is to sponsor media forums to brief news people on issues important to an organization.

It might be useful to meet with a group of reporters or editors from different news organizations who might be interested in the organization or the issues it deals with. Such a meeting can provide background and perspective for people in the media or simply break the ice and begin an ongoing relationship with them. Several nonprofits in the organization's field of interest may want to cohost such a meeting to help ensure a larger turnout of reporters.

Ask some reporters and editors what time of day and type of format that they would prefer. Then arrange for a format that lends itself to conversation, with representatives of the nonprofit or group of nonprofits providing insight into their work. The goal of such a meeting is to raise the awareness of the reporters and editors about the organization and field of interest. Make the setting and presentation as informal as possible. Distribute written materials, and make it clear that representatives from the organization are always available as resources for reporters.

Another option is to request a meeting with the reporters and editors of the local newspaper, as well as those who write the editorials. Asking for such a meeting might be a way to make the organization available for questioning by the newspaper staff, particularly if the organization or the issues dealt with are in the news. Or simply make the meetings a regular part of the organization's year, providing the organization and the newspaper staff an opportunity to talk about the issues it is involved with. Again, the goal is to build a relationship with the media based on mutual trust.

Another strategy is to work with a local college, university, or some other educational institution on a seminar or workshop to help reporters and editors do a better job of covering the nonprofit sector. Independent Sector is a national trade group for nonprofits in Washington, DC, that has worked with schools of journalism at several state universities to sponsor such forums.

The School of Journalism and Mass Communication at the University of North Carolina at Chapel Hill sponsored a daylong seminar, funded by Independent Sector, which was attended by newspaper reporters from throughout the state as well as executive directors and communications officers from several nonprofit organizations. As a result, news coverage of the nonprofit sector in North Carolina has increased noticeably.

Although reporters and editors can seem set in their ways, resources do exist to help educate them about the work of nonprofit managers. As in fundraising, achieving success in communicating with reporters and editors requires taking the time and making the effort to find ways to reach out to them. Independent Sector has a guide for journalists (Morris, 1993) that may help managers better understand the media and work with reporters and editors.

VOICING YOUR OPINION

Newspapers and radio and television stations offer forums for readers, listeners, and viewers to express their opinions. Take advantage of these options. Newspapers solicit letters to the editor and longer guest opinion columns. Radio and television stations offer opportunities to respond to news coverage. They also offer talk shows and newsmaker shows in which community leaders are interviewed. Such programs offer a golden opportunity to present an organization's case in its own words. The station representatives who schedule guests for these shows typically are grateful for the help they can get finding guests. Managers should not be shy about offering themselves or a representative of their nonprofit as guests.

USING OPTIONS BEYOND THE NEWS

The media offer numerous options other than news coverage for an organization to get its message to the public. Newspapers and television and radio stations typically publish or air community calendars. A calendar is a simple, effective way to publicize events sponsored by an agency. Television and radio stations also air public service announcements (PSAs) that can range from reading a brief news release on the air to broadcasting a television or radio spot produced and recorded by the organization. To find out about getting a PSA aired, call the local station and ask for the staff member who handles community affairs. Stations can sometimes help organizations produce your their PSA, but determine the station's deadline for submitting a request.

An organization also is likely to have a better chance of getting a message on the air if it is consistent with the types of issues the station supports. Many stations emphasize children's issues or some other cause in their own public service programming, and they are more likely to air a spot or help produce it if their favorite causes are part of the focus.

If the station will not help produce a spot but is willing to air it, the organization may be able to get the spot produced with contributed support, either in dollars or in-kind services, of a local company or organization with video production equipment. Be sure, however, that the spot does not become a promotion for whomever is underwriting its production; the local station may not want to air what it considers to be a commercial.

USING ONLINE RESOURCES

Technology has given nonprofits a set of powerful new tools to communicate. Using those tools, ranging from Web sites and e-mail to Web logs ("blogs") and "really simple syndication," or RSS, a nonprofit now can publish its own content; keep constituents, the media, and the public up to date about its work; and promote civic activism and policy change.

Organizations that are not yet taking advantage of these tools should be. To get started, turn to the growing network of nonprofit consultants and technology assistance providers that helps nonprofits map their technology needs, develop tech plans, and train staff to use technology. Tech companies also donate software and hardware for nonprofit use, and funders make grants to pay for technology. TechSoup (http://www.techsoup.org) is a good place to start. Using a Web site, e-mail, and blog, a nonprofit can become its own publisher, telling its story, targeting its audience, and creating an ongoing conversation about issues important to the organization and its constituencies, supporters, and partners.

Making online connections easier and more effective is the focus of two increasingly popular technologies: blogs and RSS. By using blogs to link to and comment on online information involving causes they care about, nonprofits can more easily share and focus attention on that information and raise their own profile with constituents, partners, and donors. By using RSS that lets visitors sign up to receive personalized notifications about new content at their Web sites, nonprofits can more easily keep constituents informed about their work.

Reporters and editors increasingly use the Web, e-mail, blogs, and RSS to keep informed. Putting these tools to work will give an organization a better chance of getting on the news media's radar screen.

MARKETING

The news media collectively represent one means of getting an organization's message to the public, but the media are beyond an organization's control. Numerous means of communicating, however, are within an organization's control, and these fall under the area of marketing. Who are the constituencies the organization wants to reach with its message, and what are the best methods of reaching them? A nonprofit typically will have many constituencies, including the people served, donors, volunteers, board members, other nonprofits, government, business, and staff and board members.

Numerous opportunities exist to communicate with those constituents: publishing a newsletter, using direct mail or targeted mailings, preparing brochures that focus on the entire organization or specific programs or projects, publishing an annual report, or creating a Web site.

Keep materials simple and easy to understand. Keep in mind the audience and focus on the message that the organization wants to communicate. Take every opportunity to promote the organization and its work, but remember that time is a luxury for everyone and the more concise the message, the more effective it will be.

An organization may lack the resources to develop and produce marketing materials itself, but the community includes individuals and organizations who might be able to help by advising staff, contributing the work, or helping fund the work. Managers need to use their imagination while seeking assistance.

CONCLUSION

Nonprofit organizations have good stories to tell and part of a manager's job is to get an organization's message to people who need to know it. By developing a media strategy and integrating it into an organization's strategic plan, managers can better ensure the organization's ability to improve its communications with board and staff, with volunteers and donors, with other nonprofits and government, and with the public and media.

When developing and putting into practice a media strategy, use common sense and keep the approach simple. A media strategy and materials should be written in language that is easy to understand and accessible. When approaching the media and preparing news releases and other materials, managers should put themselves in the place of the people they are dealing with and thus try to make their work easier. Cultivate media contacts and make the organization available as a resource for the media. When seeking media coverage, be prepared to get it by being informed, open, and accessible. And be creative by tapping into community resources while preparing a media strategy and materials. It is in a nonprofit organization's best interest to be prepared to work with the media and to be persistent and consistent in trying to get its message into print, on the air, and online.

SKILLS APPLICATION EXERCISE

You are the executive director of a reproductive health agency. You raised $1 million to build a new clinic and have scheduled a news conference to break ground for the clinic. On hand will be local dignitaries, including donors, civic leaders, local government officials, and the congressional representative from your district. Although your agency does not perform abortions, it does make referrals to physicians who do, and you are concerned that the groundbreaking event may attract abortion protesters. You also are concerned about whether and how the media will cover the event. Write a media plan for the event. Explain

- How to deal with reporters in advance of the event,
- How to focus your news release announcing the event,
- How to focus the news release to be handed out at the event,
- How to respond to reporters if protesters are present, and
- How to respond to any negative coverage stemming from the event.

Also, write a news release announcing the event, a news release to be handed out at the event, and an opinion column to run in the local newspaper after the event that focuses on the importance of the new clinic to the community and explains why newspaper coverage of the abortion protesters was overblown and out of context.

REFERENCES

Brown, M. S. (2005). *Giving USA: The annual report on philanthropy for the year 1996.* Glenview, IL: AAFRC Trust for Philanthropy.

Cohen, T. (1996). Don't skip this beat. *Foundation News and Commentary, 37*(5), 43–45.

Cooke, P. W., Reid, P. N., & Edwards, R. L. (1997). Management: New developments and directions. In R. L. Edwards (Ed.-in-Chief), *Encyclopedia of social work* (19th ed., 1997 Suppl., pp. 229–242). Washington, DC: NASW Press.

Edwards, R. L., Cooke, P. W., & Reid, P. N. (1996). Social work management in an era of diminishing federal responsibility. *Social Work, 41,* 468–479.

Gopnik, A. (1994, December 12). Read all about it. *New Yorker,* pp. 84–102.

Morris, R. (1993). *Nonprofit news coverage: A guide for journalists.* Washington, DC: Independent Sector.

Weitzman, M. S., Jalandoni, N. T., Lampkin, L. M., & Pollak, T. H. (2002). *The new nonprofit almanac and desk reference: The essential facts and figures for managers, researchers, and volunteers.* San Francisco: Jossey-Bass.

ADDITIONAL READING

Jones, C. (1983). *How to speak TV: A self-defense manual when you're the news.* Marathon, FL: Video Consultants.

Jones, C. (1991). Developing strategic media relationships. In R. L. Edwards & J. A. Yankey (Eds.), *Skills for effective human services management* (pp. 103–112). Washington, DC: NASW Press.

Hart, T., Greenfield, J. M., & Johnston, M. (2005). *Nonprofit Internet strategies: Best practices for marketing, communications, and fundraising success.* Hoboken, NJ: John Wiley & Sons.

Philanthropy Journal. Available online at http://www.philanthropyjournal.org

Prevent Child Abuse, North Carolina. (1994). *Strategies for a successful public awareness program on child abuse and neglect.* Raleigh: Author.

Strunk, W., & White, E. B. (1959). *The elements of style.* New York: Macmillan.

6

Managing Public Policy Advocacy and Government Relations

Emily D. Pelton and Richard E. Baznik

Significant cuts in federal spending for human services and more recent short-falls in state budgets have led to a reduction in resources available for many government-supported programs, particularly in health, education, social services, and the arts (Silberman, 2002). As a result, many nonprofit agencies have seen reductions in government financial support and are experiencing more intense competition in obtaining private financial support (Edwards, Cooke, & Reid, 1996; Salamon, 1997). In addition, nonprofit organizations are likely to experience a growing demand to serve individuals who were previously served by government organizations. The growth of government interest in "faith-based initiatives" is an illustration of this trend.

On the other hand, while the demands on nonprofits are increasing in some areas, profit-oriented organizations have moved very selectively into traditional areas of nonprofit operations, particularly health care (Gornick et al., 1996). Although the entry of for-profit competitors into the health care market may offer more options for consumers, many people are concerned about the growing privatization of hospitals and specialty clinics and the increasing role of the profit motive in health services delivery. Similar concerns have been expressed about the move of for-profit organizations into other areas that have traditionally been the domain of public and nonprofit organizations (Lansberg, 2004). The blurring of these boundaries leads to both opportunities and stress.

As nonprofits struggle with these pressures, they are increasingly expected to justify their funding with measurable, quantitative results. The special tax status and other unique aspects of nonprofits have historically allowed the sector to lag behind in developing financial and program reporting capabilities comparable to those of the for-profit and government sectors. Growing public attention to these factors, along with well-publicized financial and ethical scandals, have made accountability a key factor for nonprofit managers to address in their work (Gibelman, Gelman, & Pollack, 1997).

In many cases, nonprofit organizations and managers may find it necessary to initiate or support legislative changes that will help make federal and state policy transitions smoother. As policy changes unfold, lawmakers and even an emerging generation of trustees of nonprofits will be watching for results, and nonprofit managers must be able to articulate what works, what does not, and why. In cases in which new policies do not meet public needs, nonprofit leaders will need to help formulate and advocate alternatives. Similarly, when new policies are working, nonprofit leaders may be asked to share information about successful models so that others may adopt them. In any event, good advocacy skills will continue to be important in meeting the challenges now facing the nonprofit sector.

BEING A LEADER IN ADVOCACY

Regardless of professional focus, nonprofit managers will eventually find themselves participating in a public policy process or debate. To do this effectively, managers must be well-informed about their own organizations; understand their positions within particular sectors; and know how to draw strength from supporters, constituents, and partners. Similarly, managers must understand their opposition and know how to identify the key barriers to achieving their own organization's aims. All of this knowledge will help influence external processes, policies, and individuals who can help advance an organization's policy objectives.

Leading effectively in the public realm requires doing two things well. First, learn the organization's public issues and the political context in which it operates. Second, frame a clear advocacy agenda and lead the organization to advance it. These are essential elements of organizational leadership, not tasks to be left to specialists or consultants.

An organization's advocacy objectives could consist of a target goal such as increasing its share of an annual government spending bill or promoting changes to policies affecting public benefits available to clients of its programs. Sometimes advocacy can involve defending the very existence of an organization.

Some advocacy opportunities will arise in the course of an organization's normal public functions, whereas others may result from major public controversies and debates. Regardless of whether an organization is dedicated to advocacy causes or is entering the public policy realm for a specific result, managers must be aware of the public environment in which their organizations are operating. Learning about this framework—the people, institutions, and political issues that drive the system—is a basic function that should be integrated into the management of all nonprofits. This is the focus of the first section below, "Laying the Foundation."

Once an organization has a sense of the policy environment and its internal positions, its managers will be ready to assemble these into an advocacy agenda for the organization. Identifying the issues is usually easier than choosing among them, as managers will face competing pressures from both inside and outside the organization. Developing a list of criteria to guide an organization in choosing its advocacy focus will help. Once an organization has identified its advocacy interests and priorities, a manager can put together an advocacy plan with objectives and a timeline for accomplishing them. Given the chaotic nature of the policy process, the organization will want to build in measures to reevaluate and make mid-course corrections as it advances toward its goal. The organization's advocacy plan also should be clear about roles and responsibilities within the organization and partner groups. The process for launching advocacy work is the focus of the second section, "Public Advocacy."

Finally, a note: It is rare that advocacy occurs neatly and in sequential order. Sometimes an organization may be swept into an advocacy initiative defined by others before it has had an opportunity to conduct even the most basic research. Conversely, an organization may spend a great deal of time researching an issue and ultimately choose to take no action, or it may research, analyze, network, plan, and advocate simultaneously. The approach laid out below is an ideal and meant to offer useful approaches, but it is by no means meant to limit readers' thinking or even to describe the sequence of events that is most common. Advocacy is a creative, organic, sometimes random process on which the participants can impose only minimal order. Ultimately, the most successful advocates are people who are flexible, analytical, and charismatic and who embrace change and new opportunities.

LAYING THE FOUNDATION

To achieve results in advocacy, managers will need to develop a thorough understanding of both their own organization's positions, priorities, and capacity (e.g., internal factors) and their relationships with the community, supporters, opponents, and policymakers (e.g., external factors). Begin by taking the following steps to lay the foundations of policy and advocacy work:

1. Map organizational resources and positions.
2. Identify, research, and analyze the public issues.

3. Understand relevant policy and political processes.
4. Get to know the public policy players.
5. Get to know the sector players.

1. Map Organizational Resources and Positions

Before responding to a policy concern or launching a policy initiative, it is vital to understand the starting point: the organization. For example, a manager who is relatively new does not want to take a strong public position that directly contradict what his or her predecessor had said to the same policymakers last year. As a first step, map out the organization's capacity to conduct policy and advocacy, its positions, and its priorities. These, in turn, will inform the choice of advocacy issues and the formation of external policy positions.

In assessing the organization's policy and advocacy capacity, three important considerations are staff capacity, access to analysis and information, and organizational relationships. Staff are usually the most critical resource in any advocacy initiative. Colleagues who have experience with other policy advocacy initiatives can be invaluable in identifying alliances or interpreting competing internal priorities. Various staff can contribute differently. Some staff may be well-suited to research but not to advocacy and public speaking, for example, while others may be well-qualified to manage a consultant providing research products. Those with high leadership potential but little public policy experience might be developed into effective advocates.

The following criteria can help managers take stock of staff resources:

- How many people in the organization have experience in policy analysis or advocacy, and what level of effort can they devote to an initiative?
- Do staff have any experience in the particular issue of concern? Will turnover or other problems prevent them from sharing their institutional knowledge?
- Do staff themselves have experience or networks (formal or informal) that will support advocacy efforts?
- Do resources or partnerships exist that will allow bringing in outside experts to help with the work?
- Are qualified consultants or others available for policy and advocacy work in the community, and can the organization afford their rates?

Effective advocacy also hinges on access to information and analysis. Start by assessing whether the organization's information and analysis capabilities are scaled to its needs. Typically, research and analysis must be obtained from both inside and outside an organization. Policy research can be expensive if done by a private company or inexpensive (even free) if done through coalitions and "watch-dog" organization Web sites.

If the organization is a small, community-based operation, information-gathering needs might be met by a single staff person with recent experience in city government who can follow key issues via Web sites, "listservs," and the local media. Such a person also might monitor industry news bulletins and informally coordinate activities with other community organizations. However, larger organizations or those with a complex agenda may need to subscribe to professional news services or hire a consulting firm to research certain key issues.

In the research stage, learn the positions of other groups. Keeping an open mind is crucial, particularly at the beginning, because other organizations may have interpreted an issue quite differently. Some advocacy initiatives require relatively little collaboration, while others hinge on unity within a sector to succeed. Assess the ability of other potential allies to make an impact on an issue. But guard against elitism in making this assessment: The largest and most successful organizations in an industry group may not be the most credible in presenting an issue to policymakers.

Be sure to identify existing and emerging coalitions and their positions. Compare them to those of the organization. When positions are aligned, use coalitions and partnerships with other organizations. This can reduce expenditures of time and resources and can lead to more effective interactions with policymakers. For an organization with positions that are not aligned with those of others in its sector, be sure to understand why and be prepared to explain this convincingly to the organization's audiences.

Before entering the public domain, managers also must be familiar with internal priorities and public positions that relate to the organization's advocacy issues. Managers should be clear on the mission, goals, and history of the organization before forming or articulating positions on public issues. Major public policy priorities and any sensitivities can be identified by senior members of the organization, including members of the board. Managers also should assess the amount of time that internal supporters can provide. (Be sure not to underestimate the amount of time required for internal coordination of a policy initiative!)

A good first step is to research previous public positions taken by the organization or its members. In preparing testimony for a state appropriations committee, for example, review not only the preceding year's accomplishments but also any prior testimony delivered to that committee by the organization. Be sure to check whether individuals associated with the organization have spoken publicly on the same topics, even if their appearances were not on behalf of the organization.

Another step in this process is to identify linkages between public issues and organizational priorities on the opeı ational or program side of the organization's work. Managers sometimes focus only on "getting the job done" and do not have the inclination or time to consider how policies are affecting the organization's work, or vice versa. Making the connections between goals in the organization's strategic plan and barriers being encountered by staff while serving clients can help build an effective case for engaging in advocacy or public policy initiatives, especially with the board. Examples of concrete incidents affecting program delivery or clients' quality of life often are the most effective tools in an advocacy presentation.

Small nonprofits (e.g., a local shelter for homeless men) may more easily be able to identify public policy priorities than larger ones (e.g., American Red Cross), which have multiple interests at different levels of government. On the other hand, larger organizations are more likely to have the resources to conduct research and hire consultants to establish strategic plans for advocacy. Give some thought to how much time is appropriate to identifying priorities, based on where the organization falls on this spectrum.

2. Identify, Research, and Analyze the Public Issues

The mapping exercises above will help an organization identify its capacity and organizational priorities. These in turn will be useful in identifying critical public issues for the organization and developing advocacy plans to achieve its goals. Research and analysis will ensure that managers make effective choices.

There are a variety of ways to learn about issues affecting the organization: staff networks, public information (do not forget newspapers and other local media), community meetings, and information provided by constituents (e.g., members, clients, partners) or supporters (e.g., private donors, board members, public decision makers). Identifying the issues is usually far easier than choosing among them.

At the outset, a manager should identify the many public issues that could affect the organization. How will the organization decide where to put its effort? Prioritizing policy objectives is perhaps one of the most difficult decisions that nonprofit managers will make. Mapping the organization's resources will help the manager assess the internal factors that determine the organization's readiness for advocacy, although there are many external factors in the policy environment to consider as well. Remember, at this stage the manager does not need to make a final decision, only to prepare the organization to make informed choices. Factors to examine in prioritizing policy issues include the following.

IDENTIFYING TOP-PRIORITY PUBLIC ISSUES FOR THE ORGANIZATION

- Does an issue fundamentally affect the organization, for example, its ability to accomplish its mission or conduct operations?
- Does an issue substantially threaten or benefit the organization's primary constituents?
- Does the organization have credibility or a public track record that will make its positions compelling to decision makers? Or, will others wonder why the organization is engaged in the debate?
- Are other organizations better equipped to speak to the issue because of their credibility, political clout, or resources for advocacy?
- Does the organization's mapping exercise suggest that it is (or could be) part of coalitions or groups that could leverage the efforts of the organization?
- Does the issue have the potential to be resolved within the period of time that the organization plans to remain involved?

Some of these criteria, especially those related to resources, involve complex answers that may require further discussion or analysis to answer fully. Be sure not to overlook issues outside the organization's mission that nonetheless affect its work. For example, a neighborhood health clinic could easily find its operations affected by legislation about welfare reform, even though this is not strictly a "health" matter.

After narrowing the list of potential issue areas, a manager may want to prepare one or more "issue briefs" for internal review. An effective brief can be only a few pages long but should try to cover most of the elements listed as follows.

DECIDING WHAT TO TELL STAKEHOLDERS

- Information gained from the organizational mapping exercise, including capacity, internal priorities, and positions.
- Analysis of why the issue is important for the organization, its constituents, and partners (see above), including benefits or risks to the organization posed by the policy in question.
- Discussion of any major risks of involvement in the issue that might imperil the organization, its reputation, or its constituents.
- A preliminary summary of the political context of the issue and current trends, including identification of policymakers and issue supporters and opponents (see following section for more in-depth discussion).

Such an analysis lays the groundwork for further examination and will be useful in formulating an advocacy strategy later on, if one is needed.

In the early stages of research, an organization may prefer to rely on internal resources, particularly when an issue is politically sensitive or when it is not clear whether the organization has a strong stake in the outcome. As the analysis proceeds, however, determine whether a regional or national advocacy organization with centralized resources also might have useful data available. Particularly in social services fields, clearinghouse organizations frequently offer resources such as analyses of proposed legislation, background information and statistics on specific issues, and legislative action kits to promote participation in national or grassroots advocacy efforts. Obtaining information this way not only can save time and money but also can allow for greater understanding of the positions of other organizations and then help gauge the level of effort needed to make a political impact.

Note that a group that offers pre-packaged information on issues of interest to the organization will often have its own agenda. Make sure to understand that agenda and determine whether it is appropriate for the organization.

3. Understand Relevant Policy and Political Processes

In building an advocacy agenda, identify the policy and political processes that affect the organization's interests and learn how to influence them. Nonprofit managers should strive to understand the norms, processes, and actors in the political systems in which the organization will be operating. The process that determines policy outcomes for nonprofit organizations usually will have at least three dimensions:

1. A formal public dimension, which consists of information sharing and government oversight of government–nonprofit agreements (and other administrative and legal requirements).
2. An informal public dimension, which refers to how an organization and its members relate to the public officials outside formal mechanisms (e.g., through the use of media or constituent contact).
3. A "behind-the-scenes" dimension, which consists of private contacts and events that occur through networks and personal relationships.

Each aspect is important, and effective advocacy requires an understanding of all three.

FORMAL PUBLIC DIMENSIONS OF POLICY: OVERSIGHT, REVIEW, AND REGULATIONS. The formal public dimension of the policy process is governed by the legal relationship between nonprofit entities and the government, which is typically defined by specific laws, administrative procedures, and other agreements. Governmental oversight responsibilities for the activities of nongovernment organizations are designated to public officials by law or are determined by the individual interests of elected officials. These governing authorities conduct policy reviews of the activities of nonprofit organizations and usually define the expectations that they must meet in their public service.

Nonprofit organizations usually fall within the jurisdiction of several government agencies and legislative authorities. These entities play a role in defining the objectives an organization is required to fulfill to meet its obligations to the government. In addition, they provide the official venues through which the organization reports to the public. Organizations will typically interact with both legislative and executive authorities.

On the local government level, organizations will interact with the mayor's office, city council, county commission, school board, citizen advisory boards, and local departments and agencies. In state government, nonprofits will deal with the governor's office, legislative leaders and committees, state departments and agencies, and state commissions and oversight boards. At the federal level, nonprofits will interact with members of Congress (especially those representing the local district); key congressional committees; and federal departments, agencies, and commissions (See Figure 6.1 for a more complete list of regulatory entities.)

Learning the identities, functions, and norms of government entities responsible for an organization's oversight is the first step in understanding the formal public decision-making process. Over time, however, nonprofits are likely to interact on a variety of issues with many public officials and organizations, not just those who oversee their contractual obligations, funding, or core mission concerns. Thus, nonprofit managers should attempt to be informed about the full range of political issues and the policymakers in their communities.

Oversight and policy development usually involve a review process consisting of activities such as public hearings; submission and consideration of industry testimony, budget requests, or annual reports; and meetings among public officials, agency staff, and contractors. Consideration of new policies, regulations, and bills typically follows a formal procedure that includes opportunities for public comment. Nonprofit managers should be certain that they are informed and prepared to respond on key issues at each point of the formal policy process. Examples of public policy review processes in which nonprofits might wish to (or, in some cases, be required to) participate include

- Public hearings pertaining to the organization's mission or interests
- Administrative proceedings of oversight agencies
- Solicitations of public comments on proposed rules and regulations (e.g., notices of proposed rule-making in the *Federal Register)*
- Government–industry roundtable discussions of new policies or legislation.

FIGURE 6.1

AMERICA'S NONPROFIT ORGANIZATONS: WHO REGULATES WHAT?

	State Sec'y of State	State Att'y General	State Agency	Local Gov't	IRS	Federal Agency	Courts	Private Assn.	Market
Corporate Charter	■	■			■	■			■
Tax-Exempt Status		■		■	■	■			■
Nonprofit mission	■	■	■		■	■			■
Advocacy, lobbying		■	■		■	■			
Fundraising		■		■	■	■			
Financial reporting		■			■	■		■	■
Tax-exempt bonds			■	■	■	■		■	■
Employment (hiring, firing)		■	■			■	■		
Employment (tax, wrks comp)					■	■	■		
Health, safety		■	■			■	■	■	
Licensing, accreditation		■	■			■	■	■	■
Health, hospitals		■	■			■	■	■	■
K–12 schools		■	■			■	■	■	■
Colleges, universities		■				■	■	■	■
Welfare, job training		■	■			■	■	■	■
Religious legitimacy					■	■		■	■
Museums						■		■	■

(Adapted from Hammack, 2005)

Any advocacy undertaken by a nonprofit organization must be conducted within government regulations and other legal restrictions on these activities. Nonprofits must abide by the standard rules that govern political activities in the United States, including restrictions on contributions and the public disclosure of certain actions. In addition, charitable institutions are bound by even more stringent limits imposed by the U.S. Tax Code (U.S.C. 26, Sec. 501), which defines a *501(c)(3) organization* as one in which

> No substantial part of the activities . . . is carrying on propaganda, or otherwise attempting, to influence legislation (except as otherwise provided in subsection (h)), and which does not participate in, or intervene in (including the publishing or distributing of statements), any political campaign on behalf of (or in opposition to) any candidate for public office. (Internal Revenue Code)

These provisions have direct implications for nonprofits, which must abide by restrictions that apply to their donated funds. In addition, many states impose specific restrictions on lobbying that nonprofit managers should research and understand before engaging in an advocacy campaign.

INFORMAL DIMENSIONS OF POLICY: PUBLIC DISCOURSE AND INFLUENCE. The informal public dimension of policy-making consists of relationships and interactions among an organization, the public, and elected or appointed public officials, which often are fostered through the media and public interest groups. An organization's preliminary analysis should look at the influence of public figures and public opinion on particular decision-making processes. Also, consider how the media and other interest groups can influence them. Influencing decision-making outside formal government channels can range from submitting petitions or using the press (for example, talk radio, opinion–editorials, press releases) to becoming directly involved in national advocacy efforts.

Just as advocates sometimes have difficulty identifying the key public decision makers on particular issues, they may struggle to determine the role of public opinion in the policy decision-making process. Consider these questions about the role of public opinion:

- Is the public generally informed about a particular issue? If so, is the public concerned?
- Are members of the public likely to hold their elected officials accountable for decisions on the issue by taking political action?
- What evidence is available that public opinion has been used as leverage on similar issues?
- What roles do the media play in shaping public opinion about the issue and influencing the actions of public officials?
- Can the public be engaged?

If public opinion matters, then communications and media relations are likely to be important. If, on the other hand, the public is relatively uninformed or uninterested in an issue, managers must decide whether to attempt to educate the public or to deal directly with legislators and inside players. These are crucial determinants of an organization's advocacy strategy later on.

Public opinion is frequently a significant factor in advocacy. Controversial issues such as abortion rights, welfare reform, or school prayer have been debated in the public arena for many years, and it is generally safe to assume that both members of the public and elected and appointed officials have strong opinions on such matters. These positions often can be learned through news coverage, opinion polls, and information disseminated by public interest groups.

Controversy can be valuable in advocacy because it tends to generate news coverage. There is no guarantee that such coverage will be positive, however, and controversial issues tend to be cast in emotional terms that make it harder to build a case based on facts. Thus, matters of public opinion always should be handled carefully. With new or untested issues, however, there may be no way to predict how the public will react. Consider the following factors to assess the potential importance of public opinion on particular issues:

- Has the public shown an interest in similar issues in the past? Are opinion polls available? If so, what are the prevailing public opinions?
- Has any public interest, political action, or other citizen group or groups been formed that is concerned with these issues?
- Historically, how responsive have elected officials been to public opinion on such matters?
- Have similar issues been the source of debate in any recent elections?
- Does the community tend to participate in political debate? If so, on what issues?

If public opinion is well formed or seems likely to affect the policy-making process, also consider the role of the media and the organization's capacity to generate media coverage (see Chapter 5). The following are some key questions to explore:

- Do the news media regularly report on similar issues? If so, how? What does this suggest about their interest and orientation on the issue?
- Are there examples of media impact on similar issues (e.g., investigative reporting or editorials directed at elected officials)?
- What resources does the organization have available for media communications? Is this an area of strength?
- Does the organization have an existing relationship with members of the media? Is it a positive one?

Public discourse and debate can inform and influence the actions of elected and appointed officials outside officially established government structures. In many instances, nonprofits may be able to exert political influence on decision makers through the actions of their members and through public education and advocacy campaigns. Small, grassroots organizations may wish to undertake activities such as soliciting signatures for petitions or enlisting constituents to make public appearances to advocate positions on behalf of the organization. Other approaches include writing letters, running newspaper ads, submitting opinion pieces to newspapers, and coordinating grassroots campaign support for candidates (but keep in mind that there are important restrictions on participation in partisan campaigns by nonprofits). In deciding how to influence public officials, nonprofits should consider not only their own capacity to conduct these activities effectively but also the political consequences of doing so and possible effects on other areas of operations.

BEHIND THE SCENES: POLITICS AND THE BACK ROOM. The behind-the-scenes dimension is often the least accessible part of the policy-making process, but it is probably the most important. Just as an organization's annual report typically offers a helpful but incomplete picture of how it really functions, the formal public review process illustrates only part of the government–nonprofit story. Factors such as personal political alliances and rivalries, organizational politics, competing priorities, and hierarchies within agencies can have a profound impact on public policy decisions, yet they are rarely a part of the public record. To gain access to this information, a manager must develop personal contacts with decision makers and form networks with individuals and groups who can provide insights into the policy process. While this notion conjures up visions of "smoke-filled back rooms," it is not very different from other informal networks that an organization may look to for success in community relations, fund-raising, and other operational support.

In short, it is vital that managers learn the "inside game" that is often played in negotiating public policies. For example, it may be crucial to know that certain members of a legislative committee, such as the chair, wield the most power; that some agencies are more effective than others in obtaining resources from elected officials; and that certain personal relationships among legislators tend to influence policy. Additional considerations, such as campaign commitments, demands on politicians from their constituents, and the internal politics of political institutions—factors sometimes hard to glean from formal policy research—also can help you assess the organization's chances of success and influence the process.

One aspect of advocacy that can be particularly challenging is accurately identifying which individual or group in a policy-making body is most likely to determine the outcome of an issue. This uncertainty can make it difficult to prepare an effective advocacy strategy. Gaining the necessary insights often requires participation in the political process over a period of time. However, the following are good questions to ask at the outset:

- Which government entity or entities typically exert the most significant influence on the policy process?
- Who within the organization actually makes decisions (e.g., elected officials, staff, others), and who influences them?
- What are the norms and protocols for interacting with these individuals outside formal public venues?

- When are key decisions made and, if multiple interests are involved, what is the internal review process?
- What internal relationships (oppositions and alliances) exist that may affect the positions taken by key individuals?

With some of this information in hand, managers can begin to communicate— and foster relationships with—key policy decision makers.

4. Get to Know the Public Policy Players

An effective advocate will quickly learn as much as possible about the key decision makers and public groups with interests supporting or opposing those of his or her organization. Because the interests and positions of key public officials are major determinants of policy and political decision making, managers should gather general background information about decision makers as well as factors that can influence their positions; examples might include concurrent public debates, their previous votes, their constituencies, and the identity of their campaign contributors. If possible, obtain this information for each individual within the body that controls the decision-making process (much of this information is publicly available). Several public policy Web sites are listed in Figure 6.2. It is also advisable to research the individual or issue you are addressing with a Web search engine to see if unexpected information arises that warrants further investigation.

Public interest groups and coalitions with similar or opposing interests also are important players in the public arena. Understanding the role that other organizations play in the political process can help an organization anticipate and interpret events and identify potential allies or opponents.

THE DECISION MAKERS. In researching decision makers involved in particular issues, managers may want to start with known quantities, such as governing bodies that typically review the organization's activities or budget. If a relationship already exists between a government official and the organization, it may be relatively simple to assess such factors as the official's positions on various policies and his or her general level of support for the organization and its mission. Before deciding whether to request the official's political support on specific matters, however, the organization also might wish to research these additional factors:

- Who are the official's constituents (including political donors), and how would their interests be affected by the proposed policies or issues under consideration?

Managing Public Policy Advocacy and Government Relations

FIGURE 6.2
PUBLIC POLICY INFORMATION WEB SITES

Type of Web Site	URL address	Type of Information
Library of Congress/ THOMAS	http://www.thomas.loc.gov/	Comprehensive Information about U.S. Congress: bills, resolutions, laws, committee information, presidential nominations, Congressional schedule and activities. Congressional record.
US Senate and House of Representatives	http://www.senate.gov http://www.house.gov	Legislative information, links to individual member, leadership, and committee sites, member directories, Congressional schedule, and individual voting records.
US State Web sites	Example: California http://www.ca.gov (others are easily found through search engines)	Information about Governor and statewide officials, ethics and lobbying laws, information about laws, state agencies, and links to State assemblies and their members, information on laws (e.g. labor, employment, health).
The Center for Public Integrity	http://www.publicintegrity.org	Investigative journalism site that explores legislative voting records, violations of public trust, and electoral issues such as campaign finance.
OMB Watch	http://www.ombwatch.org	A nonprofit research, educational, and advocacy organization that focuses on budget issues, regulatory policy, nonprofit advocacy, and access to government.
Project Vote Smart	http://www.vote-smart.org	Library of information that provides biographical information, issue positions, voting records, campaign finances, and interest group ratings for candidates and elected officials.
Political Money Line	http://www.fecinfo.com/	Set of databases using information gathered by the Federal Election Commission on political contributions— by donor, by candidate, etc.

The sites above are generally nonpartisan. There is also a host of Web sites operated by policy advocacy and research organizations that present information from a specific point of view. The two listed below are only two of many.

Public Citizen	http://www.citizen.org	Public interest Web site focusing on lobbying, energy, trade, environment, and federal legislative process. Tends to be "left leaning" and critical of business.
The Heritage Foundation	http://www.heritage.org	Public policy organization site focused on conservative policy issues, e.g., foreign policy, tax reform, immigration. Tends to be "right leaning" and critical of government.

- What are the official's political ambitions, political affiliation, and role within the political party? How might these factors influence the official's public stances?
- What is the official's voting record on similar measures?
- What other responsibilities or political factors, such as sitting on multiple committees within a legislature, might influence the official's position?

When the public officials involved are unknown to the organization, further research is required, and the role of personal networks becomes paramount. Before preparing to approach unfamiliar individuals, learn about their reputations and modes of public interaction by asking the following questions:

- Does the official make time to meet with public groups? If so, does he or she prefer to be approached directly or through staff or surrogates?
- Is the official well informed, interested, or generally sympathetic to the type of work performed by the organization? What is his or her voting record?
- What are the other key issues with which the official is publicly associated? How do they relate to the ones at hand?

THE INFLUENCERS. In the organization's research efforts, it is important not to focus solely on the majority party or the most powerful figures. Many issues are not determined along strict party lines, and back-room negotiations can lead to unexpected outcomes. Thus, research should focus on determining not only the positions and interests of individual officials but also whether and how they can be expected to influence their colleagues on key issues.

Although it is natural to focus first on potential allies and supporters in the political process, advocacy also requires contact with officials who are opposed to the interests of the organization. Research the public record, constituencies, and backgrounds of officials expected to oppose the organization's position just as managers would research the organization's likely supporters. Also consider these issues:

- How effective are the officials who are likely to oppose an issue, versus those who may support it?
- What public groups are likely to support the opposition's stand?
- How committed are opponents to their positions? Does it appear possible to achieve a closer alignment of their positions with those of the organization?

Perhaps the best means of learning about public figures is through personal networking. Staff, board members, and other colleagues within and outside the organization can usually help shed light on the reputations, personalities, and political interests of government officials. Lateral contacts, such as government administrative program officers or legislative staff, also can offer useful insights.

5. Get to Know the Sector Players

During the organization's mapping exercise, the manager should have scanned the coalitions in which the organization is a member. While expanding the analysis, the manager will deepen the organization's knowledge of other groups in its sector that are likely to participate in advocacy efforts, including both their positions and decision-making procedures. An individual nonprofit will rarely find itself the sole advocate or opponent of any particular issue. Large-scale national issues such as welfare reform, gun control, or school vouchers evolve over many years and involve literally hundreds of organizations. Even local issues such as zoning laws, county budget expenditures, or environmental disputes can be complex and are likely to involve multiple organizations or coalitions. In many cases, organizations join together to advocate a position or hire an individual or organization to coordinate their advocacy efforts.

In some cases, an entire sector can agree on its public policy interests, but often ad hoc coalitions form at the sub-sector level to address specific policy issues. Some coalitions form over the long term, while others have little in common other than their shared position on a particular set of issues. The provisions of individual legislative proposals can sometimes divide a community, such as when resources must be split among organizations. Moreover, specific proposals can sometimes generate unusual coalitions. Groups that might normally oppose one another may learn that their interests are temporarily in alignment and join forces in a coalition to pass or defeat a particular bill. Thus, it is important to research the profiles and positions of groups involved in each public debate in which the organization is engaged.

The organization also should make informed judgments about strategic alliances in advocacy. In some instances, participation in coalitions may strengthen the organization's voice, whereas in others, the organization's positions may be watered down by the need to meet multiple interests. When joining forces with another organization or entering a coalition, assess its reliability, public legitimacy, and public interests; its political influence, access, and sophistication; and the extent to which its interests and expectations are aligned with those of the organization.

Just as the manager should research the organization's opposition within decision-making bodies, he or she must identify organizations and groups that are likely to oppose measures supported by the organization or to promote alternatives that are objectionable. Although the existence of opponents should not deter organizations from advocating their interests, the strength and resources of the opposition should help guide decisions about selecting battles to be fought and may suggest the chances of prevailing in the political process. Use the following questions to assess opposition groups:

- What are the interests of opposing groups, and who are their supporters and constituents?
- How well known, politically connected, and respected are opposition groups?
- What kinds of tactics are these groups likely to use? Could these pose long-term threats to the organization beyond the outcome of the debate on one issue?
- How committed are these groups to their positions? Is it possible to achieve a closer alignment between their positions and those of the organization?

It is not always possible to identify opposing groups at the beginning of an advocacy effort, but monitoring the political process can help identify such groups through the media, public records of events (hearings and testimony), and personal networking. The more information that is available in advance about potential opposition, the better prepared the organization will be.

PUBLIC ADVOCACY

The best way to prepare an organization for effective advocacy is to ensure that its public interests and objectives are sharply defined and that its management is well informed about the policy environment. By following the steps described earlier, managers should be in a position do both. The next step is to develop an advocacy action plan to mobilize the organization behind an agenda in the public arena. The three main steps in advancing into the advocacy process are

1. Decide when and about what to advocate.
2. Develop an advocacy action plan.
3. Engage in the political process.

1. Decide When and About What to Advocate

The ability to identify important public issues and to choose among them will largely determine an organization's success as a public advocate. Seeing an opportunity and leading the organization through a successful campaign could be the hallmark of a manager's career. On the other hand, advocacy is not always the solution to the organization's needs. Sometimes participating in an unsuccessful advocacy effort can be counterproductive for the organization. (In some cases, silence may be the best advocacy strategy of all!) Learning how to judge the political environment, how to identify advocacy opportunities even before they are clearly defined, and prioritizing among the organization's many public interests will ensure that the manager has chosen the right path.

IDENTIFYING ADVOCACY OPPORTUNITIES. The impetus for an organization to engage in advocacy can arise in a variety of ways: through government policy review processes, through public events and community activities, or through changes in the political landscape that either enable an organization to take new positions or force it to take defensive action. To be aware of these opportunities, use information resources and personal networks to stay informed about the general political climate, learn about specific new proposals that could affect the organization, monitor the actions of government agencies that affect the organization's constituents or clients, and stay in tune with other groups involved in the organization's issues and the political process.

We often think of advocacy in the context of a campaign or a high-visibility effort to change policy. Yet, many advocacy opportunities arise simply from straightforward interaction with public officials. For example, after a series of hearings on domestic violence and child abuse, several safe houses might invite members of the county board and their staff to visit their facilities. Such visits can allow officials to ask questions in a relaxed setting and to observe firsthand the results of their funding decisions and possible needs for changes in policies.

Finally, advocacy does not have to be a purely reactive process. Nonprofit organizations, particularly those that carry out public functions, often have the firsthand knowledge that legislators need to make informed public policy decisions. Use this knowledge to promote new or creative approaches to program implementation or policy reforms; new initiatives often are most effective when launched by coalitions of organizations. Establishing modes of regular contact with policymakers and their staffs is the best way to help put new issues on the table as they arise.

KNOWING WHEN TO JUMP INTO THE ARENA. Deciding *when* and *how* to enter the public policy domain—and being able to justify that decisions to others—is critically important for nonprofit managers. To help guide these choices, it is helpful to develop *criteria* to judge when advocacy is necessary or desirable for the organization.

Advocacy criteria should inform strategic questions that must be addressed in developing an advocacy action plan. Individual organizations will want to develop their own questions, but generally an organization should examine several key considerations before attempting to influence policy:

1. The organization's specific public interests
2. The organization's capacity to influence the process and whether its aims are achievable
3. The potential benefits and risks of advocacy.

Identifying Public Interests. An organization's board will typically be involved in a decision to enter public advocacy, especially when the organization will be in a visible role. Managers are typically responsible for helping the board make informed decisions. Defining an organization's interests can be relatively simple when there is internal consensus about the importance of the issue at hand and its relevance to the organization and when the consequences of possible outcomes can be predicted.

Nonprofit organizations rarely have the luxury of making decisions under such conditions, however. More often, drafting a public position involves making tough choices about how to manage competing values and priorities within an organization, particularly within large organizations with different regions or chapters to satisfy. This can be complicated when the implications of a particular policy are unclear or when a policy could affect various parts of an organization's operations or membership differently. Obtaining accurate information about the issue at hand, the political factors driving it, and other supporting analyses can make this process easier. Managers can help their boards define organizational interests by consulting with members, clients, and constituents and by conducting consensus-building activities such as internal and external focus group sessions.

Judging Capacity to Influence. Once the interests of an organization have been defined, it is equally important to assess its capacity to influence the decision-making process. Not all advocacy strategies require large budgets, and an organization should not be deterred from participating in the political process even if it has limited resources. On the other hand, many factors can limit the ability of an organization to influence public debate or the outcome of issues, and these should be assessed realistically. Before committing to a particular advocacy effort, consider these critical factors:

● What is the political climate among the general public, decision makers, and other public groups? How powerful are the organization's allies and opponents?
● What resources are available for the effort, both internally (e.g., research capability, staff, funding) and externally (e.g., partners, coalitions, public interest groups)?
● How strong are the organization's political connections? Historically, how successful has the organization and others like it been in influencing the relevant decision-making process? Does the organization have a credible and respected spokesperson?

- What does the organization have to offer that will enhance efforts already under way to influence the policy outcome? How experienced is the organization at operating in arenas such as media relations?
- Does the entire organization (e.g., staff, management, board members) back the effort, and will they lend their support?

Assessing Costs and Benefits. Finally, before embarking on a significant advocacy action, an organization should assess the potential benefits and drawbacks of doing so, including risks to the organization, taking into account the level of time, energy, and resources required to succeed.

- What does the organization stand to gain or lose as a result of the outcome of the issue under consideration? What does this suggest about the level of time, energy, and resources to devote to the effort?
- To what extent might the effort divert needed resources and organizational energy from other areas? Is this acceptable?
- What are the possible drawbacks to entering public debate? Are there long-term repercussions that should be considered, such as political tension with particular groups or decision makers?
- Can the probable outcome of the effort be estimated? What are the chances that results will be negative? What does this suggest about the need to act?
- Overall, how likely is the organization to prevail in the political process, given the factors discussed in this section? Are there alternatives to the political process for achieving desired objectives?

2. Develop an Advocacy Action Plan

Once an organization has identified an advocacy need or opportunity that satisfies its criteria, the next step is to develop an action plan (see Figure 6.3). In doing so, use the tools, resources, and information discussed in the first section of this chapter. The plan should include at least four elements:

1. Clear, time-bound advocacy objectives,
2. A timeline for action that identifies specific roles and responsibilities,
3. Advocacy messages, and
4. Specific milestones and plans for midcourse corrections.

ADVOCACY OBJECTIVES. Establishing advocacy objectives is an extension of the policy research and networking that an organization has already conducted. Advocacy objectives must flow logically from an organization's interests. However, be careful not to engage in wishful thinking that links the

---

FIGURE 6.3

SAMPLE ACTION PLAN

Issue and Interests

A nonprofit community theater receives a major share of its funding from the local county government. A new member of the county board makes a specific proposal at a public hearing to cut arts funding by one-third to finance public education programs. Given the large share of public funding received by the theater, this could force it to close. An internal county budgetary hearing is scheduled in four weeks, and final decisions will be made within six weeks.

Objectives

● Prevent severe funding cuts that will threaten the existence of the organization.
● Maintain good relations with the county board, including the new member proposing spending cuts, and the education community, which has been a strong supporter of community theater in the county.

Actions: [Weeks 1–4]

● Work through a coalition of nonprofit arts groups to develop a statement for the county board on the importance of the arts in the community. [Weeks 1–2]
● Set up meetings between board members of the organization and the new county board member as well as potential arts advocates on the county board. [Weeks 1–3]
● Work with the public arts funding agency to influence the decision-making process. Offer to provide support to agency staff who also are opposed to cuts. [Weeks 2–4]
● Show that arts programs benefit children's education. Identify teachers or influential individuals representing educational interests willing to oppose funding cuts to the county arts program. [Weeks 3–4]

Roles

● Executive director leads the nonprofit arts coalition effort, including planning meetings, distributing materials, and drafting and achieving consensus on the statement.

---

organization's ambitions to impossible outcomes. Setting realistic objectives for a particular advocacy effort can be complicated, given the number of variables influencing policy processes and the effort generally required to achieve internal consensus on organizational positions.

At the outset, be clear on whether the organization is trying to achieve incremental or fundamental change. This is important because public debates often

---

FIGURE 6.3
SAMPLE ACTION PLAN (continued)

- Public relations coordinator writes materials and gathers information.
- Education outreach staff member coordinates with arts agency staff.
- Board president sets up meetings with county board members to communicate opposition to cuts and meetings with community members to identify possible allies.

Milestone and Corrections [Weeks 4–6]

Milestone:

Budgetary hearing scheduled for 4 weeks after the hearing at which the initial proposal was made. See if new board member continues to advocate the same position or if other board members offer public opposition. Revise strategy if necessary. [Week 4]

Corrections:

- Research reveals many arts–education links in the community: Meet with the editorial board of the local paper to discuss the strong track record of community arts and the harm to both education and arts that could be caused by such a drastic funding cut. [Weeks 4–5]
- Agency arts staff do not appear to be making headway: Focus solely on direct meetings with county board members, emphasizing the link between arts and education. [Week 5]
- A strong advocate has been identified on the county board: Provide as much direct assistance to her and her staff as possible, including statistics, human interest stories, and influential contacts in the community. [Week 6]

Result [End of Week 6]

The new board member backs away from the earlier proposal. An alternative measure is passed specifying that 10 percent of the arts budget must be restricted to supporting student programs. The theater company's overall operation will be minimally affected.

---

focus on the extent to which change is required. In formulating the organization's position, managers should help the leadership of that organization assess what type of change can be achieved.

In general, advocacy efforts involve multiple objectives, and except in the most unusual circumstances, an organization probably will not achieve all of them. The nature of the political process demands engaging in debate, negotiation, and compromise. An organization ideally should have an internal list of priorities when entering the advocacy process so that staff, management, and board members can work toward common objectives. Rank the importance of each objective in terms of the most vital gains to be made or interests to be protected.

Prioritizing objectives can be useful not only for building and maintaining consensus but also for maneuvering through the political process. For example, policymakers sometimes insist that an organization define its top priorities before they will lend their support or negotiate compromises. Ranking priorities can be a risk, because some who oppose of the organization's agenda or for other reasons seek to reduce its support may take the opportunity to demand that only to top one or two priorities be considered for funding. Thus an organization may not wish to share this ranking publicly, but defining priorities provides a basis for engaging in negotiations when necessary. In addition, a priorities list can help managers and their advocacy teams develop backup positions and strategies if their initial efforts are unsuccessful.

An organization's advocacy objectives should *specify the policy that it hopes to change.* Advocacy objectives should always be linked to specific times and should specify a target audience, such as decision makers. Once advocacy is under way, or the initiative is complete, the manager should be able to evaluate (at least qualitatively) the organization's progress (and contribution) toward achieving the objective. Sometimes advocacy objectives may include outreach to "secondary audiences," those who can influence the primary target audience of decision makers. Examples of secondary audiences are the public and the media.

TIMELINE DESIGNATING ROLES AND RESPONSIBILITIES. As an organization expands its objectives into an action plan, it should define the specific steps that it will take to meet its objectives in the context of a timeline. The timeline should be based on both external conditions (e.g., political climate, strength of allies and opponents) as well as internal factors (e.g., financial and human resources). The action plan also should account for relevant political norms and procedures. If an issue requires advocacy with unfamiliar decision makers, be sure to check with others who may know them better. Recognize as well that the timeline for most advocacy initiatives will shift during the course of implementation.

The action plan should define specific *roles* for individuals and groups, usually both within and outside of the organization. Internally, managers should assign advocacy responsibilities to particular staff or themselves to ensure that the efforts will be well coordinated, particularly when public statements or actions are concerned. This assignment of responsibility must be handled with care, recognizing the respect that has been earned by managers who are viewed as effective spokespersons for the organization, as well as the potential for emerging spokespersons to gain stature in the organization. If the organization has a staff development program, it can be useful to consult with its leader while working on these assignments.

The roles of individuals and groups outside of the organization may be less well defined than those of organizational board and staff members, but it is important to incorporate them into an action plan, particularly when coalitions and other sector organizations are involved. Preliminary meetings with organizational allies should establish roles for each participant as well as expectations for how political coordination will occur. Discuss the common interests and priorities of the group (or affiliated organizations); which organizations or individuals will lead the advocacy effort; who will serve as the public representative of the group; when and how communication will take place; and what resources each organization will devote to the effort.

Sometimes action plans can incorporate roles for government officials or their staff. Although it may not be possible to obtain up-front commitments for political support, key public officials or staff can advocate with other government officials (e.g., congressional "sign-on letters" to the President that express congressional priorities). This approach to advocacy may be less time consuming, less risky, and more effective than other methods. However, do not rely solely on public officials to represent the organization's interests, because monitoring inside developments may be very difficult, and unforeseen political factors may cause even sympathetic elected officials to change their positions.

If in-house managers or existing resources are insufficient to meet advocacy needs, professional lobbyists can be hired to strengthen an organization's capacity to influence the policy process. Hiring a lobbyist generally reduces the demands on managers' time by "subcontracting" direct contacts with policymakers to a professional with inside information and political access. This may be particularly important in service delivery organizations or when an organization with little political experience conducts what it expects to be a one-time advocacy campaign.

Such services can be costly, however, and paid professionals may not be viewed as having as much legitimacy as do the members, staff, trustees, or management of the organization itself. Many public officials will give less weight to a message when they hear it from a so-called "hired gun." Also, many organizations are strictly limited by law in the amount of funds they can devote to lobbying, if it is permissible at all. In deciding whether to hire a lobbyist, managers should ask themselves the following questions (Brown, 1991):

- Does the lobbyist understand the organization's issues? Does he or she have access to the right political leaders? How is he or she regarded by those officials who will be lobbied?

- Is he or she experienced in working on the organization's issues? What is his or her track record, and have other organizations been satisfied with his or her work?
- Does he or she have a political affiliation? What other groups does he or she represent, and how might this reflect on the organization?
- What are the organization's restrictions under the IRS code in its ability to conduct lobbying, and does it have the knowledge and capacity to correctly report its lobbying activities?

The modality of advocacy that the organization chooses is another important consideration. The increasing availability of communications technology has led many nonprofits to focus on "e-advocacy" efforts to get out their messages. However, mass responses on the Internet are not always given as much weight as more traditional communications from constituents. It also can be expensive if large lists need to be maintained. The members of the management team should always consider the advantages and risks of initiating public information campaigns, acrimonious public debates with elected officials, and media coverage on issues as the organization develops advocacy action plans.

MESSAGES. Developing effective and targeted messages is the holy grail of any advocacy campaign. Even with all the best arguments, analysis, and political support, a campaign may fail if the target audience feels that an organization simply has nothing new or helpful to say. An advocacy initiative must always move the debate forward and be clear about the policy outcome being sought by its supporters.

Most campaign strategists would agree that message development is more an art than a science, but several general rules can help an organization develop effective advocacy messages:

- Every message *must* have a target audience. Be clear who the organization is trying to reach, and tailor the advocacy messages for different audiences (e.g., policymakers, media, public).
- Understand as much as possible about each of the target audiences—their knowledge base, present attitudes, and interest in the issue. Aiming too high (i.e., messages that are too complex or technical) can be equally as harmful as aiming too low (e.g., "talking down" to audiences, insulting their intelligence).
- Limit the number of messages. With too many messages—whether in a meeting, public campaign, or media opinion piece—people are less likely to retain the information or be compelled by what the organization has to say.

- Keep messages simple. Use clear language, and get right to the point. Most messages should be easily summarized in one to two sentences. The example in Figure 6.4 shows how a simple message can have a strong impact.
- Keep messages harmonized and consistent. If working in a coalition or even a large organization, agree on a common message that everyone will follow (even if each member uses different vocabulary). Conflicting messages can confuse an audience or provide an excuse for turning down a policy request.
- Reinforce messages. Most messages need to be communicated more than once. Seek multiple opportunities to convey what the organization has to say. If working in a coalition, agree on how each member can use its own access and opportunities to reach the target audience.
- Keep messages current. If advocacy objectives change, the messages may need to change, too. Or, if the messages are not having the desired effect, review their impact with key stakeholders and, if budgets allow, with focus groups that can provide feedback.

MILESTONES AND MIDCOURSE CORRECTIONS. One purpose of an action plan is to provide the organization with a shared road map. This can guide the organization initially and also determine whether it is on course. Milestones,

---

FIGURE 6.4
"CUT THE COST"

In the late 1990s, several nongovernmental organizations joined together to protest the costs being charged by large pharmaceutical companies for AIDS drugs. Doctors without Borders, Oxfam, and the South African Treatment Action Campaign mounted a high-profile international "cut the cost" campaign to oppose the practices of drug companies. In South Africa, they backed a legal effort by the government to force the companies to relax their licensing procedures, permitting cheaper generic production and sales of the drugs. The legal battle was fought out in the public relations arena for weeks, as advocates decried the industry's profit margins. Just as the judge entered the courtroom to begin the proceedings in South Africa, the pharmaceutical companies dropped their case. Although the companies' calculus was not public, the campaign appeared to have achieved its aim: to generate unwanted negative publicity for the industry, forcing a major shift in policy.

such as achieving the endorsement of key supporters or opportunities to present the organization's agenda to key audiences, should be part of the plan. If a milestone is met, the organization may end a phase of its work or expand in more ambitious directions. On the other hand, if the advocacy objectives are not being met, the organization may wish to reassess key elements of the strategy.

Every action plan is different, but it is always important to assess progress along the way to determine whether the advocacy objectives remain realistic and whether organizational resources are sufficient to accomplish the task at hand. Most importantly,

- Have sufficient resources been devoted to the action plan? If not, are more available, and how should they be used?
- Has the political environment changed, including the actions or effectiveness of the opposition? Should the objectives be revised to account for this?
- Have certain tactics failed? Is a different strategic approach necessary? For example, should the organization use a grassroots campaign versus managerial lobbying of decision makers?
- Are staff and other members of the organization carrying out their responsibilities as expected? Should any roles be reassigned?
- Are external groups carrying out their responsibilities as expected? Should the organization alter its participation in current coalitions or alliances?
- Should the organization revise its objectives to achieve less-ambitious results? If so, what should the alternative proposal be? Is the initial backup plan still the best alternative?

In the advocacy action plan, designate key points in time or events that will trigger a midcourse review and potential corrections of the objectives, timeline, and organizational roles.

3. Engage in the Political Process

Once the organization completes an action plan, it should be prepared to engage in the political process. This typically entails at least three steps:

1. Recruit supporters,
2. Choose effective tactics for communicating the messages; and
3. Monitor its impact, and revise the strategy if necessary.

As noted earlier, many advocacy initiatives are sparked spontaneously, and an organization may find itself fully engaged in the political process before it has a comprehensive plan in place. By the same token, the best-laid advocacy plans often must be totally revised as political events unfold. The ability to reframe the issues and messages is key to success.

RECRUIT SUPPORTERS. As an organization initiates an advocacy initiative, it may want to identify organizations with common interests, cultivate relationships with them, and chart a joint approach. However, efforts to recruit supporters should extend even further. The organization should target public figures and groups, as well as individual decision makers, to support its position. In the Sample Action Plan (see Figure 6.1), a community of nonprofit organizations (e.g., local arts organizations) reached out to another community (e.g., education) that shared at least some of its interests and also enlisted the help of a supportive county board member. Convincing nonaffiliated groups to endorse the organization's position can be effective, particularly when those groups can lend their legitimacy, credibility, or objectivity to the debate.

A good way to bring others into advocacy efforts is to seek their input in developing advocacy positions and messages. Although it is not always necessary to involve outsiders in the early stages of planning, it often is valuable to circulate proposals outside the organization for comment and endorsement before they are made public. This process can create a sense of shared ownership for the proposal, potentially motivating them to support the cause, and can help the organization make revisions that strengthen support for the measure. Moreover, such a review process adds different perspectives on the issue and can generate new ideas or help avert mistakes. Sharing proposals with certain groups outside the immediate community also can help the organization assess how the proposal might be received by a broader audience.

Beyond reaching out to public groups and supporters, an organization also may wish to consider sharing its proposals with certain policymakers before taking a public position. For example, the organization might ask trusted public officials and their staffs (who are known to support the organization and the position in question) to provide private feedback on such matters as

- What are the strengths and weaknesses of the position? Would managers be willing to publicly endorse it or advocate it among their colleagues? If not, what modifications would be necessary to do so?
- How are other members of the policy-making body likely to react to the position? How could it be made more politically palatable?
- What other issues could potentially affect the outcome of this issue (e.g., alternative proposals or unrelated politically charged disputes)?
- What strategies are most likely to succeed in lobbying for this position? This can be a particularly important question to ask policymakers' staff, who may be able to provide unique insights about the preferences of the governing body as well as the interests of the officials for whom they work.

When the advocacy action involves marshaling public support, the organization can consider recruiting supporters at public events. For example, major

charitable events or benefits can provide an excellent opportunity to recruit supporters and to improve the organization's name recognition within a community. Such events also can enable the organization to engender good will by inviting
volunteers, community leaders, and government officials. In large-scale and high-
budget advocacy campaigns, many other public outreach methods may be used,
such as materials (e.g., t-shirts, bumper stickers, mugs), public service announcements, earned media (e.g., opinion pieces), and paid media (e.g., advertising).

CHOOSE TACTICS FOR COMMUNICATING THE MESSAGES. Many means
are available to get messages out and influence the policy process. For example,
an organization may choose to organize or join a grassroots campaign or to
target the media (e.g., meeting with local editorial boards) as a means of conveying the message to secondary audiences that influence decision makers. Alternatively, the organization may take a direct approach to policymakers and seek to
meet with them and their staffs personally.

Public Outreach. An organization's audience can be only as supportive as it
is informed and engaged in the issues addressed in the advocacy effort. There are
a variety of ways to reach audiences, both internal and external. The means
chosen should reflect the importance of the issue, the potential role of the audience to affect policy, available resources, and expected interest in the issue. Examples of outreach mechanisms frequently used by nonprofits include

- *Speakers' bureaus.* Providing an experts list to policymakers, the media, and the community demonstrates an organization's connection to
  its constituents.
- *Events.* An organization can develop special events for a campaign, but
  most organizations already schedule many events that would interest
  policymakers.
- *Newsletters.* These can be helpful, but remember who the audience is.
  An internal staff newsletter may be boring to external readers.

Outreach can be conducted on a much broader level through grassroots campaigns. It is beyond the scope of this chapter to discuss grassroots politics and
organizing techniques, but many national organizations offer information about
how to carry out grassroots campaigning, including special restrictions for
nonprofits. Check the Web sites of one or more of the national associations
representing an organization's sector to find suggestions and guidelines.

Setting up an Internet site can be a strategic means to reach large audiences.
Numerous companies design and establish Web sites for organizations. Some businesses may provide such assistance free or at low cost. The site can meet multiple
objectives at once, such as providing up-to-date news to internal and external

constituencies, publicizing the activities and positions of the organization, and centralizing information-gathering functions (this can be particularly helpful in large organizations with regional chapters and subgroups).

By establishing links with other Web sites, publicity can be expanded even further. However, the organization should clearly define the purpose and audiences before embarking on this process, focusing primarily on content rather than form at the outset. Once established, the site should be updated frequently; a poorly maintained Web site that provides little or inaccurate information to users reflects badly on the organization.

Media. In the United States and most other Western nations, the press represents an independent voice in society, one that is assumed to have a degree of objectivity unattainable by virtually any other organization. For this reason alone, managers should consider how to communicate with editors and reporters about the objectives of the organization's advocacy efforts (see Chapter 5). To strengthen an organization's media capacity, consider the following approaches:

- *Develop contacts in the media.* An editor or reporter who already knows an organization's programs and record will most likely be much more responsive to its advocacy than one who knows nothing. Media tend to go to sources they know can provide reliable information time and time again.
- *Use technology.* Advanced information technology offers opportunities to get the word out at relatively low cost through faxes and e-mail. For example, managers can develop a list of media outlets to whom they can issue press releases and other information regularly.
- *Use news releases when needed, but sparingly.* A press release is short and designed to set up a phone call in which a manager can "pitch" the organization's issue. However, if the real target is a policymaker, a call or personalized letter can be more effective.
- *Communicate in a timely fashion.* Make sure that information is provided soon enough to take advantage of an issue's news value.
- *Be consistent and accurate.* Make sure that facts are double-checked before they are released. Coordinate information within the organization and among the members of the industry or coalition.
- *Use information strategically, but never misrepresent the facts.* Do not feel obliged to state the opposition's case, but recognize that an incomplete or misleading account will eventually backfire.

Meetings. Direct meetings often are the best opportunity to create an impression on a policymaker, and the organization may not get more than once chance. The following general rules may be helpful when approaching public officials directly in meetings or other direct communications:

- *Prepare, prepare, prepare!* Learning how public officials see their responsibilities and the demands of their constituencies can help a manager prepare good responses for the questions that they are likely to ask. (Remember that the organization and its views are not necessarily the policymaker's main concern.) Also, find out in advance whether the individual or group is already informed about the issue. Bring focused and concise analyses and timely reports or other short handouts (one-pagers) to leave behind after the meeting.

- *Be direct (if you can).* Although one may think that decision makers do not want to be asked for favors, it is often best to be clear about what one wants. Most officials and their staffs are extremely busy and will not have time to read or listen to extensive background information. Meetings may be cut short, so do not to waste time discussing tangential matters. If the proposal is favorably received, managers should make a specific request for endorsement or support, making clear exactly what actions they would like an official to take next. (Keep in mind, however, that lobbying restrictions on the organization may determine whether it is able to make a direct lobbying request concerning legislation or simply provide general educational information to a public official.)

- *Bring something to the table.* Offer reliable information and support to policymakers. Public officials and their staffs frequently lack the time and resources to conduct their own research and monitoring activities. Even keeping track of press accounts or internal developments within the decision-making body itself can be time consuming. The organization's advocates should focus on providing the type of information requested by officials and their staffs, not merely persuasive materials designed to help build a case. To maintain credibility and trust, it is crucial that information given to policymakers and their staffs is accurate.

- *Never underestimate staff.* Although officials are responsible for making policy decisions, their staff members often provide the analysis and recommendations that influence their decisions. Staff serve important functions, such as presenting information from outside groups, setting priorities for meeting schedules, and making recommendations on policy decisions and political responses. Staff also tend to engage in strategic networking and may have access to considerable information about the inner workings of their institutions. In some cases, actual decisions may be made by staff and merely executed or voiced by public officials. Do not be surprised if staff are young and seemingly junior; always treat them with respect, and do not be quick to turn down a "staff meeting" instead of a meeting with the key decision maker. This meeting could be a relationship-building opportunity.

- *Make a strong presentation.* Having the facts in order is a vital first step for a presentation, and it is easy to focus primarily or even solely on this element. Yet it is just as crucial to package information in a format that will be easily understood by the audience and useful for decision making. This includes not only written materials, graphics, and charts, but also the language used. For example, a presentation full of abbreviations, acronyms, or complex quantitative data may be as incomprehensible as a foreign language. Moreover, one can unwittingly create a condescending impression if he or she uses overly technical terminology or professional jargon. Similarly, it is important to guard against insulting the intelligence of listeners. It may help to visualize the presentation from the listener's perspective. See Figure 6.5 for several specific suggestions.

MONITOR PROGRESS AND REVISE THE STRATEGY. Once the organization has begun its advocacy efforts, its managers must remain engaged in the political process, which is ever changing. Although initial indications may suggest that a successful outcome is likely, the dynamics of most political processes make it difficult to predict results until final decisions are reached. New legislative proposals, backroom deals, and shifting coalitions can change a proposal's prospects overnight. The managers in the organization should use information resources, media, and personal networks to keep informed about the political climate as well as specific developments that occur during the stages of the policymaking process. Milestones contained in the advocacy action plan should suggest key events to monitor.

FIGURE 6.5
PRINCIPLES TO KEEP IN MIND WHEN DEVELOPING A PRESENTATION

- *Create eye-catching materials.* Brief and simple messages are generally the most effective. Put extensive quantitative information into graphic or tabular formats.
- *Develop simple, useful formats.* Consider how the information will be used. If the organization has developed a database to support its case, make it available on a CD-ROM or on the Internet so that the official's staff can use it.
- *Be prepared.* Formulate notes, or even a full text, for the person who will be presenting information. Rehearse.
- *Be ready for trouble.* Bring backup information and equipment—the projector may fail, or the audience may have to leave early (e.g., for a vote). Be prepared to give a "summary" version of the presentation.

Staying involved in the process means carefully following up on advocacy activities. After a direct meeting with a policymaker, always send a follow-up note expressing thanks, but also reiterating what was agreed to in the meeting and offering assistance in taking the next steps. For example, if a public official has offered to seek support from other members of his or her committee, has he or she done so, and what were the results of that effort? How can the organization help? This also is an opportunity to provide further information to an official's staff after a meeting.

Other follow-up actions to monitor are those of the manager's own staff and partners. If a coalition member has promised to obtain certain information and report back with the results, has this taken place? Internally, confirm that the organization's own staff members are carrying out their expected functions and assess the impact of advocacy activities on the organization. Even the activities of board members should be monitored to ensure that the organization's commitments are kept and that all elements of the advocacy strategy remain on track.

CONCLUSION

Whether managing a small, community-based organization or a large one with a national scope, understanding the policy process and advocacy methods is vital for protecting and advancing an organization's interests. The steps and process discussed in this chapter are applicable both to the executive and legislative branches of government and to such organizations as direct service providers and public watchdog groups, professional societies, colleges and universities, and beyond. The skills and capabilities described here do not require formal training, and effective advocacy campaigns can often be run with minimal resources. Nonprofit managers who engage in advocacy activities have as their most important asset their familiarity with their own organizations, the communities in which they exist, and the issues they face. The keys to successfully effecting change through advocacy and government relations activities are to articulate clear objectives; know the audience; develop and implement a coherent, realistic plan with compelling messages; and be nimble in revising the plans along the way.

On any given day, a look at a manager's busy calendar might suggest that he or she needs to devote all available time to meeting the wave of crises and demands coming toward the organization, leaving aside broader questions about the external policy environment. However, ignoring the public policy factors influencing this work will only make it more difficult for the organization to meet its regular demands in the future. Alternatively, moving aggressively and effectively on this front is likely to shore up the organization's positions, generate (or protect) its resources, and foster a more supportive policy setting in which to work.

At this point, managers need to ask themselves, Do I really have a choice?

SKILLS APPLICATION EXERCISE

Positioned as a measure to stop nonprofit organizations from spending public funds on lobbying activity and hailed as the end of "welfare for lobbyists," legislation under consideration in the U.S. House of Representatives proposes to do the following:

- Prohibit any nonprofit organization from receiving a taxpayer-subsidized federal grant if it has received more than one-third of its total income from such grants or exceeded certain limits on lobbying expenses in the previous year.
- Prohibit any nonprofit organization that receives a taxpayer-subsidized federal grant from using grant funds to purchase anything, including membership, from an organization that in the previous year spent more than 15 percent of its total income on political advocacy.

You are the senior manager of a private, nonprofit organization that promotes equal-housing opportunity in a major metropolitan area. Your organization's programs include active monitoring of the real estate industry, both sales and rentals, as well as advocacy at the local, state, and federal levels for reducing discriminatory housing practices. Your organization receives private gifts and grants and an annual operating subsidy from the county, which in total account for about one-half of your organization's operating budget. Your organization also seeks and receives major support from the U.S. Department of Housing and Urban Development for private enforcement programming. Your board of trustees and the organization's state and national membership associations have urged you to play a leadership role in developing a regional campaign against this legislation.

- What information do you need to formulate a legislative game plan?
- What channels would you use to learn the details of the proposed legislation? How would you get access to these sources of information?
- What do you need to know about your own congressional representatives as you plan this effort?
- What are the criteria that would suggest which members of Congress and which advocacy groups would support or oppose this legislation?
- Are there opportunities to build coalitions to support your objectives? What regional mechanisms might you use to identify and coordinate with other groups sharing your position?

- What kind of support should you expect to receive from the regional and national associations to which your organization belongs?
- Suggest roles in the campaign that might be played by your organization's trustees and staff.
- If your campaign will involve expenses, what are the most appropriate and likely sources for these funds?
- Suggest specific advocacy strategies you might use at various points in the legislative life of this bill.
- If you were invited to present testimony on the bill, what are the key points that you would make?
- How can you explain devoting time to long-term issues such as this legislative matter when your organization's daily workload is already overwhelming?

REFERENCES

Brown, D. (1991, May). Tracking state legislation. *Association Management*, p. 25.

Edwards, R. L., Cooke, P. W., & Reid, P. N. (1996). Social work management in an era of diminishing federal responsibility. *Social Work, 41*, pp. 468–479.

Gibelman, M., Gelman, S. R., & Pollack, D. (1997). The credibility of nonprofit boards: A view from the 1990s and beyond. *Administration in Social Work, 21*(2), 21–40.

Gornick, M. E., Warren, J. L., Eggers, P. W., Lubitz, J. D., De Lew, N., Davis, M. H., & Cooper, B. S. (1996). Thirty years of Medicare: Impact on the covered population. *Health Care Financing Review, 18/2*, p. 179.

Hammack, D. C. (2005) *America's nonprofit organizations: who regulates what?* Adapted from private communication of a chart Hammack is preparing for a forthcoming book on nonprofit law that he will coauthor in 2006 with N. Silber.

Internal Revenue Code, Title 26, Subtitle A, Income Taxes. Chapter 1, Normal Taxes and Surtaxes, Subchapter F: Exempt Organizations, Part I, General Rule, Sec. 501(c)(3). Available at http://frwebgate.access.gpo.gov/cgi-bin/getdoc.cgi?dbname=browse_usc&docid=Cite:+26USC501

Landsberg, B. E. (2004). The nonprofit paradox: For-profit business models in the third sector. *The International Journal of Not-for-Profit Law, 6*(2). Available at http://www.icnl.org/JOURNAL/vol6iss2/ar_landsberg.htm

Salamon, L. M. (1997). *Holding the center: America's nonprofit sector at a crossroads.* New York: Nathan Cummings Foundation.

Silberman, S. L. (2002). *Maintaining health and human services with diminishing resources: A survey of Ohio voters.* Washington, DC: American Association of Retired Persons.

SUGGESTED READINGS

Anderson, J. E. (2000). *Public policymaking: An introduction* (4th ed.). Boston: Houghton Mifflin.

Bernstein, J. (2005). Ballad of the beast-starvers. *The American Prospect.* Retrieved March 15, 2005, from http://www.prospect.org/web/printfriendly-view.ww?id=9335

Boris, E. T., & Steuerle, C. E. (Eds.). (1999). *Nonprofits and government: Collaboration and conflict.* Washington, DC: Urban Institute Press.

Cigler, A. J., & Loomis, B. (2002) *Interest group politics* (6th ed.). Washington, DC: CQ Press.

Cruz, J. (1997). The top ten keys to effective communication. *Nonprofit World, 15,* 24–25.

Edwards, R. L., Benefield, E.A.S., Edwards, J. A., & Yankey, J. A. (1997). *Building a strong foundation: Fundraising for nonprofits.* Washington, DC: NASW Press.

Frenza, J. P., & Hoffman, L. (1997). So you want a web site, now what? *Nonprofit World, 15*(5), 21–24.

Gibelman, M., & Kraft, S. (1996). Advocacy as a core agency program: Planning considerations for voluntary human service agencies. *Administration in Social Work, 20*(4), 51.

Haynes, K., & Mickelson, J. (1997). *Affecting change: Social workers in the political arena.* White Plains, NY: Longman.

Menefee, D. (1997). Strategic administration for nonprofit human service organizations: A model for executive success in turbulent times. *Administration in Social Work, 21(2),* 1–19.

Oleszek, W. J. (2003). *Congressional procedures and the policy process,* (6th ed.). Washington, DC: CQ Press.

Richan, W C. (1996). *Lobbying for social change* (2nd ed.). Binghamton, NY: Haworth Press.

Rosenthal, A. (2001). *The third house: Lobbyists and lobbying in the states* (2nd ed.). Washington, DC: CQ Press.

Smucker, B. (1999). *The nonprofit lobbying guide* (2nd ed.). Washington, DC: Independent Sector. Also available online from http://www.clpi.org/toc.html

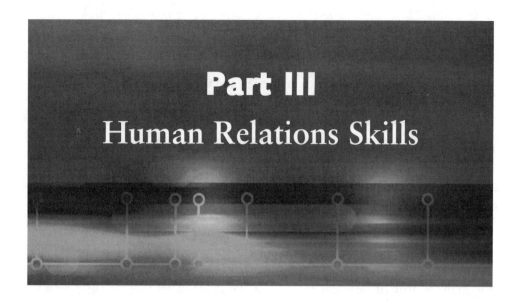

Part III
Human Relations Skills

Managerial human relations skills encompass the roles of mentor and facilitator. Competencies for the mentor role include an understanding of self and others, interpersonal communication skills, and development of subordinates. Competencies for the facilitator role include team-building, participatory decision making, and conflict management. The chapters in this section discuss these roles in effective managerial performance.

In Chapter 7, Kimberly Strom-Gottfried offers a comprehensive overview of issues crucial to the effective management of the people in an organization (i.e., human relations skills). Human resource (HR) management involves all of the choices and actions that take place in the life of an organization's employees, including job design; recruitment and selection; compensation and benefits; performance appraisal; employee support and discipline; and employee separations, including terminations, downsizing, and retirements. The effective management of these matters is crucial not only in terms of having a competent, motivated workforce but also to avoid serious legal ramifications attendant to ineffectively managing HR concerns.

In Chapter 8, Susan L. Parish, M. Jennifer Ellison, and Janice K. Parish consider the challenges involved in effectively managing employees from diverse cultural, ethnic, linguistic, and racial backgrounds. Diversity is considered in its broadest sense to indicate individual differences of gender, age, sexual orientation, race, ethnicity, cultural background, and disability status. The effective management of diversity involves recruitment, retention, rewarding, and promoting a heterogeneous mix of employees to have a productive, motivated, and committed workforce.

In Chapter 9, Darlyne Bailey and S. Kay Dunlap provide an overview of past, present, and future approaches to the design and maintenance of effective organizational teams. They present a developmental theoretical framework for examining stages of team development and the behaviors that are frequently associated with the forming, storming, norming, performing, and adjourning stages. Using two case studies, Bailey and Dunlap underscore the importance of managers understanding themselves and others, particularly emphasizing participatory decision making and managing conflict. The authors view consensus building and involvement of employees as critical aspects of managing effectively.

In Chapter 10, John E. Tropman suggests that managers can improve the decisions made in their organizations by involving groups in the process. He discusses the following components: the management of the decision process, the management of decision rules, and the management of decision results. Tropman identifies what he calls "meeting masters," managers who are particularly adept at structuring meetings of boards, committees, and the like, so that time is used wisely and important decisions are made with maximum input from all concerned.

In Chapter 11, Alice Korngold, Elizabeth Hosler Voudouris, and Jeff Griffiths trace the emergence of volunteerism in the United States from the early 1600s to the more instutionalized form of current volunteer activity. Delineating the broad scope of individual and corporate volunteerism, the authors spell out the increasingly important value that such activity holds for nonprofit organizations and society in general. They present the elements of high-impact volunteer programs and identify the key elements for establishing and effectively managing volunteer programs. Korngold, Voudouris, and Griffiths also provide their perspectives on what must be done for nonprofit organizations to "galvanize and channel the full force of volunteerism" in today's world.

7

Managing Human Resources

Kimberly Strom-Gottfried

In most nonprofit settings, services are coordinated and delivered by human beings. In contrast to some manufacturing sectors, in which equipment is a major cost of delivering goods, the greatest costs for nonprofit organizations are in their human resources (HR). The management of this element of the organization is complex. HR managers must continually negotiate the tensions of efficiency and equity in carrying out their functions, maximizing productivity while minimizing costs and using fair and respectful personnel procedures (Milkovich & Boudreau, 1997). Leaders in nonprofits also must be alert to the laws and regulations that govern their tasks and the vast knowledge base that accompanies various personnel processes.

HR management involves all of the choices and actions that take place in the life of an organization's employees, including job design; recruitment and selection; compensation and benefits; performance appraisal; employee support and discipline; and employee separations, including terminations, downsizing, and retirements. In large organizations, specific units are dedicated to each function. In smaller agencies, generalists may be responsible for the entire scope of HR activities, calling on consultants or advisors as needed for specialized expertise. In both settings, HR personnel play a key role in creating policies and procedures to ensure that the organization is competitive with other nonprofits and compliant with regulations. HR managers also play an important advisory role with supervisors, particularly around issues of fair employment practices, due process in disciplinary matters, and workplace safety. HR managers must have an understanding about the entire spectrum of personnel matters, to ensure that personnel policies and practices are consistent with each other and responsive to the changing business environment.

This chapter describes the context in which HR managers function and in which HR decisions are made. It then orients readers to five core areas of HR activity, the scope of activities in those areas, and the key concepts for effective practice in those areas.

DOMAIN OF HR MANAGEMENT: A COMPETING VALUES PERSPECTIVE

Decisions about managing an organization's workforce take place in the context of organizational, or internal, factors and environmental, or external, factors. To advance the organization's mission, effective HR decisions must be congruent with one another and other organizational units, such as operations and finance. HR professionals must be alert to changes in the service and regulatory environments so that practices comply with laws and respond to emerging societal trends.

Internal Influences

The organization's mission and practice domain provide the starting place for HR decisions (Macaleer & Shannon, 2003). These factors shape how services are delivered and, thus, the kinds of jobs that need to be created and the types of employees to fill them. For example, a residential treatment program will need personnel around the clock and, for safety and client service reasons, will need at least two staff persons on site at all times. A mental health crisis unit will need to have staff available or on call with the expertise and credentials to evaluate and respond to an array of psychiatric emergencies. A faith-based program for former prisoners re-entering the community might rely on volunteers and case managers to provide some services but also will link clients to the array of services that they will need on release.

Few social workers start an organization from scratch, so they tend to view service and staffing patterns as relatively fixed. Effective HR, though, requires managers to step back from "the way things are done" and think about how services are provided, jobs are constructed, and tasks are assigned and the ways in which these variables might be most effectively combined (Cohen, 2002). This assessment ensures that the organization has the right number of workers with the appropriate qualities and qualifications needed to carry out the agency's functions, in anticipation of changing conditions in the practice environment. Two specific concepts apply here: *job analysis* and *job design*. Job analysis refers to a systematic process of collecting data and making judgments about the nature of a specific job (e.g., a job's content, duties, tasks, behaviors, functions, responsibilities). Job analysis provides data for job design.

Job design is more all encompassing, integrating work content, qualifications, and rewards for each job in a way that meets the needs of employees and the organization. It looks at alternate ways in which the facets of jobs can be arranged (Milkovoich and Boudreau, 1997). In practice, this may mean that roles that formerly encompassed a wide variety of responsibilities are restructured to be more specialized. Or, in a growing organization, it may mean that the executive director's job spins off HR or finance tasks into two new positions. Leaders with expertise in HR can help organizations think creatively about how to organize services and personnel to best meet an agency's objectives.

Another internal consideration for HR is the financial well-being of the agency. This affects not only the number of employees but also the compensation, benefits, and services that they will be offered. New organizations and those with few financial resources will have fewer staff and will need them each to fulfill a variety of roles. They also may have difficulty retaining employees, resulting in a revolving door of hiring and resignations. Established, complex, well-to-do organizations use staff with specialized expertise and have more complex systems for staff evaluation, tracking career ladders, compensation, and benefits.

A third organizational factor affecting HR decisions is the agency's culture. Organizations that espouse a "corporate" culture will look for that fit in the employees it hires and will use more formal and explicit procedures for HR functions such as staff development, promotions, and performance appraisals. Organizations with a culture of mistrust will convey that attitude in policies that are strict and thorough. Examples might include random drug testing, requiring doctors' notes for sick time, and monitoring workers' telephone calls and e-mail correspondence. An organization that has a "family culture" will likely have broader, less-specific policies and HR actions that are highly individualized. Such an organization is likely to value a personal approach (e.g., choosing to use a person for receptionist and telephone duties over an automated system).

Personnel with HR responsibilities must be mindful of the characteristics of the agency and ensure that HR decisions are congruent with the mission, niche, service structure, culture, and financial viability of the organization. Similarly, HR managers will need to have an eye on the environment outside the agency as well.

External Factors

The environment in which the organization is situated affects HR in several ways. Two strategies for keeping informed about the changing environment are *benchmarking* and *environmental scanning*. Benchmarking refers to using internal criteria, other organizations, or available data as a basis of comparison for an agency's practices. For example, if a leading organization in the area develops a tuition payment program to encourage its employees to obtain graduate degrees, other agencies might follow suit or consider the implications for recruiting new staff when the competitor rolls out this benefit. Or, when a state nonprofit association publishes the results of a statewide salary survey and some administrators note that their caseworker salaries are well below the mean for organizations of their size, they may begin to restructure compensation and benefits in light of this benchmark.

Environmental scanning refers to the practice of regularly reviewing resources such as newspapers, listserv postings, association newsletters, and conference proceedings to be alert to innovations in HR management, to changes in the practice environment, and in laws and regulations. It means networking and being alert to all sources of information that could influence HR policies, taking into account the amount and immediacy of impact on one's setting (Milkovich & Boudreau, 1997). For example, a HR director may read about a finding from the Supreme Court about age discrimination and determine that it will have an immediate and significant impact if the agency does not change the different ways new (younger) employees are compensated compared to senior (older) workers.

Benchmarking and environmental scanning can reveal a variety of environmental effects on an organization's HR practices. The three primary external factors addressed here are the *labor conditions, economic conditions*, and *legal and regulatory influences* (Milkovich & Boudreau, 1997).

Labor conditions refer to a variety of features that affect the pool of people available for hire, the qualities of the employees, and the salaries that they may command. Key features include demographic characteristics of the workforce (e.g., gender, age, educational preparation, race, culture, citizenship), the labor market (i.e., the number of people available for employment), and geographic characteristics. For example, a Latino services agency, in a geographic area where there are few Spanish-speaking professionals, may have to offer greater compensation and benefits (or creative staff development strategies) to hire certain classes of bilingual employees (e.g., physicians, social workers, psychologists) but may find it easier to find clerical and paraprofessional staff from the surrounding community (Weinbach, 1998). Or, when the economy is growing and the labor market is tight, employers of all types will experience greater competition for applicants and will have to pay more to hire them. When corporate hiring is robust, the nonprofit sector is particularly challenged in competing for employees.

Economic conditions, of course, affect the financial health of the organization and thus the amount that the organization can pay its workers. Beyond that, the sources and stability of funding can differentially affect employees—and thus

HR policies. For example, perhaps half of an agency's direct services workforce is paid under a particular grant. This grant specifies the clients to be served and stipulates the response time required to open new cases. The grant provides a cost-of-living (COLA) increase each year and pay-for-performance incentives. This stream of funding will thus affect a variety of HR decisions in terms of staffing, job duties, merit awards, and pay increases. These changes may or may not be congruent with the HR practices for the rest of the agency's workforce. Thus, they can lead to concerns about fairness and can make the administration of HR policies more complicated.

An array of laws and regulations affect personnel decisions, from hiring to promotions, work conditions, and termination. HR managers must be conversant with them and ensure compliance in policies and organizational practices. The descriptions below provide a brief overview of key pieces of legislation. Resources at the end of the chapter can provide an in-depth examination of these laws and their workplace implications.

TITLE VII OF THE CIVIL RIGHTS ACT. Title VII of the Civil Rights Act of 1964 prohibits discrimination on the basis of sex, race, color, religion, or national origin in any employment condition, including hiring, firing, promotion, transfer, compensation, or admission to training programs. It applies to organizations "with 15 or more employees working 20 or more weeks per year, as well as to labor unions, employment agencies, and the federal government" (Noe, Hollenbeck, Gerhart, & Wright, 2004, p. 70). Groups protected under Title VII include women, Black Americans, Hispanics, American Indians, Pacific Islanders, people older than age 40, people with disabilities, and veterans. Since 1964, courts have ruled that several behaviors by employers and unions are unlawful under Title VII. These fall into two basic categories: *unequal treatment* and *unequal impact*. Disparate (unequal) treatment refers to practices in which an organization covertly treats protected group members in a discriminatory fashion, either by treating them less favorably or applying different standards to them than other employees.

Disparate (unequal) impact refers to practices that have a differential effect on the opportunities of members of protected groups. These are illegal unless they are demonstrably work related or necessary for safe and efficient operation of the business. Under disparate impact, the results of a personnel decision are important, not the intentions. The same standards for all groups can have differing consequences. For example, setting a mandatory retirement age differentially affects older employees, minimum height and weight requirements disadvantage women and individuals from small-statured ethnic groups, and inquiries about arrest records will disproportionately affect members of some minority groups. Employers must demonstrate that their personnel actions do not lead to a disparate impact for protected groups or that any such requirements are necessary, effective, and could not be achieved in any other fashion. For example, former height and weight standards for firefighters were found to have disparate impact and were replaced with strength and speed tests that better reflect the demands of the job being filled.

EQUAL EMPLOYMENT OPPORTUNITY ACT OF 1972. The Equal Employment Opportunity Act of 1972 extended coverage of Title VII to include public and private employers with 15 or more employees, labor organizations with 15 or more members, and public and private employment agencies. In 1980, Equal Opportunity Commission guidelines stated that sexual harassment is a form of sex discrimination. Generally, two types of behaviors are of concern. *Quid pro quo harassment* occurs when an employee offers to reward another in return for sexual favors (or to punish the person for rejecting those advances). The second form of sexual harassment involves the creation of a *hostile work environment* through offensive language or sexually suggestive jokes, posters, or actions.

THE EQUAL PAY ACT. The Equal Pay Act of 1962 mandates that employees on the same jobs be paid equally, except for allowable differences in seniority, merit, or other conditions unrelated to sex. It includes both direct and indirect compensation (e.g., benefits, paid time off).

PREGNANCY DISCRIMINATION ACT OF 1978. The Pregnancy Discrimination Act of 1978 states that pregnancy is a disability and qualifies a person to receive the same benefits as would those with other disabilities.

FAMILY AND MEDICAL LEAVE ACT OF 1993. The Family and Medical Leave Act (FMLA) of 1993 requires that organizations with 50 or more employees grant up to 12 weeks of unpaid leave for the birth or adoption of a child, to care for a spouse or an immediate family member with a serious health condition, or when unable to work because of a serious health condition (Noe et al., 2004).

AGE DISCRIMINATION IN EMPLOYMENT ACT. The Age Discrimination in Employment Act of 1967 protects people ages 40 and older and prohibits arbitrary discrimination on the basis of age. The exceptions in the provision prohibiting mandatory retirement ended in 1994.

AMERICANS WITH DISABILITIES ACT. The Americans With Disabilities Act of 1990 prohibits discrimination on the basis of physical or mental disability by employers with 15 or more employees. While it does not set numerical goals for hiring or promotion, it does require reasonable accommodations to support employees with disabilities. These may include redesigning jobs, installing ramps, purchasing facilitative equipment, changing work space, and examining training and promotion opportunities.

SOCIAL SECURITY ACT OF 1935. The Social Security Act of 1935 provided old-age, disability, survivor's, and health benefits and established the basis for federal and state unemployment programs.

FAIR LABOR STANDARDS ACT OF 1938. The Fair Labor Standards Act (FLSA) of 1938 set minimum wages and hours, child labor standards, and overtime pay provisions. It distinguished between "exempt" and "nonexempt" jobs or employees. Workers who are exempt from the FLSA include managers, executives, and professionals, such as a mental health agency's clinical staff. Employees who are not exempt, such a child care workers, clerical staff, and maintenance personnel, are covered by the regulations, and thus must be provided overtime pay and other provisions of the Act.

Effective personnel management requires carefully balancing the conflicts inherent in balancing the organizational and environmental factors described earlier. For example, a 60-employee agency may embrace the spirit of the FMLA, but offering extended leave (even without pay) may place a terrific burden on service provision if several employees from a particular unit use the leave unexpectedly or at the same time.

An organization may value seniority in its workforce and have retention program in place to ensure that, once hired, employees will stay. The strategy, though, may result in compensation costs that are top-heavy with senior, higher paid workers, and the low turnover may make it difficult to restructure programs to respond to changing economic conditions and encourage the innovation that new workers might bring.

Also, an organization, because of its mission and culture, may actively seek to hire workers who might otherwise have difficulty finding employment, such as high school dropouts, people with criminal histories, or those in recovery from drug problems. In response, the personnel department may offer flexible schedules and job tasks, onsite literacy programs, generous wellness benefits, and supportive supervision. The challenge in living its values, though, may mean that the agency has higher staff development and health insurance costs and excessive staffing demands due to greater turnover in the workforce.

Imbedded in these conflicts is the continuous tension between efficiency and equity. Immediately dismissing an underperforming employee is efficient, but it is not fair or just. Hiring only healthy, able, single employees may yield a productive workforce, able to devote long hours to the job, but it is not legal or equitable.

The effective HR manager must use strategies to keep informed of changing organizational and environmental conditions, be familiar with the agency's personnel policies and practices to interpret the effects of those changes, and balance the competing values that those conditions create. Those considerations are illustrated further in this chapter in the discussion of each step in the HR process.

Recruitment and Selection

Attracting and selecting employees begins with a clear impression of what qualities the position demands. A precise and current job description is essential for making this determination (see Figure 7.1). Flowing from job analysis and design, the job description should specify the reporting relationship of the position,

---

FIGURE 7.1
SAMPLE JOB DESCRIPTION

Title: Clinician–Supervisor

Reports to: Director of Mental Health

Position is responsible for providing mental health and substance abuse treatment in the agency's catchment area. The Clinician–Supervisor is responsible for providing administrative and clinical supervision for at least three professional or paraprofessional staff.
Specific duties required for carrying out this role include but are not limited to

1. Assist in the development of cooperative working relationships with referral sources and other agencies essential for case coordination
2. Assist in the assessment of area needs for new programming and services in mental health and substance abuse
3. Provide treatment at a level consistent with the prevailing direct service standard
4. Provide consulting and education services to public groups and community agencies
5. Open and maintain case records in keeping with agency policies
6. Assist supervisees in professional development and effective agency practice
7. Complete performance appraisals at least once annually
8. Practice and provide supervision in an ethical manner, upholding agency policies, and procedures
9. Provide emergency and on-call coverage on a rotating basis.

Qualifications: This position requires a master's degree in social work, psychology, or a related field and clinical licensure in the respective discipline. The position further requires appropriate experience to ensure that applicant is able to adequately perform the required duties and supervise the practice of others.

---

job tasks, and qualifications and credentials needed. Job descriptions may be organized by areas of responsibility or by the knowledge, skills, and abilities needed to successfully fulfill the position (Noe et al., 2004).

The organization's HR department can develop procedures for filling vacancies so that the hiring process is cost efficient, fair, and legal. HR policies might specify who is involved in personnel decisions (e.g., immediate supervisor, search committee, unit team?) and who must be consulted for signoff at various points in the process (e.g., when an advertisement is posted, when finalists are selected, when an offer is made). Personnel specialists also should develop the selection process and train those involved in recruitment and selection to ensure that their practices are effective and ethical. The selection process would include decisions about the format applicants should use in expressing interest (e.g., résumés vs. standardized application forms), the process and criteria for reviewing the documents submitted, and the steps in the application process, which could potentially include initial screening, preliminary telephone interviews, agency interviews, reference contacts, and drug tests or criminal background checks. HR can assist those responsible for hiring in structuring their interviews so that questions are legal and relevant to the job and the qualifications sought and help them to develop evaluative criteria to weigh what they learn about a candidate in light of the expectations of the job. The HR staff also will implement affirmative action strategies to attract a diverse pool of candidates and equal opportunity measures to ensure that the hiring process is free from intentional or unintentional discrimination.

RECRUITMENT. The nature of the organization, the position, and the labor market will affect the strategies used to advertise for applicants and the information sought. A small local grassroots agency will primarily use referrals from current workers, local media, and networking with other organizations and local schools or colleges to announce position vacancies. Larger organizations may have a "job postings" section on their Web site, hold open houses, and have procedures for promotion from within, in addition to using conventional advertising. Recruiting for a clerical or entry-level direct practice position will primarily involve a local search and resources, whereas the search for a chief executive officer (CEO) may be regional or national, involving advertising in national newspapers or association journals and perhaps using a search firm to ensure a strong and diverse candidate pool.

Letters, e-mail announcements, and advertisements for positions should use unbiased language, clearly state the type of job and the relevant qualifications (including years of experience, if appropriate), and provide direction about steps applicants should take (e.g., "Send cover letter, résumé, and references to . . . ," "See our Web site for an online application," "Come to our open house on . . .").

Remember that the announcement must attract relevant candidates and discourage unsuitable candidates. An announcement that is too broad or poorly worded may result in a deluge of applicants who are incompatible with the position, thus complicating the selection process. Including the salary range in the announcement similarly may help narrow the pool of applicants, but it also may prematurely discourage desirable candidates, allowing the salary to overshadow other benefits associated with the position.

SCREENING. The first step in the selection process is to screen résumés or applications to ensure that they meet the criteria advertised. Any that do not indicate the proper level of education, experience, license, and so forth should be set aside. Pecora (1998) recommended the use of a matrix or spreadsheet to evaluate the résumé or application against the qualifications of the position. The required and preferred qualifications would be listed across the top of the matrix, and the applicants would be listed down the left-hand side, to capture in one document the relative qualifications of a large pool of candidates. This process helps differentiate the strongest candidates from the pool of applicants who meet the established criteria. Based on the data collected on the matrix, the organization can prioritize those it will pursue through the rest of the process.

Although not common in the nonprofit sector, some large organizations use employment tests and work samples to further narrow the field of candidates. Tests may include those that determine how well a person can learn or acquire skills (aptitude tests), their level of knowledge (achievement tests), personality type, physical abilities, and word-processing and other clerical skills (Noe et al., 2004). These testing programs all share similar challenges: their validity relative to the job's requirements and their legality if they unfairly disadvantage certain classes of employees. A more common strategy in the nonprofit sector is to use application materials to generate a list of interviewees and conduct any necessary testing as a condition of the job offer after a finalist (or set of finalists) has been selected.

Before inviting candidates for interviews, the organization must decide who should serve as interviewers at various points in the process, whether one-on-one or group interviews will be more effective, and what types of information it is seeking from this part of the process (see Figure 7.2). Ideally, interviews help reveal or bring to light information beyond that which is available in the résumé or application, and the information sought is directly relevant to the position being filled. Interviewers should be able to identify the knowledge, skills, and abilities related to the position that are tapped by each of the interview questions. In other words, "What answer is the organization looking for? What will this answer tell about this applicant's suitability for the job?" The interview also should provide the applicant with an accurate impression of the position and the organization so that he or she can evaluate the goodness of fit with his or her skills and interests.

Some suggestions for interviews include the following:

- Use interviewers from a variety of backgrounds who represent the diversity within the organization.
- Use the same interviewers for all candidates.
- Have interviewers review the position description, equal employment opportunity requirements, and the candidate's application materials before each session.
- Create a comfortable, private environment that is free from distractions.
- Use open-ended, nonleading questions.
- Be aware of interviewers' vocal tone and body language (Hindle, 1998).
- Take notes or use an evaluation form to identify important responses by each candidate.
- Ask the same questions of each candidate, but use follow-up questions as needed for clarity or greater depth of response.
- Ask for examples that illustrate the applicant's handling of past incidents that are relevant to the position (e.g., "Tell us about—an experience when you handled a conflict with a coworker," "your experience in working with suicidal clients," "a mistake that you made and what you learned from it," "a time when you experienced an ethical dilemma," "your efforts to build a pluralistic work team;" Falcone, 2002).
- Use hypothetical situations to assess the applicant's judgment and abilities. For example, "How would you respond—if a client asks to see his record?" or "a supervisee comes back from lunch with alcohol on her breath?"
- Anticipate questions the candidate may have and allow him or her enough time to ask them.

SELECTION. Interviews typically help narrow the field of candidates or rank the preferences for hire. However, before a finalist is chosen, the organization should conduct both *background* and *reference checks*. Background checks ascertain that the information the applicant provided about his or her education, experience, and credentials is accurate. Misrepresentation of these facts should be a significant source of concern and prompt further examination and discussion if not outright disqualification for the position. Information from references may be less helpful, in that applicants usually select references that are inclined to give favorable feedback. Other references, such as former employers, may have policies that confine the information that they provide to the

---

FIGURE 7.2
FAIR INQUIRY GUIDELINES OF THE
EQUAL EMPLOYMENT OPPORTUNITY COMMISSION

The following guidelines were established by the Equal Employment Opportunity Commission to provide specific protection from discrimination in hiring certain protected classes:

Subject: **Relatives, marital status**
Unlawful Inquiries: Whether the applicant is married, divorced, separated, engaged, widowed, and so forth: "What is your marital status?" "What is the name of relative/spouse/children?" "With whom do you reside?" "Do you live with your parents?" "How old are your children?"
Lawful Inquiries: "What are the names of relatives already employed by the company or a competitor?" No other questions are lawful.

Subject: **Residence**
Unlawful Inquiries: Names or relationship of people with whom applicant resides; whether applicant owns or rents a home: "Do you live in town?"
Lawful Inquiries: Inquiries about address to the extent needed to facilitate contacting the applicant (a post office box is a valid address). "Will you have problems getting to work at 9 a.m.?"

Subject: **Pregnancy**
Unlawful Inquiries: All questions relating to pregnancy and medical history concerning pregnancy: "Do you plan on having more children?"
Lawful Inquiries: Inquiries about the duration of stay on a job or anticipated absences that are made to both men and women alike. "Do you foresee any long-term absences in the future?"

Subject: **Physical health**
Unlawful Inquiries: Overly general questions ("Do you have any disabilities?") that would tend to divulge disabilities or health conditions that do not relate reasonably to fitness to perform the job. "What caused your disability?" "What is the prognosis of your disability?" "Have you ever had any serious illness?" "Do you have any physical disabilities?"
Lawful Inquiries: "Can you lift 40 lbs?" "Do you need any special accommodations to perform the job you've applied for?" "How many days did you miss from work (or school) in the past year?" The questions must relate to the job.

FIGURE 7.2
FAIR INQUIRY GUIDELINES OF THE
EQUAL EMPLOYMENT OPPORTUNITY COMMISSION (continued)

Subject: **Family**
Unlawful Inquiries: Questions concerning spouse or spouse's employment, spouses' salary, and child care arrangements or dependents. "How will your husband feel about the amount of time you will be traveling if you get this job?" "What kind of child care arrangements have you made?"
Lawful Inquiries: Whether applicant can meet specified work schedules or has activities or commitments that may prevent him or her from meeting attendance requirements. "Can you work overtime?" "Is there any reason why you can't be on the job at 7:30 a.m.?"

Subject: **Name**
Unlawful Inquiries: Any inquiries about name that would divulge marital status, lineage, ancestry, national origin, or descent: "If your name has been legally changed, what was your former name?"
Lawful Inquiries: Whether an applicant has worked for the company or a competitor under any other name and, if so, what name. Name under which applicant is known to references if different from present name: "What name are you known to the references you provided us?"

Subject: **Sex**
Unlawful Inquiries: Any inquiry. "Do you wish to be addressed as Mr., Mrs., Miss, or Ms.?" or *any* inquiry as to sex such as "Do you have the capacity to reproduce?" "What are your plans to have children in the future?"
Lawful Inquiries: None

Subject: **Photographs**
Unlawful Inquiries: Requests that an applicant submit a photograph at any time before hiring.
Lawful Inquiries: May be requested after hiring for identification purposes.

Subject: **Age**
Unlawful Inquiries: Any questions that tend to identify applicants ages 40 or older.
Lawful Inquiries: "Are you 18 years of age?" "If hired, can you furnish proof of age?"

FIGURE 7.2
FAIR INQUIRY GUIDELINES OF THE
EQUAL EMPLOYMENT OPPORTUNITY COMMISSION (continued)

Subject: **Education**
Unlawful Inquiries: Any question asking specifically the nationality, racial, or religious affiliation of a school.
Lawful Inquiries: All questions related to academic, vocational, or professional education of an applicant, including the names of the schools attended, degrees/diplomas received, dates of graduation, and courses of study.

Subject: **Citizenship**
Unlawful Inquiries: Whether an applicant is a citizen. Requiring a birth, naturalization, or baptismal certificate. Any inquiry into citizenship would tend to divulge applicant's lineage, descent, and so forth.

- "Are you a citizen of the United States?"
- "Are your parents or spouse citizens of the United States?"
- "On what dates did you, your parents, or your spouse acquire U.S. citizenship?"
- "Are you, your parents, or your spouse naturalized or native-born U.S. citizens?"

Lawful Inquiries: Whether applicant is prevented from being lawfully employed in the United States because of visa or immigration requirements. Whether applicant can provide proof of citizenship (passport), visa, or alien registration number after hiring. "If you are not a U.S. citizen, do you have the legal right to remain permanently in the United States?" "What is your visa status (if "no" to the previous question)?" "Are you able to provide proof of employment eligibility upon hire?"

Subject: **National origin/ancestry**
Unlawful Inquiries: Everything. "What is your nationality?" "How did you acquire the ability to speak, read, or write a foreign language?" "How did you acquire familiarity with a foreign country?" "What language is spoken in your home?" "What is your mother tongue?"
Lawful Inquiries: "What languages do you speak, read, or write fluently?" This is legal only when the inquiry is based on a job requirement.

Subject: **Race or color**
Unlawful Inquiries: Any question that directly or indirectly relates to a race or color.
Lawful Inquiries: None.

FIGURE 7.2
FAIR INQUIRY GUIDELINES OF THE
EQUAL EMPLOYMENT OPPORTUNITY COMMISSION (continued)

Subject: **Religion**

Unlawful Inquiries: Any question that directly or indirectly relates to a religion. "What religious holidays do you observe?" "What is your religious affiliation?"

Lawful Inquiries: None except "Can you work on Saturdays [Sundays]?" and that only if it is relevant to the job.

Subject: **Organizations**

Unlawful Inquiries: "To what organizations, clubs, societies, and lodges do you belong?"

Lawful Inquiries: "To what professional organizations do you belong? (Exclude those whose name or character indicates the race, religious creed, color, national origin, or ancestry of its members.)" These inquiries must relate only to the applicant's professional qualifications.

Subject: **Military**

Unlawful Inquiries: Type or condition of military discharge. Applicant's experience in other than U.S. armed forces. Request for discharge papers.

Lawful Inquiries: Inquiries concerning education, training, or work experience in the U.S. armed forces. (Note that, in many areas, veterans are a protected class.)

Subject: **Height and weight**

Unlawful Inquiries: Any inquiries not based on actual job requirements.

Lawful Inquiries: Inquiries about the ability to perform a certain job.

Subject: **Arrests and convictions**

Unlawful Inquiries: All inquiries relating to arrests. "Have you ever been arrested?" (Note that arrests are *not* the same as convictions. An innocent person can be arrested.)

Lawful Inquiries: None relating to arrests. Legal inquiries about convictions are "Have you ever been convicted of any crime? If so, when, where, and what was the disposition of case?" "Have you ever been convicted under criminal law within the past 5 years (excluding minor traffic violations)?" It is permissible to inquire about convictions for acts of dishonesty or breach of trust. These relate to fitness to perform the particular job for which an applicant applies.

Note. Available from the Equal Employment Opportunity Commission at http://www.stat.washington.edu/www/jobs/questions/.

dates of service and whether or not the individual is eligible for rehire. Others may limit their feedback to "observable, job-related behaviors" (Noe et al., 2004, p. 181). References and background checks may not differentiate among acceptable candidates, but they may identify unacceptable ones. Even if reference checks are not always fruitful, it is incumbent on the hiring agency to thoroughly pursue them. The costs of missing potentially troubling data about an applicant are high.

If hiring is contingent on successful completion of other steps such as drug testing or criminal background checks, those should be completed at this stage before a final offer is made.

When the candidate has been selected, the job offer should explicitly state the job responsibilities, pay, benefits, schedule and starting date, and the date by which the candidate should accept or reject the offer (Noe et al., 2004). Until the position is officially filled, other finalists should not be notified, lest the first offer fall through. However, once a candidate has accepted the job, all applicants should be contacted and thanked for their interest in the position. This information often is communicated by letter, accompanied by a phone call to other finalists or a personal meeting with internal candidates for the position. The agency also should carefully document the pool of applicants at each stage of the process, the person selected, and the specifics of the job offer.

INTERNAL STAFFING. Internal staffing presents some special conditions for screening and selection. Successful internal candidates affect not only the position they assume but also their original or "source" position (Milkovich & Boudreau, 1997). Filling vacancies from within can be an effective strategy for fostering employee retention and satisfaction, but it leads to a ripple effect in creating vacant source positions that then must be filled. The aggregate result may be that the agency primarily hires only entry-level employees because senior positions are filled internally. Another outcome is the effect on the supervisors in the source positions, who may resent their investment of time and effort in what may amount to a stepping stone for employees whose aspirations lie elsewhere in the organization.

Another challenge of internal staffing occurs when an employee is not selected for advancement. That person may be stellar in his or her current role but be ill-suited or unprepared for the new position. Yet, unlike external applicants, this person will continue with the agency after being rejected for the new position. It is therefore essential that the notification process be handled in a tactful and timely manner. The failed application should be used as an opportunity to explore additional education or work experiences that may enhance the worker's portfolio for future promotions.

Compensation and Benefits

Compensation typically refers to a worker's salary or hourly wages, merit pay or incentives, and COLA adjustments. *Benefits*, or *indirect compensation*, include paid time away from work, health insurance, pension, employee services (e.g., wellness center, day care, smoking cessation program), and payments on legally mandated benefits (e.g., social security, unemployment compensation, workers' compensation, FMLA leave in organizations with more than 50 employees). Compensation decisions are shaped by other laws as well, including those setting the minimum wage and overtime rules and those forbidding discrimination on the basis of gender, race, age, and ability. Compensation decisions also are shaped by organizational goals, external competitors, and the wages paid to existing employees.

An organization's structure and strategic objectives will shape the type of compensation system it adopts (e.g., flat or steep, closely guarded or transparent), its interest in using pay-for-performance incentives (Brody, 1993), and the degree to which it seeks to match or exceed the pay offered by competitors. Some organizations that embrace an egalitarian pay policy will have little differentiation among salary or wage levels. Other, often larger, organizations will use a more hierarchical system, with ranges or salary bands and explicit rules about how people move up the salary scale (e.g., seniority, performance, or both).

Organizations must be alert to competitive pressures and may make a conscious decision to pay less than the going rate offered by similar agencies, making up for the deficit with more generous benefits, flexible hours, or enjoyable working climate. Agencies also must be alert to internal pressures. Two are of particular importance. *Compression* occurs when new hires are brought on at higher pay than that of existing workers with similar seniority. Typically compression results from stagnant salary increases within an organization and robust increases at other organizations in an environment. Thus, the new worker's pay has progressed further outside the organization than it has for those workers who have remained in an agency with a history of offering uncompetitive raises. *Equal employment opportunity concerns* also arise when pay differences among positions are unjustifiable. Differences in pay of equal work are allowed if they result from differences in seniority, in the quality of performance, and in quantity and quality of production or from other factors such as shift differentials (e.g., for working an overnight shift) or hazard pay (e.g., for undesirable or riskier work). Differences in race, gender, marital status, and age cannot be used to legitimize differences in pay.

Beyond base salary or hourly wages, many organizations offer merit pay: bonuses or percentage increases on base pay offered for achieving various goals (e.g., attendance, productivity, exemplary service). Bonuses differ from merit increases in that the former are one-time occurrences and do not alter the recipient's base pay. These are easier to administer, in part because they create no long-term financial obligations, but they may be less satisfying to employees who would like the promise that a permanent increase in wages affords. *Profit sharing* refers to merit awards that are given to units of employees based on the organization's profitability at the close of the operating year; in *gain sharing,* rewards may be obtained by cost savings as well as profits. Neither is common in the nonprofit sector, and they may have questionable capacity to motivate employees if workers have little hope that the rewards are within their control. In fact, merit pay systems can be problematic for the following reasons:

- The proportion of variable pay to base pay is so small that the merit system has little leverage.
- Some merit systems have high "risk" in that there is a low probability of an increase in pay commensurate with the amount of additional effort needed to get it.
- The system by which merit is measured and distributed is perceived as unfair.
- The agency lacks sufficient funds for the system to have much impact on employees.
- Merit systems can have unintended consequences; for example, incentives to reduce length of hospital stays may lead to premature patient discharges.
- Annual rewards are not proximal to the efforts that workers took to achieve them, thus they lose their motivational impact.
- It can be difficult to measure the qualities that nonprofit seeks to reward.
- Workers become discouraged and unmotivated when limited rewards are available and thus only go to a few top performers.
- Employees may overrate their performance or the availability of merit funds and are disappointed when merit awards fail to meet their expectations (Brody, 1993).

An agency must carefully review its direct compensation system to determine the legal and strategic advantages of different options. It must do the same with its indirect compensation, or benefits package. What benefits, beyond those mandated, will employees receive? Will those differ by classes of employees or seniority? What benefits can the organization afford, in terms of financial obligations and staffing? How much choice will the worker have in selecting the benefits that best suit him or her? It is appealing to offer a *cafeteria plan,* by which employees can select the array of benefits that best meet their individual needs. However, such programs can be expensive to design and complex to administer, rendering them unfeasible for small organizations.

Staff Orientation and Staff Development

In most organizations, the HR director or department is responsible for creating and administering the staff development program. The overall goal of staff development activities is to improve the employees' current and future performance. Staff development generally encompasses those programs designed to meet the employees' needs and those designed to meet the organization's needs, although effective training is generally of benefit to both parties. Staff development on behalf of employees may include providing or funding attendance at workshops to help workers meet the continuing education requirements of their licenses. It also may involve financial support, schedule adjustments, or time off so that employees can pursue education to fulfill their personal interests. For example, a bachelor's degree may not be a requirement for an administrative support position, but the agency may support the worker in that role who wants to pursue a degree for his or her personal development.

Staff development for an organization's benefit typically includes mandatory training needed for accreditation or regulatory purposes, such as CPR certification, compliance with universal health precautions, and procedures for safe client restraints. Organizations also may promote training that helps advance their strategic objectives (e.g., education in a particular therapeutic technique to respond to new service demands or in a new philosophy for work with abusive families to respond to changes in service philosophy at the statewide level; Alderson & Jarvis, 2003).

Orientation is a particular form of staff development designed to acquaint new workers with the agency's formal and informal rules and expectations. It has several purposes, including helping workers learn job procedures; begin to establish relationships with colleagues, subordinates, and superiors; and familiarize them with the ways their role fits with larger organizational structure and mission (Abramson, 1993). Orientation is more than a tour of the building and a long afternoon spent reading the policy and procedures manual. It should be an ongoing process designed to provide workers with the information that they need at the points that they need it.

Those responsible for planning staff development must decide

- How to assess job, organizational, and individual needs
- What kinds of skills and knowledge should be targeted (e.g., literacy, technical skills, interpersonal skills, broad knowledge on particular topics)

- Who should participate in what kind of training
- Who should provide the training
- Under what auspices the training should be offered
- How training transfer (use of new information on the job) will be assured (Kraiger & Aguinis, 2001).

While organizations can have highly sophisticated methods for tracking employees' existing abilities and aspirations for career and personal development, in most small to medium-sized organizations, the supervisors are the keys to uncovering and tracking this information. HR personnel may encourage supervisors to be attuned to this information in supervisory conferences with workers, and at the very least, during the annual performance review and planning process. Employee communication vehicles (e.g., newsletters, e-mail announcements) also can be used to solicit ideas for continuing education and encourage individual employees to identify training needs.

At least one person in the organization will need to keep track, through environmental scanning and coordination with administrators and personnel records managers, the training topics that are required by contracts, licenses, and regulations; the frequency necessary; and the requisite certification of competence or completion. Once a schedule of compulsory training has been created, administrators should consider the resources available for other forms of staff development and the strategies that the agency might use to deliver it.

Each of the many types of training delivery methods has particular strengths and disadvantages. They involve different costs to the organization in terms of travel, instructional expenses, and time away from the workplace. Various methods are suited for different learning objectives; Figure 7.3 captures some of these distinctions (Asamoah, 1995; Beckett & Dungee-Anderson, 1996; Griffin, 1995; Johnson, 2001; Milkovich & Boudreau, 1997; Weinbach, 1998).

Organizations can meet multiple objectives through an effective staff development program. They can ensure various forms of regulatory or legal compliance and improve workforce relations by helping employees meet their needs for growth and for meeting mandatory continuing education hours without incurring a cost or losing time off. In that respect, a robust staff development system may be seen as a form of employee benefits. Last, a strategic examination of the workers' ambitions and the workplace's internal and environmental conditions will lead to staff development plans that ensure a stable pool of workers who are prepared with the skills and knowledge to meet the agency's changing needs.

Performance Appraisals

Performance appraisal is the formal, structured system of measuring, evaluating, and influencing an employee's job-related attributes, behaviors, and outcomes.

FIGURE 7.3
STAFF DEVELOPMENT MODELS

Type of Staff Development	Common Uses	Considerations
On-the-job training; supervision	Orientation; improving performance; safety training; student internships	Relevant to job; trainer can evaluate comprehension or mastery and provide immediate correction; some elements of job may be hard to observe or replicate; costs include supervisor's or trainer's work time and development of curriculum or ancillary materials
Mentoring	Orientation; grooming for promotion	Highly individualized; linked to personal development and career planning; content typically relevant to job; helps with employee retention; can be difficult to find suitable mentor; can be part of affirmative action strategy
Coaching	Orientation; grooming for promotion; addressing performance problems	Highly individualized; linked to personal development and career planning; content typically relevant to job; can be costly if coach is not "in house"; not cost efficient for large numbers of employees
Videos/DVDs	Skills training; suicide lethality assessment; child-abuse detection	Low interaction; less transferability of content to job; cost effective (once purchased, video can be reviewed for refresher or by other employees; timing (can be viewed at employees' convenience); better for knowledge acquisition than skill development
Teleconferences	New knowledge; emerging issues	Timing generally fixed; may conflict with employee schedules; may be coverage or scheduling problems if several employees want to attend

FIGURE 7.3
STAFF DEVELOPMENT MODELS (continued)

Type of Staff Development	Common Uses	Considerations
Workshops (in house; using internal or external educator)	Mandatory training; commonly needed training (e.g., ethics hours for licensure, CPR); multicultural practice	Cost effective; convenient for workers; using coworker as educator can diminish innovation and sense of legitimacy of content; need to arrange office coverage/staffing when workforce is at training
Off-site workshops and retreats	To fill continuing education hours; organizational integrity; networking; new skills and knowledge	Can expose workers to innovations; can give workers a break, sense of respite from work; may incur travel costs and additional time away from the office; may be challenging to transfer training
Conferences	Networking; respite	Usually offer an array of topics, so attendees have high latitude in choice of content; training transfer may be limited, depending on what sessions employees select and quality and relevance of delivery
Credit-bearing coursework	To achieve a degree or additional credentials; to obtain new knowledge or abilities	Expensive; time consuming; assignments/coursework may benefit agency; may help with employee retention; worker may not stay at the agency after attaining degree
Web-based instruction	Ethics compliance; training on regulations; education on new fields (e.g., disaster preparedness)	Can be self-paced to worker schedule; easy to update content; feedback or evaluations immediate; can be delivered to large numbers of workers; may be difficult to ensure that worker thoroughly completed program

Organizations use performance evaluations to accomplish a variety of objectives, including providing feedback to improve work performance, acquiring data for merit pay determinations, developing a candidate pool for internal promotions, identifying training needs and career goals, documenting and addressing poor performance, reorganizing work assignments, and preparing for long-range planning (Milkovich & Boudreau, 1997). Some authors have contended that performance assessments should be uncoupled from pay-for-performance strategies (for example, Matheson, Van Dyk & Millar, 1995; Millar, 1998). They have argued that the developmental goals of such assessments are distorted when linked with pay and that what should be a constructive process becomes a charged and potentially punitive experience. Others have criticized performance systems for being too vague, biased, and punitive (for example, Clifford, 1999). Some have contended that the evaluative element in performance reviews undoes the developmental and supportive functions and, further, it undermines morale and teamwork (for example, Roberts, 1998). These critiques should be taken into account in designing and implementing an effective, meaningful system of employee evaluation and feedback.

In nonprofit organizations, administrators must develop, implement, and evaluate the performance management system. The steps in doing so include determining the performance criteria (for example, What performance will be measured? What will constitute exceptional or unsatisfactory performance?), identifying and preparing the personnel who will carry out the appraisals, determining the frequency and types of evaluation instruments to be used, and linking the results to other systems in the organization (for example, compensation, staff development, discipline).

Performance criteria typically result from the job analysis, which reflects the demands of the job and how the performance of that job affects the agency's outcomes. Examples of performance criteria (Milkovich & Boudreau, 1997, p. 104) include the following:

Skills/Abilities/Traits	*Behaviors*	*Results*
Job knowledge	Performs tasks	Contacts made
Dependability	Follows rules	Caseload/clients served
Creativity	Regular attendance	Client satisfaction
Leadership	Maintains records	Initiated new project

These criteria then should be reflected in the instrument used to evaluate performance and in the data sources (or evaluators) who should participate in completing the appraisal. In some workplaces, the evaluative instruments are highly individualized, with the elements of the worker's job description forming the basis of the appraisal. In others, a more universal form is used, reflecting broad objectives that apply to the majority of the organization's personnel.

As indicated in Figures 7.4 and 7.5, many sources of data can be incorporated into an evaluation of performance, and evaluation systems can use single or multiple evaluators. Although the direct supervisor typically has primary responsibility for conducting the evaluation and discussing it with the employee, he or she may seek the input of others. Sources of data include client satisfaction

---

FIGURE 7.4
SAMPLE POSITION-SPECIFIC PERFORMANCE APPRAISAL

Position: Assistant to the Director

Reports to: Executive Director (ED)

Directions: Under each Principal Function, list the Performance Expectation(s). Record the Performance Indicator(s) at the "Acceptable Performance" level and the Source(s) of Data used to evaluate it.

Function 1: Coordinates the Center's Administrative Office. Informs ED of client or staff issues as they arise, notifies ED of approaching deadlines, aids in the anticipation of concerns and offering assistance in troubleshooting. Maintains confidentiality regarding sensitive information as it applies to staff, clients, and regulatory bodies.

Performance Expectations:

Performance Indicator(s): Exchanges timely information exchange with the ED through written and verbal communications. Develops systems for supplying needed information. Consults with ED regarding staff, client, or community issues; timelines; and their subsequent impact. Generates options for addressing problems. Maintains confidentiality of information exchange specific to this role.

Sources(s) of Data: Self-report. Direct observation and feedback from ED, board, staff, clients, and other constituents.

Function 2: Communicates effectively with staff regarding policies, policy changes, and procedures under the auspices of the ED. Serves as information resource on established policies by directing parties to sources regarding procedures, rules, and regulations.

Performance Expectations:

Performance Indicator(s): Provides timely, clear, accurate written and verbal communication with staff regarding policies and procedures.

---

surveys, peer or team feedback, self-appraisal (verbally or on ratings forms), records, service statistics, and other forms of quantitative data.

When to Measure Performance. Performance appraisals are generally conducted annually, either on the employee's annual date of hire or during a specified period, such as the end of the fiscal year, when all workers are reviewed simultaneously. An advantage of doing all evaluations at the same time is that

---

FIGURE 7.4

SAMPLE POSITION-SPECIFIC PERFORMANCE APPRAISAL (continued)

Sources(s) of Data: Self-report. Direct observation and feedback from ED and staff.

Function 3: Provides back-up support for finance and client data managers. Is familiar with accounting and client file systems, has the ability to use them, and offers resolutions to problems associated with those systems in the absence of the assigned personnel.

Performance Expectations:

Performance Indicator(s): Whenever the assigned staff are unavailable, individuals who have financial or other data inquiries are assisted promptly. Problems that arise are resolved satisfactorily and complete; accurate information is provided.

Sources(s) of Data: Self-report. Direct observation, feedback from staff and related departments such as the funding agencies and insurance companies.

Function 4: Provides coordination and editing support for the agency's publications, including brochures and reports. Writes the agency's newsletter. Coordinates press releases and requests from the media.

Performance Expectations:

Performance Indicator(s): Documents are completed in a timely manner (within the realm of the staff member's control) and are in the correct format so that deadlines are rarely missed. Information is complete and accurate so that follow-up requests are rare. Errors noted are corrected promptly and rarely require a second request for correction.

Sources(s) of Data: Self-report. Number and quality of documents produced. Review of completed documents and works in progress. Observation and feedback from collaborators and end users.

FIGURE 7.5
SAMPLE GENERAL APPRAISAL INSTRUMENT

Rate the employee using the following scale:

1 = Seldom 2 = Occasionally 3 = Usually 4 = Frequently 5 = Always NA = Not Applicable

To what extent does this employee—

_____ Consistently produce an acceptable quantity of work?

_____ Complete tasks in an accurate and timely manner?

_____ Complete tasks with a minimum of supervision?

_____ Accept responsibility for new or difficult projects?

_____ Follow appropriate agency procedures?

_____ Seek appropriate input from supervisor or colleagues?

_____ Communicate clearly and concisely?

_____ Actively advance the organization's mission and objectives?

_____ Work cooperatively with staff from other units to advance the organization's goals?

_____ Arrive at work and return from breaks on time?

---

performance review does not get "misplaced" among other projects or activities, as can happen when they are done individually, throughout the year. Mass reviews also can be advantageous when an organization uses a pay-for-performance compensation system, because the financial obligations for merit awards are all determined and allocated at the same time. This helps in financial planning. A disadvantage of the clustered evaluation is that employees may have different lengths of service that are not accommodated by such a system. And, there is a danger that appraisals will not be sufficiently individualized or will get the short shrift amid the volume of evaluations to be completed in a fixed time.

Variations to the annual use of appraisals occur at the outset of employment, when workers on provisional status may get evaluated at three- or six-month intervals until they have completed their probationary period. Likewise, some progressive discipline programs will require more frequent interim appraisals for employees with performance problems.

How to Measure Performance. After deciding what to measure, the sources of information for evaluation, and the timing of appraisals, the organization must then determine its system for measuring performance. The methods below can be used alone or in various combinations to capture the data the organization values.

A commonly used method is the *graphic rating scale* (Milkovich & Boudreau, 1997). It involves statements of performance criteria (e.g., "Submits forms in a timely manner" "Successfully matched volunteer tutors with students") followed by a graph of three to seven boxes indicating levels of performance (e.g., "outstanding–good–fair–poor," "all the time–usually–rarely–never"). A key in effectively using this method is ensuring that evaluators are properly trained with a common understanding about what each anchor or score is meant to reflect. For example, an employee may only *rarely* start new projects, because of the nature of her job, but whenever she is supposed to start one, she *always* does. Which rank should that item be given? Organizations also must consider what it is they are trying to rate: the frequency with which something occurs or the quality with which the task is done? Different priorities or objectives will lead to different ranking schemas.

Two other techniques provide nice complements to the graphic rating scale. *Essays* are open-ended narratives about the worker's strengths and weaknesses (or any aspect of performance) during the evaluation period. *Critical incidents* are statements describing very effective and ineffective behaviors critical to job tasks. Both strategies help illuminate numerical scores and thus are more useful when combined with quantitative methods.

A *management-by-objective (MBO)* performance review system is highly individualized. For each evaluative period (e.g., six months, one year), the worker and supervisor set several highly specific and measurable goals that are relevant to the person's job or the organizational goals. The supervisor and supervisee should set clear time lines and indicators of quality that will reflect superior, acceptable, or unacceptable performance (e.g., *Superior* = Employee will complete all charting within 48 hours of a client's session; *Acceptable* = Employee will complete charting on at least 80 percent of assigned cases within one week of client session. *Unacceptable* = Employee fails to update any charts within two weeks of client session). The worker is then evaluated on whether or not the objectives were met in the time frame indicated. An advantage of an MBO performance review system is that the expectations placed on employees can be tailored to their interests and ambitions and to the organization's needs in a changing environment. Two disadvantages are that the system is time consuming and carries risks for inequity in the treatment of various employees. For example, are the goals selected by all employees of equal feasibility or difficulty? Do some supervisors set the bar unreasonably high or unreasonably low for superior performance?

Checklists and *behaviorally anchored rating scale (BARS)* are two evaluation systems that use different strategies to limit the potential for unfair variability in raters. Checklists involve a list of statements about characteristics of the worker (e.g., "requires extensive prompting to complete paperwork on time"). The supervisor checks it if it is true of the worker, leaves it blank if it is not. This reduces the potential for differing interpretations about the frequency or quality of behaviors, as may happen with scales. Unfortunately, some important worker characteristics (e.g., initiative, autonomy, communication skills) do not lend themselves to simple "yes" or "no" determinations, in part because of the nuances in how and where these skills are used.

BARS address the variability problem by providing examples or critical incidents to serve as "anchors" for each point on the scale. For instance (Milkovich & Boudreau, 1997),

Position: Home Monitor

Performance dimension: Displays concern for nursing home residents and responds to their needs with genuine interest. A "home monitor" should

GOOD				POOR
Recognize when a resident is depressed and has a problem he or she wants to discuss.	Respond to residents' need for information on financial support or other resources in the community.	See a person and recognize him or her as a resident and say "Hello."	Respond to a resident's need to talk: get into a discussion but fail to follow up later on the concern with either resident or other staff.	Criticize a resident for being unable to solve his or her own problems.

The challenge in a BARS system is that it is time consuming and complex to create an instrument that meaningfully captures unique examples of performance for the array of tasks that encompass any particular job. The system is most useful in large organizations in which multiple employees are covered by the same job description. The time invested up front in instrument development reduces the potential for evaluator error or inequity and is cost effective in the long term.

LIMITING ERRORS AND BIAS IN PERFORMANCE APPRAISALS. Whatever evaluation system the agency uses, supervisors should be thoroughly trained in the instruments used and in the evaluative process. Likewise, employees must be informed about their job expectations and the ways in which those will be measured. An employee should not learn at the interview session that colleagues will be consulted about his performance or that his dress would be considered as an indicator of professionalism. The National Association of Social Workers Code of Ethics (2000) speaks to both of these issues: "Social workers who provide supervision should evaluate supervisees' performance in a manner that is fair and respectful" (3.01d); "social workers who have responsibility for evaluating the performance of others should fulfill such responsibility in a fair and considerate manner and on the basis of clearly stated criteria" (3.03).

Beyond avoiding employee discomfort and ethical challenges, communications about performance expectations serve to motivate employees to live up to the expectations associated with their positions. In understanding the supervisor's expectations, the employee can better prioritize tasks, seek assistance in areas in which growth is needed, and use supervisory sessions to receive periodic feedback on progress (Langdon & Osborn, 2001). The performance review is thus not an annual process but an ongoing discussion of strengths and weaknesses, culminating in a written appraisal at least once per year. It also is not a unidirectional process but rather an interchange between the worker and reviewer, where self appraisal is combined with other sources of data to form an overall impression of how the employee is meeting the organization's expectations. Ideally it also should be an opportunity to evaluate how the organization is meeting the worker's expectations and how a better fit between the two may be achieved. In addition to seeking worker input, all performance review systems should include a mechanism for employees to comment on their ratings, indicating their agreement or disagreement with the appraisal.

Evaluators should be especially alert to several common errors in reviewing employees. HR managers can help educate supervisors about these mistakes and can construct systems that mitigate these problems. They include (Langdon & Osborne, 2001; Milkovich & Boudreau, 1997) the following:

- *Halo or horn error.* This occurs when a worker's performance on one dimension influences ratings on all dimensions. For example, all ratings may be marked down if the worker fails to get to work on time, or up because of his or her friendly customer service.
- *Leniency.* This refers to giving a worker a higher rating than he or she deserves. It typically occurs because the rater wishes to avoid conflict or does not want the worker's eligibility for a raise to be jeopardized by less-than-excellent performance.
- *Strictness.* This refers to giving a more harsh rating than performance deserves, usually due to the rater's inexperience, prejudice, low self-confidence, or inability to take a range of variables into account. Strictness (and also leniency) can result from the absence of clear evaluative standards.
- *Central tendency.* This error occurs when everyone is given average ratings, regardless of differences in performance, usually to avoid complaints

from or dissent among workers. It also can result from the reviewer giving insufficient time or attention to his or her evaluation responsibilities.

- *Primacy and recency effects.* These errors result when first impressions or more recent events inappropriately influence the evaluation rather than taking into account the totality of performance over entire appraisal period. Those who criticize the efficacy of performance appraisals note the rise in worker productivity in the weeks immediately preceding the review, with a corresponding drop in performance after the review is complete. A good appraisal arrangement and proper training for reviewers helps ensure that the system is not skewed by such recency effects.

- *Contrast effects.* These errors are most likely to occur when job-based evaluation criteria are not used, as employees are compared against each other (e.g., making an average employee appear outstanding when compared to a group of poor employees). This type of forced ranking also can present an inaccurate and unfair picture of employee performance when all employees perform above expectations but are treated differentially when ranked against each other.

THE EVALUATION SESSION. As noted earlier, a successful appraisal system means that employees know what is expected of them, and these criteria are evaluated throughout the year. The evaluation should thus take place in the context of a trusting relationship, built through the supervisory process, where the worker is free to share job-related successes and challenges, seeking the supervisor's guidance and support. As the date for the evaluation session approaches, the reviewer should gather the necessary data, including that from the employee, and set a mutually agreeable time for the session.

The nature of the feedback will affect the way that the session is structured, although all sessions should involve an opening in which the purpose of the meeting is established, a middle section in which strengths and areas for improvement are addressed, and a closing in which follow-up steps are enumerated (Millar, 1998). When the employee's performance is exemplary, the interview will largely be an opportunity to review the ratings and share those impressions with the worker, using more time to look forward to the year ahead rather than at the year past. These sessions are a great opportunity to get feedback from the worker and to learn more about staff development needs and career aspirations as part of the goal setting process for the years ahead (Langdon & Osborne, 2001).

When there are concerns about areas of the employee's performance, the supervisor should offer specific, behaviorally focused feedback and clear expectations about what would constitute improved functioning. Figure 7.6 provides

---

FIGURE 7.6

EXAMPLES OF INEFFECTIVE AND EFFECTIVE FEEDBACK

DON'T—"You make the whole team look bad by never showing up on time."
DO—"The team needs your expertise. When you were late three times last week, we couldn't proceed until you arrived. We expect all of the team members to be here at 8 a.m."

DON'T—"You need to be more reliable."
DO—"On at least five occasions in the last month, the intake worker was unable to reach you when you were on call. The expectation is that on-call staff will leave a number where they can be reached. If you fail to leave a number or cannot be reached at it during the next six months of on-call service, you will be placed on probation, and the progressive discipline process will be initiated."

---

examples of general, ineffective feedback, and descriptive, effective feedback. The reviewer should avoid excessive tangents that are focused on assigning blame or determining *why* the performance was unsatisfactory and instead use the time to ensure that the employee understands the nature of the concerns and the conditions for improvement. If the detrimental review initiates a progressive discipline program, the elements of that process must be made clear to the employee. If accommodations are called for to assist in improving the employee's performance (e.g., closer supervision, additional training, referral to an employee assistance program for personal difficulties), the expectations of both parties must be clearly discussed and documented.

Whether the review addressed stellar performance or poor performance, the reviewer must ensure that all documentation is properly completed and submitted. Because evaluative processes are often linked to other HR decisions (e.g., promotions, bonuses, merit pay, disciplinary procedures), the failures in record keeping here have reverberating consequences.

Supervisors and others involved in the evaluative process should regularly evaluate their own performance and the effectiveness of the appraisal process. Areas to address might include the following: "Have I taken steps to improve my appraisal skills?" "How well did I prepare for the session?" "How much did I talk and how well did I listen?" "Have I treated all staff equally?" (Langdon & Osborne, 2001). Honest and consistent self-appraisal helps ensure that performance assessment processes are efficient and equitable. Like performance appraisals, such a self-review also identifies areas for work and growth.

Employee Separations

In HR, the term *separations* refers to the circumstances in which the employee and the organization part company. This typically happens in four unique circumstances: (1) when employees quit, (2) when they retire, (3) when they are dismissed, and (4) when they are laid off. Note that the first two types are typically initiated by the employee (although the agency can influence those decisions), and the last two are initiated by the workplace (although the worker's position or performance may have a role in the decisions).

Separations are not necessarily negative phenomena. Terminations can be good when they involve someone who has not been a productive or constructive part of the workforce or when the loss of a worker improves morale or makes way for new organizational direction or energy. Separations are most negative when they involve unnecessary or illegal losses or when the separation process creates dissent or discouragement among continuing employees.

Terminations are linked to other HR decisions. For example, policies on compensation and benefits may specify the conditions under which those continue when an employee leaves. Policies on paid time off may limit the amount that an employee can accrue or carry over from year to year to control the expenses the agency may incur when an employee leaves. Managing layoffs by freezing vacant positions may differentially affect staffing in units rather than spread cuts evenly across the organization. Discharging ineffective employees can lead to a reexamination of hiring and supervisory practices to determine whether improvements might mean future disciplinary actions could be avoided. Separations also are linked to each other. For example, a financial crisis that might ordinarily necessitate layoffs might be addressed by early-retirement incentives that reduce high payroll expenses associated with long-term employees. Special considerations go with each type of separation (Milkovich & Boudreau, 1997).

RESIGNATIONS. Employee decisions to resign are influenced by a variety of factors, some of which may not be in the organization's control. Typically they involve the worker balancing the satisfaction and expectations from their current job against the satisfaction or expectations in the alternative. When there are fewer alternatives (e.g., in a tight job market), there are fewer resignations, but there also may be more *withdrawal behavior*, such as absenteeism, work slowdowns, and unwillingness to undertake new projects.

Too often, employers assume that workers are motivated solely by money, and they therefore resign themselves to excessive turnover, failing to take steps to study and address other sources of dissatisfaction. By researching the amount and pattern of resignations and by conducting exit interviews, employers can better assess the causes of resignations and the personnel, policy, or programmatic changes that might be initiated to keep valued employees. For example, if workers under one supervisor are quitting at a higher than usual rate, is there something going on with that unit or that individual that might need to be addressed? If employees typically leave after a very brief period on the job, is there something that must change in the screening and selection process to ensure that applicants understand the nature of the work and so that the employer does not hire those who are ill-suited to the job? Perhaps workers in single-parent households find on-call or evening hours untenable. Could another scheduling or service delivery system be developed that would be more accommodating? It is expensive to search for and hire new employees. Taking the time at the end of their service to get feedback on the organization may cut down on those costs by avoiding unnecessary losses.

RETIREMENTS. Retirements differ from other resignations in that they occur at the end of a person's career, and the worker is opting for a lifestyle change rather than another work environment. Retirements may be prompted by employer incentives like adding time to years of service for pension calculations, offering severance pay, or providing part-time employment with full-time benefits. Sometimes, however, the organization may want to institute measures to retain experienced employees who might otherwise retire, especially if there are negative implications of mass retirements, such as diminished quality of the remaining workforce, less variability in seniority, or expensive buyouts.

DISCHARGES. Discharges also are known as "fires." Employee dismissals are a complex and challenging process, regulated by laws and agency policies. As discussed in Chapter 13, they also are a significant area of organizational risk when poorly managed. A key concept to introduce at this point is the notion of *employment at will*. In essence, employment at will means that within state law, the employer–employee relationship at private organizations exists at the will of both parties, subject to whatever contractual obligations were arranged at the outset of employment (e.g., requirement of two-week notice before termination; Gibelman, 2003). The implications for poor-performing workers, then, would be that the employee can be let go for any reason at any time, as long as the process and the rationale is in keeping with the organization's policies and procedures. However, as noted in the section on the regulatory influences of HR, employees are protected from wrongful discharge due to age, sex, religion, and other factors. They also are protected from termination for such actions as whistleblowing, refusing to engage in unlawful acts (such as insurance fraud), filing a worker's compensation claim, engaging in lawful union activities, and others (Falcone, 2002).

Therefore, even when an employment-at-will relationships exists, administrators should institute and use a progressive discipline system, whereby performance concerns are addressed in a multistage process escalating from verbal warnings to written warnings and to termination, should performance problems continue unabated. The system should spell out unacceptable behaviors and consequences. Of course, all evidence and material related to each step in the disciplinary process, including efforts to assist the employee to improve performance, and the ultimate decision to discharge must be thoroughly documented.

Employees can be terminated for

- Incompetence in performance that does not respond to training or accommodation
- Gross or repeated insubordination
- Civil rights violations such as harassment
- Too many unexcused absences or repeated lateness
- Illegal behavior, such as theft
- Drug activity or intoxication on the job
- Verbal abuse
- Physical violence
- Falsification of records.

These behaviors vary in their severity and in the degree of risk they pose for the organization, its clients, and its workers. Therefore, organizations may differentiate, in the disciplinary policy, the ways in which each category of infraction will be handled (e.g., by suspension, automatic discharge, discipline). Organizations can establish *just cause* for discipline by ensuring that workers are adequately informed of the consequences of certain forms of conduct, that the agency's performance expectations are reasonable and appropriate for safe and efficient operations, that the agency engaged in a fair and objective investigation before determining that the worker was in error, that the investigation yielded support that a violation took place, that policies were applied without discrimination, and that the discipline was appropriate for the infraction (Falcone, 2002).

The discipline system should thus be characterized by clarity and fairness, not only in the way that policies are applied but also in the way that people are treated throughout the process. Noe and his colleagues (2004) referred to the latter as *interactional justice*, wherein an organization "took the employee's feelings into account" in carrying out its disciplinary policies (p. 311). Fairness is conveyed by treating the employee with respect and empathy, listening to the employee's perspective, providing opportunities for improvement, and preserving the worker's dignity, even in the face of a decision to discharge the worker. The principles of progressive discipline are sometimes summarized as the *hot-stove rule*, because like, hot stoves, effective discipline provides fair warning, reacts at once, is consistent and objective, applies equally to all, and does not apologize for what it is (Noe et al., 2004).

Once the decision has been made to terminate the employee, it should be swiftly, firmly, and privately carried out. The person conducting the dismissal meeting should begin with a clear statement of the purpose of the meeting, the basis for the decision, and the next steps in the process (Rivas, 1998): For example,

> Paul, we are meeting today to discuss your discharge from the organization. Today you missed a case staffing despite the stipulation in your performance plan that you attend those meetings. As described in your last disciplinary warning, such an absence is cause for termination from the agency. Today will be your last day. This sheet describes your options for appealing this decision and the payment of your remaining salary, vacation days, and benefits.

These are difficult conversations, and it is often helpful to practice or role-play them with a superior before to the actual meeting. It also may be helpful to have a third party attend the meeting (e.g., another manager, HR professional) to ensure that the steps are carried out properly and to provide corroboration should the employee dispute the facts of the meeting at a later date. Having support at the meeting also may enhance the sense of safety if concerns exist about the employee's reaction (Falcone, 2001). Practice can help the supervisor avoid pitfalls in the dismissal meeting, including backpedaling from the decision, negotiating, and blaming others for the decision (Rivas, 1998).

LAYOFFS. When an organization determines that downsizing is necessary, the first step is diagnosis: what is the nature and extent of the budgetary shortfalls? Are they time limited? Are they due to miscalculations in income or overexpenditures? Do they center in one department or program? This analysis should lead to tentative options, which must then be weighed in terms of their adequacy for addressing the problem and the ramifications for clients, services, personnel, and morale. Must staff be cut? (Sometimes cutting staff also will diminish the ability to generate revenue.) Should cuts be across the board, or should they eliminate an entire service line or division? What are the pros and cons of options to layoffs, such as hiring freezes, downsizing through attrition, early retirements, voluntary furloughs (unpaid days off), or mandatory across-the-board furloughs (during traditionally "slow" periods)? The decisions should ensure equity, taking into account the organization's objectives, the maintenance of key programs, the needs of the workers who remain, and the costs of the layoffs (e.g., paying out unused vacation time or arranging job-search assistance).

The downsizing process must be carefully managed, and communications should be characterized by honesty and frequency. To the extent that agency functioned effectively before the financial crisis, the better able it is to weather the layoffs. To the extent that it is characterized by unhappiness, distrust, and hopelessness, the more difficult the downsizing experience will be.

CONCLUSION

HR management involves an array of interlocking steps and strategies that are used to help the agency achieve its goals through an effective and stable workforce. HR decisions are shaped by variables that are specific to the organization and by external factors, such as labor market characteristics, economic factors, and laws and regulations. Across the array of personnel actions, from employee selection to compensation, training, and evaluation to separations, HR managers must be mindful of the competing tensions of equity and efficiency and understand the interlocking and sometimes unintended consequence of HR actions.

SKILLS APPLICATION EXERCISE

- In small groups, develop a set of interview questions for candidates for a position within a nonprofit organization. Select one group member to role-play an applicant for the position, select another member to lead the interview, and assign other groups members particular questions to ask the candidate; then conduct a candidate interview. After the interview, discuss what went well and what could be improved.
- Obtain a performance evaluation instrument from a nonprofit organization and interview individuals responsible for overseeing performance evaluation, such as the director of HR management or the CEO. Assess the strengths and weaknesses of the organization's performance evaluation system.

REFERENCES

Abramson, J. S. (1986). Orienting social work employees in interdisciplinary settings: Shaping professional and organizational perspectives. *Social Work, 38,* 152–157.

Age Discrimination in Employment Act of 1967, Pub L. No. 90–202, 29 USC §§ 621 et seq.

Alderson, J., & Jarvis, S. (2003). *Cornerstone 2: What's good for families is good for workers* [curriculum]. Raleigh: North Carolina Division of Social Services.

Americans with Disabilities Act of 1990, Pub L. No. 101-33, 42 USC. §§ 12101 et seq.

Asamoah, Y. (1995). Managing the new multicultural workplace. In L. Ginsberg & P. R. Keys (Eds.), *New management in human services* (2nd ed., pp. 115–127). Washington, DC: NASW Press.

Beckett, J. O., & Dungee-Anderson, D. (1996). A framework for agency-based multicultural training and supervision. *Journal of Multicultural Social Work, 4*(4), 27–48.

Brody, R. (1993). *Effectively managing human service organizations.* Newbury Park, CA: Sage.

Clifford, J. P. (1999). The collective wisdom of the workforce: Conversations with employees regarding performance evaluation. *Public Personnel Management, 28,* 119–150.

Cohen, B. J. (2002). Alternative organizing principles for the design of service delivery systems. *Administration in Social Work, 26*(2), 17–38.

Equal Employment Opportunity Act of 1972, Pub L. No. 92-261, 42 USC §§ 2000.

Equal Pay Act of 1962, Pub L. No. 88-38, 29 USC §§ 206d.

Fair Labor Standards Act of 1938, 29 USC §§ 201 et seq.

Falcone, P. (2002). *The hiring and firing question and answer book.* New York: Amacom.

Family and Medical Leave Act of 1993, Pub L. No. 103-3, 29 USC §§ 2601 et seq.

Gibelman, M. (2003). *Navigating human service organizations.* Chicago: Lyceum.

Griffin, W. V. (1995). Social worker and agency safety. In R. L. Edwards (Ed.), *Encyclopedia of social work* (Vol. 2, 19th ed., pp. 2293–2305). Washington, DC: NASW Press.

Hindle, T. (1998). *Interviewing skills.* New York: DK Publishing.

Johnson, C. E. (2001). *Meeting the ethical challenges of leadership.* Thousand Oaks, CA: Sage.

Kraiger, K., & Aguinis, H. (2001). Training effectiveness: Assessing training needs, motivation, and accomplishments. In M. London (Ed.), *How people evaluate others in organizations* (pp. 203–219). Mahwah, NJ: Lawrence Erlbaum.

Langdon, K., & Osborne, C. (2001). *Performance reviews.* New York: DK Publishing.

Macaleer, B. & Shannon, J. (2003). Does HR planning improve business performance? *Industrial Management, 45,* 15–20.

Matheson, W., Van Dyk, C., & Millar, K. (1995). *Performance evaluation in the human services.* New York: Haworth Press.

Milkovich, G. T., & Boudreau, J. W. (1997). *Human resource management* (8th ed.). Homewood, IL: Irwin.

Millar, K. I. (1998). Evaluating employee performance. In R. L. Edwards, J. A. Yankey, & M. A. Altpeter (Eds.), *Skills for effective management of nonprofit organizations* (pp. 219–243). Washington, DC: NASW Press.

National Association of Social Workers. (2000). *Code of ethics.* Washington, DC: Author.

Noe, R. A., Hollenbeck, J. R., Gerhart, B., & Wright, P. M. (2004). *Fundamentals of human resource management.* Boston: McGraw-Hill.

Pecora, P. J. (1998). Recruiting and selecting effective employees. In R. L. Edwards, J. A. Yankey, & M. A. Altpeter (Eds.), *Skills for effective management of nonprofit organizations* (pp. 155–183). Washington, DC: NASW Press.

Pregnancy Discrimination Act of 1978, Pub L. No. 95-555, 42 USC §§ 2000 et seq.

Rivas, R. F. (1998). Dismissing problem employees. In R. L. Edwards, J. A. Yankey, & M. A. Altpeter (Eds.), *Skills for effective management of nonprofit organizations* (pp. 262–278). Washington, DC: NASW Press.

Roberts, G. E. (1998). Perspectives on enduring and emerging issues in performance appraisal. *Public Personnel Management, 27,* 301–320.

Social Security Act of 1935, Pub L. No. 74-271, 42 USC §§ 301 et seq.

Title VII of the Civil Rights Act of 1964, Pub L. No. 88-352, 42 USC §§ 2000.

Weinbach, R. W. (1998). *The social worker as manager* (3rd ed.). Boston: Allyn & Bacon.

8

Managing Diversity

Susan L. Parish, M. Jennifer Ellison,
Janice K. Parish

In the private for-profit sector, effectively managing employees from diverse cultural, ethnic, linguistic, and racial backgrounds is widely accepted as an imperative to maximize organizational efficiency and profits. Extensive evidence suggests that proactively managing diversity can improve organizational performance and support core business values of fairness and equity, enhance creativity, enhance problem-solving and innovation, improve the caliber of the workforce, and expand marketing capacities and strategies (for example, Cox, 2001). A well-managed diverse workforce makes numerous contributions to the larger organization. While a diverse workforce offers numerous benefits for organizations, managing a heterogeneous contingent of employees is challenging. This is particularly the case in terms of communication, collaboration, and conflict resolution.

For nonprofit managers, less evidence is available regarding the impact of managing diversity on the organizations that they typically manage. And yet nonprofit managers face complex and often competing values as they strive to recruit and manage a diverse workforce. This chapter provides an overview of the exigencies that require nonprofit administrators to proactively manage diversity, including demographic shifts, ethical obligations, and improved service outcomes. (The legal basis for managing diversity is described in Chapter 7.) A brief overview of emerging organizational models of diversity management is then presented, followed by concrete strategies for actively managing diversity across domains of managerial responsibility. The chapter concludes with vignettes that offer examples of effective approaches to managing diversity.

For the purposes of this chapter, *diversity* is meant in its broadest sense to indicate individual differences of gender, age, sexual orientation, race, ethnicity, cultural background, and disability status. We adopt the definition and application of *managing diversity* advanced by Ivancevich and Gilbert (2000), that is, the organization's commitment to "recruit, retain, reward, and promote a heterogeneous mix of productive, motivated, and committed workers" (p. 77).

DEMOGRAPHIC CATALYSTS FOR MANAGING DIVERSITY

Major demographic shifts are underway in the United States, and these compel nonprofit leaders to proactively manage a diverse workforce. The demographic changes include the aging of the general population, the increasing racial and ethnic diversity of the population, and the increased life expectancies of people with disabilities.

Aging America

Like most of western Europe and Japan, the U.S. population is aging. In the United States, this trend is spurred by the baby boom generation and is arguably the most pressing force that will shape the nation's domestic policy in coming decades. The oldest, or leading edge, of baby boomers will turn 65 in 2010, and the elderly proportion of the population will accelerate for decades. Fully one-fifth of Americans are projected to be ages 65 or older by 2030 (U.S. Bureau of the Census, 2000). Demographers and economists predict that state and federal budgets will be strained as health care, retirement, and disability benefit costs soar to accommodate the needs of this cohort of elderly adults (Lee & Skinner, 1999).

The aging of the general population will have critical consequences for the human services sector as well. The elderly care system will increasingly require more caregivers, therapists, professionals, and administrators. Meeting the need to expand the workforce will further squeeze the entire nonprofit sector, whether it serves elderly people or not. Managers will thereby need to rely on a diverse workforce as never before, or else they will not be able to compete for an increasingly scarce labor pool.

The "Browning" of America

Demographers are projecting that the combined forces of immigration and childbirth will result in Latinos displacing African Americans as the largest racial minority group in the United States by 2010 and that white Americans will decline to 50 percent of the population by 2050 (U.S. Bureau of the Census, 2000). Rodriguez (2003) has termed this phenomenon the "browning" of America. He has argued that, while American culture has always existed at the convergence of heterogeneous racial, ethnic, and cultural traditions, the browning of America is evident in the emerging centrality of Latin American cultural influences in the United States.

The increasing racial and ethnic diversity will require nonprofit managers to have the skills to manage diversity for two reasons. First, the diversity of Americans has become a central characteristic of the workforce—the homogeneity within some organizations of previous generations is gone. Second, diverse clients will demand that the nonprofit organizations that serve them reflect similar diversity. As such, nonprofit leaders interested in providing responsive services must effectively recruit, retain, and manage a fully representative workforce.

Increased Life Expectancies of People With Disabilities

A third demographic shift that also will affect nonprofit managers results from the past century's advances in medical care and technology, which have contributed to a significantly longer lifespan for people with disabilities than was typical or even possible in the early and mid-1900s. Because people with disabilities presently have approximately the same life expectancy as the population without disabilities, for the first time, children with many disabilities are outliving their parent–caregivers in large numbers. Increased life expectancies result in people requiring services for longer periods of time, and these prolonged care needs will strain existing, under-funded service systems. Service systems for people with disabilities have not sufficiently increased funding and support to meet the growing demand for care across the lifespan.

For nonprofit managers, the increased longevity of people with disabilities, similar to the aging of the population, also has consequences for the workforce. As people with disabilities age, they will require greater levels of care and support than has ever been required in the past. As such, the service system that supports them will compete for workers with the rest of the human services industry.

Another important aspect of the improved technologies is that people with disabilities are now working in unprecedented numbers. People with disabilities represent the single largest minority group in the United States, at approximately 20 percent of the civilian population (Jans & Stoddard, 1999), and their employment is protected and encouraged by the Americans with Disabilities Act (see Chapter 7).

FINANCIAL INCENTIVES FOR MANAGING DIVERSITY

Although managing diversity effectively and ethically in the workplace can seem a daunting and complex task, there are powerful incentives for doing so. Most compelling for many organizations are the economic benefits and the potential financial losses incurred when employees' diversity is not harnessed to the organization's advantage; diversity is viewed as a "business issue" first and foremost (Cox, 2001), at least in the for-profit world.

Another frequently cited motivation for managing diversity is compliance with legal mandates, as organizations are usually very aware of the damage that lawsuits and negative publicity can cause to funding sources, organization reputation, and staff morale. Financial inducements are the most commonly cited reason for managing diversity among businesses and for-profit organizations; thus, most research about implementing diversity initiatives in the workplace has promoted the agenda of maximizing profit by maximizing diversity. Economic benefits are a considerable incentive for businesses and nonprofits alike, the latter often functioning on carefully allotted budgets with little room for waste of resources. In the present era of states' fiscal hardships and subsequently ensuing cutbacks (U.S. General Accounting Office, 2003) to nonprofit health, education, and human services organizations' budgets, fully using the creativity and industry of each employee is necessary to fulfill organizational missions. Effectively managing diversity promotes just such utilization.

When diversity is valued in the workplace, employees' interpersonal communication improves, resulting in increased creativity and collaboration (Cox, 2001). Employees who feel that their individuality is valued and do not feel pressured to conform to dominant culture may experience increased identification with their organization and work. This contributes to lower turnover rates, higher job satisfaction, and employees who place greater value on the quality of their work (Thomas & Ely, 1996). Members of minority groups who work in organizations invested in valuing and promoting diversity tend to be more committed to the employer (Mattis, 2001). In addition, being able to draw from a multicultural staff increases an organization's competitiveness and ability to work sensitively and competently with diverse populations (Cox, 2001).

If positive economic inducements are not reason enough to manage workplace diversity, there also is the consideration of the negative financial consequences for the organization that either ignores or superficially addresses diversity. Diversity is a demographic reality that organizations cannot avoid. Thus, organizations that disregard the significance of workplace diversity only harm themselves: They are less competitive (Cox, 2001) and are subject to discrimination lawsuits that can ruin their financial stability as well as their reputations (Hubbard, 2004).

Employees who lack an appreciation of diverse coworkers, clients, or customers are more likely to have difficulty with interpersonal relationships and communication, which can result in higher turnover, reduced collaboration, and reduced sensitivity to colleagues' values and backgrounds (Bucher, 2000). High levels of staff turnover are particularly expensive for organizations, even without considering its impact on morale. The costs of replacing employees, including recruitment, selection, training, and reduced productivity of departing and newly hired employees, are even higher when replacing workers of color because of a longer time-to-fill rate (Hubbard, 2004).

ETHICAL INCENTIVES FOR MANAGING DIVERSITY

For human services or other nonprofit organizations actively working for social justice, the ethics of valuing diversity is the crux of the issue: putting organizational ideals into practice and combating the historical legacy of systemic oppression. For employees and managers of organizations with social justice missions, ethical considerations compel managers to move from the economic "status quo" of addressing diversity toward a valuation of diversity that truly prioritizes the ideals of the organization and of social work.

Very little research has examined the ethical underpinnings of managing diversity effectively, but the root of such considerations for social work organizations, for example, stems from the National Association of Social Workers (NASW) *Code of Ethics* (2000), which cites "social justice" and "the dignity and worth of the person" as two of the social work profession's six core values. The *Code of Ethics* compels social workers to fight for social justice, and social work organizations are therefore mandated to be institutions of cultural competence, with policies and practices that promote equity and full participation of staff with diverse backgrounds.

Nonprofit organizations face barriers to implementing diversity management initiatives. Hyde (2004) found that the burden for implementing diversity management initiatives typically rests with the executive director or chief executive officer of the organization. Nonprofit leaders often face a daunting array of competing values and priorities that challenge their efforts to manage diversity (Hyde, 2004). In addition, although nonprofits may be the most committed to valuing diversity from an ethical standpoint, they often are the least financially able to prioritize training their employees (Chambers & Riccucci, 1997).

Another crucial element in ethically valuing diversity is avoiding tokenism and the pigeonholing of employees who are members of minority groups. Using multicultural employees for their "niche" knowledge of their racial or ethnic group—or expecting them to provide such knowledge—can contribute to a negative workplace environment and higher turnover. Such minority employees are likely to feel that being valued only for their insider knowledge about particular groups is demeaning and stereotyping (Thomas, Mack, & Montagliani, 2004).

Organizations that value diversity from a social justice perspective must take extra care not to exploit employees of color to maximize their own profits or legitimacy as progressive organizations.

ORGANIZATIONAL MODES OF DIVERSITY MANAGEMENT

Recognition of pervasive institutional discrimination in the workforce catalyzed the creation of Equal Employment Opportunity and Affirmative Action policies (see Chapter 7). The earliest organizational approaches to managing diversity were therefore responses to these policies.

The leading theorists of managing diversity formulated organizational change models that sought to explain managerial responses to diversity (e.g., Powell, 1993; Thomas, 1991). These models described trajectories through which organizations typically moved. At the least responsive end of the continuum, organizations maintained reactive postures and responded, often under duress, to affirmative action requirements and political considerations. At the most responsive end of the continuum, structural and ideological changes were made in which organizations actively embraced a diverse workforce and made having a diverse workforce became a centerpiece of the core business strategy (Agars & Kottke, 2004). The earliest theorists (e.g., Powell, 1993; Thomas, 1991) generally categorized organizations in terms of their climate's receptiveness to issues of workforce diversity—that is, did the organization "react" to the potential threat of lawsuits, or was it proactive in actualizing and implementing a new valuing of the diverse workforce (Agars & Kottke, 2004)?

These latter organizations that proactively worked to implement diversity values represent the progressive end of the spectrum. They include organizational actions that result in the complete integration of women and members of minority groups as valued members of a multicultural workforce. This latter approach is not "color-blind" or assimilationist (Chrobot-Mason & Ruderman, 2004), but values the distinct, individual contributions that workers from diverse backgrounds can make to the organization. The uniqueness and heritage of diverse workers are honored and used in this latter approach, which is when the active management of diversity succeeds.

An emerging managing diversity model articulates the characteristics of organizations that are engaged in effective diversity management. This so-called integrative model (Agars & Kottke, 2004) postulates that effective organizations progress through three stages: (1) issue identification, (2) implementation, and (3) maintenance. The transition between stages includes organizational factors (e.g., top management initiatives, mission changes) and individual factors (e.g., management role modeling, attitudinal changes) that influence the extent to which movement progresses. From these theorists' perspective, managing diversity entails multilevel organizational and individual factors that interact across the individual and organizational level to facilitate (or hinder) progress toward successful diversity management.

REQUISITE SUPERVISORY BEHAVIORS AND APPROACHES FOR EFFECTIVELY MANAGING DIVERSITY

What then, is required for competent and effective management of diversity? Chrobot-Mason and Ruderman (2004) have identified opportunities for active, assertive intervention in three key managerial responsibilities: (1) recruitment and selection, (2) professional development, and (3) enhancing teamwork. Across the scope of their core job functions, successful managers of diversity must have multicultural knowledge—a clear understanding of the different values, customs, rituals, norms, and beliefs across cultures. Managers also must situate this knowledge in a thoughtful awareness of themselves—understanding their own biases and expectations of people from dissimilar backgrounds. In addition, managers must possess four key skills: (1) conflict management, (2) interpersonal communication, (3) feedback seeking, and (4) role modeling (Chrobot-Mason & Ruderman, 2004).

Actively promoting cultural inclusion must begin with recruitment and selection because effectively managing diversity requires a workforce that is, first and foremost, diverse (Chrobot-Mason & Ruderman, 2004). The research suggests that members of minority cultures still face considerable disadvantages in the hiring process. While overtly hostile discrimination in hiring has largely disappeared, there is compelling evidence that it has been replaced by more subtle forms of discrimination, in which white male managers are more likely to hire white male candidates and justify their choices in hiring criteria that are ambiguous (Chrobot-Mason & Ruderman, 2004). To address these problems, managers must first become aware of their own biases and improve their comfort with people from disparate backgrounds. The use of systematic, standardized selection procedures, clear evaluation criteria, and recruiters and interviewers who themselves represent diverse backgrounds also will strengthen recruitment and hiring (Fernandez, 1999).

Managers' professional development responsibilities encompass employee training, providing challenging job assignments that promote employees' growth, evaluation, mentoring, and role modeling. All of these responsibilities provide managers different contexts in which diversity can be valued and enhanced.

Women and members of minority groups are less likely to receive adequate training and mentoring and are less likely to be given challenging tasks that develop their skills and competence. People of color and women also are less likely to receive informal feedback (Chrobot-Mason & Ruderman, 2004), a valuable professional development mechanism. Cognizant of this likely deficit, managers can take steps to ensure that formalized feedback processes are systematically implemented. Such plans should include the requisite annual performance appraisals, but also mentoring, the provision of networking opportunities, recognition programs, and the use of support groups. All of these strategies can enhance multiculturalism in nonprofit organizations.

Evaluation procedures that use so-called "360-degree feedback" (Chrobot-Mason & Ruderman, 2004) enable supervisors, subordinates, and peers to provide feedback in a formalized, anonymous process. This procedure enables all workers, whether from dominant or nondominant groups, to benefit from the counsel of others.

The frequent lack of informal mentoring for minorities and women across organizations can be addressed by formalized processes in which supportive mentors are identified and work time is available for the development and ongoing maintenance of mentoring relationships. When mentors and protégés have different backgrounds, particular attention needs to be paid to communication. Training in active listening can help mentors improve their skills to ensure that they are communicating effectively with their protégés.

Formal employee reward programs often fail to recognize workers from minority groups and women. This is likely the case because the values and contributions of white men, the dominant group, tend to be valued, while the contributions of others are easily overlooked (Chrobot-Mason & Ruderman, 2004). The equitable distribution of recognition should include not just pay and promotion but also awards, special invitations, training opportunities, credit for performance, and praise. Leaders should monitor the distribution of rewards and work diligently to ensure that they are equitably allocated.

Management-sponsored support groups in which minority members can confidentially share experiences and encourage one another can also contribute to organizational efforts to value diversity. Facilitating these groups by providing space and work time to participate can also provide workers from minority groups with powerful messages that their success and contributions are valued by the organization.

Managers' third major responsibility related to supervision is the area of enhancing teamwork (Chrobot-Mason & Ruderman, 2004) and facilitating employees' productivity and cooperation. Many women and minorities are marginalized and ostracized within their worksites, and organizational environments contribute to the lack of integration workers feel. Supervisors can use several strategies to address this critical issue. First, managers must enable all workers to have a valued voice within the organization. To do so, managers must be cognizant of the different communication and participation styles workers with different backgrounds have. For instance, some workers may feel that it is disrespectful or inappropriate to speak during meetings. As such, brainstorming sessions that rely on the spontaneous generation and articulation of ideas are unlikely to be fruitful. To encourage everyone's participation, managers can use strategies like nominal group techniques (originally developed by Delbecq, Van de Ven, & Gustafson, 1975). To use this technique, group members silently generate and write down their own responses to a question or problem, share them verbally with the group, and then everyone privately ranks the ideas. This technique respects the different participation styles of the group and provides a way for everyone to participate.

In addition to attending to the different communication and participation styles of workers from different background, managers interested in embracing and truly valuing diversity must lead by example and serve as role models. Managers' ongoing communication, whether written, oral, or by e-mail, offers opportunities to affirm diversity values. Consistent, public messages can be powerful for workers from dominant culture and minority subgroups alike.

Proactive strategies to managing diversity are preferred, but managers also must intervene and assertively address conflict among workers as it arises. To tackle this challenging responsibility, managers must have the courage to exercise their leadership authority and cannot brook attitudes and actions from staff that undermine diversity values. Leaders must be unequivocal about giving voice to and valuing minority employees, cannot tolerate prejudice, and must mediate intergroup conflict. These tasks are intimidating to many social services professionals and require considerable skill in the areas of communication, negotiation, problem-solving, and team-building.

In all of these areas, managers should be held accountable for their decisions related to diversity. Simple data collection efforts and monitoring of recruitment, selection, and distribution of recognition, particularly, can identify patterns in managers' decisions, a useful and important first step in ultimately addressing bias.

COMMUNITY CONTEXT OF MANAGING DIVERSITY

Markedly different from the for-profit managers' usual situation, nonprofit and social services leaders often have job responsibilities that include considerable interaction with the larger community. These tasks create opportunities to improve the centrality of multiculturalism to the organization.

Most nonprofit leaders are compelled to work cooperatively with other social services organizations in their communities. Referrals for mental health services, for example, may come from food pantries, organizations that address intimate partner violence, or advocacy organizations for families of children with disabilities. Leaders who are fully involved in their communities and working cooperatively with peers from other organizations can strengthen their organization's multicultural capacities. Networking with similarly concerned colleagues from different fields presents contexts for sharing experiences and engaging in ongoing discussions about disparate and effective diversity management approaches. Managers can reach out to leaders in other social services organizations to learn how they handle this aspect of their management responsibilities.

Analysis of the client population often presents imperatives for engaging in targeted outreach and ensuring that organizational missions to serve diverse client populations are met. Networking with organizations that serve racial/ethnic minorities, gay men, lesbians, and people with disabilities can expand the diversity of an organization's clientele. Managers can conduct focus groups and needs assessments with community members who are from minority groups to determine how the organization can best serve diverse constituencies. These actions also send an important message to employees about the organization's commitment to serving a diverse clientele, which reinforces the value of having a diverse workforce.

BOARD INTERACTIONS AND DIVERSITY

Nonprofit managers typically have extensive contact with a volunteer board of directors. The board's oversight of the organization can be exploited to meet objectives of increasing workforce diversity and effective diversity management. While nonprofit executive directors generally report to the board or its executive committee, in fact the relationship is typically more fluid, and the organization's paid staff often provides leadership to the board in helping it set priorities and policies. As such, paid managers may facilitate prioritizing diversity issues and concerns for the board.

Active involvement of the board in diversity management efforts should begin with the organization's bylaws. Bylaws that require a proportion of the board to be representative of different population subgroups can help ensure that the organization addresses diversity issues on an ongoing basis, regardless of staff or board member turnover. Recruiting board members from diverse groups should be a central consideration in helping organizations shift toward a more inclusive culture. Such recruitment efforts must be undertaken in ways that are not tokenistic but instead convey a true interest in the perspectives and values of diverse populations.

Ongoing board training and education, a valuable strategy for the competent leadership of all nonprofits (Robinson, 2001), should emphasize the critical nature of serving diverse clients and maintaining a diverse workforce. Paid organization leaders can be instrumental in ensuring that board members remain informed about current developments in managing diversity. Nonprofit managers should share their experiences and what they learn from other managers with their boards to facilitate an ongoing dialogue around these issues. Maintaining the board's attention on this issue is critically important to support the success of diversity initiatives.

Finally, board members should be expected and encouraged to provide leadership in setting policy to support or require initiatives that promote valuing diversity in the workforce. Paid managers can provide information about management trends that support workers with disparate backgrounds and needs. For example, the federal Family and Medical Leave Act (FMLA, P.L. 103-3) does not require employers to grant unpaid leave time for the care of gay or lesbian partners as it does for married heterosexual couples. Boards can exhibit leadership by setting organization policy that is more progressive and supportive of gay and lesbian workers than the federal standards. Similarly, boards can establish policies that promote flextime, job sharing, and paid caregiving leave that support women's (and, increasingly, men's) dual roles as employees and caregivers (Hooyman & Gonyea, 1995; Williams, 2000).

CONCLUSION

Leaders in human services organizations face compelling inducements to effectively manage an increasingly diverse workforce. These imperatives include dramatic demographic changes, financial considerations, and the shared ethical values that undergird most social services organizations. Managers have opportunities to strengthen their organization's multicultural capacities through all aspects of their responsibilities: recruitment and selection of personnel, professional development, staff evaluation, recognition programs, feedback and mentoring programs, teamwork management, productivity and cooperation, community interactions, and board development. Consistently using the skills required to support these responsibilities is essential for managers truly committed to embracing, valuing, and benefiting from a diverse workforce. The case studies that follow illustrate some of these issues.

CASE STUDIES

Case 1

BACKGROUND. Joan, the group manager, holds regular monthly staff meetings. This month, she assigns three small teams a separate continuous quality improvement project for completion and presentation at next month's meeting. Each team comprises three members, and the team themselves will choose their own leader, who will present results and findings next month.

Two days later, one of the group leaders, Julie, requests a meeting with the manager to discuss her concerns and questions. During the meeting, Julie explains to the manager that she is having a lot of trouble with another team member, Angelo. Julie states that Angelo has not contributed anything to the project and that she "just cannot work with him. He is uncooperative, lazy, and disrespectful toward me." Julie looks at Joan and says "You know how men are. They just can't handle a woman supervisor."

POSSIBLE SOLUTION. Joan probes further and learns that Angelo made at least one disrespectful comment to Julie when the group was meeting. Joan also decides that this may be a learning experience for Julie if she is able to work out a different solution rather than just not working with Angelo. Joan meets privately with Julie to discuss options for approaching Angelo with this problem, and they decide that the best approach is a direct one from Julie to Angelo. Julie rehearses what she will say to him with Joan, including telling him that she did not appreciate the comment he made and that she expects him to contribute his fair share of work to the assigned task. Joan lets Julie know that she will support what she says and will certainly step in with Angelo if his attitude and contributions do not change, but that the first step is the two of them talking things out. Joan also reinforces to Julie that she may be unfairly judging Angelo by asserting that all men do not like women supervisors. Julie reports back to Joan that, when she confronted Angelo, he apologized for making the remark and expressed a desire to complete his part of the team project.

Case 2

BACKGROUND. Tom is a new part-time clerk in the organization. He has a developmental disability and has a job coach who helped him learn his job. His job coach is from a disability services organization and does not work for Tom's employer. When Tom first began his new job, the job coach was with him daily, helping him learn the ropes. Tom's manager, Joe, met with the staff and made it clear that he expects everyone to make Tom feel comfortable.

Tom learned his job quickly and after approximately one month, he, Joe, and the coach decide that the coach is no longer needed every day. They agree that the coach will help Tom set up his weekly routine each Monday and will check in again on Thursday. In another month, they agree to re-evaluate Tom's progress. The coach has asked Joe to reinforce two main goals with Tom: (1) to increase his productivity by completing four tasks every day and (2) to improve positive interactions with his peers, as Tom tends to avoid all conversation with others.

At a subsequent staff meeting during which Tom is not present, a staff person states that she speaks for herself and others in reporting that Tom is "just not working out." She says that he is too slow getting his work done and thus creates difficulties for everyone. "Plus," she says, "he is rude and will not even answer a question asked directly to him. "We," she says, gesturing to others in the room, "don't think that people like him should get special treatment. We all have work to do."

POSSIBLE SOLUTION. Joe has never worked with an individual with developmental disabilities before and is honest with the staff that he is not sure how to best handle the problem but that he would really like to give Tom a chance to succeed. Joe lets the staff know that he and the organization greatly values a diverse team and that people from different backgrounds, with different skills and abilities, can learn and grow from one another, Tom included. While not asking for "special treatment," Joe asks them to focus on the positive changes that have occurred since Tom's employment. He reminds them that, although Tom may be a little slow, his work is always completed perfectly. He lets the staff know that he will address the issue with Tom. Afterward, Joe decides to give the job coach a call to discuss the issues. Joe and the job coach have a great conversation, during which the job coach volunteers to come to a staff meeting to speak with the staff and provide them with some additional information and assistance in working with Tom or others with disabilities. Progress is slow, but two months later, Tom has become more comfortable at work and even has lunch with other staff once in a while in the lunchroom.

Case 3

BACKGROUND. A manager is observing two staff members work together, Ayana, a new staff member and recent immigrant from Africa, and Lewis, who has worked for the organization for more than 12 years. The manager overhears this conversation between the two:

Ayana: "I am missing a data collection sheet from last Monday. Do you know who I should get it from?"

Lewis: "Listen, I don't know how you people did things over on the big continent, but here we just go with the flow, don't make waves, if you know what I mean. Just do the form, and we are done."

POSSIBLE SOLUTION. The manager realizes that she has two problems on her hands: (1) the fact that Lewis made a disparaging racial remark and (2) the fact that he told Ayana to complete the form herself. Deciding to deal with the former issue first, she meets privately with Lewis. She closes the door and tells him that she overheard the comment that he made to Ayana about being "over on the big continent." She explains to him in no uncertain terms that negative comments such as those or any others that devalue someone's identity will not be tolerated and that further comments will be grounds for disciplinary action. She explains to Lewis that this organization, from the executive director down to the direct-line staff, is composed of individuals from different backgrounds. The success of their team is due largely to the fact that they all bring different ideas and perspectives to the table. She reminds him that when he first started in the organization, he needed support and assistance from senior staff as well and not a disrespectful attitude. She requested that if he needed to discuss serious concerns with her regarding his or his peer's work, he could request a meeting with her at any time. She then requested that he apologize to Ayana for the remark and that he teach her where to obtain and how to complete data sheets.

After Lewis apologized, the manager met privately with Ayana. She explained to Ayana that she had overheard Lewis's remarks and was troubled by them. She reinforced that the organization valued Ayana's work and contributions and that management would not tolerate racist remarks or other comments that devalued individual staff. The manager encouraged Ayana to come to her if she experienced any further negative interactions with Joe or any other staff. The manager reiterated that the organization was committed to supporting a diverse workforce and would not tolerate staff behavior that undermined this commitment.

Case 4

BACKGROUND. Ruth, a direct care staffer, requests a meeting with Mark, her supervisor. Ruth requests a leave of absence for 1 week to care for her life partner, who is ill. At present, the organization does not have a policy that extends to unmarried partners, and as such, Mark cannot grant the request.

POSSIBLE SOLUTION. Mark realizes that the organization's existing policy, as well as the FMLA, which permits unpaid leave of up to 12 weeks for employees wishing to care for an ill family member (or a newborn or newly adopted child), does not include provisions for unmarried life partners. In addition, current organization policy prohibits the use of such leaves. Because the existing policy is not supportive of the needs of lesbian or gay staff, Mark drafts a policy revision and pushes for its adoption within the organization. To support Ruth's specific situation, Mark reviews her file and informs her that she can use her accrued sick or vacation time to care for her partner. However, Mark continues to press for policy change within the organization.

SKILLS APPLICATION EXERCISE

- Contact the director of human resources at your nonprofit organization and request a breakdown of the personnel by their racial, disability, gender, and ethnic group membership. Are any staff openly identified as lesbian, bisexual, gay, or trans-gendered? Do the organization's supervisors come from diverse backgrounds? What about the agency's board of directors? Are the supervisors and board representative of the larger community in which the organization is situated?

- Conduct a diversity audit for your organization. Examine and evaluate all facets of the organization's practices related to recruitment and selection, professional development, evaluation, and enhancing teamwork. In what ways are these practices welcoming to people from diverse backgrounds? In what ways do they promote the inclusion of a workforce that is diverse and representative of the larger community in which the organization is located? Develop a plan with specific tasks and strategies to improve the organization's management of diversity across population subgroups. Meet with your executive director and review your plan. Can you convince him or her to adopt it?

REFERENCES

Agars, M. D., & Kottke, J. L. (2004). Models and practice of diversity management: A historical review and presentation of a new integrated theory. In M. S. Stockdale & F. J. Crosby (Eds.), *The psychology and management of workplace diversity* (pp. 55–77). Malden, MA: Blackwell.

Bucher, R. D. (2000). *Diversity consciousness: Opening our minds to people, cultures, and opportunities*. Upper Saddle River, NJ: Prentice Hall.

Chambers, T., & Riccucci, N. (1997). Models of excellence in workplace diversity. In C. Ban & N. Riccucci (Eds.), *Public personnel management: Current concerns, future challenges* (pp. 73–90). New York: Longman.

Chrobot-Mason, D., & Ruderman, M. N. (2004). Leadership in a diverse workplace. In M. S. Stockdale & F. J. Crosby (Eds.), *The psychology and management of work-place diversity* (pp. 100–121). Malden, MA: Blackwell.

Cox, T. H. (2001). *Creating the multicultural organization: A strategy for capturing the power of diversity*. San Francisco: Jossey-Bass.

Delbecq, A., Van de Ven, A., & Gustafson, D. (1975). *Group techniques for program planning*. Glenview, IL: Scott-Foresman.

Fernandez, J. P. (1999). *Race, gender, and rhetoric*. New York: McGraw-Hill.

Hooyman, N., & Gonyea, J. (1995). *Feminist perspectives on family care*. Thousand Oaks, CA: Sage.

Hubbard, E. E. (2004). *The diversity scorecard: Evaluating the impact of diversity on organizational performance*. Burlington, MA: Elsevier.

Hyde, C. A. (2004). Multicultural development in human service agencies: Challenges and solutions. *Social Work, 49*, 7–17.

Ivancevich, J. M., & Gilbert, J. A. (2000). Diversity management: Time for a new approach. *Public Personnel Management, 29*, 75–92.

Jans, L., & Stoddard, S. (1999). *Chartbook on women and disability in the United States*. Washington, DC: U.S. Department of Education, National Institute of Disability and Rehabilitation Research.

Lee, R., & Skinner, J. (1999). Will aging baby boomers bust the federal budget? *Journal of Economic Perspectives, 13*, 117–140.

Mattis, M. (2001). Advancing women in business organizations. *Journal of Management Development, 20*, 371–388.

National Association of Social Workers. (2000). *Code of ethics*. Washington, DC: Author. Available online at http://www.socialworkers.org/pubs/code/code.asp

Powell, G. N. (1993). Promoting equal opportunity and valuing cultural diversity. In G. N. Powell (Ed.), *Women and men in management* (pp. 225–252). Thousand Oaks, CA: Sage.

Family and Medical Leave Act, Pub. L. 103–3, 1993.

Robinson, M. K. (2001). *Nonprofit boards that work: The end of one-size-fits-all governance*. New York: Wiley.

Rodriguez, R. (2003). *Brown: The last discovery of America*. New York: Penguin Books.

Thomas, D. A., & Ely, R. J. (1996). Making differences matter. *Harvard Business Review, 74*, 79–90.

Thomas, K. M., Mack, D. A., & Montagliani, M. (2004). The arguments against diversity: Are they valid? In M. S. Stockdale & F. J. Crosby (Eds.), *The psychology and management of workplace diversity* (pp. 31–52). Malden, MA: Blackwell.

Thomas, R. R. (1991). *Beyond race and gender: Unleashing the power of your total work force by managing diversity*. New York: AMACOM.

U.S. Bureau of the Census. (2000). *Projections of the resident population by age, Hispanic origin, and nativity: Middle series*. Washington, DC: Author.

U.S. General Accounting Office. (2003, May). *Recent state policy changes affecting the availability of assistance for low income families* (GAO/HEHS-03-588). Washington, DC: Author.

Williams, J. (2000). *Unbending gender*. New York: Oxford.

Designing and Sustaining Effective Organizational Teams

Darlyne Bailey and S. Kay Dunlap

The presence of teams in the workplace has a long history. However, as the type, amount, and complexity of the demands on America's human services establishment increase, organizational leaders are continuing to rediscover the productivity of effective teams.

Teams are being used in a wide range of activities, including researching new programs and services, developing clinical treatment plans for the improved care of patients, and redesigning the organizational environment. The literature supports this posture. Almost every new book on organizational effectiveness stresses the importance of teamwork. However, despite this recognition, a study by Dyer (1987) showed that few managers actually take the time to understand when and how to develop and sustain these teams. In interviews with 300 managers from various organizations, Dyer found that less than 25 percent had instituted programs to ensure the continued success of teams. Moreover, while all these managers were on teams themselves, only 10 to 15 percent had supervisors who had addressed this issue with them. Surprisingly enough, this trend continues today.

A lack of information may be the reason for this inattention. Despite the literature in this area, managers seem to still not realize that effective teams require at least these conditions:

1. An environmental context in which the organization's goals and resources support the team's needs,
2. Team members with the skills and areas of knowledge necessary to accomplish the task, and

3. A team leader who appreciates the dynamics of change throughout and can keep the focus on both the task and interpersonal processes.

While this chapter focuses on the creation and maintenance of teams whose members interact face-to-face, these three conditions also are true for "virtual teams" that use largely technology-supported communications to accomplish their tasks.

Thus, this chapter explores three issues:

1. The process of team development (how teams are formed and how they become functional);
2. Typical behaviors of team members during the course of the team's existence; and most importantly,
3. The requisite values, embodied in behaviors and skills that effective team leaders must learn and enact (why *wanting* a team to be productive is just not enough).

This chapter presents these issues through an analysis of one model for the development of teams and two case vignettes and concludes with suggestions for the further development of skills in working with teams. The words *team* and *group* are used interchangeably herein to describe a work unit that "has a particular process of working together, one in which members identify and fully use one another's resources and facilitate their mutual interdependence toward more effective problem solving and task accomplishment" (Hanson & Lubin, 1988, p. 77).

Organizations need leaders who understand the needs of human services organizations and their teams: leaders who can clearly assess their teams' abilities and reach out for help in attending to their limitations. The future of our human services organizations depends on the ability to design and sustain effective teams.

PAST, PRESENT, AND FUTURE OF ORGANIZATIONAL TEAMS

Recognition of the strength of people when they work together in organizations dates back to the 1800s. Several scholars have made notable contributions in this area during several eras.

Late 1800s and Early 1900s

German sociologist Max Weber preached the need for (and potential dangers of) authority and rationality in working with organized groups of people (see Weber, 1930). Le Bon (1903/1960) discovered the powerful effects of this collectivity on the individual group member. Frederick Taylor (1911/1978), the subject of the novel and film *Cheaper by the Dozen,* studied the process of efficiency and proposed that large systems are most efficient when their organizational members are scientifically managed. At about the same time, Mayo (1933) conducted his Hawthorne Western Electric Studies and noted the relationship between group identity and cohesion in informal groups and worker productivity. Concurrently, Sigmund Freud (1922) analyzed the effects of conflict in groups.

Mid-1900s

Kurt Lewin (1947), credited as the father of modern group dynamics, explored the phenomena of the formation and development of groups through laboratory and experience-based reaming. Psychologists Abraham Maslow (1965) and Carl Rogers (1970) wrote about the almost limitless quality of human potential when fundamental needs are met within a culture of positive self and other regard. Almost simultaneously, Katz and Kahn (1966), McClelland (1961), McGregor (1966), and Von Bertalanfy (1968), each working separately, generated a collective description. They viewed organizations as open systems composed of subsystems of people whose level of satisfaction with the tasks, coworkers, and authorities plays a major role in determining the productivity of organizations.

Late 1900s

Ouchi (1981) and Pascale and Athos (1981) have suggested that Americans have much to learn from studying alternative forms of management, such as those used in some of the highly successful Japanese organizations. One example is the quality circle, a method in which a team of employees actively participates in the resolution of the organization's problems. Although the quality circle, as a variant of team building, continues to receive mixed reviews among American workers, an article in *Business Week* ("The Payoff From Teamwork," 1989) helped bring the role of work groups up-to-date.

In some companies, the problem-solving nature of quality circles first evolved into what were called special-purpose or project management teams that focused on specific tasks through the collaboration of staff and management. Then, in the mid to late 1980s, teams of employees began producing entire products instead of parts of products (e.g., a whole car instead of just the doors). Called *self-managing teams,* they also have assumed responsibility for some management-level decisions. While studies continue to explore the dynamics of self-managing teams (e.g., their cost and benefits and the role of external leadership), the literature described this form of organizational work group as the wave of the future (Courtright, Fairhurst, & Rogers, 1989; Manz & Sims, 1987).

Early 2000s

Management essayist Charles Handy (2000; now a self-described social philosopher) viewed teams as more self-than-other organized "collections of individuals" who share not only a common purpose but, more importantly, a camaraderie that manifests itself in each member's sense of loyalty to the team itself (p. 101). It is this clarity of commitment that Handy used to differentiate teams from committees, defining the latter as "collections of representatives" who work to find a compromised resolution to their charge (pp. 101–102).

While evaluations of teamwork can vary widely in terms of focus, degrees of complexity, and methodology (Gant, 2004), this view of the team as an interdependent entity unto itself that collaborates with others in the organization also is frequently evident in determining a team's success. Hackman (2002), for example, suggested that, in addition to offering a deliverable (service or product) that is "acceptable to clients," the other two criteria that should be used to measure a team's effectiveness are "growth in [the team's] capability" and a group experience that is "meaningful and satisfying" for its members (pp. 23–33). Inherent to these criteria is a high level of trust and fair play both within the team in terms of its internal actions and between the team and its interactions with the rest of the organization through policies and systems of reward and compensation that are consistent and fair (Frost, 2003; Lencioni, 2002).

In short, as historians readily tell us, the future carries the thumbprints of the past. The first need for order within groups of people was recognized in the 1800s. The scientific management of people (often referred to as "Taylorism") was proposed in the early 1900s, only to be ameliorated by the role of social support and the need for managing conflict. The mid-1900s brought recognition of the dynamics of the evolution of groups and of how groups are most effective in raising organizational productivity when the members' individual and social needs are met. In the late 1900s, organizations worldwide in the for-profit and nonprofit sectors alike began experimenting with innovative designs for organizational teams.

Now in the early 2000s and into the near future, effective task-oriented teams are best understood as collections of people who are held together by a common purpose, a sense of loyalty and accountability to themselves, a culture of trust and confidence that attends to results but does not require certainty of consensus, a concomitant agenda for a positive experience for all its members, and a clear understanding of measures of success. The degree of effectiveness in today's teams must therefore include not only the perceptions of the "client" (internal or external to the surrounding organization) but also the resultant level of satisfaction of each of the members.

The next section covers the general activities and requisite skills inherent in successful teams. It presents many of the aforementioned values and ideologies of some of the major contributors to the current understanding of organizational teams.

TEAMS: STAGES, BEHAVIORS, AND SKILLS OF LEADERS

Given the long-standing and robust history of organizational teams, it is not surprising that many models can be used to describe their evolution. Regardless of the differences in specific responsibilities, size, and the length of duration, once formed, all these groups seem to go through similar stages.

Small-group theorists tend to see these models as developmental, with the successful movement through one stage dependent on the satisfactory completion of the stage or stages that preceded it (see, e.g., Bennis & Shepard, 1956; Dunphy, 1974; Moosbruker, 1988; Neilsen, 1972). These models may have anywhere from three to seven stages, but one five-stage model is comprehensive, descriptive, easily remembered and, therefore, continues to be widely used. The Tuckman and Jensen (1977) model includes the stages of forming, storming, norming, performing, and adjourning.

In the preceding review of the literature on organizational teams, the conception of the "person-in-charge" evolved from the command-and-control manager, through the socioemotional leader (or leadership, as a function that rotated among team members in relation to different members' skills), to leaders who, in the words of Mosskanter (2004), "espouse the standards, values, and visions; exemplifying the power of serving as a role model; [and] establish processes, routines, and structures" for the team (pp. 326–327).

Over the past two centuries, the focus of the team leader has moved from one's self (style and needs) to attending to others (styles and needs) to today's dynamic interrelationship among self-and-others (styles and needs). Knowing all of this, it is now more than ever necessary to augment the Tuckman and Jensen (1977) model to include the role of the leader. What has been constant now must be more explicit—the need for the leader to be an agent of change, fully appreciating the difference yet interdependence between change and transitions (Bridges, 2003). Therefore, this chapter expands the Tuckman and Jensen model by describing the developmental challenges and skills of the leaders of organizational teams that are necessary to facilitate the team's successful movement through the stages.

Table 9.1 shows the developmental stages, general types of behaviors that team members exhibit at each of these stages, corresponding tasks for the team leader, and behavioral skills that are necessary for the leader to help the team

TABLE 9.1
TEAM DEVELOPMENT: STAGES, BEHAVIORS, TASKS, AND SKILLS

Stages	Members' Behaviors	Leaders' Tasks	Leaders' Skills
1. *Forming*: People volunteer or are recruited to work together on a common task.	Questioning the leader about the group's purpose, appropriate behaviors of members, and leader's role Attributing in-team status to members on the basis of outside-of-team information Obeying the leader Discussion patterns are jerky and there are long periods of silence	Provide structure regarding boundaries of the team (e.g., frequency and place of meetings, the organization's reason for forming the team, timelines for achieving the team's task) Offer guidance in setting directions for the accomplishment of the task Solicit each member's opinions and ideas Encourage dialogue	Awareness of a personal leadership style as a "change agent" Effective communication Thorough knowledge of the fit between the team's task and organizational goals
2. *Storming*: Individual and subgroup differences of opinions, values, skills, and interests start to surface.	Expressing opinions and disagreements Exploring the degrees of individual power and challenging the leader's role and style Attending to and avoiding the team's task Emergence of cliques and bonds	Discuss the team's decision-making process Model appropriate awareness of self and others Provide the team with the resources necessary to accomplish the task Help the team establish procedures and norms for the resolution of conflict	Management of different values behaviors, and skills Awareness of personal strengths and limitations Use of process and content

Stage			
3. *Norming*: The team focuses on the need for order and guidelines for how to work together.	Stabilizing the team's purpose, authority relationships, individual levels, and types of participation Exhibiting in-group humor Emergence of informal leadership Establishing procedures for the resolution of conflict and the accomplishment of the task	Adhere to the team's established structure and procedures Ensure that the team's actions are in accordance with what the team *really* wants to do Infuse the team with enthusiasm and energy Reward individual and team efforts Acknowledge and reinforce the informal leadership Protect the team from outside interferences	Mentoring Management of agreement Balancing work with play Buffering the team from ongoing operations
4. *Performing*: The team delivers the completed task.	Producing results: alignment of members' energies and interests with the team's task	Vigilance: attend to the team's need for fine tuning its skills and attitudes Develop mechanisms for the continued monitoring of the team	Visioning Listening with the "third ear" Evaluation
5. *Adjourning*: The original need for the team no longer exists.	Assessing process and product Dissolving the team	Publicly acknowledge the team's accomplishments	Positive regard of self and others

Note. From B. W. Tuckman and M. A. C. Jensen, "Stages in Small Group Development Revisited," *Group and Organization Studies*, 2, 419–427. Copyright © 1977 by Sage Publications, Inc. Reprinted by permission of Sage Publications, Inc.

accomplish its goals in ways that are efficient in terms of time and resources and satisfying to the individuals and the group as a whole.

STAGES OF DEVELOPMENT

In the *forming* stage, people come together to work on a common task. Whether some of these people have previously worked together on a similar project or all have joined in the past to accomplish a different goal, the point remains that this is the first time that all these individuals are uniting to work on this task. Amid individuals' questions about what is expected of them, the purpose of the group, the role of the leader, and their attributions regarding each member's potential power in the group and real influence outside the group, the leader must provide general guidelines for the group and take steps to establish a group culture that fosters and rewards the free exchange of ideas and opinions.

To accomplish these tasks, at this stage the leader must have both a strong sense of self-awareness and an understanding of the interrelatedness of the team's task and the organization's goals. Moreover, the leader must be able to communicate this personal and professional information in a way that models candor and appropriate self-disclosure and acknowledges the value of the team to the effectiveness of the total organization. It is these skills that will help the group members begin to risk sharing their ideas, an activity that facilitates the group moving from forming into storming.

In the second stage, *storming*, as individual group members and small subgroups continue to share their different perspectives, other differences become more noticeable. Differences in values, types and levels of skills, and degrees of interest in and commitment to the group's task are only a few of the many areas that may become reasons for members to be attracted to or to seek distance from one another. As these differences emerge, members also begin to explore their own leadership abilities, often by challenging the role and style of the designated leader. At this time, the leader must continue to model self-awareness and help the group understand how some types and levels of conflict are productive by helping them to establish guidelines and procedures for resolving conflicts and making group-level decisions. While ensuring that the team has access to the concrete resources (e.g., time, space, materials) that are required to accomplish the task, the leader must now demonstrate additional skills to equip the team members with the necessary intellectual and emotional tools. The leader's ability to recognize and appreciate the sundry differences that arise in this group will serve as a guide for how the members can use these differences to make the team's time together more productive. The leader's knowledge of the difference between the group's *process* (the methods and procedures the group uses to achieve its goals) and its *content* (the activities and issues that a group discusses and

"We had a wonderful group established. Harmonious. Supportive. Even established our own goals and norms. Then our boss came back from her meeting, and we got task oriented very quickly."

enacts to achieve its goals) must be used to help the group work effectively in both areas. It is only when the group as a whole agrees on how it will disagree that it is able to move into the third stage of development.

In the stage of *norming,* the team must continue its work on establishing "codes of conduct" for how the members will interact. With the abatement of the tensions surrounding the issues of individual and subgroup identities and authority, informal leaders become apparent as the group rallies around the purpose of the team and determines exactly how it will complete the task. Amid a strong sense of group identity, the leader must continue to focus on content and process by helping the group adhere to its procedures; ensuring that the necessary resources are maintained; enthusiastically rewarding the efforts of individuals, subgroups, and the team as a whole; and supporting the members who assume leadership roles. Moreover, the leader must help the group build on its new process for disagreeing by teaching its members how to manage agreement—how to avoid the trap of agreeing just to agree that members often submit to at this stage to maintain the group's harmony. When the group learns how to balance work with play and agreement with disagreement, it is then able to accomplish the task and moves into the performing stage.

This fourth stage, *performing*, is really the payoff, when the team's energies and interests are focused on completing the task. The leader's role is now akin to offstage directing—attending to the fine tuning of the members' skills and feelings of being team players while assisting the team to develop skills to use in monitoring the execution of the task. Modeling skills of visioning (communicating a sense of what this team can be like when the task is completed); responding to the individuals' and team's felt yet often unspoken needs, desires, and fears; and joining the team in the collective evaluation of the finished product move the team to the final stage.

In this fifth stage, *adjourning*, members acknowledge and assess the total process and content of the team as they move toward dissolution. Concurrently, the leader informally and publicly recognizes the team's accomplishments as belonging to the *entire* team. The primary skill at this time is the leader's ability to have a positive regard for her or his role in this process and for the roles and responsibilities of the other members. The worth of the product is thus a symbol of a job well done by an effectively functioning team.

Although these team behaviors and the accompanying motivators and requisite skills of leaders are understandable, teams often get "stuck" in one or more of these stages. At these times, the leader's skills are best appreciated for their combined effect of facilitating the group's development. To understand these leadership skills better, consider some key moments in two very different teams— the first case study looks at the development of one social services agency's planning team. This group consists of members of the board of trustees and the staff. The second case study looks at a professional development project that consisted of administrators and staff from two school districts. The latter project actually enabled these districts to form a (albeit temporary) partnership best described as a consortium (Bailey & Koney, 2000). Although both case studies are recounts of actual events, in both settings all participants are fictitious. Additionally, it should be noted that for purposes of clarification, each stage in each vignette is discussed separately. In reality, the stages of the teams in each of the following move between and among all events.

CASE OF THE EAST SIDE YOUTH CENTER

Because of rapidly shrinking resources, particularly money and appropriately trained personnel, as well as the changing needs of the community and the demand for increased accountability from funding bodies, the East Side Youth Center (EYC) has decided to develop a three-year strategic plan. This process will enable EYC to revisit the agency's mission statement, staffing patterns, and programs and to forecast the changes that are needed in the structure or operations to help the agency become a multiservice family center.

At a recent monthly meeting, the board unanimously decided to hire a local consultant to outline the strategic planning process and help the organization move through it. Because of limited funds, the consultant agreed to meet with a planning team at the beginning and six months later and, if necessary, to meet periodically with the team leader to answer questions and suggest subsequent steps.

The executive director and members of the board selected a planning team of four board members and three staff members. The president of the board was quickly appointed the team leader for the same reason she had earlier been voted president: a sound background in leadership training, some of which she had obtained on her own and the rest of which her place of employment had provided.

Forming

At a half-day workshop for the team, the consultant described the major steps and issues of a good strategic plan. The team members asked many questions, and everyone left the meeting feeling comfortable and confident about the pending process. However, two weeks later, at the first real meeting, the members focused the discussion more on themselves than on the plan. They began to refer to their community and business status and to position themselves to influence the others.

The group also began to question the expertise of the team leader. Whenever the leader would try to refocus the conversation, the group fell silent. The leader then began to make fewer statements and ask more questions, such as "Given the fact that the team is to develop a plan to recommend to the board at the end of six months, how frequently do you want to meet?" And, "What ideas do each of you have about the process as a result of our workshop with the consultant?" The members slowly began to respond to the leader's questions, offering their ideas and deciding that the group would meet for three to four hours every other week.

In the next two meetings, the group began to explore the specifics of the task more actively, with the leader modeling skills of active listening, asking open-ended questions, and providing basic information about the mechanics of the planning process.

Storming

In the fourth meeting, the leader noticed that the members were talking to her less and arguing more among themselves. A week earlier, she had telephoned the consultant and had happily reported the team's progress. The consultant reminded her of the "calm before the storm" and urged her to remember her conflict mediation skills. So when the members began to quarrel about the superiority of one person's ideas over another's and to imply that the board members' and staff's intentions were different, the leader pointed out what they were doing. She noted the benefits of each subgroup's perspective and asked the entire team to decide the type of process they would use for appreciating and then using the differences they had identified earlier.

At first, the leader was accused of not being direct enough. Then she was told that she was too dictatorial. The leader maintained her position and noticed that the next three meetings were attended by only two board members and two staff members. She began to urge the group to talk about the content of planning, as well as the process they were using to work as a team.

Norming

In the eighth meeting, the members began to talk about wanting more guidelines for the team. A lively discussion ensued about requirements for attendance and procedures to use for resolving disagreements. The leader told the story of the "Abilene Paradox" (see Harvey, 1974), in which an entire group of people agreed to do something that actually was bad for the group and that no one really had wanted to do—a case of mismanaging agreement. Sprinkled throughout this otherwise serious conversation were quips and jokes about the leader and the team members. There was a general feeling of camaraderie and anticipation as the group reviewed its progress to date and articulated future steps.

During the next two meetings, the leader began to notice that one board member was taking a leadership role within the group by starting the meetings, soliciting comments, and then summarizing a seemingly disparate list of ideas. She began to support this man's behavior and met with him twice outside the group to get his ideas about how the group could finish the plan. Once, during a monthly meeting of the entire board, when a motion was made to expand the team's responsibilities, the man supported the leader in refusing this additional work. At the leader's suggestion, a prepresentation party was held for the team members at this man's house—a celebration of all the work that had been done and a rehearsal of the team's recommendations to the rest of the board.

Performing

Just before the team submitted its plan, it had its final meeting with the consultant to get another perspective on the recommendations. The leader encouraged the team to be strategically creative with its suggestions and then facilitated a discussion about its work as a team. All the members were animated about their work together over the past several months and felt as though each had played a significant role in the process. The consultant also was satisfied with the results and suggested that the team volunteer to monitor the effectiveness of the plan, pending its ratification by the rest of the board. The group agreed and immediately began to formulate a mechanism for the continued evaluation of both the implementation of the plan and the process of the team.

It is not surprising that when the team presented the three-year strategic plan for the agency, the board and the executive director were pleased. The discussion was animated, creative, and productive. The board voted to continue the team for another 6 months to oversee the plan and assess future steps, such as installing another monitoring team and rotating members through it. The meeting ended with the team leader publicly thanking her colleagues and distributing framed certificates of appreciation to each member of the team.

Adjourning

Even though the original team was going to stay intact, the new tasks and responsibilities were different. The leader encouraged the team to celebrate the ending of the initial work. She began this closing by sharing her perceptions of the team's progress, focusing on both the process and the product. All the members expressed their views and, while praising themselves and the leader, began to talk about the first steps to take in their new roles as monitors of the plan.

CASE OF THE MATHEMATICS PROFESSIONAL DEVELOPMENT COLLABORATIVE

The districts involved in the collaboration in this case are from two inner-ring suburbs in a large northeastern metropolitan area (herein referred to as Reichards and Pointer). The districts came together as a result of administrative leadership and private grant funding. Both districts shared common struggles in supporting teachers to implement new national mathematic standards with an eye toward increasing mathematics achievement scores in both districts. While there were some economic and sociopolitical differences between the two districts, both shared important realities: a dedicated teaching faculty and common professional development needs.

Forming

Two central office administrators met and discussed how collaboration would benefit each district. The two leaders discussed their respective attempts to implement the national math standards and to support teachers with in-service training. Both district leaders realized that while helpful, short-term workshops resulted in short-term change. In addition, their faculty members were complaining that "Every year there is something new we're expected to do" and that the traditional faculty development was not as productive as any of the stakeholders wished. Moreover, research informed them of the need for classroom-based change to affect long-term results.

As leaders continued their discussion and acknowledged the dedication of many of their teachers, they likened instructional change to learning a new sport: One sees a skill being modeled, he or she analyzes it with the help of an experienced other, analyzes it again on his or her own, receives specific feedback, practices, and returns for new lessons. Thus, the concept of a math "coach," working alongside teachers in the classroom, was born. With later funding from a private grant, the two leaders were ready for the next step—a staff development plan that acknowledged the contribution of dedicated teachers.

Storming

Recognizing the importance of teacher involvement for staff development was a critical understanding for each central administrative leader. As a result, classroom teachers with a strong interest in math education were chosen from both Reichards and Pointer. These representatives (later referred to as the "Design Team") took the initiative to communicate with their peers about math instruction needs. With teachers as the major force in the design and implementation of the collaboration, and with the use of the two district math coaches, everyone was enthusiastic about the potential new "design" in staff development.

As the initial enthusiasm became bogged down with time and resource constraints, as well as with instructional needs, barriers became evident. Both the members of the Design Team and the teacher participants focused on the differences between Reichards and Pointer and not their similarities. Members of each design team argued about time commitments, differences in physical resources, and central administrative leadership style differences. In addition there was some jockeying for power as members challenged the leadership styles of various individuals on the team.

As the central administrators observed this they realized that they needed to implement some "top-down" general guidelines about how to agree to disagree. However, they were careful to acknowledge the individual strengths of each member and of the importance of candor plus respect. They modeled active listening and risk-taking about concerns and moved the teachers in the direction of their commonalities.

Norming

As members of each district's Design Teams began to appreciate the specific needs of each district, the central administrators assumed a more from-a-distance support stance. Each group met and established their goals. The year's activities ranged from curriculum mapping to math-literature connections and sharing of ideas. As a result, when the Design Teams of Reichards and Pointer met together, communication channels opened up with a greater flow of sharing successful as well as challenging instructional strategies.

While the meetings were not disagreement free, greater trust was evident. The central administrators continued to concentrate on common content and processes. Additionally, they authentically praised the individual efforts of all participants. Sometimes this praise was verbal and at other times through written notes of appreciation for genuine effort and growth, always with the focus on what instructional change best benefited the students in each district. In time this spawned greater teacher-to-teacher and district-to-district sharing.

Performing

The Design Teams of both Reichards and Pointer continued to work closely with their respective math coaches. The central administrators began to include more Design Teams' decisions regarding the goals and format of future meetings. The district coaches met twice weekly during the latter part of the year to plan strategies that aligned with specific math "strands." The teachers who participated assumed greater responsibility for requesting specific support with strategies in particular strand areas in which they felt the most need. Together the teachers and coaches received some stipend reimbursed writing for demonstration lessons. This writing ranged from lessons on strategy implementation to assessment materials specific to grade levels.

During this time the central administrator leadership modeled skills of visioning, supported the Design Team and the coaches, and joined the teams in evaluating the finished products—the strategy lessons and assessment materials.

Adjourning

Both district's Design Teams and building teachers continued to work on specific instructional strategies aligned with the national mathematic strands. The teachers became more respectful of the expertise of the math coaches and in turn the math coaches became more sensitive to the multiple demands of the classroom teacher. Gradually the leadership of the Design Teams transferred to the building grade-level leaders in math curriculum. As a result, the teacher-to-teacher communication continued and building principals supported their efforts with common blocks of planning time.

The true results of this collaborative were felt five years after the project when the achievement results began to reflect increased achievement scores in both districts, a tangible indicator of long-term instructional change and staff development for the two school districts. Moreover, both districts continued to support a math coach position through district funds when grant funds were no longer available.

By the third year the Design Team representatives rotated with the continued support of the coaches and the central administrators. Their work together continues and remains animated and productive.

Both these case vignettes demonstrate the five stages of Tuckman and Jensen's (1977) model of team development. It is now important to note four facts: First, while a team progresses through these stages, it also may regress owing to a change in the membership, responsibilities, or the need to work through the issues presented at an earlier stage.

Second, a team's developmental stage may have nothing to do with its age. Depending on the roles and responsibilities of a team, its relationship to the rest of the organization, and the effectiveness of its leader, a team that has been working together for two years may be stuck in an early stage, such as storming. It is likely to stay at that stage unless it is helped, whereas a much newer team may rapidly progress through the various stages.

Third, although there are clear benefits to establishing work teams, there also are some costs, or what Schindler-Rainman (1988) called "negative aspects," to using teams. Some reasons to avoid forming a team include the incompatibility of the members' commitments, the lack of a sense of purpose and direction, a member who cannot work as part of the team, or the lack of organizational support. Thus, organizational managers must weigh the costs and benefits of forming work teams before they actually form the teams.

Fourth, as stated at the beginning of the two vignettes, the team does not usually move from one clearly differentiated stage to the next. As with all models, this one represents an ideal type. In reality, the stages tend to be less obvious, and a team may even remain between stages for a while.

The identification of the typical behaviors of members and the skills that the management needs the team leader to possess, as well as an analysis of Tuckman and Jensen's (1977) model, all help organizational managers become aware of the dynamics of work teams. This knowledge, combined with a clear sense of their own abilities and limitations, enables managers and leaders alike to help their teams become more productive for the organization and highly rewarding for their members.

CONCLUSION

This chapter covered the evolution of the concept of organizational teams, from part of Weber's (1930) work on authority relationships to its current usage as collections of people who share both a common purpose and a sense of camaraderie (Handy, 2000). A developmental model was used to study the stages of the processes of the team's formation, maintenance, and termination. Two vignettes provided specific examples of the relationship among these stages, the members' behaviors, the tasks of the leader, and the skills that the leader needs to accomplish his or her primary task—the facilitation of the team's development toward productivity.

Nonprofit managers should realize that the needs of teams change over time. Yet recognizing the team's stage of development at any point in time is only part of the challenge. It also is important that the organization at-large must remain ready and capable to provide the resources the team needs to effectively function. Another important message is that team leaders must be willing to share their own thoughts and feelings while recognizing and aligning their abilities with the needs of the group to help the team understand their group-level process. Finally, perhaps the most important message for the organization and the leader to remember is that the work of effective teams is always led by someone who has knowledge of, skills in, and values the processes of transition and change while staying committed to a positive experience for all through the team's evolution.

As organizational leaders and scholars, we know that the synergy that comes from effectively operating teams is limitless. Building teams is an ongoing process, one in which all members have critical roles.

SKILLS APPLICATION EXERCISES

Here are some suggestions for exercises that can be used for experiential learning opportunities:

- You are assigned to lead a work team that has been meeting for several months. After reading the organization's charge to the team, you call a meeting and discover that only a third of the members have come. They are the same third that usually comes, and they call themselves the "real workers" on the team. What do you do and say? Why?
- You are hired as a consultant to facilitate the merger of two small nonprofit organizations. As part of the premerger agreement, the management teams of both agencies have been asked to form the leadership of the new organization. How would you get these people to work as a team? What initial problems or issues would you expect to encounter?
- You are asked to write a chapter in a new book about the development of teams, highlighting the major principles and skills that managers need to learn. What do you write about and why?
- With a partner or small group, create a microcase study that reflects each of the five stages. Be prepared to share your "case" with course mates.
- From the case studies identify specific examples that align with the Tuckman and Jensen (1977) model.

REFERENCES

Bailey, D., & Koney, K. M. (2000). *Strategic alliances among health and human services organization: From affiliations to consolidations.* Thousand Oaks, CA: Sage.

Bennis, W. G., & Shepard, H. (1956). A theory of group development. *Human Relations, 9,* 415–437.

Bridges, W. (2003). *Managing transitions: Making the most of change.* Boston: Perseus Group.

Courtright, J. A., Fairhurst, G. T., & Rogers, E. L. (1989). Interaction patterns in organic and mechanistic systems. *Academy of Management Journal, 32,* 773–802.

Dunphy, D. C. (1974). *The primary group: A handbook for analysis and field research.* New York: Appleton-Century-Crofts.

Dyer, W. G. (1987). *Team building: Issues and alternatives* (2nd ed.). Cambridge, MA: Addison-Wesley.

Freud, S. (1922). *Group psychology and the analysis of the ego.* London: Hogarth Press.

Frost, P. J. (2003). *Toxic emotions at work: How compassionate managers handle pain and conflict.* Boston: Harvard Business School Press.

Gant, L. M. (2004). Evaluation of group work. In C. D. Gavin, L. M. Guttierrez, & M. J. Galinsky (Eds.), *Handbook of social work with groups* (pp. 461–475). New York: Guilford Press.

Hackman, J. R. (2002). *Leading teams: Setting the stage for great performances.* Boston: Harvard Business School Press.

Handy, C. (2000). *21 ideas for managers: Practical wisdom for managing your company and yourself.* San Francisco: Jossey-Bass.

Hanson, P. G., & Lubin, B. (1988). Team building as group development. In W. B. Reddy & K. Jamison (Eds.), *Team building: Blueprints for productivity and satisfaction* (pp. 76–87). Washington, DC: NTL Institute-University Associates.

Harvey, J. (1974, Summer). Managing agreement in organizations: The Abilene paradox. *Organizational Dynamics,* pp. 63–80.

Katz, D., & Kahn, R. L. (1966). *The social psychology of organizations.* New York: John Wiley & Sons.

Le Bon, G. (1960). *The crowd.* New York: Viking. (Original work published 1903)

Lencioni, P. (2002). *The five dysfunctions of a team.* San Francisco: Jossey-Bass.

Lewin, K. (1947). Frontiers in group dynamics: Concept method and reality in social equilibria and social change. *Human Relations, 1,* 41.

Manz, C. C., & Sims, H. P., Jr. (1987). Leading workers to lead themselves: The external leadership of self-managing work teams. *Administrative Science Quarterly, 32,* 106–129.

Maslow, A. H. (1965). *Eupsychian management: A journal.* Homewood, IL: Irwin-Dorsey.

Mayo, E. (1933). *The human problems of an industrial civilization.* New York: Macmillan.

McClelland, D. C. (1961). *The achieving society.* New York: Van Nostrand Reinhold.

McGregor, D. (1966). *Leadership and motivation.* Cambridge, MA: MIT Press.

Moosbruker, J. (1988). Developing a productivity team: Making groups in work. In W. B. Reddy & K. Jamison (Eds.), *Team building: Blueprints for productivity and satisfaction* (pp. 88–97). Washington, DC: NTL Institute-University Associates.

Mosskanter, R. (2004). *Confidence: How winning streaks and losing streaks begin and end*. New York: Crown Business.

Neilsen, E. H. (1972). Understanding and managing intergroup conflict. In T. W. Lorsch & P. R. Lawrence (Eds.), *Managing group and intergroup relations* (pp. 329–343). Homewood, IL: Irwin-Dorsey.

Ouchi, W. G. (1981). *Theory Z: How American business can meet the Japanese challenge*. Cambridge, MA: Addison-Wesley.

Pascale, T., & Athos, A. G. (1981). *The art of Japanese management: Applications for American executives*. New York: Wagner Books.

Rogers, C. (1970). *Carl Rogers on encounter groups*. New York: Harper & Row.

Schindler-Rainman, E. (1988). Team building in voluntary organizations. In W. B. Reddy & K. Jamison (Eds.), *Team building: Blueprints for productivity and satisfaction* (pp. 119–123). Washington, DC: NTL Institute-University Associates.

Taylor, F. (1978). The principles of scientific management. In J. Shafritz & P. Whitbeck (Eds.), *Classics of organizational theory* (pp. 12–19). Oak Park, IL: Moore. (Original work published 1911)

Tuckman, B. W., & Jensen, M. A. C. (1977). Stages in small group development revisited. *Group and Organization Studies, 2,* 419–427.

Von Bertalanfy, L. (1968). *General systems theory*. New York: George Brazillier.

Weber, M. (1930). *The Protestant ethic and the spirit of capitalism* (T. Parsons, trans.). New York: Charles Scribner's Sons.

Producing High-Quality Group Decisions

John E. Tropman

Nonprofit managers have many tasks. Managing, improving, and transforming their organizations is a constant challenge. Accomplishing these tasks means working with groups to achieve high-quality decisions.

The first executive tasks involve *managing* the organization. Many of these concern issues of human resources, budgets and capital resources, and the general work involved in keeping the organization running. So the very first task of nonprofit managers is to keep the organization in the "on" position to deliver a product that produces outcomes that help clients and consumers to achieve positive change.

The second task is to *develop a high-performance organization,* which is different from actually running the organization. In this case, the manager is challenged not only to do the job, but to do it faster, better, and cheaper. Achieving these goals involves innovation (doing things we already do in new ways) and invention (doing things we have not done before.)

The third task is to *transform* the organization. Nonprofit organizations need to be periodically reinvented, and it is the mandate of managers to initiate and lead those efforts. In today's financially strapped environment margin can replace mission. This process—sometimes called "mission creep," occurs when the organization slips off its mission and follows the funding. That said, the mission needs to be periodically refurbished and refinished to remain current.

Success in each of these task bundles requires decisions. Executives manage the many elements of these decision process. This chapter focuses on a package of crucial elements in that process, providing both analysis of the decision process and suggestions about how executives can improve their work in this area.

IMPORTANT CONCEPTS IN THE DECISION PROCESS

As managers think about decision making in the organization, it is important to reemphasize decision verities and introduce some new decision concepts (Tropman, 2003). This chapter, then, examines problems in decision making and concludes with some ways to address them.

Choosing Often Means Losing

Decision making usually means "the painful necessity of choice." This observation is surely a well-known decision truth but one that people often forget because of the very pain of choice, and because it is hard for winners and losers to work together after choice is made. One cannot avoid choosing, as the office motto "not to decide is to decide" reminds regularly. Choosing often means losing—someone wins and someone loses. There are ways to maximize the gain of multiple stakeholders and interests; however, there will still be losses. Some sets of values will be maximized, others minimized. Creative decision management is the management of competing values and interests in which "losses" move into the less acceptable or unacceptable range and feelings and emotions run high. There are always at least two points of view, interests, ideas, or perspectives that must be blended, prioritized, selected, and organized as managers go about their decision-making work. Often, there are several perspectives about which people feel strongly.

Decision Quality

Decisions are a product of a decision-building process. As such they can be considered in terms of excellent, good, satisfactory, poor, and awful. Many people do not think of decisions as being qualitatively ranked from awful to excellent, like a restaurant meal, but that is an important perspective to adopt. A high-quality decision does not mean "I win," however satisfying that might be. Generally, an *excellent* decision is an "all-win" decision in which all stakeholders gain, although not necessarily equally; a *good* decision is one in which many stakeholders win, although there are a minority of those who do not; a *satisfactory* decision is one in which the specific winners and losers shift around, but there is no net gain or loss; a *poor* decision is one in which some win big, but a majority lose. Finally, an *awful* decision is one in which every stakeholder is worse off after the decision is made.

Conflicting Values

One element of decision making that creates continuous issues is the problem of conflicting values. If one considers that a *value* is an idea to which commitment is attached, then "losing" becomes "wrong" very easily. Managing conflicting values becomes a key task of nonprofit executives.

Decision Rules

One package of conflicting values is the set of rules (or norms) that groups use to legitimize decisions, called *decision rules*. There are no **neutral** decision rules; any rule (e.g., one person, one vote) conflicts with one or more others (honoring deeply felt preferences of minority groups who could never win a vote) in a typical decision situation. Group members often become committed to the rightness of one or another decision rule. (One person, one vote is "best," for example, and "right.") Finding solutions (decision candidates) that "fit" or address several rules is a vital task of nonprofit executives.

Decision Culture

Decision culture is a situation in which one package of decision rules, meeting rules, and preference schedules attain a privileged status and are routinely, almost automatically, used.

Decision Building/Constructing versus Decision Making

Decision-making is a popular phrase in common parlance. But are decisions really "made"? A better, more effective and accurate description of decision work might be decision "constructing." Language like *decision constructing* or *decision building* conveys the step-by-step process of decision work that is obscured in the phrase *decision making*. It is truer to say that decisions are built—piece by piece, element by element—very much like a menu for Sunday dinner might be "built." One thinks about the main course, then one thinks about the vegetables, the starch, and the dessert, and these components are assembled piece by piece. And then, once the entire range of possibilities is in place, the chef looks at the overall fit and sees whether or not everything harmonizes with everything else, and some adjustments might be made at that point. We might call that *decision sculpting*. *Decision management* is my name for the skill set of helping a group through a decision-building process.

The Decision Mosaic: Some Assembly Required

The word *decision* is really a collective noun. The concept of a decision mosaic invites thinking of a "decision" as made of many smaller parts called *elements*. These are assembled together to make the whole picture, often called "a decision."

Decision Management

Decision management is the competent operation of a mindful and intelligent process of decision production. Competence involves *knowledge* of the decision process and skill in its application. Knowledge involves understanding the steps in the *decision process (need/problem specification, alternative/option develop-ment, appropriate consideration of gains and losses for the options,* and *selec-tion).* Skill in decision management involves helping the *decision community* (decision builders plus stakeholders) move through the decision process in a timely and productive manner.

Decision Manager

A decision manager is the person who designs and "operates" the decision pro-cess and guides decisions through it. It is one of the important roles of the non-profit executive. One might also use the phrase "decision guide."

High-Quality Meetings

Decision production usually involves a series of meetings in which various stake-holders are gathered. These meetings need to be effectively and efficiently struc-tured so that the chances of securing a high-quality decision are enhanced.

Meeting Rules

Meeting rules are norms that collectively create effective and efficient meetings. They are the best practices that, if followed, create the greatest chance of success.

Solo versus Ensemble Process

In the decision-building approach, it is more usual that many parties are involved and very frequently there are meetings, conferences, and discussions during which the decision construction occurs and through which decision building occurs. Hence, nonprofit managers must manage competing values in the decision-making process itself because by implication, construction occurs over time rather than at a single moment in time.

ISSUES IN THE DECISION PROCESS: CONFLICTING DECISION CULTURES

Conflicting values and their resultant cultures have an important place in thinking about the job of the nonprofit manager. A theory of competing values (Tropman, 1989) that emphasized the diversity of values that everyone entertains addressed the importance of understanding that competing values are not either–or types of situations but rather are both–and types of situations. For example, one was committed not to *either* equality *or* to achievement, but rather one was committed to *both* equality *and* achievement in some mix, the proportions of which may change over time and space.

When packaged or bundled, competing or conflicting values become conflicting cultures. In thinking about decision making and the skills required in it, it often is helpful to think about organizations as being characterized by differing and competing subcultures. In the management area, Quinn (1988) perhaps has been the most articulate spokesperson on competing values. He has identified four cultures based on differing positions an organization might assume on the dimensions of flexibility and control (Figure 10.1). Each organizational subculture has dominant skills and a dominant basis around which decisions are informed and built. These are (1) consensus, (2) information and data, (3) results, and (4) influence. As decision making progresses, certain organizational styles—decision cultures—emerge and become typical.

Each quadrant has its own cultural archetype or cultural name. In the upper left is the *clan* subculture, low on flexibility and formal control. It is a culture driven by membership, and the main reward is acceptance into membership. Key skills are facilitating and mentoring. Decisions are built around consensus.

In the lower left is the *hierarchy* subculture, low on flexibility and high on formal control. It is driven by adherence to rules and structure, and the reward is promotion. Important skills are coordinating and monitoring. Decisions are built around data.

In the lower right, the *market* subculture is juxtaposed to the clan subculture. High on flexibility and control, this subculture pays almost no attention to membership (e.g., how long one has been with an organization, who one is, who one's parents are) and stresses results almost entirely. Control comes through results only. Someone who produces is in; someone who does not is out. In the market culture, the question is, "What have you done for me lately?" Whereas the clan subculture is more like a country club or sorority, the market subculture is more like an investment bank—no one cares how nice his or her investment

---

FIGURE 10.1
FOUR ARCHETYPICAL AGENCY CULTURES AND AGENCY PROPERTIES
IN RELATIONSHIP TO LEVEL OF CONTROL AND AMOUNT OF FLEXIBILITY

Level of Organizational Control	Amount of Flexibility	
	LOW	**HIGH**
LOW	**Clan**	**Adhocracy**
	Skills: Facilitating, mentoring	*Skills:* Innovating, brokering
	Decision method: Consensual, decision building[1]	*Decision method:* Political
		Decision bases: Influence
	Decision bases: Consensus	
HIGH	**Hierarchy**	**Market**
	Skills: Coordinating. monitoring	*Skills:* Producing, directing
	Decision method: Empirical decision building	*Decision method:* Results, decision building
	Decision bases: Data and information, position in the agency	*Decision bases:* Probability of results

Note. Adapted from Quinn, Rohrbaugh, and McGrath (1985). See also Robert Quinn, *Beyond rational management,* San Francisco: Jossey-Bass, 1989.
[1]In the original, Quinn had "decision making," which I have changed to "decision building" to reflect the emphasis here.

banker is, we just want results. Core skills are producing and directing. Decisions are built around results.

Finally, in the upper right, there is the adhocracy as opposed to bureaucracy. Adhocracy is high on flexibility and low on control. Whereas bureaucracy is focused on rules and structure and the "routinization" of events, adhocracy is like a pick-up baseball game or a jazz band. Whoever is around may do what needs to be done. There is an exciting openness, fluidity, and porosity to the adhocratic sub-culture, but it also can be chaotic and undirectional. Central skills are innovating and brokering. Decisions are built around influence.

These organizational and decision cultures are, in some sense, all present in all organizations. Everyone needs some consensus, some results-based work, some political activity and the uses of influence, and some work based on data and information. The problem for executives as decision managers is to balance the competing demands and styles over the course of the day, week, and year. Different issues arguably would require a different mix—or perhaps a different sequence of skills bases and methods. In decision management and decision building, one important job of the executive is to assemble the right package of conflicting values and bases for the appropriate situation. But, of course, they clash each with the other, so the executive is continually managing them—like prickly guests at a dinner party—so that their benefits can be enjoyed and their contentions minimized.

ISSUES IN THE DECISION PROCESS: SUBCULTURE SOLIDIFICATION— WHEN STRENGTHS BECOME PROBLEMATIC

Each decision subculture has great strengths. One problem—the one just discussed—is its clash with another decision subculture. However that is not the only potential problem. Difficulties arise when any one subculture becomes too overweening. These are well illustrated by Quinn, Rohrbaugh, and McGrath (1985) in their perspective chart (see Figure 12.2; 1985). Quinn et al. wrote of the decision-making perspectives of each subculture. I have adapted their perspective slightly here.

Employees will frequently want one or the other perspectives to obtain. Indeed, conflict with those in the agency wanting other emphases and foci is common. The role of executives here is to encourage and support *all* decision approaches, as appropriate, and also to manage the conflict that will inevitably result.

The clan subculture uses a consensual perspective. Participation in and commitment to decisions is high. All members of the organization characterized by this subculture would typically be involved and would participate. Members of this subculture feel that if one participated in the process, he or she must and will support the resulting outcome. But too much participation leads to a poky and sometimes stalled decision process. Attending to and caring about membership involvement is of course important; overattention to member wishes means that one member with a different view can hold up the whole process. Nonprofit organizations are heavily represented in the clan quadrant, and delay in decision making is a common problem.

The strength of the hierarchy subculture is twofold. One strength is in its empirical perspective—doing it by the numbers. The other is in its rules and position-based processes. Decision makers here use database processes and explicit decision accountability. Knowing where the buck stops is a hallmark of a hierarchical subculture's decision-making process. And it is important to touch base with each of the relevant positions and follow all the appropriate rules. But going by the numbers alone can lead to a decline in effective participation and empowerment. As numbers go up, people frequently go down. Database processes are fine, but qualitative perspectives also are important. Then, too, rules are fine, but usually formed on past experience and not always relevant to current situations. Positional involvement is fine as well, but sometimes the person in a particular position at a particular time does not have the expertise or the perspective needed for the job.

In the market subculture, goal attainment and efficiency—results, results, and more results, and fast—become crucial. Decisions are made quickly and rationally, usually by those closest to the possible result rather than by the "right" official or all of the members. Premature decisions are often characteristic of the market culture. Short-run, immediate perspectives are dominant, and a longer-run perspective is driven out by the need for "more for me, sooner."

In the adhocracy subculture, adaptable and stakeholder buy-in elements are strong. Who makes decisions often depends on who is around to do it. But the decision making is less focused on the decision maker than on the decision supporters. In thinking politically, the decision maker is more often the decision packager, seeking views from others and putting them into an acceptable package. Hence, who makes the decision is less important than the success of the decision. Of course, getting everyone on board is important. But adhocracies can let leadership shift from the decision-making core to the periphery and suggest only what will pass, as opposed to what is right.

Cultural solidification is the problem of overemphasis on one particular decision subculture. Organizations may have a default style, but if executives manage in a way that uses a diversity of decision subcultures and manages the

FIGURE 10.2
FOUR ARCHETYPICAL AGENCY CULTURES AND AGENCY DECISION STYLES IN RELATIONSHIP TO LEVEL OF CONTROL AND AMOUNT OF FLEXIBILITY

Level of Organizational Control	Amount of Flexibility	
	LOW	HIGH
LOW	Clan	Adhocracy
	Consensual perspective	Political perspective
	Supportability of decision	Legitimacy of decision
	Participatory process	Adaptable process (who is in the room?)
HIGH	Hierarchy	Market
	Outputs perspective	Outcomes perspective
	Accountability of decision	Efficiency of decision
	Empirical/data and rules/position-based process	Expertise/experience-based decision process

Note. Based on Quinn, Rohrbaugh, and McGrath, 1985.

resulting conflicts from that diversity, then the organization can remain reasonably healthy.

The problem is that too few executives recognize the need for decision subcultural diversity, and the organization tends, rather, to follow the rule of "the more, the more." This rule means that the more one uses one particular style, the more he or she is likely to use it. That is why management is "work." The chief executive needs to be the "outrigger" on the decision canoe—balancing with his or her weight the preferred approaches. Hence, if an organization is tending toward clan styles, the executive needs to ask about results; if the agency emphasizes numbers and rules, the executive needs to introduce adhocratic considerations. The executive, in short, often acts as a counterweight. If the executive supports conventional decision cultures too much or too often, the organization enters culture lock—and uses that method exclusively. That is when the strength becomes fatal.

Executive overemphasis is one cause of cultural solidification. A second has to do with agency stress. Individuals tend, under stress, to "revert" or "default" to preferred comfortable ways of acting, even if they are inappropriate for the moment at hand. Agencies are the same. Hence, agency stress and pressure tends to "encourage" or "force" agencies to revert to preferred decision styles even if they are absolutely wrong.

ISSUES IN THE DECISION PROCESS: SUBCULTURE CULTURE LOCK—
WHEN STRENGTHS BECOME FATAL WEAKNESSES

One might think that solidification is a problem. It is. But the problems can get worse. That problem is "culture lock." Solidification still allows—or can allow—for a bit of decision diversity. Culture lock not only goes for exclusivity but, because the strengths are unchecked or balanced, they "morph" into problematic practices and become fatal flaws. The agency has moved into "the negative zone."

Quinn (1988) dealt with this idea of strengths and weaknesses in his concept of positive and negative zones (Figure 10.3). Every strength becomes a weakness if pushed too far. On the outer circle of the figure is familiar problems of group decision making. When the strengths of a subculture are pushed too far or overstressed, they pass the utility point and become overdone. Then problems occur.

In the clan subculture, extreme permissiveness and inappropriate participation become key, sprinkled with a good helping of unproductive discussion. In the hierarchy subculture, procedural sterility and trivial rigor become hallmarks (as in the saying, "You have erroneously initialed the attached memo; please erase your initials and initial your erasure"). Iron-bound tradition also is common in the hierarchy subculture ("It's the weekly meeting; we have it every week;

FIGURE 10.3
THE POSITIVE AND NEGATIVE ZONES

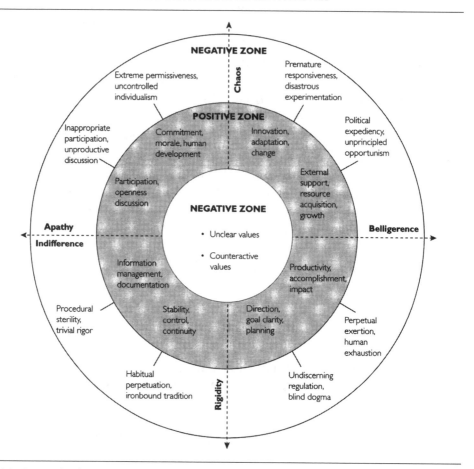

we always have"). In the market subculture, perpetual exertion and human exhaustion can become problems ("What results have you produced THIS morning?"). In the adhocratic subculture, premature responsiveness and unprincipled opportunism can become difficulties as well.

How might an executive actually approach "managing" these issues? The next section discusses three managerial foci that can provide help. One involves managing meetings, where decision opportunities occur in any culture. The second involves managing decision rules, which are the cultural norms that make decisions "okay." And the third is managing decision results—avoiding problematic results like groupthink and the Abilene Paradox.

The group context of decision making is key because one setting—meetings—is where much decision making happens, because groups are a key locus in which values are enacted and expressed, and the group decision contest is a place where executive success is seen and judged. It is the "playing field" of executive work.

The myth that it is lonely at the top suggests that chief executive officers (CEOs) and other managers work alone. Decision work is presented as a solo operation—an executive gets the information and retreats to her or his office to "make" the decision. A common observation is that "I didn't get any work done today; I spent my whole day in meetings." The perspective here is that decision building is an ensemble event, with many points and stops along the way. These stops are often called *meetings*.

That approach suggests that American culture assumes that "work" is not done in a collective setting. It suggests that the collective setting is something of a waste of time and that real work is done alone in one's office. That idea is not only erroneous but also pernicious, because it devalues the most common setting in which a decision construction goes on—the group context or group setting. It devalues work that might be undertaken to improve one's skill as a decision manager within the group context and it offers stereotypic and negative views of the group context. However, in most nonprofit organizations today, the group context is ubiquitous. We spend a lot of time in meetings. The degree of their formality varies, and they are run using whatever technology the individual in charge has picked up in his or her training. However, people's experiences with meetings is often—in fact almost regularly—negative. Jokes about meetings abound. For example, someone commented that a camel is a horse assembled in a staff meting. Someone else commented that a nonprofit board is a group that takes minutes to waste hours. Somehow, negative and hostile humor is an attempt on the part of the culture to either control or make understandable and comprehensible the ubiquity of meetings.

But meetings can be viewed as an organizational process, the output of which is a decision stream. What that means for the CEO is that, like other organizational processes (e.g., the budget process, capital improvement process, fundraising process), meetings must be managed carefully.

Finally, because of its ubiquity and its centrality in organizations, efforts in managing the group decision context—that is, the meeting—is one place in which management success can be most telling. The most successful CEOs and top-level managers have had the ability to manage group decision making at the board level, staff level, community level, and other levels where they sit with colleagues, superiors, subordinates, peers, and citizens and try to create policies that will be a positive force for their communities.

What, then, might be the antidote to some of these problems? A common meeting structure that allows the difficulties to be avoided and the strengths to be blended is part of the answer. A research project on the "meeting masters" suggests some things that nonprofit managers might do to manage competing values and eliminate the difficulties of moving to extremes in any one of these four cultural cases (Tropman, 2003). The meeting masters, whom I have interviewed and videotaped over the years, have meetings that are astonishing because they are so different from all of the other meetings that one might typically experience. They ran terrific meetings—terrific in this case meaning that high-quality decisions were made and the participants enjoyed themselves.

As one of the masters observed,

> Here is the deal. My groups give me their time and their effort; I give them accomplishment in the form of participation in high-quality decisions. Each of us needs to keep our end of the bargain.

What did these meeting masters do differently? First, they thought about the decision-making process differently. From their point of view, the decision-making process was something like an orchestra performance or a play. It required preparation and organization. As they met with their boards, staffs, citizen groups, and volunteer groups, those meetings were at the end of a process of preparation rather than at the beginning. They never said, "Let's get together and see if there's any reason for having gotten together." They always had some sense of what needed to be done, although they never had a sense of the exact output. Thus, the gatherings they orchestrated were never rubber stamps; instead, they were honest, open, participatory forums, organized within decent, reasonable time frames and with decent and reasonable alternatives available to the participants. Attendees were always alerted ahead of time to the topics and the hoped-for outcomes, whether it was a decision outcome or a brainstorming outcome, so they could prepare intellectually and conceptually before they came. One of the meeting masters told me,

> You know, there are only three things done at meetings. You announce things, you decide things, and you brainstorm about things. The way I organize my meetings is that I gather all of the announcements and put them at the beginning. Then I take the decision-making items and put them in the middle. And finally, when it comes to the brainstorming items, I put those at the end. It works out very well.

This way of organizing meetings can be called the "three-characters rule."

Because the meeting masters felt that the play or drama was an apt metaphor for a meeting, they put less emphasis on the personalities of the participants and more emphasis on the scripts that they did or did not have. The meeting masters, through the agenda and other preparatory processes, spent a good deal of energy on providing scripts for the individuals coming to the meeting. This allowed individuals to come prepared, participate authentically and fully achieve decisions, and have a good time.

The meeting masters followed several rules to enhance the ability of members to fully participate. Among the most important was the rule of halves, under which the masters simply asked the participants, whether it was a board, staff, or volunteer meeting, to hand in agenda items that they wanted considered at the next meeting at least halfway between the meeting dates. That meant that, for a typical staff meeting on Monday, the staff had to turn in items by the previous Tuesday or Wednesday. This gave the meeting master a chance to see what was afoot, organize the material sensibly, and get the necessary information and people set up to attend the meeting. Very little is worse than getting together with colleagues, board, or staff and having an issue come up for which one could have been prepared if he or she had known about it. No one likes to look foolish.

Another rule the meeting masters followed is the rule of sixths. This rule was described in the following way by one of the meeting masters:

> When I put my agenda together, I like to think of it this way. About a sixth of the material should be from the past. And if we have more than that, we're simply not moving quickly enough through the material that we have. About four-sixths of the material should be from the here-and-now; and about one-sixth—and this is the fun part, for my board—is from the future. Each meeting, we take time to look ahead and to speculate about what are the issues that are coming down the pike that might or will affect us. We share ideas and feelings, we brainstorm about them, then begin to prepare ourselves intellectually and, I might add, emotionally, for what's just ahead. This process means that my board is never surprised by issues. They've always had a chance to think them through. And I do the same thing with my staff, as well.

This manager used the rule of sixths to create a sense of anticipation, to get a feel for where her board and her staff were in terms of issues of the future.

Having talked with the board and staff, I also can share their reactions. One of the board members remarked,

> This is a great system. We always go through things in about the same way. We finish some leftover matters, usually rather quickly, get to matters at hand, and then wrap up our meeting with brainstorming, anticipating the future, and getting our ideas. I have a really deep sense of participation in this board, and it's more than I can say for the other boards I'm on, let me tell you.

The meeting masters also followed the rule of three-quarters. About three-quarters of the way between meetings, whatever the schedule was, they sent out a package including the agenda, the minutes, and any reports. Although many people do this for boards of directors, it is infrequently done for staff. But the same principle applies. Individuals need a chance to think about the material that is coming up. As one of the masters said,

> It's a little bit like playing a musical instrument. If I give you a piece of music and say, "Play this on the piano," we call that sight reading in music. And it has all the squeaks and grunts that a sight-reading rendition frequently has. And how much better we sound if we have a chance to practice a bit. Yet, in meetings, we routinely engage in sight-reading, except we don't recognize all those crazy little bits of participation as a result of the fact that individuals have just gotten the agenda and the materials, are struggling through it, are struggling to understand it, and struggling to make sense of it. It doesn't make any sense to me not to send stuff out a little bit ahead.

The meeting masters also followed the rule of the agenda bell outlined in Figure 10.4. The agenda bell is a system for organizing the agenda itself. It contains seven items. The first is the minutes for the previous meeting. If a group has minutes, they should be approved right away. If it is a board meeting and a quorum is not present, my experts said, "Approve them anyway and reapprove them later. It's important to begin on time, and you don't want to wait, punishing those who have shown up on time and rewarding those who, for whatever reason, can't seem to make it."

The second item represents announcements. These are short, factual, non-controversial statements of things that might be of interest. Announcements are

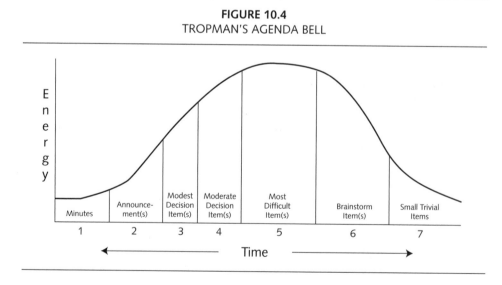

FIGURE 10.4
TROPMAN'S AGENDA BELL

not discussed except for a quick factual question, and they should not contain matters that people would logically wish to discuss.

The third, fourth, and fifth items on the agenda bell structure are items for decision. Here, the meeting masters did an interesting thing. They divided the items for decision (and they knew which items needed a decision because they had already gotten them under the rule of halves) into three categories—easy ones (for example, items 3a, 3b, 3c), moderately difficult ones (items 4a, 4b, 4c), and one really tough one (item 5). Here is a sample:

Item#	Item Content	Time	Notes
1	Minutes	2–2:05	
2	Announcements— New desks ordered	2:05–2:10	
3	Retreat Location— Key West seems best— ACTION	2:10–2:15	
4a	Vendor Selection— A new software vendor wishes to make a presentation ACTION	2:15–2:25	
4b	Medical Coverage Should we extend medical coverage to staff's gay or lesbian partners? ACTION	2:25–2:35	
5	Dress Code Should we retain casual Friday, go casual all week, or return to professional dress all week? ACTION	2:35–3:00	
6	Annual Community Appreciation Event Ideas for an exciting, different way to show our stakeholders that we appreciate their support BRAINSTORMING	3:00–3:38	
7	Adjournment	3:38–3:40	

The idea behind this structure is that the group begins by taking action on those items that are fairly easy to deal with but require formal approval. There is a transition into the somewhat more difficult items, and at about the halfway point of the meeting, the group tackles the toughest item. After that item has been dealt with, the group moves to item 6, a category containing the brainstorming items. Finally, an easy item, perhaps a thank you or even a motion for adjournment, is put in as item 7.

One of the meeting masters explained the rationale behind this structure in the following way:

> The way I set up my meetings is a little bit like the way I exercise. There's a get-go period, a heavy work period, and a decompression period. You know, decision making tears at the fabric of the group, so I try to finish up the big decision item about two-thirds of the way through the meeting. This means that we can spend the last part of the meeting working together—because, of course, in many instances, when you're making decisions there's conflict—on items for the future. It really works well.

It also turns out that the division of decision items into an easy group, a somewhat more difficult group, and the toughest group means that individuals are more likely to be buoyed by success on some easy items as they tackle harder items, and hopefully are buoyed by success on those when they tackle the toughest item. Thus, the agenda is shaped rather than handled in a random fashion.

These basic processes—getting information ahead of time; shaping and structuring the agenda, including items from the future; sending the agenda and attendant documents out ahead of time; and structuring the actual meeting according to the agenda bell principle—prove immensely helpful in managing conflicting values. Although people might have different perspectives, they will all be singing from the same music. Common structure, although it is not a total antidote to uncommon participants, serves a useful function. People with a clan orientation can have an adequate chance at appropriate participation, whereas people with a market orientation (all see that there is a structure that will probably lead to action). Thus, those two kinds of commitments are balanced. The agenda itself provides the kind of structure often preferred by those with a hierarchy orientation, whereas the rule of sixths and the brainstorming and speculative material at the end of the meting provides something that those with an autocracy orientation value and cherish. In this sense, then, a common structure is a tool for managing conflicting cultural orientations.

There also were some practices that the meeting masters avoided or changed from traditional practice. One of these was the no-new-business rule. Using the rationale of the rule of halves, participants were encouraged to present new business in agenda items they submitted before the meeting rather than at the meeting itself. As one of the meeting masters said,

> New business is the worst enemy that a meeting can have, in my opinion. People come in with half-thought-out concerns and worries, no one has had a chance to adequately prepare, and it tends to draw people away from the agenda at hand. We try to get people to think ahead about what they want to discuss at the meeting and let us know. Then we can have the information and people ready.

Another thing that the meeting masters eliminated was the traditional report. One of the masters described the no-more-reports rule:

> Many meetings are just oral newsletters. They go around the room, and people try to put the best face on whatever they're doing. It's a curious mixture of announcements, decisions, and discussions, and nobody knows really when to cut in or how. I've been able to get rid of all of that and have completely reorganized. Now, I ask people to "break up" what would have been their report into an announcement item—and then I put it in the announcements section, or a decision item—and then I put it in the decision section, or a brainstorming item—and then I put it in the brainstorming section. This means that we don't have a finance committee report anymore. If the finance chairperson has a simple announcement, as I said, it goes there. If there are items from the finance committee that we need to act on from a decision point of view, they go into the middle section. If the finance committee wants us to brainstorm around some issues, I put that at the end. It works very well.

Naturally, these techniques will not be the full answer to the problem of managing competing or conflicting values in a group decision-making setting. But they provide a different kind of answer. Typically, when people think about managing conflicting values, they tend to think about people getting together on the values themselves. The problem is that the structures or processes that we use for these kinds of settings often exacerbate their very differences, leading to worse fissures and cleavages than there were at the beginning. Providing a common structure and an indirect way of managing conflicting values appear to be successful (Figure 10.5).

PUTTING IN THE FIX: BUILDING HIGH-QUALITY DECISIONS THROUGH MANAGING CONFLICTING DECISION VALUES AND RULES

Decision rules are norms that make decisions legitimate. People bring them into decision-making settings—board meetings, staff meetings, volunteer meetings—

FIGURE 10.5
KEY MEETING RULES FROM THE MEETING MASTERS

Three-characters/Agenda bell	Announcement items first.
	Decision items second.
	    Easy decision items.
	    Then tougher decision items.
	    Then the toughest decision items.
	Brainstorming discussion items third.
	Organizes items according to what must happen with them

Rule of halves	Get upcoming items halfway between meeting times. Then one can organize them and get the information and people you need. **Gets people to think ahead**
Rule of sixths	About one-sixth of the items should be for brainstorming and discussion only and should relate to the future. **Reaches ahead far tough items and dealing with them proactively**
Rule of three-quarters	Send material out about three-quarters of the way between meetings so that people can read and think about it. **Invites people to prepare intellectually and psychologically before the meeting**
No-new-business rule	New business is sent in ahead of time so it can be structured into the ongoing flow of the meeting. **Creates the expectation of getting items in early and preparing for them rather than bringing them up at the last minute**
No-more-reports rule	Individuals who might have given reports now divide up that content into three parts that appear at the appropriate place under the rule of the agenda bell. **Reports are gone, replaced by individual items**

from their wider life. In effect, decision rules represent different cultural preferences about how decisions should be made. So managing decision rules is, in effect, managing conflicting cultures.

The most common decision rule is the *extensive* decision rule, which says basically that one person has one vote. Everyone has a say, and everyone's say is weighted equally. This rule is preferred by clan culture.

The second decision rule is the *intensive* decision rule—Who cares most? This view says that decisions are driven by intensity. It is a favorite of adhocracy culture because individuals within this culture get deeply and heavily involved in particular projects and tend to think of these projects as most important.

The third decision rule is the *involvement* rule. Who might have to carry out a particular decision? This rule gives preference to the implementers—the doers—and it is a favorite of the market culture. Market culture is, after all, a can-do culture, and its view is typically "let the person who has to do the job have the most say about it."

A fourth decision rule is the *expert* rule—what do the lawyers, doctors, and scientists have to say about this? Have they signed off? This rule is a favorite of the hierarchy culture, organized in lines and boxes as it tends to be. They have the right experts and officials sign off.

A fifth rule is the *power* rule, sometimes known as, "What does the boss think?" The power rule can reflect individual preferences on the one hand or reflect cultural preferences on the other. If the boss happens to be a clan-oriented person, then the extensive rule might get priority, and so on.

The key element to understand decision rules is that all five operate in almost all groups, and they conflict with each other. In this context, "conflict" means that the distribution of outcomes would be different if only one rule was followed, as opposed to a blending of all five. Two kinds of problem can arise.

The first problem is in the mixed-culture organization, in which all rules are simultaneously operating. This means that the CEO has to continually manage the situation to be sure that breadth, depth, involvement, expertise, and power all have their proper place. The proposals most likely to go forward and reach a decision point in a timely fashion are those that can meet and be shown to meet the interests of most of these decision rules. Formulating and expressing options that are linked to these rules is the process of decision crystallization.

For example, suppose a group is discussing where to have lunch. There is much talk, and among the issues coming up are what most people want to do (the extensive rule), what the vegetarians want to do (the intensive rule), who is going to drive (the involvement rule), whether they have harmful additives at the place everyone might be thinking of (the expert rule), and what would the boss say (the power rule). A meeting master in this discussion suggested that they go to the nearby Chinese restaurant because it would satisfy most of their

"The first meeting of the coalition 'Groups Organized to Conserve Humorous Acronyms (GOTCHA)' will now come to order."

preferences (the extensive rule addressed). It appealed to the vegetarian colleagues because it had vegetarian dishes (the intensive rule addressed). The meeting master said that she would drive (the involvement rule addressed) and that the restaurant did not put monosodium glutamate in their food (the expert rule addressed). Last, she stated that the boss did not care where they spent their lunch money (the power rule addressed).

This was an amazing occurrence, because the group understood that issues of concern to them in decision making, including breadth, depth, involvement, power, and expertise, were addressed. Everyone in the group agreed, and off they went. Although the issue was small, the performance was masterful. And the example is one that managers might wish to keep in mind in mixed cultures when there are conflicting bases people will accept as a reason for a decision being legitimate.

The second problem can occur when one culture is very dominant. In this type of organization (e.g., clan, market, hierarchy, adhocratic), one rule tends to be very dominant over all others. Hence, in the clan culture, the extensive decision rule might be given preference. This means that people who feel strongly—experts, people with power, and people who might have to carry out decisions—are not given the kind of weight that a high-quality decision truly deserves. In these instances, the manager wants to be sure that the other bases of decisions are articulated and brought into play. Obviously, agencies will have their preference for decision rules, but the exclusion of appropriate alternative bases will create a weaker, poorer-quality decision than might otherwise be expected.

For example, a task force from a clan-oriented organization was working on a proposal. In this group, experts were not well regarded, power was very well regarded, and involvement was not well regarded. Depth of preference was given short shrift. After a considerable amount of time, effort, and work, a proposal was voted on, to the great satisfaction of the task force, and proudly presented to upper management. The proposal was quickly rejected. The first mistake was that the task force had not considered the wishes of the boss. The second mistake was that it had not considered certain legalities. The third mistake was that the individuals who had to carry out the recommendation had serious questions about it. And the fourth mistake was that the people who felt deeply but differently about the proposal had not been consulted or involved. Hence, if the chairperson had articulated the alternative decision bases and pointed out that these perspectives needed to be included and addressed, there would have been a much better result.

PUTTING IN THE FIX: BUILDING HIGH-QUALITY DECISIONS THROUGH MANAGING CONFLICTING VALUES IN DECISION RESULTS

A good deal of thought has been given to documenting awful decisions or awful types of decisions. Perhaps the most famous kind of bad decision is the groupthink decision, a concept developed by Janis (1972). Cohesion of the group is very high and individual members of the group test hate to bring up contrary points of view because they do not want to put stress on the cohesion of the group and disturb the peace. Groupthink is typically a problem of the clan organization.

A second kind of decision problem is decision randomness, exemplified by what has been called a "garbage can model of organizational choice" (Cohen, March, & Olsen, 1972). For high-quality decisions, four types of people or perspectives are needed in the same room at the same time: (1) the problem knowers (individuals who know the problems the organization faces); (2) solution providers (creative individuals who can solve problems if they know what the problems are, but they often do not); (3) resource controllers (individuals who sign off on the allocation of money and people and therefore are crucial to implementation); and (4) "decision makers looking for work" (usually the top-level managers who have to bless a decision if it is to go forward). Cohen and colleagues argued that most organizations assemble these individuals at random, as if tossed into a garbage can. This randomness is a feature of the adhocratic culture. A few people get together and do this, then a few more get together and do that, then others get together and do yet a third thing, and there is a huge amount of rework and very little orchestration and organization.

A third decision problem is the "do-it, fix-it method," This phrase, which has become common, is associated with Wal-Mart's strategy for evolutionary growth. Collins and Porras share the following from a Wal-Mart executive: "We live by the motto 'Do It. Fix It. Try Something Else.'" (1994, p. 148), which is characteristic of a group that is so eager to act that it often takes premature action. This also could be called the "fire, ready, aim" group. Although groupthink becomes mired in process and the failure to surface authentic alternatives, the do-it, fix-it group grabs the first gold ring that seems reasonable, proceeds with it, and often winds up needing to repair, sometimes very quickly.

The last decision problem is "same as last year," a decision type characteristic of hierarchical cultures. Given the rigidities and often ponderous nature of hierarchies, making decisions that are new, different, risky, or odd is very difficult. This method seems to fit with the conservative mentality. After all, hierarchies are very good at doing something on a repeated basis over time and space. In a sense, this method continues that skill or competence into the decision-making area.

Each of these bad decisions occurs because of an overemphasis on the particular strengths of a particular culture and because those strengths get carried over into the decision-making process. For example, the adhocracy structure tends toward chaos, and so it has a tendency toward randomness in its decision-making process. The clan subculture, with its skills at involving participants and processing issues and concerns, may never reach a decision or it succumbs to groupthink.

The antidote to these problems is complex. First, the commonly used decision processes ensure that a certain amount of structure, openness, participation, and promptness will be simultaneously present. Thus, the potential perils of using only one cultural preference as the basis for decision making are reduced. Second, the management of decision rules goes a long way toward creating the balance culturally necessary for a high-quality decision. Third, one can do assessments of the decisions themselves. One way to assess decisions is to go back into the history of a particular group, such as a nonprofit's board. Look at the decisions the board made and ask these questions: Are these decisions good? Why or why not? A discussion about the quality of the decisions can be useful.

The announcement ahead of time that decisions will be evaluated in the future changes the nature of the process itself. People pay more attention when they know that they are going to be evaluated. If a man knows that he will be weighed at the end of the week by his physician, he will probably be careful, during that week at least, to exercise and watch his diet. Hence, what the physician sees when she looks at the man's weight is a modified weight, not a true weight. Similarly boards, staff groups, and volunteer groups working on a decision will be more careful and articulate and will participate with more authenticity if they know that they are going to be evaluated.

In addition, a no-fault discussion of why certain decisions were good and why certain decisions were not so good helps everyone understand their mission, task, and role as a group working together for the organization's good.

CONCLUSION

The management of group decision making or decision building is one of the most important tasks that nonprofit managers can undertake simply because so much of their time is spent in decision-making groups. Many CEOs and other top-level managers spend more than half of their time in meetings. Most of them express mild disbelief to vigorous dislike of this allocation of their time and consider this time largely wasted, ceremonial, useless, and not productive. One can only imagine what it would be like if the decision-making groups that everyone participates in so frequently were to become so productive and useful that people looked forward to attending. And yet, the meeting masters created such groups and sustained enthusiasm in them over considerable periods of time. Their peers, superiors, and subordinates turned to them to undertake difficult tasks and chair difficult task forces, and they almost always did an outstanding job. Their goal was to make high-quality decisions, and the tips and suggestions presented in this chapter will help nonprofit managers move in that direction.

SKILLS APPLICATION EXERCISES

- Thinking of the four quadrants, rank your organization according to the dominance of the clan, hierarchy, market, and adhocracy subcultures. Consider whether your organization has the decision-making problems discussed in this chapter. Feel free to add more problems, other problems, and different problems.
- Think specifically of the kinds of problematic decisions discussed in the chapter: group-think; garbage can or randomness; do-it, fix-it; and same as last year. Considering the past six months at your organization, count how many of these decisions your organization has been involved with. Think of one or two really awful decisions. Try to understand what went wrong, and think about some of the ways the material in this chapter (and other chapters) could help you fix it.
- Review Figure 10.5 and then make some plans for your own action at your organization to implement these rules.
- Observe a meeting at your organization (or somewhere else) and see if you can observe the decision rules in action (or more likely, in nonaction). Develop a plan to practice thinking up possible solutions that meet and can be shown to meet most of these rules. It will be a little bumpy at first, but you will be surprised at how quickly you become good at it.

REFERENCES

Cohen, M., March, J., & Olsen, J. (1972, March). A garbage can model of organizational choice. *Administrative Science Quarterly,* pp. 1–25.

Collins, J., & Porras, J. (1994). *Built to last.* New York: Harper Collins

Janis, I. (1972). *Victims of groupthink.* Boston: Houghton-Mifflin.

Quinn, R. E. (1988). *Beyond rational management: Mastering the paradoxes and competing demands of high performance.* San Francisco: Jossey-Bass.

Quinn, R. E., Rohrbaugh, J., & McGrath, M. R. (1985). Automated decision conferencing. *Personnel,* 62(11), 49–55.

Tropman, J. (1989). *American values and social welfare: Cultural contradictions in the welfare state.* Englewood Cliffs, NJ: Prentice Hall.

Tropman, J. E. (2003). *Making meetings work* (2nd ed.). San Francisco: Jossey-Bass.

11

Managing Volunteers Effectively

*Alice Korngold, Elizabeth Hosler Voudouris,
and Jeff Griffiths*

When a major earthquake and tsunami hit Asia and Africa in December 2004 and when a major earthquake struck Afghanistan, Pakistan, and India in 2005, volunteers came from all corners of the world to feed the hungry, find survivors, work in clinics, erect and repair homes, purify water, and perform multiple and arduous tasks needed to help rebuild lives and communities. Companies from far and wide organized workforces in addition to donating funds. Estimates place the level of America's private giving at more than $1 billion (USA Freedom Corps, 2005). Much of these efforts were coordinated by international as well as local nonprofit organizations, including the Red Cross, Oxfam America, Feed the Children, US Fund for UNICEF, and USA Freedom Corps. Similarly, when major hurricanes have struck the United States, the response of the American people has been significant.

From the 1600s when volunteers and generous donors formed universities, libraries, and museums, to September 11, 2001, when planes struck the twin towers of the World Trade Center and groups and individuals donated to the families of those killed and to the public safety organizations that responded to the emergency, America has demonstrated its strength in making the country and world a better place. The movement toward the country's independence from Great Britain was won through organized volunteer efforts: citizens made up the armies, supplied medical support, and drove public policy. The antislavery movement was powered and staffed by volunteers; the Underground Railroad represents one of the largest organized volunteer efforts in the country. During the period of industrialization and immigration, volunteers established movements to eradicate poverty, crime, vice, and civic disorder; this era marked the formation of organizations such as the Children's Aid Society and settlement houses. The women's suffrage movement was volunteer driven; volunteers who lectured, wrote, marched, lobbied, and practiced civil disobedience ultimately won the right for women to vote with the passage of the 19th amendment to the U.S. Constitution in 1920. Volunteers sent packages to soldiers during world wars I and II. Volunteers marched for civil rights in the 1950s and 1960s. Major national and world-wide events, including the Olympics and political conventions, are heavily dependent on and supported by volunteers.

Volunteer movements are powered by a passion to make things better. The needs today are as great as ever. The nation's nonprofit sector is battling severe financial constraints while facing growing demands to provide quality education to all children, job training and placement for those who are on welfare, health care services to those who are sick, prevention and wellness to improve people's lives and opportunities, and arts and cultural experiences for learning and inspiration.

The 21st century marks the emergence of even more institutionalized forms of volunteer activity. Today's volunteerism is inclusive of people of all ages from all walks of life. As communities face new challenges, now is the time to drive this infectious movement to new heights to improve lives throughout the world. Now is the opportunity for broad participation in furthering health and human services, arts and culture, education, environmental protection, and civic development.

Aside from addressing disasters of calamitous consequences, nonprofits and their volunteers provide vital daily services. To understand the magnitude and impact of charity and volunteerism, simply imagine cities without schools, hospitals, day care, museums, concerts, public parks, homes for senior citizens, and services for those with disabilities. In fact, in the United States, 44 percent of adults volunteer; that is 83.9 million adults who represent the equivalent of more than 9 million full-time employees at a value of $239 billion (Independent Sector, 2001). Every nonprofit organization has it in the power to establish a mini-movement by galvanizing volunteers to support its mission. This chapter shows how organizations can engage productive volunteers and channel their energies, with their hearts, to improve the lives of citizens of communities here and abroad.

VOLUNTEERS OF ALL AGES AND STAGES

Fueled by powerful institutions like the Points of Life Foundation and rapidly growing Internet volunteer-matching services, volunteering is a burgeoning industry that is capturing the hearts, minds, and hands of young and old; rich and poor; and urban, suburban, and rural. Following are a few examples.

Youth

The Millennials, young adults who graduated from high school around the year 2000, are touted as a uniquely volunteer-oriented generation. By the Millennial era, the notion of volunteering gave way to a more compulsory "service learning," which is now often required for graduation from middle or high school. Bolstered by acts of Congress in 1990 and 1993 that created the Learn and Serve America program, the integration of community service with academic study has spread to schools everywhere. From 1984 to 1999, the share of high schools offering any kind of community service program grew from 27 to 83 percent, and the share with "service learning" grew from 9 to 46 percent. Two-thirds of all public schools at all grade levels now have students engaged in community work, often as a part of the curriculum.

A new Millennial service ethic is emerging, built around notions of collegial (rather than individual) action, support for (rather than resistance against) civic institutions, and the tangible doing of good deeds (Howe & Strauss, 2000). According to Peter Gomes (2002), chaplain at Harvard University, the Millennials are unique in their interest in seeking what he calls "the good life," including service to the community:

> In this generation the search for goodness, both institutional and personal, has reappeared as a defining characteristic in young people's renewed search for the good life. . . . The fundamental question of the young . . . is, simply, "what will it take for me to make a good life, and not merely a good living?" (p. 23)

As Millennials move into the job market, employers are already seeing evidence of their interest in service and the community. Managing partners of many professional-services firms are establishing and expanding their volunteer programs to attract and retain the most highly qualified new graduates. Furthermore, many of these graduates have taken newly created college and graduate school courses in nonprofit governance and management with the intention of becoming involved in service to their communities. As the best-educated generation in this nation's history, and with the support of their employers, Millennials can become a powerful force in contributing their knowledge and passion to strengthening the nonprofit sector (Korngold, 2005, p. 23).

Several national organizations have been established in the past two decades to capture and engage this spirit of volunteerism among young adults. Here are a few examples:

- Americorps, created in 2003 by the Corporation for National and Community Service, has involved more than 250,000 people in helping communities advance education, public safety, health, disaster relief, and environment issues (see http://www.americorps.org/).
- City Year, founded in Boston in 1988, is an "action tank" to improve society through policy and action in service. City Year involves 17- to 24-year-olds in a full-time year of service in 14 communities nationwide (see http://cityyear.org/).
- Teach for America, formed in 1990, is a movement to eliminate education inequity. More than 12,000 individuals have joined, committing two years to teach in low-income rural and urban communities, affecting the lives of more than 1.75 million students (see http://teachforamerica.org).
- Net Impact is a network of more than 10,000 MBA students and professionals who perform pro bono services by providing business skills to help nonprofits with management issues (see http://net-impact.org/).

Senior Citizens

America's senior citizen population is growing, as is their presence in community service. Older people represent 21 percent of the nation's population; they number more than 57 million, of which 47 percent volunteer. Their contribution amounts to more than 4.8 billion hours a year. The Baby Boom generation is expected to inflate the number of senior citizens to 80 million; they are living longer and seeking ways to make a difference (Saxon-Harrold, McCormack, & Hume, 2000). Organizations that are engaging senior volunteers include the following:

- AARP, representing 35 million members, involves seniors in service through a variety of programs, such as driver safety, tax help, and the Senior Community Service Employment Program, as well as through AARP chapters, its Educators Community, and its Day of Service and Community Builders (See http://www.aarp.org).
- Volunteers of America, a national nonprofit that promotes health and independence for senior citizens, engages its members in service through their National Retiree Volunteer Coalition (see http://www.voa.org/tier3_cd.cfm?content_item_id=746&folder_id=421).
- National Senior Service Coalition sponsors Foster Grandparents, Senior Companions, and the Retired and Senior Volunteer Program, through which more than half a million Americans ages 55 and older serve their communities (see http://www.seniorcorps.org/about/index.html).

Corporations

Volunteerism is a powerful new phenomenon in the business sector, taking hold among employees and encouraged and celebrated by the chief executive officers (CEOs) of multinational corporations and small businesses alike. In today's competitive environment, businesses recognize that volunteerism offers many benefits to employees; to the company itself; and most of all, to the community. Businesses are understanding that volunteerism builds teamwork, morale, and loyalty to the company, not to mention visibility and good will in the community. Furthermore, companies realize that when communities are strong, business is strong; hence, corporate investments in education, health and human services, and the arts are in everyone's best interests (Korngold, 2005).

The prevalence of corporate volunteerism is documented by the Conference Board, the Points of Light Foundation, Boston College's Center for Corporate Citizenship, Harvard Business School, and others. Furthermore, companies are beginning to assess the benefits of their charity and service in strengthening communities. This is a clear sign that community service is gaining traction as a serious endeavor for businesses. Korngold and Voudouris noted the following in 1996:

> Although many companies accept the premise that volunteerism is good for business, it is important to establish mechanisms to document and measure the benefits to the company, employees, and the community. After all, in other corporate endeavors, top management expects consistent reporting from all departments in order to determine where resources should be allocated, which programs are effective, and which initiatives should be continued. Furthermore, a carefully documented evaluation of the program's impact provides information that is needed to enhance opportunities to serve corporate and community interest. Finally, a report of the program's impact reinforces volunteers, inspires others to join in the effort, increases the program's visibility, strengthens support for the program both internally an externally, and maximizes the public relations benefits to the company. (p. 24)

Korngold (2005) also noted that, although

> Nonprofits are not in a position to measure the benefits to businesses... it helps for nonprofits to understand the compulsion of companies to do so. [Furthermore,] outcome data can often serve as a lever to move businesses to invest even further in nonprofits. (pp. 45, 47)

Businesses are not only mobilizing employees to volunteer in the United States but also their employees at their plants and sites in countries throughout the world. Judith Binney, director of Global Volunteer Initiatives for Citigroup, has noted that

> Volunteerism is new to many cultures and, consequently, the movement takes hold at a variety of levels and paces. It is exciting to see that people who have never so much as considered hands-on service—such as building houses through Habitat for Humanity—brand-new volunteers experience such delight that they are prepared to participate again and again and to encourage others to do so as well. (personal communication, March 21, 2005)

Business volunteers are a resource of extraordinary potential given the size of multinational corporations and the millions of people that they employ throughout the world.

Communities

As interest in volunteerism races ahead, communities are organizing matchmaking services and larger scale days of service. United Way organizations, volunteer centers, and Hands On Network provide useful vehicles for citizens to learn about volunteer opportunities and participate. Online matching services such as volunteermatch.org and idealist.org provide nationwide access to information about nonprofit organizations and volunteer needs. Furthermore, foundations and corporations are investing in these volunteer-matching services to make it easier for people of all ages and from all backgrounds to participate.

BROAD SCOPE OF VOLUNTEERISM

Volunteering takes many forms, ranging from "done-in-a-day" activities—such as planting trees, fixing up shelters, repairing homes for senior citizens, and painting schools—to longer-term commitments, such as tutoring children or teaching adults who are illiterate how to read. Various types of volunteering are sometimes categorized as follows:

- *Episodic*—a one-time or occasional event, such as an organized day to plant trees and bulbs in public parks;
- *Recurring*—such as weekly tutoring children in after-school programs, teaching adults who are illiterate, or mentoring young people;
- *Family volunteering*—such as serving food in a homeless shelter on a holiday; and
- *Team volunteering*—such as building houses, or collecting and arranging cans and cartons of food for distribution to shelters.

Volunteering also ranges from direct service, "hands-on" activities such as those mentioned earlier, to fundraising, management assistance, and nonprofit board membership. These are described as follows:

- *Fundraising*—This activity is often organized through volunteer committees that reach out to prospective donors, sometimes through events such as luncheons and dinners honoring role models or major contributors.
- *Management assistance*—Individuals provide volunteer expertise in a variety of areas, such as finance, investments, law, real estate, public relations, marketing, strategic planning, human resources, and information technology.
- *Service on nonprofit boards of directors*—Each nonprofit is governed by a board of directors, whose primary role is to provide financial and strategic oversight; boards ensure that the mission is paramount and the organization has the resources to produce compelling outcomes that benefit the community.

THE VALUE TO NONPROFITS

Volunteers are a workforce that expands the capacity of nonprofits to address increasing demands for health and human services, education, arts and culture, and civic and economic development. Volunteers provide time, money, specialized technical expertise, business acumen, and leadership.

Volunteerism is a powerful means to promote better understanding among diverse groups of people. When a group of employees from the suburbs work hand-in-hand with families in rural areas or the inner-city to build homes for Habitat for Humanity, the volunteers engage in new communities. When Black Americans, White Americans, Latinos, and Asian Americans serve on nonprofit boards together, they provide diverse perspectives for the strategic vision of the organization while also reaching new constituents and supporters. When Americans venture to Sri Lanka to help victims of the tsunami, they learn a new culture and environment while spreading understanding and good will. Volunteerism brings people together; it makes the world a smaller and better place.

Volunteers are ambassadors spreading knowledge and passion for vital matters. As they become better educated about an issue—a disease and its impact, the relationship between education and economic development, or the alienation of young people in impoverished urban neighborhoods—volunteers, in turn, create better understanding among a broad variety of constituents. Moreover, citizens who are knowledgeable about challenges facing society will be better-informed voters and public policy advocates.

Additionally, the Independent Sector (2001) has shown that volunteers are more likely to make charitable contributions and their financial gifts are greater than those of nonvolunteers. Consequently, widespread volunteering ultimately leads to greater public investment in important causes.

INVESTING IN VOLUNTEERS FOR HIGH-IMPACT

Contrary to popular misconceptions, volunteers are not free. Volunteerism requires a serious financial investment to yield desirable outcomes. Imagine workforces of millions of people who are motivated to do good works but who lack guidance and direction. Chaos would result, and volunteers would be woefully discouraged, never to return again.

There is still a long way to go for the nation's nonprofit sector to galvanize and channel the full force of volunteerism. Volunteers continue to be a highly underused resource. To maximize the opportunity, the following needs to take place:

- *Further national investments* in recruiting, matching, training, and recognizing volunteers will leverage this growing national human resource; examples of federally supported initiatives include City Year, Americorps, and the Points of Light Foundation. Funders, both private and public, must realize that funding for volunteerism will yield a high return on investment.
- *Communities* that seek to expand volunteerism need to invest in the infrastructure to match people with opportunities—through local volunteer centers, for example.
- *Businesses* that seek to strengthen the communities where their employees live and work need to fund programs to organize and recognize employees who volunteer.
- *Nonprofit organizations* need to invest in identifying, recruiting, training, coordinating, and recognizing volunteers. Too many volunteers are discouraged when they arrive with their hearts full of good will only to be discouraged by the lack of time and attention that is required to direct their energies. This happens in nonprofit of all sizes, from neighborhood recreation centers to large-scale urban zoos to international relief organizations.

To maximize the potential of volunteers, nonprofits require resources. Nonprofits that seek to leverage the time and talents of volunteers must fund paid staff positions to run effective, productive, and high-impact volunteer programs. Nonprofits will need capacity in human resources, technology, marketing, secretarial and administrative, transportation, and sometimes events management to build and deploy the volunteer workforce. Each dollar that is invested in supporting volunteerism can yield multiple dollars of volunteer time and value. For example, by funding the position of a well-qualified volunteer coordinator, a nonprofit can potentially "employ" the equivalent of 10, 20, 30, or even 100 full-time employees who are "free" (depending on the degree of training and oversight needed).

High-impact volunteer programs recognize the importance of the following key ingredients for success:

- *Top-level support*—The nonprofit's CEO must recognize the worth of the investment; support fund-raising to establish and maintain an effective volunteerism program; extol the value of volunteers among board and staff members; recognize and appreciate volunteers publicly and privately; and ensure that a well-run, centralized volunteer program is properly staffed.

- *Staffing the volunteer program*—The organization needs a staff member whose role is to ensure the effective administration of the volunteer program; in larger nonprofits, the volunteer director (sometimes called a "coordinator" or "administrator") will need additional staff as well. The volunteer director's role is to identify and create volunteer opportunities that will be useful to the organization and attractive to potential volunteers; ensure good training and oversight of volunteers; and enable positive and rewarding volunteer experiences. The volunteer director needs to be skilled in decision-making, leadership, management, training, public relations, and public speaking. The coordinator must be an advocate for the volunteers within the organization.

- *Budgeting*—The nonprofit needs to develop an annual budget for its volunteer program and then assess the outcomes. Expenses might include the position of volunteer coordinator, administrative or support staff, transportation, meals, and recognition events. At each year end, the organization should assess the investment and the results (i.e., a cost–benefit analysis).

- *Policies*—Written policies need to be established related to the purpose of the volunteer program, insurance coverage for volunteers, background checks and screening, confidentiality, personnel policies (modified for volunteers), and reimbursement of expenses.

The most effective volunteer programs are centralized, with one key person being accountable. A high-impact volunteerism program has the following key elements:

- *Assessing organizational needs*—The volunteer director, together with the support and input of the CEO and program heads, needs to survey the organization and be creative in developing volunteer opportunities that will expand the nonprofit's capacity for serving the community. Each volunteer position needs a clear job description (although one job description—e.g., for a tutor—might apply to many volunteers in that position).

- *Recruiting*—The volunteer director needs to be highly visible and present in the community, reaching out to diverse constituents and many "feeders" of potential volunteers. Feeders might include businesses, volunteer centers, colleges and universities, schools, religious organizations, youth groups, and senior citizens.

- *Screening*—The volunteer director, in collaboration with the various program heads, needs to establish clear criteria and qualifications for each volunteer position and ensure a diligent screening process.

- *Placing*—In concert with program heads, the volunteer director needs to determine the best possible matches of volunteers to positions, taking the organization's and the candidate's interests into account.

- *Orienting*—The volunteer director must educate volunteers about the larger mission and purpose and the organization's compelling value to the community. Volunteers who understand the organization will be inspired to do as much as possible; they also can be valuable ambassadors and advocates. The volunteer orientation is a perfect opportunity for the CEO to meet the volunteers, inspire them about the vision for the organization and the value of the volunteers, and recognize their generosity. It also is important to create and provide a volunteer manual, including information about the mission and the organization, expectations of volunteers, schedules, and other useful information.

- *Training*—Volunteers must be trained just as other employees are trained. This is necessary to ensure a win–win for the nonprofit and the volunteer and to maximize the volunteers' value. For some volunteer positions, the training will be extensive—e.g., for tutors. For others, a little guidance with hammer and nails is sufficient.

- *Scheduling*—Volunteers need to be scheduled for the benefit of the organization and its clients. At the same time, flexibility, when it is possible, will make volunteer opportunities more feasible for many volunteers. Food banks, for example, offer a variety of times throughout the week for volunteers to sort cans and boxes for distribution to various sites. There are, however, organizations, that need volunteers during the school day or afternoons directly after school.

- *Supervising*—Just as with paid employees, volunteers need to be supervised and monitored. This is the only way to ensure that they are contributing value and also are having a positive and rewarding experience. By supervising volunteers and knowing each person's ability, the volunteer director also will be able to recognize opportunities to promote or shift volunteers to new experiences for which they have talents.

- *Motivating*—Volunteers do it for the psychic rewards. People volunteer because it feels good and makes their lives more fulfilling. Volunteer directors, program heads, and the CEO will get the most out of volunteers' efforts by making sure that the volunteers feel part of the team, to see how their work advances the mission and make the community a better place. Volunteer directors need to consider how these messages can be communicated to charge up volunteers' enthusiasm and energy. The greatest motivator of all is seeing the connection between the volunteer's time and a good result—whether the volunteer has helped build a playground where children laugh and play; tutored a child who gains greater pleasure in reading; helped an immigrant to navigate in his new community; arranged for employment for a mother who is on welfare; or planted a flower garden that makes people smile as they stroll around the home for senior citizens. Volunteers also appreciate the chance to learn and grow, so education and training are important, as are opportunities to perform a variety of tasks.

- *Recognizing*—Thanking, appreciating, recognizing—nothing is more fundamental. Everyone in the organization—including and especially the CEO—should greet volunteers as they pass, say "Thank you," and smile. Beyond conveying the daily courtesies and pleasantries, nonprofits should honor and recognize volunteers at special events, whether formal or informal. Volunteers will stay and do their best for the organization only if they feel welcome and appreciated.

- *Evaluating*—In collaboration with the program heads, the volunteer director should evaluate volunteers. This is particularly important with volunteers who provide a skilled service, such as tutoring or teaching. Also, by evaluating volunteers, the coordinator might see ways to expand a volunteer's role or responsibilities or shift someone to a more suitable position. With volunteer groups doing one-day service projects, individual evaluations are not necessary, but an assessment of the project is useful. By reviewing the project and the experience, plans can be made for improvements in the preparation or follow-up. For example, if the organization did not have enough tools or materials for volunteers, it can remedy this in the future.

- *Keeping records*—An important role for the volunteer coordinator is to track who, what, where, when, why, and how. This information is important for thanking volunteers, aggregating volunteer information for reports to foundations and the board regarding volunteer value and impact, creating a list of "friends" of the nonprofit for appeals for volunteers and gifts, and assessing the volunteer program to continually strengthen and improve it.

- *Managing risk*—The nonprofit should consult its attorney and insurance company regarding its volunteer policies and positions, qualifications and screening, confidentiality, and safety. The CEO and the board should ultimately approve the volunteer employment policies and insurance.

A BETTER WORLD

The saying goes that "there is a lid for every pot." This is often used in referring to matchmaking. Similarly, there is a rewarding volunteer opportunity for every person who wishes to volunteer.

Given the needs of American communities, the interest among so many to volunteer, and expanding volunteer-matching services, now is the time for nonprofit organizations to draw on this powerful resource and channel the good will. The contributions of countless volunteers can be put to good use to make this world a better place.

SKILLS APPLICATION EXERCISES

You are the director of volunteers for a large, urban, family services organization that offers an array of programs, ranging from counseling to education to feeding programs. Although the organization has an annual budget approaching $14 million, much of its success relates to an outstanding volunteer program that engages some 350 volunteers in a variety of activities from serving on the organization's board members to serving in its soup kitchen. As the director, you are responsible for providing leadership and oversight to recruiting, training, placing, supervising, evaluating, and recognizing these volunteers. Your volunteer program—often held out as a national model—has led to your being asked to be the keynote speaker at a city-wide conference on volunteerism. Your keynote speech is to last approximately 30 minutes. You have been requested to

- Speak to the value of volunteers' contributions to nonprofit organizations
- Define the scope of volunteerism in modern American society
- Describe the profiles of today's volunteers
- Highlight the ingredients of high-impact volunteerism efforts
- Identify key elements in successful volunteer programs.

Please prepare a four- to five-page outline, with key talking points for this speech.

REFERENCES

Gomes, P. J. (2002). *The good life: Truths that last in times of need.* New York: HarperCollins.

Howe, N., & Strauss, W. (2000). *Millennials rising: The next great generation.* New York: Vintage Books.

Independent Sector. (2001). Giving and volunteering in the United States, 2001. Available online at http://independentsector.org/programs/research/gv01main.html

Korngold, A. (2005). *Leveraging Good Will: Strengthening Nonprofits by Engaging Businesses.* San Francisco, CA: Jossey-Bass.

Korngold, A., & Voudouris, E. (1996). Corporate volunteerism: Strategic community involvement. In D. Burlingham & D. Young (Eds.), *Corporate philanthropy at the crossroads* (pp. 23–39). Bloomington: Indiana University Press.

Saxon-Harrold, S., McCormack, M., & Hume, K. (2000). *America's senior volunteers.* Available online at http://www.independentsector.org/pdfs/SeniorVolun.pdf.

USA Freedom Corps. (2005). USA Freedom Corps tsunami relief efforts. Accessed online March 8, 2005 at http://www.usafreedomcorps.gov/content/about_usafc/newsroom/announcements_dynamic.asp?ID=853)

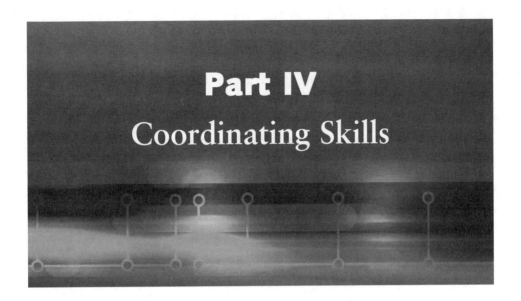

Part IV
Coordinating Skills

Managerial coordinating skills encompass the roles of monitor and coordinator. Competencies for the role of monitor include receiving and organizing information, evaluating routine information, and responding to routine requests for information. Competencies for the role of coordinator include planning, organizing, and controlling work. The chapters in this section focus on these internal, control-oriented roles and competencies as nonprofit managers seek to create conditions of organizational stability and continuity.

In Chapter 12, Marci S. Thomas provides a primer on financial management of nonprofit organizations. Given that an organization's finances are critical to its effectiveness and even to its survival, nonprofit managers need to be familiar with basic accounting and financial management concepts and practices. Thomas enables nonprofit managers to become familiar with basic terms and concepts that are crucial for the effective financial management of an organization.

In Chapter 13, Paul A. Kurzman emphasizes the risks and liabilities that nonprofit organizations encounter and the monitoring and coordinating roles of managers in establishing and overseeing risk management activities. He identifies the most frequently encountered risks and discusses recommended responses, including insurance protection, legal counsel, staff training, and internal risk audits, urging nonprofit managers to deal proactively with the risks their organizations face.

In Chapter 14, Andrea Meier and Charles L. Usher discuss the changing context of program evaluation in nonprofit organizations, suggesting that the traditional separation of the roles of manager and evaluator have begun to blur in response to increased demands for organizational accountability. They review different types of program evaluation approaches and strategies and provide helpful tools for managers.

In Chapter 15, Laura I. Zimmerman and Andrew Broughton provide an overview of issues related to computing and information technology, with attention to networks and the Internet. Further, they recommend that nonprofit managers engage in strategic planning for technology and suggest specific management steps that can be taken to plan for technology in an organization.

12

Managing the Finances
of Nonprofit Organizations

Marci S. Thomas

Nonprofit organizations are formed to serve either a public purpose or mutual benefit. Generally they are distinguished from business enterprises because they

- Receive significant contributions from donors who do not expect a commensurate or proportionate return;
- Have charitable, religious, or educational operating purposes; and
- Are not owned by individuals.

Nonprofits can have these characteristics in varying degrees depending on the nature of their mission and operations. Examples of nonprofits include voluntary health and welfare organizations, colleges and universities, churches and synagogues, federated fundraising organizations, civic and community organizations, trade associations, and social and country clubs. There also are entities such as health care organizations that are formed as nonprofits but are less reliant on contributions and more on the fees charged for services.

The Internal Revenue Service (IRS) provides certain benefits to nonprofits if they meet certain criteria, the most important of which would be that no part of the net earnings of the entity may benefit a private individual or shareholder of the nonprofit. In addition to exemption from federal and state income tax, other benefits of tax-exempt status include the ability to attract donations that are tax deductible to the donors and issue debt at lower interest rates. Nonprofits are required to pay federal payroll tax and also may be required to pay real estate tax and sales or other local taxes as required by state law.

For many people, the word *nonprofit* conjures up the image of an entity created to do good works in an environment in which there is an abundance of donors. Unfortunately, this is far from the truth. Nonprofits exist in a very competitive environment. There are more than 1 million nonprofits in the United States today competing for dollars, not only in the form of donations but also in the form of grants and contracts from federal, state, and local governments; foundations; and larger nonprofits.

Donors and other funding sources are concerned about how nonprofits manage their resources. Based on "hits" to Guidestar's database of nonprofit financial information on the Internet, it is evident that the public is carefully scrutinizing the financial activities of nonprofits before making donations. GuideStar, a national database of nonprofits, uses data from nonprofit's informational tax return Form 990 to populate its database with financial information about them. It is important to remember that nonprofits serve the community and as such have a responsibility to function with integrity and efficiency.

FOCUS ON ACCOUNTABILITY

There is considerable focus today on the accountability of entities in general. In response to high-profile frauds and corporate failures, Rep. Michael Oxley (R-OH) and Sen. Paul Sarbanes (D-MD) authored the Sarbanes–Oxley Act, became law in 2002. Although it applies to publicly traded entities, there has been a trickle-down effect to nonprofits and other nonpublic companies. Sarbanes–Oxley requires, among other things, that the chief executive officer (CEO) and chief financial officer attest to the fair presentation of the financial statements on a quarterly (and yearly) basis and that the entity undergo an audit of internal controls over financial reporting. In addition, some provisions govern the use of audit committees and auditor independence.

Many believe that it is just a matter of time before nonprofits of significant size are required to comply with this law in some form, mainly because of the support that the U.S. General Accounting Office (2003) has given to the idea. In anticipation, larger nonprofits are beginning to adopt certain of its provisions, in part because of the increased awareness of board members, many of whom work for public companies. A 2003 survey conducted by Grant Thornton, a national public accounting firm, indicated that nonprofits are taking steps to institute policies and procedures to enhance their governance structures and internal controls over financial reporting. All entities, regardless of corporate form, are required to comply with two Sarbanes–Oxley provisions: the prohibition of retaliation against whistle blowers and the prohibition against the destruction of documents when an entity is under criminal investigation.

It is clear to see that, in these complex times, nonprofit executives need a basic knowledge of financial management principles. This chapter introduces the basic financial concepts that executives need to understand to manage a nonprofit. It is important that management has sufficient knowledge to know when to call on accounting and finance professionals for assistance.

FINANCIAL STATEMENTS

Financial statements summarize the activities of the nonprofit and are used to communicate this information not only to those responsible for leading and managing the entity but also to its board of directors and external parties such as donors and other funding sources, bond holders, and creditors. Generally accepted accounting principles require that a nonprofit present a statement of financial position, a statement of activities, a statement of cash flows, and notes to the financial statements. The financial statements should be read as a complete set. Each one presents a different perspective on the financial condition of the nonprofit. Relying on one statement alone can give readers a misleading picture.

The discussion that follows describes the financial statement elements that are most important to nonprofit executives to understand. It is important to understand that nonprofit accounting is complex. An accounting professional specializing in nonprofits should be consulted when preparing financial statements for outside parties.

To illustrate nonprofit financial statements, we use the statements for a hypothetical homeless shelter that is a 501(c)3 organization. Its mission is to provide assistance to homeless individuals. It also provides job placement services in the community on a sliding-scale basis. The entity derives the majority of its support from small contributions from individual donors and government grants.

Statement of Financial Position

The statement of financial position presents the finances of an entity at a given point in time: the end of a month, the end of a quarter, or the end of a year. The statement lists, in order of liquidity, the assets, the liabilities, and the equity of the entity. As nonprofits rarely issue stock, the net assets are the cumulative results of operations and restricted donations of the entity since inception. Net assets are categorized according to the level of restriction specified by the donor: unrestricted, temporarily restricted (as to purpose or time), and permanently restricted.

Nonprofits may, but are not required to, issue classified financial statements. When statements are classified, the current assets and liabilities are separated from the noncurrent items. *Current assets* are expected to be collected or used within one year, and *current liabilities* are expected to be paid within one year. Even if statements are not classified, like those of the hypothetical homeless shelter, the assets and liabilities should be listed in order of liquidity. The statement of financial position for the shelter and a description of its elements are shown in Figure 12.1.

FIGURE 12.1
SAMPLE HOMELESS SHELTER STATEMENTS OF FINANCIAL POSITION,
JUNE 30, 2005, AND 2004

	2005	2004
ASSETS		
Cash and Cash Equivalents	$18,366	$311,984
Investments	265,019	14,859
Pledges Receivable Less Allowance for Doubtful Accounts	56,933	36,059
Grants Receivable	187,507	251,089
Inventories	50,550	65,550
Prepaid Expenses	21,365	20,251
Property and Equipment:		
Land	358,092	358,092
Buildings	780,258	780,258
Equipment	475,142	335,114
Less Accumulated Depreciation	(295,847)	(256,889)
	$1,917,385	$1,916,367
Other Assets	55,349	57,999
TOTAL ASSETS	$1,972,734	$1,974,366
LIABILITIES		
Accounts Payable	$87,912	$71,945
Accrued Expenses	22,350	25,409
Deferred Revenue	-	108,529
Mortgages and Notes Payable	1,092,517	1,060,057
Other Liabilities	3,202	1,823
TOTAL LIABILITIES	1,205,981	1,267,763
NET ASSETS		
Unrestricted	698,553	601,603
Temporarily restricted	18,200	55,000
Permanently restricted	50,000	50,000
TOTAL NET ASSETS	716,753	656,603
TOTAL LIABILITIES AND NET ASSETS	$1,972,734	$1,974,366

CASH AND CASH EQUIVALENTS. Cash can be held in checking or savings accounts or in the case of petty cash, in a locked safe. Many nonprofits keep a supply of petty cash on hand, but this should be carefully controlled. Cash equivalents are short-term financial instruments such as certificates of deposit and money market funds with an original maturity of three months or less.

INVESTMENTS. Short-term investments can be in the form of debt or equity securities. Accounting literature prescribes that, although they are initially recorded at cost or if donated, at fair value, they are written up or down to the market value at each financial statement date. Nonprofits also may have other types of investments such as derivatives, investments in split-interest agreements, investments in other entities, and investments in real estate or other tangible property. These are initially recorded at fair value, but the accounting for subsequent valuation is complex.

Derivatives are investments in which the value of the investment is derived from an underlying asset. Derivatives require no initial net investment or one that is smaller than would be required for contracts that would have similar response in market factors. An example of derivative would be an option to purchase stock. Derivatives may or may not be short-term investments. They are complex instruments and should be used only by someone with the knowledge and skills to be sure that they are used appropriately.

Nonprofits are frequently the beneficiaries of split-interest agreements. There are numerous types of split-interest agreements, but all involve an interest going both to the nonprofit and donor. Some agreements call for the donor to receive a periodic annuity (e.g., yearly, monthly) for life, and the remainder of the investment goes to the nonprofit at the death of the donor. Some provide the nonprofit with an annuity during the life of the donor, but the remaining assets revert to the donor's heirs at death. With today's life expectancies and lower rates, some nonprofits are having problems with these investments, as the payment to the donor may be greater than the income generated by the investment. Before accepting them as donations, the nonprofit should consult with professionals that have experience with this sort of investment if the requisite knowledge is not available in house.

Nonprofits also may have investments in for-profit entities or other nonprofits. For example, an educational institution may have created a foundation for the purpose of fund-raising. The rules that govern when the entities are consolidated or if one merely has an interest in the net assets of another are complex. Management should consult financial professionals to determine the appropriate accounting treatment for a given situation.

PLEDGES AND ACCOUNTS RECEIVABLE. Nonprofits are required to record pledges when the pledges are made at the amount that the entity expects to collect. This is especially important in a building campaign when experience suggests that not all of the donors will pay on their pledges. In addition, if donations are long term (more than one year before they are paid), they should be discounted to reflect the time value of money. Each period management should evaluate the collectibility of pledges and, if necessary, establish an allowance for those that may not be collectible. Pledges should be segregated by net asset class (i.e., whether the donor meant the pledge to be unrestricted, temporarily restricted, or permanently restricted.

Accounts receivable arise when the entity sells goods or services. Receivables should be recorded when the goods have been delivered or services rendered. An allowance should be established at the end of each period for those accounts receivable that may not be collected.

GRANTS RECEIVABLE. A nonprofit may be the recipient of different types of grants. Reimbursement grants require that the entity spend the money for the intended purpose and then bill the grantor. At the point that the money is spent, the entity has a grant receivable. This receivable is recorded even if it has not yet been billed. It would be rare that a grantor agency would default on a grant. But grants, like other receivables, should be evaluated for collectibility. If the grant is paid in advance of the service being performed, the entity still owes the grantor the service. It is recorded as a liability called *deferred revenue,* until the service is performed.

INVENTORIES. Inventories are not generally a major item on the statement of financial position of a nonprofit because most nonprofits provide services as opposed to selling products. However, when a nonprofit has product inventories (such as publications), they are recorded at cost and periodically evaluated for obsolescence or any kind of damage that would cause them to lose value and trigger a write down.

PREPAID EXPENSES. Nonprofits are sometimes called on to prepay certain items such as insurance or rent. This means that the cash is paid before the item is being used. The asset reflects the unused portion of the insurance, rent, or other prepaid item.

PROPERTY AND EQUIPMENT. Property and equipment typically consists of land, buildings, computer and other devices, or tools and leasehold improvements. These are recorded at cost if purchased. If donated, assets are recorded at the fair value at the date of donation. Each period, a portion of the asset is recorded as expense. Accumulated depreciation represents the cumulative depreciation since the asset was placed in service. Land is the only asset in this category that is not depreciated. Property and equipment accounts are periodically evaluated for impairment.

OTHER ASSETS. Other assets is a category in which items without financial significance are aggregated. An example might be a deposit on leased space or equipment.

ACCOUNTS PAYABLE AND ACCRUED EXPENSES. Accounts payable are liabilities to vendors for goods purchased or services that have been rendered for which payment has not been made. Accrued expenses are liabilities for which there typically is no invoice. Examples might be amounts owed to employees for time worked within a period for which they have not been paid or amounts expected to be paid for worker's compensation claims.

DEFERRED REVENUE. Deferred revenue is a liability to the party that paid the entity to perform service before the service being performed. An example might be when a company has paid the nonprofit in advance to perform contract research. The service was not yet performed even though the payment had been made. As discussed earlier, grants that are paid in anticipation of work to be performed are recorded as deferred revenue until the service is performed.

MORTGAGES AND NOTES PAYABLE. Mortgages and notes payable are debt instruments that are generally long term. In classified statements of financial position, the amounts would be separated into the amount to be paid within the coming year and the long-term portion. The notes to the financial statements would disclose the interest rate, the maturity of the debt, and any kind of debt covenants with which the entity must comply.

Nonprofits also may enter into lease agreements. Operating leases are not recorded in the financial statements, but the information is disclosed in the footnotes. Capital leases have more characteristics of ownership due to the duration of the lease or amount of the minimum lease payments. Capital leases are recorded as both an asset and a liability. The asset is the amount of the asset, and the liability is the amount of the minimum lease payments less the amount representing interest.

OTHER LIABILITIES. Other liabilities is a category in which items without financial significance are aggregated. For example, these could be amounts owed on for health insurance payments or amounts to be paid for property taxes or anything that is not significant in amount.

Statement of Activities

The statement of activities represents the activities of the entity over the past year (or less in the case of interim financial statements). It is divided into three classes of assets: (1) unrestricted, (2) temporarily restricted, and (3) permanently restricted. Health care organizations have a slightly different presentation because they are required to report a performance indicator so that they can be compared to their for-profit counterparts. The statement of activities for the hypothetical homeless shelter and a description of its elements are in Figure 12.2.

SUPPORT AND REVENUE. Support and revenue has several components.

Contributions. These are unconditional, voluntary gifts from a donor who does not receive equal value in exchange. An example of a condition would be a gift that is contingent on raising a certain amount of matching donations or amounts specified in a will to be left to the nonprofit. A will can be changed, hence the condition. Contributions may have restrictions on them. Restrictions are stipulations put on the gift by the donor that might affect the purpose for which the gift is used or the timing of when the gift is used. For example a donor might restrict her gift of $1,000 to be spent for research or might state that it should be used for operations in 2006. When the restrictions are met, the amounts are reclassified as unrestricted, as the restrictions are released. This is the only way that the gift can be used. The statement of activities shows a line item titled "net assets released from restriction."

Gifts also can be permanently restricted. This means that the principal cannot be spent, although generally the return on the investment may be. The donor also may make stipulations on how the return can be spent. The return on investment refers to the interest or dividends plus any appreciation or depreciation in the investment. However, if the donor makes no stipulations, then the investment return will be unrestricted. Certain states have laws governing how returns on endowment (permanently restricted) funds are recorded.

Nonprofits also may receive contributions of goods and services. Donated goods should be recorded at the fair value of the gift. Contributed services may be recorded only if they meet two criteria: (1) They either create or enhance a nonfinancial asset (i.e., building an addition to a building) or are provided by a professional working in that capacity (i.e., an attorney offering services), and (2) the nonprofit would have purchased those services if they had not been given in donation. Services of volunteers not meeting these criteria are disclosed in the notes to the financial statements.

Government grants. These grants are generally exchange transactions, which means that the government is providing resources to the nonprofit to perform services that they would have performed if the nonprofit did not do it for them. Because this is value exchanged for value, it is referred to as an *exchange*

FIGURE 12.2

EXAMPLE HOMELESS SHELTER STATEMENTS OF ACTIVITIES,
YEARS ENDED JUNE 30, 2005, AND 2004

	2005	2004
UNRESTRICTED NET ASSETS		
Unrestricted Revenues		
Contributions	$971,650	$1,121,729
Government Grants	560,554	622,649
Program Revenues	1,104,816	896,857
Investment Income	3,135	3,973
Other Revenue	13,446	15,854
TOTAL UNRESTRICTED REVENUES	2,653,601	2,661,062
Net Assets Released From Restriction		
Expiration of Time Restriction—United Way	12,800	10,000
Restrictions for Training	25,000	25,000
TOTAL UNRESTRICTED REVENUES AND OTHER SUPPORT	2,691,401	2,696,062
EXPENSES		
Salaries and Wages	1,334,735	1,247,349
Payroll Taxes	209,084	197,431
Contract Services	157,200	150,209
Supplies	125,144	117,271
Telephone	82,306	80,489
Postage and Shipping	14,502	12,689
Occupancy	38,752	39,932
Equipment Rental and Maintenance	74,500	76,249
Printing and Publications	1,502	1,488
Travel	9,300	9,470
Drug Testing and Treatment	38,500	34,043
Relocation Assistance	18,443	19,322
Interest	88,500	90,501
Depreciation	85,550	84,000
Utilities	76,003	73,537
Food	91,020	82,916
Auto and Truck	2,200	5,997
Marketing	13,222	13,091
Professional Fees	34,262	58,885
Security	12,355	12,326
Bus Tokens	12,235	14,716
Licenses and Fees	13,133	12,422
Insurance	62,003	62,500
TOTAL EXPENSES	2,594,451	2,496,833
INCREASE IN UNRESTRICTED NET ASSETS	96,950	199,229
TEMPORARILY RESTRICTED NET ASSETS		
Contributions Restricted for Use in Training Program	1,000	1,800
Net Assets Released From Restrictions	(37,800)	(35,000)
DECREASE IN TEMPORARILY RESTRICTED NET ASSETS	(36,800)	(33,200)
INCREASE IN NET ASSETS	60,150	166,029
NET ASSETS AT BEGINNING OF YEAR	656,603	490,574
NET ASSETS AT END OF YEAR	$716,753	$656,603

transaction. These transactions are always unrestricted, as the revenue is earned. Not all grants are exchange transactions. Foundations and other nonprofits may refer to their contribution to the entity as a grant.

Program revenue. This category is used for instances in which an entity has charges for goods or services associated with a program. These also are exchange transactions.

Investment income (or return). This category includes dividends, interest, rents royalties, and other types of payments. The income is recognized when it is earned. As note earlier, investment income should be reported in the appropriate net asset class.

Expenses. These are recognized when they are incurred. They may be reported in the statement of activities by natural classification (e.g., payroll, rent) or by functional classification (e.g., program, management and general, fundraising). If the entity chooses not to present functional expenses in the body of the statements, the information must be disclosed in the notes to the financial statements. Voluntary health and welfare organizations, those that derive the majority of their support from the public, must prepare a supplemental statement of functional expenses.

Other requirements. Other required items related to expenses that are specific to nonprofits are

- The requirement to show both the revenue and expenses related to special events (e.g., golf tournaments) and
- The option to relate certain expenses to more than one functional activity.

Nonprofits are held by donors to a very high standard when it comes to how money is spent. Donors tend to prefer their donations be spent on programs. As noted earlier, donors will look at the entity's financial statements or informational tax return Form 990 to see how much of the entity's resources are being spent on support services (e.g., management, fundraising). To make these percentages as favorable as possible, management should consider looking for ways to move as much of those costs into program as possible by inserting program components in these other activities. This enables them to allocate the costs to both activities. For example, a newsletter may contain a request for donations and may serve an administrative function to notify interested parties of the nonprofit's activities. If the entity inserts information in the newsletter that is program related, the portion of the costs to produce and mail the newsletter can be allocated to program as well. There are very specific accounting rules governing joint costs to prevent abuse. The activity must be relevant to a program, it must include a call to action on the part of the recipients of the newsletter (e.g., a plea to stop domestic violence by reporting instances to authorities), and the distribution must be wider than just the donor base.

Statement of Cash Flows

The statement of cash flows is the financial statement that illustrates the cash inflows and outflows of the entity over the reporting period. Cash inflows and outflows can be from operations, investing activities, and financing activities.

Notes to the Financial Statements

The notes to the financial statements provide additional disclosures on the financial statement elements as well as other information that is important to external users. Examples of disclosures that enhance the user's ability to make decisions related to the entity are

- Description of the nonprofit including tax status (e.g., 501(c)3);
- Significant accounting policies;
- Composition of receivables, including maturity dates;
- Composition of investments, including unrealized and realized gains and losses;
- Composition of property and equipment if not shown on the face of the statements;
- Composition of long-term debt, including interest rates and maturities;
- Concentrations of risk;
- Contingencies;
- Transactions with related parties;
- Litigation; and
- Commitments (e.g., rental commitments).

AUDITS

Many nonprofits obtain audits of their financial statements. An audit may be required annually by lenders or funding sources as a condition of obtaining a loan or grant. Some nonprofits obtain audits at the request of their boards or because it is good business practice.

If a nonprofit receives more than $500,000 in federal awards, it is subject to an audit under Government Auditing Standards and OMB Circular A-133. This audit consists not only of that of the entity's financial statements but also that of its federal awards. The A-133 audit has two components: One relates to the testing of internal control over major grant programs, And the other relates to auditing the entity's compliance with requirements of Circular A-133 and grant agreement related to those major programs.

"For your convenience we've consolidated all our forms into one, which I'll ask you to take a few minutes to review."

TAX RETURNS

Nonprofits that have more than $25,000 in gross receipts are required to file an informational tax return, Form 990, with the IRS. A nonprofit may be required to pay income tax on earnings that are not related to its tax-exempt purpose.

BUDGET AND CONTROL MECHANISMS

Budgeting is a very important exercise for a nonprofit. It provides the nonprofit with a focal point for management to plan and prioritize the activities of the entity. A well-thought-out budget also provides a basis for financial analysis and monitoring of the nonprofit's activities.

Several techniques can be used in the budgeting process. The most thorough is *zero-based budgeting*. With this method the entity starts with the premise that all activities should be challenged and a determination made as to whether they are appropriate for the entity given its mission, vision, and values as well as its strengths and weaknesses and the opportunities and threats in the marketplace. Zero-based budgeting is rarely used because it is time consuming. However, it is a valuable exercise that should be undertaken periodically.

The more common method is the *incremental/decremental approach.* In this method the nonprofit examines the activities from the prior year and creates a budget based on anticipated changes. No matter which method is used, budgeting should be treated as an important part of the nonprofit's planning and administrative processes.

Once the budget is constructed, a variance analysis should be performed to measure the budget to the actual results of operations. The nonprofit also should consider performing a *horizontal analysis,* which measures the actual results of operations against the operations in the prior year. Another important form of financial analysis is *vertical analysis,* which attempts to factor out the growth in the entity by comparing the different sources of revenue as a percentage of total revenue and the expense line items as a percentage of revenue. These analytical techniques are illustrated in Figure 12.3.

Ratio analysis is another useful tool for analyzing operations. A *ratio* is an expression of the relationship between two numbers as a single number or a percentage. Ratios can be computed using financial information in both the numerator and denominator. They also can be computed using both financial and nonfinancial information. They can be compared to ratios computed in the prior year or years as well as to published information for similar entities. Table 12.1 illustrates some of the more common ratios used in analyzing nonprofits.

Once the calculations have been completed, management should review the results with an eye toward how much they differ from their expectations. For example, if the entity hired three additional employees during the year, management's expectation would be that salaries and benefits would increase. Expectations are not always easy to develop, however. For example, management may have a difficult time forecasting certain financial statement items, such as contributions, because they are influenced by factors such as the economy's effect on individual donors, bequests, natural disasters such as hurricanes, or issues such as terrorism. These things tend to influence a donor's decision to give and are beyond the control of the nonprofit. These and other factors, such as those listed below, should be considered when forming expectations and when determining the threshold over which the variance warrants investigation:

- Personnel hired or terminated during the year;
- New or terminated contracts or grant agreements;
- Fundraising constraints;
- Loan covenants;
- Change in number or square footage of facilities;
- Changes in inflation, interest rates, or other economic factors;
- Changes in the level of programs and services;

FIGURE 12.3
TECHNIQUES USED IN ANALYTICAL REVIEW

Comparison of budget to actual

Step 1

Actual amount – budgeted amount = variance

The variance is the difference between the budgeted and actual amounts.

Step 2

$$\frac{\text{Variance}}{\text{Budgeted amount}} \times 100$$

The variance is expressed as a percentage of the budgeted amount.

Horizontal analysis

Step 1

Amount current year – Amount prior year = variance

The variance is the difference between the current and prior year amounts.

Step 2

$$\frac{\text{Variance}}{\text{Amount prior year}} \times 100$$

The variance is expressed as a percentage of the prior year amount.

Vertical analysis

Step 1a

$$\frac{\text{Revenue item}}{\text{Total revenue}} \times 100$$

Comparison of each revenue or expense item to total revenue. Then compare the percentages from the prior year to current year.

Step 1b

$$\frac{\text{Expense item}}{\text{Total revenue}} \times 100$$

TABLE 12.1
COMMON RATIOS USED BY NONPROFITS

Days in accounts receivable	$\dfrac{\text{Average accounts receivable}}{\text{revenue per day}}$	Measures average time to collect. Useful also for donations if they are not long term.
Current ratio	$\dfrac{\text{Current assets}}{\text{current liabilities}}$	Measures liquidity and how well the entity is poised to pay expenses
Program expense to total expense	$\dfrac{\text{Program expenses}}{\text{total expenses}}$	Measures how much of the entity's resources are used for programs
Fundraising expense ratio	$\dfrac{\text{Fundraising expenses}}{\text{total expenses}}$ or $\dfrac{\text{Total fundraising expenses}}{\text{amounts raised}}$	Measures how much of the entity's resources are used for fundraising. Measures productivity of fundraising expenses
Contribution revenue ratio	$\dfrac{\text{Contribution revenue}}{\text{total revenue}}$	Measures how much of the entity's total revenue comes from contributions
Average contribution per donor	$\dfrac{\text{Contributions}}{\text{Number of donors}}$	Measures per average donation
Revenue raised per person at fund raising event	$\dfrac{\text{Revenue raised per event}}{\text{Number of participants per event}}$	Measures relative success of the event
Compensation cost	$\dfrac{\text{Compensation and benefit cost}}{\text{Average number of employees}}$	Measures average cost per employee

- Changes in certain expense line items due to outside factors (e.g., increase in postage or insurance rates); and
- Increased marketing or fundraising efforts.

INTERNAL CONTROLS AND RISK OF FRAUD

Those who work in nonprofits should not be misled into thinking that they are not likely to be the victims of fraud. The Association of Certified Fraud Examiners (2004) found that the most costly fraud and abuses occur in entities with less than 100 employees. In fact, it is likely that nonprofit entities, by their very nature, are more susceptible to fraud because of the following characteristics:

- An atmosphere of trust that assumes that all employees and others who work for or with the entity are honest;
- Revenue sources that are difficult to estimate and control; contributions may come to the entity in the form of cash, an asset highly susceptible to theft;
- Employees who lack business experience;
- Financial constraints that keep them from being able to hire sufficient people to properly segregate duties;
- Use of volunteers as board members who may have a personal relationship to the cause but do not have sufficient knowledge and understanding of business issues; and
- Leaders such as an executive director or CEO who have passion for the mission of the nonprofit and less respect for the business processes of the entity.

All nonprofits, regardless of size, should institute strong internal controls to help prevent both errors and fraud. Internal control is a process designed by the entity's executive and principal financial officers or people performing similar functions to provide reasonable assurance regarding the reliability of financial reporting as well as to promote the timely detection of unauthorized acquisition, use, or disposition of the entity's assets.

In 1992, the Committee of Sponsoring Organizations of the Treadway Commission published an integrated framework for internal controls. As illustrated in Figure 12.4, five categories of internal control should be considered when designing an entity's system of internal controls

1. The *control environment* is the foundation for all of the other controls and provides the "tone from the top." Factors are integrity and ethical values, commitment to competence, management's consideration of the knowledge and skills necessary to accomplish an employee's responsibilities, attention and direction provided by a board of directors or audit

FIGURE 12.4
COMPONENTS OF INTERNAL CONTROL

Control environment	• Integrity and ethical values • Commitment to competence • Management's consideration of the knowledge and skills necessary to accomplish an employee's responsibilities • Attention and direction provided by a board of directors or audit committee • Management's approach to taking business risks • Emphasis on meeting financial targets • Manner of assigning authority and responsibility • Human resource policies and procedures
Risk assessment	• Management's risk assessment process • Board approved policies that address significant business control and risk management practices
Control activities	• Top level reviews • Comparing budget to actual results, actual results to benchmarks or industry standards, prior year against current year. Investigating variances (These are also a monitoring control) • Information processing controls • Segregation of duties • Controls designed to safeguard assets
Information and communication	• Obtaining and disseminationg information where appropriate necessary to run the business. • Adequate information technology
Monitoring	• Management and supervisory activities

committee, management's approach to taking business risks and emphasis on meeting financial targets, manner of assigning authority and responsibility, and human resources policies and procedures. The control environment may be the most important of all controls. Without the appropriate tone coming from management and the board of directors, it is less likely that other controls will operate as designed to prevent fraud and error.

2. The entity should engage in a *risk-assessment* process. Generally, risk pertains to operations, compliance with laws and regulations, and financial reporting (including the possibility of theft of assets). The entity should perform an analysis of the likelihood that these types of issues could occur and the magnitude of the problem should they occur.

3. *Control activities* generally consist of an entity having a policy as well as a procedure to implement the policy. Examples of control activities are top-level reviews, including comparing budget to actual, actual results to prior period performance, or actual results to benchmarks or industry standards. The key with top-level reviews is that management investigates unusual relationships and takes corrective action. If performed by supervisory personnel reviewing the work of others, these reviews also

may be monitoring controls. Other examples are information-processing controls, those designed to safeguard assets and records, and segregation of duties.

4. *Information and communication* relates to the identification, capture, and communication of information, both financial and nonfinancial, to parties that need it. An information system that is able to handle the number and complexity of the entity's transactions also is important.

5. *Monitoring* involves assessing the design and operation of controls on a timely basis and determining whether they are still relevant and effective so that corrective action can be taken when necessary. Monitoring activities can be ongoing or separate evaluations and include management and supervisory activities, comparisons of budget to actual, reconciliations of account detail to the general ledger, and review of exception reports generated by the company's information system.

SEGREGATION OF DUTIES

As noted earlier, nonprofits are frequently under financial constraints that limit the number of administrative personnel that they are able to keep on staff. This leads to concern around the segregation of duties. Fraud is more likely to occur when employees have duties that are incompatible and give them the opportunity to commit fraud. For example, if an employee has the ability to create a new vendor in the accounting system, approve invoices for payment, and post transactions to the general ledger, theft could occur. The employee could set up a fictitious vendor in the system, create an invoice and submit it for payment, approve the invoice, post it to the accounting system, and then wait for the check to be sent to them.

Duties can be segregated even with a limited number of people in the office. In addition, management should consider using program personnel and the executive director to help segregate duties. Figure 12.5 illustrates ways to segregate duties when there are two and three people available. Figures 12.6 and 12.7 illustrate the common fraud schemes that can be prevented by proper segregation of duties.

CONCLUSION

Financial management of nonprofits deserves significant attention from management and the board of directors. Today's economic and regulatory climate represents a challenging new environment especially for nonprofits with their financial constraints. Nonprofits are stewards of public resources, and it is important that they demonstrate fiscal responsibility and accountability to their boards, donors, grantors, and the community.

FIGURE 12.5
SEGREGATION OF DUTIES FOR SMALL NONPROFITS

With two people

Accountant or other financial personnel
- Record pledges
- Mail checks
- Write checks
- Reconcile bank statement
- Record credit/debits
- Approve payroll
- Disburse petty cash
- Authorize purchase orders
- Authorize check requests
- Authorize invoices for payment

Executive Director
- Receive and open bank statements
- Sign checks
- Make deposits
- Perform interbank transfers
- Distribute pay checks
- Review petty cash
- Review bank reconciliations
- Approve vendor invoices
- Perform analytical procedures
- Sign important checks
- Make compensation adjustments
- Discuss matters with BOD or audit committee

A receptionist or administrative employee could open mail and create a deposit log for incoming checks.

With three people

Accounting Staff
- Record pledges
- Write checks
- Reconcile bank statement
- Record credit/debits
- Reconcile petty cash
- Distribute payroll

Accountant or other financial personnel
- Approve payroll
- Process vendor invoices
- Mail checks
- Perform analytical procedures
- Approve invoices for payment
- Disburse petty cash
- Open mail and log cash
- Receive bank statements

Executive Director
- Make compensation adjustments
- Sign important contracts
- Discuss matters with BOD or audit committee
- Sign checks
- Complete deposit slips
- Perform interbank transfers
- Perform analytical procedures
- Review bank reconciliation

FIGURE 12.6
PREVENTION OF FRAUD SCHEMES BY SEGREGATION OF DUTIES

Segregation of Duties	Helps prevent
Person who opens mail and logs in cash receipts should be different from the person who functions as cashier or posts to accounts receivable. Lock box Restrictive endorsements on checks	Skimming cash
Bank reconciliations should be performed by persons independent of cash receipts (and disbursements).	Theft and alteration of checks
Periodic statements to donors/customers are mailed by a person other than the one responsible for posting to receivables.	Lapping of accounts or pledges receivable
Customer follow-up on complaints is independent of cash handling or receivables posting.	Lapping of accounts receivable
Credit memos are handled by those who handle cash or post to accounts receivables.	FS 5
Person who signs checks should be different from the one initiating purchases, approving purchases, shipping, receiving, cash receipts, accounts payable, and custody of cash. Check signer should be authorized by board of directors.	Kickbacks, fictitious invoices, inflating invoices
Mechanical check signers and signature plates should be under the control of management. That person should be independent from the person initiating purchases, approving purchases, shipping, receiving, cash receipts, accounts payable, and custody of cash.	Fictitious invoices, inflating invoices, stealing checks

FIGURE 12.7
PREVENTION OF FRAUD SCHEMES BY SEGREGATION OF DUTIES

Segregation of Duties	Helps prevent
Purchasing should be separate from requisitioning, shipping, and receiving.	Excessive purchasing
Requisitioning, purchasing, and receiving should be different from those who process invoices, accounts payable, cash receipts and disbursement, and the general ledger functions.	Stealing to make personal capital improvements Ficticious or inflating invoices or altering checks
Invoice processing and accounts payable should be separate from the general ledger function.	Duplicate payments
Persons who are independent of purchasing and receiving should follow up on unmatched open purchase orders, receiving reports, and invoices.	Ficticious or altering invoices
Persons who prepare payroll should be independent of time keeping, distribution of checks, and hiring. They should not have access to other payroll data or cash.	Ficticious employees Overpayment of wages Stealing payroll checks Diverting payroll taxes Embezzling wages Keeping terminated employees on payroll and stealing checks or colluding with them

SKILLS APPLICATION EXERCISES

- Obtain a balance sheet and operating statement from a nonprofit organization. Review these, trying to apply the definitions and concepts in this chapter. Classify the various accounts, identifying assets, liabilities, fund balances, revenue, and expenses.
- Review the financial statements, assessing the financial status of the organization, identifying any concerns or issues that may be indicated by the financial statements.
- Identify any strategies in place in the organization aimed at preventing fraud.

SUGGESTED READINGS

American Institute of Certified Public Accountants. (2004). *Not-for-profit organizations: Audit and accounting guide.* New York: Author.
American Institute of Certified Public Accountants Committee of Sponsoring Organizations. (1992). *Internal control—Integrated framework.* New York: Author.
Association of Certified Fraud Examiners. (2004). *Report to the nation on occupational fraud and abuse.* Austin, TX: Author.

Bryce, H. J. (1999) *Financial and strategic management for nonprofit organizations* (3rd ed.). San Francisco: Jossey-Bass.

Grant Thornton LLP. (2003). *National board governance survey for not-for-profit organizations.* Chicago: Author.

Saul, J. (2004). *Benchmarking for nonprofits: How to measure, manage and improve performance.* St. Paul: Amhearst Wilder Foundation.

Thomas, M. S. (2003). *Fraud in not-for-profit organizations.* Red Bank, NJ: Loscalzo.

U.S. General Accounting Office. (2003). *Government auditing standards.* Washington, DC: Author.

Zelman, W., McCue, M., Millican, A., & Glick, N. (2003). *Financial management of healthcare organizations* (2nd ed.). Oxford, England: Blackwell.

13

Managing Liability and Risk in Nonprofit Settings

Paul A. Kurzman

The life of the law has not been logic, it has been experience, the felt necessities of the time, the prevalent moral and political theories, intuitions of public policy, avowed or unconscious, even the prejudices which judges share with their fellow men, have a good deal more to do than syllogism in determining the rules by which men should be governed.

—Justice Oliver Wendell Holmes, Jr.

For nonprofit managers, few topics cause more concern than the issue of risk management. This concern is well founded given the increase in litigation against nonprofit organizations and their boards and staff. Much of the current vulnerability results from changes in the practices and funding of organizations. Human services agencies, for example, no longer are seen merely as compassionate caretakers but as professional service providers. Youth recreation programs, senior citizens' outings, crafts projects, and remedial reading programs have been supplemented (if not supplanted) by sophisticated employment, child development, group homes, employee assistance, and family treatment programs. Similarly, voluntary charitable contributions to fund programs in nonprofit organizations (through theater benefits, bequests, thrift shops, community foundations, and United Way contributions) have, in many cases, given way to major contracts and fee-for-service arrangements with governmental agencies, which now provide the bulk of the income. Human services agencies are no longer playing "sandlot ball"; they are playing in the "big leagues" and have correspondingly big risks to manage (Bernstein, 1981; Kurzman, 1995; Tremper, 1994).

As nonprofit organizations come of age, they find that maturity involves new risks and responsibilities. This is true for such disparate entities as museums, hospitals, camps, research institutes, public television stations, zoos, libraries, orchestras, philanthropic foundations, colleges, churches, civic associations, historical societies, technology institutes, private schools, nursing homes, missionary societies, fraternal lodges, community improvement districts, literary guilds, botanical gardens, university presses, and animal welfare societies. Using social work and social agencies as a template for discussion, one may view the nature and complexity of the change for nonprofit organizations more broadly.

LEGAL ENVIRONMENT

In tandem with rapid social change has come the recognition of social work as a full-fledged mental health profession. Social workers are, by far, the largest professional group today in the human services arena. However, 33 years ago, in 1973, only 11 states provided for the legal regulation of social work practice, while in 2006, all 50 states do. Similarly, professional social workers enjoy the status of qualified providers of mental health services under state insurance laws in 32 states today, whereas such vendorship status for social work did not exist in a single state 25 years ago (Association of Social Work Boards, 2005). With licensure and vendorship has come the authority to be direct and independent providers of clinical treatment services, generally without referral from or supervision by psychologists or physicians.

Increasingly, clinical social workers make the diagnoses, provide the treatment, authenticate clients' claim forms, and authorize third-party reimbursements, not only with private insurance carriers but also with TRICARE (formerly CHAMPUS) and Medicare. Today, social workers serve as expert witnesses in courts of law, as mental health managed care experts for major health insurance carriers, and as framers of clinical service regulations in the departments of both state and federal governments.

As lawyers have noted, "professionals are held to a higher standard of behavior in their professional capacities than that of the general population" (Watkins & Watkins, 1989, p. 36). Hence, the recent recognition of social work's autonomous professional stature by the government, insurance companies, courts of law, and the public has helped create new forms of exposure and greater risk in practice. Some service settings, of course, involve inherently higher levels of potential peril than do others. Nonprofit organizations with foster care, adoption, day care, debt management, family planning, protective services, group homes, camping, residential treatment, and sexual dysfunction programs, for example, place practitioners and managers at particularly high levels of risk. Even the public sector of social work practice is no longer protected. As Besharov (1985) has noted,

> Courts have all but abolished the doctrines of sovereign, governmental, and public official's immunity, so that it has become easier to bring tort suits against public social service agencies and their employees. Similarly, the abolition of the doctrine of charitable immunity has exposed private agencies and their employees to greater liability. (p. 13)

Today, nonprofit managers also must "look within" to managing their risks as employers in a competitive and heterogeneous world. For example, do women have access to senior positions in the same way that men traditionally have? Are people of color well represented on staff, not just at the clerical or custodial level but in professional, supervisory, and managerial positions? Are appropriate accommodations made for people with disabilities, both as staff and as clients, in a barrier-free environment? Are ageist and homophobic biases toward colleagues and clients dealt with promptly, honestly, and openly? Many of these issues are dealt with, in part, when a union represents staff or when strong organizations are present in the broader community to ensure nondiscrimination and the ongoing accountability of organizations to their consumers of service—but increasingly, such intermediaries are not at hand.

The foregoing realities would be cause enough for concern if professionals were well prepared for risk management issues in their graduate education; however, many are not (Besharov, 1985; Madden, 2003; Reamer, 2003; Schroeder, 1995; Stein, 2004). Professional codes of ethics are rarely mentioned in the curriculum; moreover, the legal dimension of ethical issues in practice receives scant attention in higher education curricula, despite the guidelines of accrediting bodies.

Hence, managers may have little preparation for this critical dimension of their professional responsibility. This situation is certainly no better with respect to members of other disciplines who are involved in nonprofit organizations. Indeed, managers may be skilled supervisors, wise administrators, and even creative fundraisers, but managing the institution's legal obligations and vulnerability is an area for which they often are apt to be unprepared and unqualified. Moreover, because staff members are likely to perceive themselves as "gooddoers" and "do-gooders," risk management may seem an oxymoron (Albert, 2000; Barton & Sanborn, 1978; Dickson, 1995; Everstine & Everstine, 1986).

COMPETING VALUES

As Quinn and Rohrbaugh (1981) have suggested, competing values underpin any assessment of an organization's effectiveness. Organizations that follow an "open-systems" model, for example, may value behaviors and outcomes that would be perceived as less important to leaders who pursue a "rational-goal" model. Simply put, "the Competing Values Approach suggests that the selection of various criteria of effectiveness reflects competing value choices" (Edwards, 1987, p. 5). As a manager, should one emphasize chance taking, creativity, and innovation, or rules and regulations that may reduce risk, exposure, and potential organizational jeopardy, from without and within? Does promoting innovation and decision making at the level closest to the client enhance the organization's posture, or place its stability (in an unstable world) at too great a risk (Kurzman, 1977).

To many observers, the term *risk management* connotes caution, collaboration, and consultation. Professionals, who are trained to have expertise in autonomous practice, may perceive such an agenda as a series of illegitimate boundaries circumscribing their judgment, discretion, and freedom to maintain service-centered interventions. Too much management of risk indeed may inhibit the freedom one wishes to promote to keep the organization at "the cutting edge"—competitive and therefore stable in an ever-changing external world.

As Lewin (1997) noted, a dynamic field of forces conditions and constrains managers' decisions. In fact, recognition of and a healthy respect for the inevitable competing values just noted can lead managers to a different use of self that may strike a proper balance among the several forces over time. A competing-values approach gives recognition to this reality and provides a useful framework for analysis and conceptualization. The approach both highlights elements and values that are often overlooked (e.g., risk management activity) and encourages the manager to place the need for action in this arena in a broader perspective that may condition implementation. Quinn and Rohrbaugh's (1981) perspective can prod nonprofit managers to initiate instrumental activities toward the legitimate protection of the organization, its staff, and those whom it serves without placing an inappropriate or exclusionary value on this activity over others. In Simon's (1961) terms, an acknowledgment of competing values can lead to the development of a "satisficing" model of management that recognizes legitimate contending interests among the field of forces, without and within.

RISKS

As the references to this chapter indicate, many books have addressed the vulnerabilities and the liabilities inherent in professional practice. However, less emphasis has been placed on the nonprofit agency per se and on the role of the executive or manager in establishing and managing risk management activities. This section examines the major risks that require management and the complexity of the competing values that must be squarely addressed (Bullis, 1995; Reamer, 2003).

*"According to the **Tarasoff** decision, I'm obligated to warn the people below of your intention to jump on them."*

Six risks in prototypical human services practice are most frequently noted. If these risks are not understood and approached from a preventive posture, they most likely result in litigation or claims of unethical practice. (Note: Although the following is addressed primarily to the human services, with social workers as one example, it also is applicable to other professionals in similar voluntary, charitable, nonprofit organizations.)

Best known perhaps may be the employee's and organization's duty to warn if the client discloses an intent to harm himself or herself or others. Codified in what has become known as the *Tarasoff* decision, a ruling by the California Supreme Court in 1976 imposed on therapists the duty to "exercise reasonable care" in the protection of potential victims from the violent acts of clients (Barker, 1984; Weil & Sanchez, 1983). The court concluded that therapists have "an affirmative duty to warn and protect" when they determine, through appropriate standards of their profession, that their clients present a serious danger of violence to a particular person or persons *(Tarasoff v. Board of Regents of the University of California,* 1976). Although the *Tarasoff* case was decided by a state court and thus technically may be of limited jurisdictional value, few cases have had as far-reaching an effect (Hull & Holmes, 1989). Several landmark decisions in subsequent years affirmed the *Tarasoff* principle and extended its intent to cover nonlicensed "mental health counselors" and licensed mental health providers *(Hedlund v. Superior Court of Orange County,* 1983; *Jablonski v. U.S.,* 1983; *Peck v. Counseling Service of Addison County,* 1985). In the *Tarasoff* decision, the court said, in part,

> When a therapist determines, or pursuant to the standards of his or her profession should determine, that his or her patient presents a serious danger of violence to another, he [or she] incurs an obligation to use reasonable care to protect the intended victim against such danger. The discharge of this duty may require the therapist to take one or more of various steps, depending on the nature of the case. Thus it may call for him [or her] to warn the intended victim or others likely to apprise the victim of the danger, to notify the police, or to take whatever other steps are reasonably necessary under the circumstances.

A second area of risk to human services organizations comes ironically from the duty to keep confidential all material that is shared with them and their practitioners in the course of a professional relationship. Section 1.07(c) of the *Code of Ethics* of the National Association of Social Workers (NASW, 2000), for example, states that "Social workers should protect the confidentiality of all information obtained in the course of professional service" (p. 10). However, confidentiality is not absolute, which is why the sentence continues, "except for compelling professional reasons" (see also Davidson & Davidson, 1998; Polowy & Gorenberg, 1997). What the *Tarasoff* decision did was to delineate one such compelling professional reason and to clarify that the word *should* may imply an obligation to act and disclose. In the words of the *Tarasoff* decision, "The protective privilege ends where the public peril begins." Indeed, the concept of client confidentiality is governed for social workers in law in 48 states as *privileged communication.* The state statutes provide protection for service recipients similar to the protection they enjoy in the context of their relationships with attorneys, members of the clergy, and physicians (Dickson, 1998; Knapp & Van de Creek, 1987). However, almost all such statutes make exceptions to privilege when such disclosure is necessary to avert serious foreseeable and imminent harm to self or other identifiable people or to prevent the abuse or neglect of children. In fact, all states today have a specific law that mandates professionals to report known or suspected cases of child abuse and define nonreporting as a prima facie case of unprofessional conduct.

A third professional obligation involves the duty to ensure continuity of service to people under care. The expectation is that the institution does not abandon or neglect a client who needs immediate care or currently is under its care without making reasonable arrangements for the continuity of service. Such a duty obligates the organization to uncooperative and "undesirable" clients, whose hostility and initial unresponsiveness may indeed be a symptom of their need and their disorder. Being able to demonstrate outreach, empathy, flexibility, and appropriate referral to an alternate provider may be essential (Meyer, Landis, & Hays, 1988; Salzman & Furman, 1999). Similarly, the duty adequately to record services provided is incumbent on all providers and practitioners (Schrier, 1980). As social workers and other human services providers achieve the status and recognition of vendors, accurate and timely recording becomes essential to ensure that both institutions and clients are properly protected for the receipt of third-party payments. The failure to support a diagnosis from the current American Psychiatric Association's (2000) *Diagnostic and Statistical Manual of Mental Disorders,* commonly known as *DSM-IV-TR,* in recording that has been provided to an insurance carrier to justify a fee payment may be defined as an act of fraud within state statutes. In addition, many states that license professional practitioners define the failure to provide adequate recording of services and to retain such records for a specific number of years as grounds for charges of professional misconduct. Practitioners also have a duty to diagnose and treat their clients properly.

This is a major issue for organizations that have weak procedures for supervisory review and few standards to support interprofessional consultation and referral (Corey, Corey, & Callanan, 2002; Houston-Vega, Neuhring, & Daguio, 1997; Reamer, 1989). The failure to refer a client to a physician to rule out biological, organic, or genetic conditions that may trigger psychological symptoms is perhaps the largest arena of risk. Alexander (1983) noted that half the claims for erroneous diagnoses made under an Insurance Trust's professional liability insurance program were based on a charge that the clients' problems were actually medical, not psychological. In addition, organizations need to provide for consultation in psychosocial areas for which individual providers may still be poorly trained, such as learning disabilities, eating disorders, and substance abuse.

The expectation that practitioners reach an appropriate *DSM-IV-TR* diagnosis also implies that this correct assessment is recorded on insurance forms to Medicaid, Medicare, and private insurance carriers such as Blue Cross/Blue Shield. Because social workers and other human services providers are often recognized as eligible vendors of psychotherapeutic treatment, care must be taken that errors in diagnosis, whether intentional or inadvertent, are not recorded. Research (Kutchins & Kirk, 1997) has shown that service recipients may place pressure on providers to report less severe diagnoses than are indicated because of their fear of the potential adverse effects of labeling. Staff may conversely feel pressure to increase the severity of the diagnosis falsely or to exaggerate symptoms so the consumer can qualify for third-party payments.

Finally, a risk to practice is inherent in the duty to avoid sexual impropriety. Sexual acts performed under the guise of therapy are not permitted between clients and staff (Gabbard, 1989; Schultz, 1982). Virtually all the codes governing the professional conduct of social workers, for example, in the 50 states (and four jurisdictions) that regulate their practice make this prohibition explicit. Moreover, Section 1.09(a) of the NASW *Code of Ethics* (NASW, 1999) makes no exceptions to its unequivocal statement "Social workers should under no circumstances engage in sexual activities or sexual contact with current clients" (p. 13). The codes of ethics of other mental health professions have somewhat similar prohibitions against sexual activities between therapists and their clients. Such activity cannot be defended under the guise of "supporting the transference" or helping to "overcome sexual inhibition or dysfunction."

Given the position of trust that the employing organization shares with its practitioners, courts may view employers as having culpability as well. The potential perils here are even greater than with the risks previously described, because most insurance policies exclude coverage for intentional wrongdoing, such as sexual involvement with clients. Managers and supervisors, moreover, generally are viewed in the role of *respondeat superior* and share vicarious liability for such tortuous acts committed by those under their supervision or in their employ (Watkins & Watkins, 1989; Weiner & Wettstein, 1993).

These most serious risks and duties have been highlighted to demonstrate that great caution and sound judgment are needed by those who lead nonprofit service organizations today. The litigious environment in which professionals currently practice makes it imperative that managers reduce their organization's exposures while preserving a spirit of flexibility and innovation. Risk management procedures have to be put in place because good intentions provide insufficient protection. In addition to the possibility of government-sponsored criminal actions against nonprofit employers and their practitioners, civil actions by consumers are becoming more common and more successful. The defense against torts, such as the negligence of employers and the malpractice of individuals, requires as careful thought as do preparation of the budget and staffing of the board of directors. These exposures are shared by all nonprofit organizations, including churches, libraries, schools, civic associations, hospitals, museums, and cultural organizations.

RECOMMENDED RESPONSES

Four major recommendations flow from this discussion. They reflect a focus on the competing values that are intrinsic to the issues at hand and therefore deal with process and goals, maintenance of and competition among systems, planning and training, and internal and external loci of organizational concern.

Insurance Protection

Today, no nonprofit organization can afford to be without adequate forms of insurance. Such coverage should include

- *Premises liability,* covering all sites at which services may be delivered;
- *Professional liability*, including the activities of all paid staff, volunteers, and consultants;
- *Coverage of officers and directors,* to shield executives and members of the board of directors from individual and collective personal liability in the performance of their fiduciary duties;
- *Vehicular insurance,* generally at a level higher than the mandated state minimum; and
- *Bonding* for all officers and staff who have the authority to sign contracts or manage the institution's income and assets.

Such casualty policies should cover the organization and key participants for most losses and damages, including negligence, provided that one cannot prove nonfeasance or malfeasance (Angell & Pfaffle, 1988; Reamer, 1995). In addition, insurance generally provides for the funding of the potentially expensive legal defense against charges that may be brought, regardless of the outcome. Without adequate insurance, winning a case in court may actually be a pyrrhic victory (Jones & Alcabes, 1989). Out-of-pocket legal fees and court costs may be so high that, in effect, one "loses" even when one wins. In summary, it is essential for the organization to obtain insurance coverage that is commensurate with the organizational scope and program complexity of its services (Tremper, 1989).

Legal Counsel

Every nonprofit organization should establish legal counsel in the same way it sets up an ongoing relationship with an accountant or program consultant. One should not wait until a crisis occurs and then select an attorney under pressure. Most managers try to ensure that one or more attorneys serve on their advisory board or board of directors, so they can get the frequent informal advice they may need on such issues as reviewing a lease, framing an amendment to the bylaws, or signing a governmental contract, usually on a pro bono basis. However, an independent counsel often is warranted. First, some legal opinions may involve a potential conflict of interest for a board member because the questions involve actions by the board itself or one of its members. Second, the legal issues may be outside the board member's legal specialization and expertise. Third, the individual (or organization) that is taking legal action may be a client of the board member's firm.

Whether done by a board member or an external counsel, new legal agreements and contracts should be fully reviewed before they are signed. Given the principle of *respondeat superior* noted earlier, it also is important for an attorney to ensure that insurance covers those people, for example, who are agents of the facility's service (under the supervision of organizational employees), such as student interns, AmeriCorps workers, community volunteers, and trainees (Cohen & Marino, 1982). On a proactive basis, an attorney should regularly explore the major federal, state, and local statutes (and evolving case law) that govern the organization, its funding, and its services.

Staff Training

The best way to avoid trouble is to prevent it from occurring. Professionals know the value of education and prevention, often deploying these skills on behalf of customers and clients with remarkable creativity and success. As managers, however, they often forget to apply what works in their own practice to the organizations for which they now are responsible.

In addition to ongoing service-centered training activities that may accompany monthly administrative meetings or periodic case conferences, it may be wise to institute quarterly half-day sessions for formal administrative training. Such sessions not only provide line staff with the information they need for advancement into managerial positions, but they also send the message that organizational issues are everyone's concern (Besharov & Besharov, 1987; Kurzman, 1998). Experts can be invited to speak, or staff with special expertise can lead the sessions. From a risk management perspective, important items to cover may include

- State laws governing the requirements and procedures for reporting known or suspected cases of child or elder abuse or neglect;
- Principles that are embodied in the *Tarasoff* decision with regard to the "duty to protect" when there is serious potential danger posed by a client to self or to others;
- Current federal and state regulations on record-keeping and retention;
- Statutes on privileged communication governing the several mental health professions and the specific principles of confidentiality embodied in the professions' ethical codes;
- The proper completion of insurance forms for third-party reimbursement, including the appropriate use of the several axes of the *DSM-IV-TR;*
- Additional training for proper differential diagnoses in areas in which many professionals may be poorly trained, such as learning disabilities, organic pathology, psychopharmacology, and chemical dependence; and

- Relevant state rules and standards of professional conduct for the licensed professions, as appropriate, including nursing, social work, marriage and family counseling, psychology, nutrition, audiology, architecture, and accounting.

Special emphasis must be given to the need to train staff to avoid even the appearance of sexual impropriety. Occasionally, it may be appropriate, for example, for a therapist to hug clients momentarily to console them; to stroke their wrists briefly during a moment of stress; or to compliment clients on their dress or appearance if this is a new sign of strength and self-esteem. It would be naive, however, not to understand that there is a thin line that would be easy for staff to cross. Moreover, one must remember the clinical dictum, especially in working in the context of a helping relationship with troubled clients, that "perception is reality." The alarming rise in charges of professional misconduct that have been brought before disciplinary committees of licensing boards and committees of inquiry in various professional associations in recent years (charging service providers with both heterosexual and homosexual sexual misconduct) must be understood and underscored. As was noted, such charges against social workers, for example, have become so prevalent in recent years that a cap has been placed on professional liability insurance coverage when a sexual impropriety by a practitioner has been documented (Besharov, 1985).

Furthermore, managers should note that this issue is not profession specific. An American Psychological Association study showed that, during a 10-year period, 45 percent of all malpractice awards through its professional liability coverage dealt with therapist–patient intimacy ("Therapist–Patient Sexual Intimacy," 1988). Bringing in members of appropriate professional associations' committees on inquiry to discuss the respective provisions of the various professional associations' codes of ethics in this area is warranted. In addition, it may be wise to invite a member of the disciplinary panel of relevant state licensing boards to speak about standards for licensure and case law experience regarding sexual impropriety. Training staff members to avoid giving even the possible suggestion of improper behavior in their speech, conduct, and presentation of self is crucial to limiting a facility's exposure. If such a transgression occurs, the staff person should be quickly identified as "an impaired professional" and referred for appropriate help, and the consumer's needs and rights must be served and protected (Reamer, 1992).

Internal Audit

All nonprofit organizations conduct a fiscal audit each year, if only because it is required by funding bodies and the Internal Revenue Service as a condition for maintaining their tax-exempt status. However, most managers do not retain outside experts to conduct a periodic program and management audit to ensure that risks are being properly managed (Reamer, 2001). An external auditor, a board member, and a senior member of the managerial staff should review the following items:

- Are the organization's governmental licenses and accreditations in order?
- Are all eligible professional staff currently licensed and registered for practice?
- Are provisions for emergency actions (e.g., fire drills, reporting of theft, involuntary hospitalization of clients, safety of staff, responding to accidents) well known and regularly updated?
- Have premiums for all forms of casualty insurance coverage been paid?
- Are procedures for the management of records being properly followed?
- Are governmental vouchers and records of insurance reimbursements being maintained in keeping with legal and contractual requirements?
- Are supervisory evaluations being conducted and reviewed in a timely fashion?

A biennial internal management audit of the appropriateness of such standard operating procedures and the staff's adherence to their provisions is a preventive risk management activity that may pay big dividends for the organization, the staff, and those they serve.

CONCLUSION

New opportunities have brought new risks. As professionals who often are managing regulated organizations in the context of a litigious society, nonprofit managers can no longer consider risk management a luxury. The demands of clients, funding sources, and the standards of the professions suggest that managing risks is part of the prudent manager's responsibility for implementing a strategy of primary and secondary prevention. That is, risk management is better conceptualized as a proactive strategy of affirmation than as a reactive response to a crisis. Managers who organically build in this function as a normative component to their administrative role and function should not find this activity any more burdensome than hiring staff and balancing the budget. Although managers have to respond to many competing values and demands as they control and adapt to their environment, the growth and stability of organizations are dependent on the managers' competent performance of risk-management functions. Nonprofit service organizations have legitimate "survival needs" because they must coexist with internal and external forces that constantly impinge on them. In a sense, they are social organisms that reflect the legitimate competing values to which they must respond. In this context, they must manage risks to thrive and survive, often in turbulent times, because consumers—often with few options in life—depend on them.

SKILLS APPLICATION EXERCISES

- You are the manager of a hospital-based employee assistance program (EAP) that provides free and confidential professional mental health and substance abuse services to all hospital employees and their families. An emergency room nurse voluntarily comes to the EAP to see a counselor on your staff about her cocaine and alcohol addiction, which she says "seems to be getting worse." Because she is exceedingly good at what she does and generally careful about when she "snorts" and drinks, her addiction has not been detected by supervisors or peers. She wants help for her problem, but only if she can stay on her job and only if the EAP promises her confidentiality. Provided that the EAP staff make these two promises, she indicates that she will do whatever they recommend, including coming in for daily EAP sessions, gradually eliminating her use of alcohol and cocaine, and joining Alcoholics Anonymous and Cocaine Anonymous in the community. She reminds your staff person that she is a voluntary self-referral and of the EAP's long-standing and well-known promise of confidentiality (Kurzman, 1988). Without revealing the client's identity, your EAP counselor wants to know whether you will permit him to honor the client's requests. What do you do, and why?

- Your private community college has received a letter from a prominent negligence attorney alleging that a male faculty member at the college made explicit verbal and physical advances to a female student after evening classes and during advising sessions held in his office. It is said that the student, in the context of a relationship of unequal power, was told that her course grade and letter of recommendation for senior college depended on her willingness to become sexually intimate with the faculty member. The attorney says that these advances made her physically ill and unable to function at her well-paid job as an executive secretary, because she could no longer concentrate at work. She further claims, through her attorney, that your faculty member's actions alienated the affection of her husband, a prominent physician, who wants a divorce. The client's attorney wants to meet with you to explore a $1-million settlement, in lieu of a protracted, public, and potentially more costly outcome of litigation against you, the faculty member, and the college. As the college's vice president for academic affairs, would you meet with the client's attorney? What are your short- and long-range plans of action?

- You are the new executive vice president of a center for the performing arts that has a symphony orchestra, theater repertory, opera company, music conservatory, experimental drama workshop, modern dance ensemble, and a ballet. You have several state-of-the-art facilities, many prominent performers, and a large number of performance support personnel. Your center receives income not only through sales and subscriptions but also from government arts and humanities grants, rental agreements, teaching and training contracts, corporate sponsorships, foundation grants, and an endowment. You have a diverse professional, paraprofessional, and support staff and the immediate aid of three experienced deputies (for program, development, and administration). What is your plan of action, during your first year, to assess the adequacy and sufficiency of your organization's risk management policies and procedures?

REFERENCES

Albert, R. (2000). *Law and social work practice* (2nd ed.). New York: Springer.

Alexander, C. A. (1983, November). *Professional liability insurance: Jeopardy and ethics.* Paper presented at the Professional Symposium of the National Association of Social Workers, Washington, DC.

American Psychiatric Association. (2000). *Diagnostic and statistical manual of mental disorders* (4th ed., text rev.). Washington, DC: Author.

Angell, F. J., & Pfaffle, A. E. (1988). *The whole field of insurance and risk management* (3rd ed.). Mt. Vernon, NY: Chase Communications.

Association of Social Work Boards. (2005). *Social work laws and regulations: A comparison database.* Available online at http://aswbdata.powerlynxhosting.net

Barker, R. L. (1984). The *Tarasoff* paradox: Confidentiality and the duty to warn. *Social Thought, 10*(4), 3–12.

Barton, W. E., & Sanborn, C. (Eds.). (1978). *Law and the mental health professions.* New York: International University Press.

Bernstein, B. E. (1981). Malpractice: Future shock of the 1980s. *Social Casework, 62,* 175–181.

Besharov, D. (1985). *The vulnerable social worker.* Silver Spring, MD: National Association of Social Workers.

Besharov, D., & Besharov, S. H. (1987). Teaching about liability. *Social Work, 32,* 517–522.

Bullis, R. K. (1995). *Clinical social worker misconduct.* Chicago: Nelson-Hall.

Cohen, R. J., & Marino, W. E. (1982). *Legal guidebook in mental health.* New York: Free Press.

Corey, G., Corey, M., & Callanan, P. (2002). *Issues and ethics in the helping professions* (6th ed.). Belmont: CA: Wadsworth.

Davidson, J. R., & Davidson, T. (1998). Confidentiality and managed care: Ethical and legal concerns. In G. Shaimess & A. Lightburn (Eds.), *Humane managed care?* (pp. 281–292). Washington, DC: NASW Press.

Dickson, D. T. (1995). *Law in the health and human services.* New York: Free Press.

Dickson, D. T. (1998). *Confidentiality and privacy in social work.* New York: Free Press.

Edwards, R. L. (1987). The competing values approach as an integrating framework for the management curriculum. *Administration in Social Work, 11,* 1–13.

Everstine, L., & Everstine, D. S. (1986). *Psychotherapy and the law.* Orlando, FL: Grune & Stratton.

Gabbard, G. O. (Ed.). (1989). *Sexual exploitation in professional relationships.* Washington, DC: American Psychiatric Association.

Hedlund v. Superior Court of Orange County, 34 Ca. 3d 695 (1983).

Houston-Vega, M. K. Nuehring, E. M., & Daguio, E. R. (1997). *Prudent practice: A guide for managing malpractice risk.* Washington, DC: NASW Press.

Hull, L., & Holmes, G. (1989). Legal analysis and public agencies: The therapist's duty to warn. *New England Journal of Human Services, 9*(2), 31–34.

Jablonski v. U.S., 712 F. 2nd 391 (1983).

Jones, J. A., & Alcabes, A. (1989). Clients don't sue: The invulnerable social worker. *Social Casework, 70,* 414–420.

Knapp, S., & Van de Creek, L. (1987). *Privileged communication for mental health professionals.* New York: Van Nostrand Reinhold.

Kurzman, P. A. (1977). Rules and regulations in large-scale organizations: A theoretical approach to the problem. *Administration in Social Work, 1,* 421–431.

Kurzman, P. A. (1988). The ethical base for social work in the workplace. In G. M. Gould & M. L. Smith (Eds.), *Social work in the workplace* (pp. 16–27). New York: Springer.

Kurzman, P. A. (1995). Professional liability and malpractice. In R. L. Edwards (Ed.-in-Chief), *Encyclopedia of social work* (19th ed., Vol. 3, pp. 1921–1927). Washington, DC: NASW Press.

Kurzman, P. A. (1998). Workplace ethics: Issues for human service professionals. In R. Chadwick (Ed.), *Encyclopedia of applied ethics* (Vol. 4, pp. 555–560). San Diego: Academic Press.

Kutchins, H., & Kirk, S. A. (1997). *Making us crazy, DSM: The psychiatric bible and the creation of mental disorders.* New York: Free Press.

Lewin, K. (1997). *Field theory in social science.* Washington, DC: American Psychological Association.

Madden, R. G. (2003). *Essential law for social workers.* New York: Columbia University Press.

Meyer, R. G., Landis, E. R., & Hays, J. R. (1988). *Law for the psychotherapist.* New York: W. W. Norton.

National Association of Social Workers. (2000). *Code of ethics.* Washington, DC: Author.

Peck v. Counseling Service of Addison County, 499 A-422, VT (1985).

Polowy, C. I., & Gorenberg, C. (1997). Legal issues: Recent developments in confidentiality and privilege. In R. L. Edwards (Ed.-in-Chief), *Encyclopedia of social work* (19th ed., 1997 Suppl., pp. 179–190) Washington: NASW Press.

Quinn, R. E., & Rohrbaugh, J. (1981). A competing values approach to organizational effectiveness. *Public Productivity Review, 5,* 122–140.

Reamer, F. G. (1989). Liability issues in social work supervision. *Social Work, 34,* 445–448.

Reamer, F. G. (1992). The impaired social worker. *Social Work, 37,* 165–170.

Reamer, F. G. (1995). Malpractice claims against social workers. *Social Work, 40,* 595–601.

Reamer, F. G. (2001). *The social work ethics audit. A risk management tool.* Washington, DC: NASW Press.

Reamer, F. G. (2003). *Social work malpractice and liability* (2nd ed.). New York: Columbia University Press.

Salzman, A., & Furman, D. M. (1999). *Law in social work practice* (2nd ed.). Chicago: Nelson-Hall.

Schrier, C. (1980). Guidelines for record-keeping under privacy and open-access laws. *Social Work, 25,* 452–457.

Schroeder, L. O. (1995). *The legal environment of social work* (rev. ed.). Washington, DC: NASW Press.

Schultz, B. M. (1982). *Legal liability in psychotherapy: A practitioner's guide to risk management.* San Francisco: Jossey-Bass.

Simon, H. A. (1961). *Administrative behavior* (2nd ed.). New York: Macmillan.

Stein, T. J. (2004). *The role of law in social work practice and administration.* New York: Columbia University Press.

Tarasoff v. Board of Regents of the University of California, 17 Cal. 3d 425,551, P 2d 344 (1976).

Therapist–patient sexual intimacy. (1988, September–October). *EAP Digest,* p. 13.

Tremper, C. R. (1989). *Reconsidering legal liability and insurance for nonprofit organizations.* Lincoln, NE: Law College Education Services.

Tremper, C. R. (1994). Risk management. In R. D. Herman (Ed.), *The Jossey-Bass handbook of nonprofit leadership and management* (pp. 485–508). San Francisco: Jossey-Bass.

Watkins, S. A., & Watkins, J. C. (1989). Negligent endangerment: Malpractice in the clinical context. *Journal of Independent Social Work, 3*(3), 35–50.

Weil, M., & Sanchez, E. (1983). The impact of the *Tarasoff* decision on clinical social work practice. *Social Service Review, 57,* 112–124.

Weiner, B. A., & Wettstein, R. M. (1993). *Legal issues in mental health care.* New York: Plenum Press.

14

Designing New Approaches to Program Evaluation

Andrea Meier and Charles L. Usher

As the operating environments of nonprofit organizations have changed in recent years, so have managers' roles. Managers used to be responsible primarily for monitoring and controlling the processes and functions within their organizations. Now they also are called on to act as facilitators and mentors for staff members within their organizations, as innovators in program development, and as brokers between their organizations and surrounding communities (see Chapter 1). These multiple roles can be mutually enhancing, or they can conflict. Spurred by this progressive expansion in their responsibilities, nonprofit managers have sought new ways to get feedback on how well they perform their roles and assess their organizations' effectiveness.

Nonprofit managers must be able to function effectively in this environment of competing values and demands. In addition to their other duties, managers also must function as monitors and coordinators of activities within their organizations and of their organizations' performance relative to mission and external environment. This chapter reviews how the field of social program evaluation has developed over the past 30 years and describes the changing roles of evaluators, program staff, consumers, and policymakers in the evaluation process. Before going forward, note that the information provided here can serve only as an introductory survey of these evaluation methodologies. The appendix in this book provides information about Internet links to funders who support and document program experiences with innovative approaches to evaluation and the different research organizations that promote each type of evaluation approach described here.

CHANGING POLITICAL CONTEXT OF HUMAN SERVICES EVALUATION

Although most nonprofit organizations now incorporate evaluations into their program activities, the strongest demand for accountability has always been within the human services sector. Because of this historical emphasis, this chapter begins with a summary of how changes in human services policy in the past decade have created a need for new systems of accountability in the public and nonprofit human services sector, one that traditional approaches to evaluation cannot support.

The mid-1990s saw a clear conservative shift in American politics, most evident in new Republican majorities in Congress and in many state legislatures. The legislation that emerged from these bodies resulted in less federal support for human services and a shift in authority and responsibility from the federal government to the states and from the states to local government. Fundamental premises of the social welfare system, such as the entitlement of poor families to support under the Aid to Families with Dependent Children program, were discarded, and states were required to establish new principles of social responsibility.

This shift in power was consistent with the recommendations of liberal social reformers who saw community-based decision making and resource allocation as essential to the renewal of disadvantaged neighborhoods and communities (Alexander, 1999; Nelson, 1994). A key difference, however, was the expectation that federal financial support would continue or possibly even expand in certain areas, such as prevention and early intervention programs (Usher, 1995). Thus, the devolution of power grew out of demands from both ends of the political spectrum, although from two quite different sets of motivations.

The political transformation of the mid-1990s was, of course, the culmination of a conservative shift that began with the election of Ronald Reagan in 1980 and has continued at an increasing scale to the present time. Managers of nonprofit organizations and public agencies have increasingly faced pressure to eliminate fraud, waste, and abuse and to control caseload growth in the programs they administer (Terry, 1997). A variety of strategies, such as total quality management (Walters, 1994) and results-oriented management (Gitlow & Gitlow, 1987), were devised to help managers improve the efficiency and effectiveness of their organizations. Moreover, the concept of managed care emerged during this period in an effort to create incentives for cost-effective delivery of services (Usher, 1998). Changes in federal funding mechanisms that resulted in the increased use of purchase-of-service agreements enabled new nonprofit and for-profit organizations to enter into the "market" for services provision.

To compete effectively with public agencies for resources and satisfy consumer demand, these newcomer organizations began to incorporate new management strategies (Edwards, Cooke, & Reid, 1996; Fine, Thayer, & Coghlan,

1998). Public and nonprofit human services agencies have not been the only entities affected by these trends. In the 1990s, many state and local arts programs experienced funding cutbacks caused by national campaigns to eliminate the National Endowment for the Arts (Loyacono, 1995; McCarthy, Brooks, Lowell, & Zakaras, 2001). Even less-controversial arts programs have been forced to justify the value of their programs to their funders using evaluation techniques to show how their services are culturally enriching to their communities (McCarthy et al., 2001).

In addition to attacks from political conservatives, the federal government also came under criticism from other sources. Some social policy analysts, such as Sar Levitan (Levitan, 1992) and Lisbeth Schorr (Schorr, 1997), have charged that federal social experiments have not been useful to policymakers or administrators and were not a worthwhile investment of resources. Indeed, they challenged the very scientific approach on which many programs were based as inconsistent with the premise that the most effective programs are those that are responsive to the interests, needs, and resources of given communities as opposed to conforming to a "one-size-fits-all" program model (Usher, 1995).

In response to these critiques, some evaluators began experimenting with and advocating new approaches to program evaluation that they perceived to be more appropriate to a more decentralized political system (for example, Fetterman, Kaftarian, & Wandersman, 1996). The emergence of these new approaches is described below.

Although the program evaluation concepts and methods discussed here are relevant and applicable to public agencies, for-profit, and nonprofit organizations, much of the research in program evaluation has been done to assess the effectiveness of human services programs. The examples of different types of evaluations presented in this chapter reflect the authors' personal experiences with this kind of program evaluation and the richness of this body of research.

CONCEPTUAL ROOTS OF PROGRAM EVALUATION

Contemporary approaches to program evaluation draw on two conceptual foundations: (1) policy analysis (see, for example, Quade, 1979; Wildavsky, 1979) and (2) social psychological and educational assessment (e.g., Dugan, 1996). As a result, evaluators differ in the aspects of programs (e.g., process, outcome, impact) that they accord top priority and the research approaches (e.g., qualitative, quantitative) that they consider valid and appropriate. Policy analysts typically draw heavily on political and economic theory. If their work is grounded in these theories, evaluators will focus on program cost-effectiveness and the impact of programs on institutional power relationships. Evaluators trained in educational and psychological theoretical frameworks tend to be more concerned with the developmental processes associated with individual and collective learning.

Policy Analysis and the Rational Decision-Making Model

In the 1970s, policy analysis emerged as an intellectual discipline to help decision makers make choices that produce results that are "systematic, efficient, coordinated, and rational" (Wildavsky, 1979, p. 127). From the point of view of the elected officials and taxpayers, this means that things are "done well and cheaply" (Quade, 1979, p. 45). However, the meanings of done well and cheaply vary according to who is making the judgments. The policy analyst's goal is to promote decision makers' understanding of the costs and benefits of using different strategies to achieve social objectives. Originally, policy analysts labored at "pure planning," generating alternatives without regard to the political contexts in which the decisions were being made (Wildavsky, 1979). Now with a more mature discipline, analysts are more likely to take interactions between planning objectives and power relationships into account (Durning, 1993).

Policy analysts use a five-stage, rational decision-making model to identify and compare various policy alternatives. Analysts first work with decision makers to define the policy's objectives as explicitly as possible. They gather data to establish base rates for existing conditions. They then try to identify all reasonable alternatives available for achieving those policy objectives and the conditions and constraints under which each alternative is likely to perform. After identifying several alternatives, analysts examine each strategy in terms of its legal, economic, technical, and political feasibility and its positive and negative effects in the short and long terms. As part of this exploration, analysts develop conceptual models to link decisions explicitly to outcomes. Because each alternative has positive and negative features, analysts then work with decision makers to develop criteria to be used to decide which alternatives are preferable (Quade, 1979).

Applying the Rational Decision-Making Model to Program Design and Evaluation

Human services programs constitute the products of the policy analysis process. Programs represent the realization of decision makers' specific decision criteria and the alternatives that they have selected to deal with social problems. Within the context the rational decision-making model, program design procedures parallel the five stages of policy analysis (see Table 14.1). Program planners begin by specifying the target problem and identifying salient factors that contribute to that problem and the relationships among those contributing factors. They then

TABLE 14.1

OUTCOMES-ORIENTED APPROACHES TO PROGRAM EVALUATION

Evaluation Approach	Key Stakeholders	Values and Evaluation Outcomes Promoted	Methods	Typical Questions
Experimental evaluations	High-level policy makers and decision makers	Theoretical, causal understanding Efficiency Accountability	Experimentation Systems analysis Causal modeling Cost–benefit analysis	Did the program achieve its desired outcomes? Are the outcomes attributable to the program? Is the program the most efficient way to achieve the desired outcomes?
Performance audits	Program funders and administrators	Efficiency Accountability	Cost finding Process evaluation Output measurements	Has the program met or exceeded pre-established program standards?
Decision-oriented or utilization-focused approaches	Local decision makers and mid-level program managers	Practicality Pragmatism Program effectiveness Quality control Resource utilization	Case studies Key informant interviews Systematic observation Document reviews	Which parts of the program work well? Which parts of the program need improvement? How effective is the program?

create conceptual models of the problem. They identify interventions that address the focal problem and implement the one that seems most appropriate for local conditions.

Evaluators work with program staff from the start to collect data on baseline conditions and intervention processes. They then interpret findings and, where possible, compare the effects of alternative strategies. Policymakers use evaluation findings help them decide whether they should continue to allocate resources to a program, while program managers use the information to improve program operations.

Social-Learning-Based Evaluations

Evaluations designed to promote social learning have their conceptual roots in educational, community, and organizational psychology. From this perspective, people confronted with new challenges try to set meaningful goals, map out plans of action, and take action in ways that they believe will help them attain their goals (Bandura, 1977). Self-assessments are an integral part of this complex, ongoing learning process. When people engage in self-assessments, they can obtain information that they need to know to help determine whether they are making progress toward achieving desired goals. If their progress is slower than anticipated, the information may suggest ways that they could modify their behavior so that success becomes more likely. When goal-oriented efforts appear to be productive, people experience feelings of self-efficacy and are more likely to persist in the face of obstacles (Bandura, 1986; Fetterman et al., 1996).

According to the social-learning perspective, system change within organizations and communities involves similar learning processes. People with common interests learn together by gathering information to better understand the nature of their shared problems; to identify alternatives, taking action to remedy those problems; and to assess how well they succeeded. If these processes are carried out effectively, such collective self-evaluations can contribute greater cooperation between organizational units, more trust in participants' ability to collaborate in problem solving, higher levels of participation, and a stronger sense of ownership among employees or individual citizens (Nelson, 1994).

Pressures for Change in Evaluation Research

As with policy analysis and other social sciences, educational evaluation research before the 1970s reflected the prevailing experimentalism of the social sciences research paradigm (Campbell & Stanley, 1963). In the 1970s and 1980s, the civil rights and feminist movements gave rise to radical critiques of positivist social sciences research methods. Activists challenged the validity of these learning and research models on the grounds that such methods submerged the perspectives of historically disenfranchised groups (Harding, 1993; Sayer, 1992). In addition, evaluation researchers began to point out that experimental models for evaluation were not providing the information needed by policymakers or program staff (Dugan, 1996; Usher, 1995).

While evaluators continued to use conventional social sciences research methods, many researchers began to advocate alternative contexts within which to apply these methods. Newer approaches take into account the ways in which both programs and their evaluations are implemented and sample a wider range of stakeholder viewpoints. Some evaluators now draw on the critical theories of Freire (1971) and newer theories of learning organizations (Chawla & Renesch, 1995).

Evaluators who endorse this position believe that stakeholders' perspectives should not only be widely sampled but also that the evaluation itself constitutes an important opportunity for individual and collective learning and community mobilization (Fetterman et al., 1996). They have argued that the evaluation process should be demystified and that stakeholders' experiences should be taken as a valid form of expertise. Furthermore, evaluations should empower stakeholders, promoting a sense of ownership in programs and their evaluations, by including them as active and ongoing participants in the evaluation process. In this way, they can learn how to design evaluations for themselves, collect and interpret data, and apply those findings to making their programs more effective.

Each evaluation approach described in this chapter has particular strengths and limitations. When designing programs and choosing strategies for evaluation them, managers are confronted with the challenge of finding ways to approximate the methodological rigor offered by the rational decision-making model without losing the dynamic complexity revealed by process and participatory evaluations. Recognizing this reality, evaluation researchers have begun to investigate how these different research paradigms can be integrated to maximize their methodological strengths and minimize their weaknesses (Greene & Caracelli, 1997).

Evaluations vary along several dimensions. The purpose of an evaluation determines its research design (see Figure 14.1). Its scope may be limited to a single program or be a more complex examination the interrelationships between several programs. It may focus on program implementation, program outcomes, or both. The evaluation may use quantitative data collection methods (e.g., surveys, administrative data), qualitative methods (for example, interviews, focus groups, case records, archival documents), or combinations of both. The purpose of an evaluation and the values expressed through it also will determine which stakeholders participate and how, and the roles that evaluators are asked to play.

Intervention Research Design Components

Evaluation Scope and Focus. The staff time and energy needed to collect data and the added expense of the consultants' expenses make conducting evaluations a costly enterprise. Because of this fact, evaluators are usually asked to limit their investigations to single programs. When stakeholders are more concerned with governance issues, the evaluation will assess how successful administrators and staffs of various community services have been in creating and sustaining collaboratives that maximize available resources (Center for the Study of Social Policy, 1996; Mulroy, 1997). When stakeholders are concerned with increasing an organization's or a community's capacity, the evaluation is designed to monitor program activities, assess outcomes, and train stakeholders to do their own evaluations and monitoring.

Evaluation approaches also can be categorized according to the degree to which they focus on outcomes or process. When the primary stakeholders are elected officials and policymakers who are concerned with efficiency and cost-effectiveness, evaluations are designed to measure program outcomes in ways that enable comparisons with other programs. If stakeholders' primary concern is program improvement, the evaluation will be designed to measure aspects of both program implementation and outcomes.

EVALUATION RESEARCH DESIGNS. The constellation of stakeholders also influences decisions about the focus of the evaluation and the evaluation design (see Campbell, 1963). Because evaluations of community services must usually respond to the information needs of multiple stakeholder groups, program evaluators often accommodate them by using "mixed-method" evaluation designs that combine outcome and process evaluation strategies (Greene, 1997).

Stakeholder Involvement, Information Needs, and Social Values

Regardless of how they are carried out, evaluations of human services programs must be responsive to many societal pressures (Usher, Gibbs, Wildfire, & Gogan, 1996). Policymakers and funding organizations are removed from the day-to-day operations of programs, but they are concerned with resource allocation issues. Program managers and frontline staff are much more in touch with how their programs function. Consumers and their families are directly or indirectly affected by how well programs are designed and implemented. Individual programs are nested within larger networks of interdependent community services, which must coordinate their efforts with one another to maximize their effectiveness (Center for the Study of Social Policy, 1996; Mulroy, 1997).

Be they individuals or collectives, all of these actors are program stakeholders. Each is motivated by different values and needs different kinds of information to perform their roles competently. Because the stakeholders who initiate an evaluation generally determine the purpose and scope of the evaluation, they also have strong vested interests in the results. In recognition of this power, the community of evaluation stakeholders has expanded. Over the past two decades, groups composed of service recipients, their families and, sometimes, whole communities have mobilized and demanded to be included explicitly in the community of stakeholders. Empowered with information about program operations and effectiveness, they too have begun to influence decisions about community services and how to make them better suited to local conditions (Weiss & Greene, 1992).

Evaluators' Roles

Evaluators are stakeholders in evaluations, too. Their professional reputations as researchers depend on their being able to conduct evaluations in ways that produce reliable and valid findings while satisfying other stakeholders' needs. Their roles depend on program structure and the type of evaluation. Evaluators may be employees of an organization that runs programs. Among their duties, they also are responsible for monitoring program operations. Alternatively, evaluators may be brought in by the organization as outside consultants with specific evaluation expertise solely to conduct an evaluation.

Depending on the evaluation design, evaluators' roles range from "program auditor" to "community facilitator." If the evaluation is based on an experimental, social sciences research paradigm, evaluators are expected to keep themselves separate from the program operations so that they can maintain their objectivity. Evaluators in this kind of role are charged with judging the outcomes and counterbalancing the vested interests of program staff and management (Lowi, 1993; Usher, 1995). The more participatory evaluation models legitimize evaluators' roles as facilitators for organizational learning, helping stakeholders learn how to design and run their own evaluations and use that information to make ongoing refinements in program operations (Usher, 1995). They also may draw on their expert status to help programs obtain needed resources (Fetterman, 1996).

RELIABILITY AND VALIDITY IN PROGRAM EVALUATION

Reliability and validity have multiple meanings within the context of program evaluation. For programs, reliability denotes the ability to produce consistent results using specified methods under a given range of conditions. Validity refers to the appropriateness of the program design and content for addressing the needs of target populations. Well-designed program services and the plans for delivering them are based on state-of-the-art knowledge. This knowledge is derived from personal experience, experience reported by others ("practice wisdom"), and scientific knowledge about the problem and appropriate remedies. Program staff success or difficulties in applying this knowledge appropriately when designing services or service delivery processes that support or diminish the accessibility and effectiveness of the service also affect program validity.

Because program evaluation also is a form of applied social sciences or behavioral research, researchers' definitions of these concepts apply. Here reliability refers to the integrity of program and evaluation implementation. Evaluators must monitor the implementation of their programs to ensure that they have been implemented as planned and to determine whether the evaluation procedures themselves have been carried out as intended. In this context, reliability also functions as an index of generalizability—that is, the degree to which a program design can be replicated in other sites with similar results. Program stakeholders differ in the importance that they place on program generalizability, and evaluation designs reflect those priorities (Patton, 1990).

To justify their conclusions, evaluators must use reliable data collection strategies. If data collection methods are deemed reliable, and significant differences in program outcomes are found over time, stakeholders can plausibly claim that the differences are attributable to the program or other factors and not to the ways in which the phenomena were measured (Frankfort-Nachmias & Nachmias, 1992). If a program does not adhere to standards for intervention reliability and validity, its perceived benefits may not be attributable to program activities. If the evaluation procedures do not meet such standards, it is impossible to know whether the program was effective because it is impossible to know what was actually evaluated.

COMPETING-VALUES FRAMEWORK AND EVALUATION APPROACHES

Policy analysts view public agencies and human services programs as tangible responses to conditions that are defined politically as social problems (Wildavsky, 1979). From a social–ecological perspective of organizational behavior, each organizational system is a subsystem within a larger institutional political system, within which subsystems compete with each other for scarce resources (Hall, 1991). Whereas each organization or program satisfies a specific set of societal values, the value systems themselves may conflict. Policymakers and program managers routinely face decisions that involve shifting resources from one program or organization to others. Ideally, the best decisions lead to courses of action in which available resources are used to provide the greatest increase in social benefits to the greatest number of people. However, such decisions are never simple. Often they are driven by political pressures and local crises whose effects unexpectedly spill over into programs that were directed at resolving apparently unrelated problems.

Organizations are effective to the degree they are able to maintain a dynamic equilibrium between their internal needs and the demands of society (Quinn, 1988). They vary in their internal operational stability, social cohesion, and employee morale. They also differ in the efficiency with which they are able to achieve their institutional missions, adapting to changing conditions or exploiting emerging opportunities in their operating environments. Managers play different roles in each organizational domain. To be effective, managers must use different and sometimes conflicting sets of skills: boundary-spanning skills, human relations skills, coordinating skills, and directing skills (see Chapter 1). Similarly, managers need different types of information to know how well they are performing in each skill area.

When choosing among possible evaluation approaches, savvy managers assess their information needs and those of other key stakeholders. Managers typically have used conventional outcome evaluation strategies based on rational decision-making principles to determine how effective they have been in directing their programs' progress toward their goals. As changing conditions compel them to expand the scope of their roles, they have begun look to newer participatory approaches. For example, managers now may use evaluation approaches, based on social- and organizational-learning principles, to obtain feedback on their performance of internal coordination functions. Growing demands for comprehensive services, interagency collaboration, and greater consumer involvement often call for systemic perspectives. Under these conditions, managers may be better served by participatory evaluation approaches that enable them to assess their effectiveness in using human relations and boundary-spanning skills to respond to changes in their communities, institutional collaboratives, and social policies. Each form of evaluation approaches is described in detail in this chapter.

TYPES OF EVALUATION

Outcome Evaluations

Outcome evaluations emphasize results that can be assessed after a program cycle has been completed or the entire program has been terminated. The strengths and limitations of the three most common types of outcome evaluations—experimental evaluations, performance audits, and decision-oriented approaches—are summarized in Table 14.1.

EXPERIMENTAL EVALUATIONS. Traditionally, experimental outcome evaluations are mandated by high-level policymakers or other distant stakeholders. They typically incorporate research designs that reflect the assumptions and values of policy analysis and the rational decision-making model. This kind of evaluation often relies on the "gold standard" of research methodologies: experimental and quasi-experimental research designs (Usher, 1995; Weiss & Greene, 1992). For this type of research design, the goal is to establish that independent variables (e.g., program activities) and dependent variables (e.g., program outcomes) are causally related (Frankfort-Nachmias & Nachmias, 1992). To confirm this, researchers use strategies of comparison, manipulation, and control. In a laboratory setting, for example, researchers can use random assignment of participants into treatment and control groups to help rule out the possibility that factors other than the program caused the observed association between the "treatment" and specific outcomes. In classic experimental protocols, data are collected before the start of a program or program cycle and then again after a given program cycle has been completed.

Program evaluators use various statistical techniques to assess the degree to which changes in program outcomes are related to provision of program services. They also seek to understand causal relationships by trying to control the internal and external conditions of the study systematically. It is impossible to impose the level of control required for experimental research. Pragmatic evaluators seeking to approximate the rigor of experimental designs may use quasi-experimental research designs that do not require randomization. Instead of randomized assignment and carefully matched control groups, researchers may use comparison groups that share critical characteristics. They may gather samples from various sites or make multiple observations of the same groups over time as supplementary data to support their conclusions about the extent and range of program effects (Frankfort-Nachmias & Nachmias, 1992).

Experimental evaluations provide the strongest evidence for program effectiveness. However, the requirements of this type of research design limit its usefulness as the basis for policy making. If the evaluation design requires random assignment of individual program participants, the experiment is usually limited to a few select sites. The information produced by such a study cannot explicitly account for widely varying organizational, political, and community contexts. Further, experimental designs often have the unintended consequence of alienating program staff from the evaluation effort with evaluators viewed as adversaries. Staff members with vested interests in meeting the needs of their clients may view random assignment as an unethical limitation of services. Worries that the evaluation findings will be unfavorable also may precipitate staff concerns about job security (Usher, 1995). Faced with these perceived threats, staff choose not to implement new interventions or carry out evaluation tasks as prescribed. Such coping strategies can compromise the evaluation design to such an extent that it does not measure what was intended. Other circumstances that occur during the course of an evaluation may threaten the validity of evaluation findings, such as organizational policy changes, the departure of key staff, or high dropout rates among experimental or control group participants (Lipsey, 1990).

PERFORMANCE AUDITS AND CONTRACTS. Performance audits are used when decision makers want a "nonsympathetic" third-party review of program outcomes. They tend to be investigative in tone and assume an adversarial relationship between program evaluators and program managers and staff (Usher, 1995). Although the purpose of performance audits may be to promote efficiency, the true cost of providing services and the full range of program benefits may never be calculated. Performance audits are inflexible in that measurement of outcomes does not take into account the effects of changes within the organization or in the conditions within which the program operates (Wedel, 1991). From the standpoint of community governance, performance auditing may be self-defeating. Because its goal is to promote efficient use of resources, it spurs competition between providers to capture scarce resources rather than cooperation to create synergistic effects for communities as a whole (Nelson, 1994).

Performance contracting is an outgrowth of performance auditing. In performance contracts, funders and program administrators negotiate performance contracts before the program begins. Such contracts specify the degree of change in specific conditions to be accomplished by the end of the funding cycle, the criteria to be used for measuring those changes, the means for monitoring them, and the incentives for meeting or not meeting these goals (Eikenberry & Kluver, 2004). Here the funders are interested in knowing whether a program has met or exceeded pre-established standards of performance. The evaluator may be either a project or contract manager with specific responsibilities for program monitoring or an independent consultant brought in from outside. Performance contracts may be linked to linear or stepwise standards. When linear standards are used, incentives and penalties are keyed to incremental improvements. Performance contracts incorporating step structure criteria reward or penalize programs on the basis of the proportion of overall change in the criteria over the course of a program cycle using some predetermined baseline (Eikenberry & Kluver, 2004; Wedel, 1991).

DECISION-ORIENTED APPROACHES. Program managers and local decision makers often need to make programmatic and budget decisions based on information about which parts of their programs are working well and which need improvement. These circumstances call for evaluations that use a decision-oriented approach (Weiss & Greene, 1992). This approach (also known as utilization-focused) is appropriate for smaller-scale evaluations. Whether evaluators are appointed from within the organization or brought in from outside, they are expected to maintain a degree of objectivity. Findings from decision-oriented evaluations are site specific, so stakeholders do not have to be concerned with their generalizability. However, evaluators must be concerned about the reliability of the data they are given, so they "triangulate" perspectives. By drawing on multiple data sources, (e.g., administrative data; structured and unstructured surveys; questionnaires, interviews, and systematic observations), they can confirm their conclusions. If different data sources lead to contradictory findings, evaluators may work with administrative stakeholders to interpret such discrepancies and their implications for program planning.

Process-Oriented Evaluations

Process-oriented evaluations are used to gain insight into the ways in which a specific program is experienced by staff and participants at a specific time under specific conditions (Weiss & Greene, 1992). These evaluations are principally used for two related purposes: (1) They are used when managers need to understand the relationship between a program's implementation and stakeholders' feelings of satisfaction or frustration with the way services are delivered and (2) they also are used to gain insight into the strengths and weaknesses of programs and to assess whether the program is working as planned (Patton, 1990). These evaluations use a variety of qualitative research methods, such as ethnographic and case studies, interviews with key informants, focus groups, and opinion surveys (Weiss & Greene, 1992).

Because qualitative research requires a unique kind of expertise in relating to the program staff and consumers who provide the information, evaluators are usually brought in from outside. Evaluators themselves are data collection instruments. Their interpersonal skills, sensitivity to verbal and nonverbal cues, and perceived personal integrity affect whether their informants trust them enough to disclose sensitive information. These evaluator characteristics largely determine whether such evaluations are considered reliable and valid (Patton, 1990). The validity of process-oriented evaluation findings can be challenged if the evaluators are unskilled in the systematic observation, in-depth interviewing, and survey design needed for this approach.

Participatory Evaluations

Participatory evaluations represent an important shift away from the deductive, researcher-centered approaches to more inductive, community-centered efforts (Langton & Taylor, 1992). Participatory evaluations also vary in approach and purpose. Some focus on remedying specific problems, whereas others explicitly aim to promote community empowerment through social criticism and long-term structural changes (see Table 14.2). The following sections describe different participatory approaches to evaluation.

PROGRAM THEORIES OF CHANGE. A cross-cutting theme that has recently emerged and is compatible with all of these approaches, however, is the importance of strategic planning. More specifically, it is the recommendation that

TABLE 14.2

PROCESS-ORIENTED AND PARTICIPATORY APPROACHES TO PROGRAM EVALUATION

Evaluation Approach	Key Stakeholders	Values and Evaluation Outcomes Promoted	Methods	Typical Questions
Process	Program directors, staff, and clients	Pluralism Understanding diverse populations Deficit based	Case studies Key informant interviews Systematic observation Document reviews	How do various stakeholders experience the program?
Action research	Community activists Stakeholders who are directly affected by the problem under study	Pluralism Building capacity to achieve social change Deficit based	Content analysis of reports in mass media Focus groups with stakeholders Key informant interviews with stakeholders Systematic observation	What do people in the system need? What research needs to be done to understand the system? What interventions are needed to improve the system?
Program self-evaluation	Program funders Evaluators Program administrators, staff, and clients Representatives from other community organizations	Community self-governance Organizational learning Enhanced capacity for self-evaluation Implementation integrity Program effectiveness Asset based	Multimethod (quasi-experimental and qualitative methods) Surveys Record reviews Focus groups	Is the program serving the intended population? To what extent is the program being implemented as planned? How do various stakeholders experience the the program? To what extent and in what ways is the program effective?

TABLE 14.2
PROCESS-ORIENTED AND PARTICIPATORY APPROACHES TO PROGRAM EVALUATION
(continued)

Evaluation Approach	Key Stakeholders	Values and Evaluation Outcomes Promoted	Methods	Typical Questions
Program self-evaluation (continued)				To what extent is the program coordinating its efforts with other community services?
Cluster evaluation	Program funders Evaluators Program administrators Staff	Pluralism Mutual understanding Organizational learning Inclusion of multiple interests Deficit based	Biannual networking conferences Focus groups	How do various programs respond to common problems? To what extent and in what ways do programs? To what extent and in what ways do programs identify and address the needs of disenfranchised groups?
Empowerment evaluation	Disempowered groups (including program clients and others) Representatives of the dominant system	Empowerment Social change Deficit based	Stakeholder involvement in identifying ways to develop outcome measures (e.g., structured and unstructured questionnaires and surveys) Systematic observation Historical analyses Social criticism	In what ways to do the program's premises, goals, and activities maintain structural inequities in the distribution of power and resources?

TABLE 14.2

PROCESS-ORIENTED AND PARTICIPATORY APPROACHES TO PROGRAM EVALUATION
(continued)

Evaluation Approach	Key Stakeholders	Values and Evaluation Outcomes Promoted	Methods	Typical Questions
Appreciative inquiry	Same as above	Empowerment Organizational learning Worker engagement Asset based	Stakeholders conduct in-depth interviews with each other to describe data	What are participants' best experiences with the organization? What do participants value most about themselves, the nature of their work, and the focal organization? What do participants experience as the core values of the organization? What three wishes would participants make to enhance the vitality and health of the organization?

participants in an evaluation consciously and deliberately develop a "theory of change" to guide the development and implementation of new programs and policies (Connell & Kubisch, 1997). A theory of change articulates the stakeholders' notions of what will make the program work. It differs from the rational decision making process, in which logic models are used that start by characterizing the problem and identify inputs needed at each stage of the program (W. K. Kellogg Foundation, 2003). To create a theory of change, stakeholders work backward from the ultimate goals that they want to achieve, specifying what interim goals must be attained to create the conditions for attaining later ones (see Table 14.3; Connell & Kubisch, 1997). As they identify goals at

TABLE 14.3
THEORY OF CHANGE AND EVALUATION MODEL

Theory of Change Step	Program Characteristics	Evaluation Questions
1. Long-term outcomes	What are the program's three main objectives? What knowledge bases (e.g., theory, research, best practices) have been used to select these objectives? What are the relationships among the program's objectives?	How are these outcomes measured? When are they measured? How are these data currently being analyzed?
2. Penultimate outcomes	How long can consumers remain in the program? How and when do program staff (or consumers) determine that consumers are approaching completion of the program? What do consumers have to do to successfully complete the program? What program activities contribute most directly to consumers' completion of the program? How do these activities contribute to the attainment of the programs' goals? How do program activities enhance or interfere with each other?	How are consumers' participation levels documented? What key aspects of consumer participation (if any) are currently *not* documented? What kind of follow-up does the organization do (if any) to assess the program's long-term effectiveness? How does the organization use program evaluation and client satisfaction survey data to improve services?

TABLE 14.3
THEORY OF CHANGE AND EVALUATION MODEL (continued)

Theory of Change Step	Program Characteristics	Evaluation Questions
3. Intermediate outcomes	How and when are program plans for individual participants or groups reassessed?	When and how are changes in program plans documented?
	What circumstances lead to changes in program plans?	How are program interactions documented?
	Who is involved in negotiating changes in program plans?	How and when are revised program activities reassessed for appropriateness and effectiveness?
	What criteria are used to decide which program services should be added or dropped at this stage?	
	What combinations of activities appear to enhance or conflict with each other, and in what ways?	
	Under what circumstances are consumers terminated or diverted from the program?	
	Organizational Learning	
	What organizational structures and processes interfere with effective delivery of services?	How are problems with organizational structures and processes documented?
	When, how often, and under what circumstances do these problems occur?	When organizational conflicts are resolved, how are these events documented?
	How are they resolved?	
	How does the organization feed back organizational learning to managers and staff?	

TABLE 14.3
THEORY OF CHANGE AND EVALUATION MODEL (continued)

Theory of Change Step	Program Characteristics	Evaluation Questions
4. Early outcomes	*Participants' Entry Into the Service System*	
	What must a person do to be considered a participant in the program?	How are these behaviors documented?
	When must these requirements be completed?	What key behaviors (if any) are not documented? Why?
	What tasks must staff do when enrolling new participants?	How are staff actions documented?
	What are the deadlines for completing these tasks?	
	Early-Stage Treatment or Service Management	
	When are treatment or service plans established?	How are these planning procedures documented?
	Who is involved in treatment or service plan negotiations?	What planning procedures (if any) are not documented? Why?
	What criteria (if any) are used to individualize plans?	How are final plans documented?
	What staff are involved in implementing plans?	What plans (if any) are not documented? Why?
	What is the schedule for supervisors' review of plans?	How is the implementation of plans monitored?
	How are plans' appropriateness and adequacy assessed at this stage?	
	When and how is feedback given to staff?	

TABLE 14.3
THEORY OF CHANGE AND EVALUATION MODEL (continued)

Theory of Change Step	Program Characteristics	Evaluation Questions
5. Initial conditions	*Participant Characteristics*	
	What are participants' sociodemographic characteristics?	How are these characteristics measured?
	What are participants' problem baseline levels?	How often are these characteristics measured?
		How recently were these characteristics measured?
	Predisposing and Precipitating Environmental Conditions	
	What are the baseline levels of these conditions?	How are these factors measured?
	How are staff members informed about changing conditions in the operating and community environment?	How often are these factors measured?
		How recently were these factors measured?
	How is this information incorporated into on-going program planning?	
	Stakeholders	
	Who are the key stake-holders for the organization or project?	How are contacts with stakeholders documented?
	How does the organization define its stakeholders?	When do they need information?
	What different kinds of information do various stake-holders need?	
	How will they use program or client information?	

each program stage, stakeholders also specify the kinds of data that they can use to determine that those goals have been met (see Table 14.2).

To develop a theory of change demands a substantial level of commitment by participants coupled with the self-discipline to think through the intentions and expected consequences of plans, but the effort can be expected to pay significant and varied dividends. One important benefit is that evaluators can introduce stakeholders to research evidence about effective interventions while tailoring the intervention design to local needs and priorities (Usher & Wildfire, 2003). In cases in which there are no standardized measures for capturing progress on interim program goals, evaluators help participants develop them.

PROGRAM SELF-EVALUATIONS. Program self-evaluation is a specialized form of participatory evaluation used within individual programs. The aim here is to help organizations integrate their management and evaluation processes in such a way that "information about program performance feeds back into policy and program planning, [enabling] corrective action and quality improvement to become routine" (see Table 14.2; Usher, 1995, p. 62). Variants of such integrative approaches are also being promoted as complementary monitoring systems to conventional financial measures of productivity in for-profit corporations (Kaplan & Norton, 1996). In contrast to the adversarial relationships so common in conventional evaluations, the self-evaluation approach is based on the assumption that stakeholders at different levels have a shared interest in making programs as effective as possible.

Instead of imposing a research design on the program, the evaluator acts as a consultant, working with groups of managers, staff, and stakeholders to help them identify and articulate their program's theory of change. Once they have developed their program models, staff members and the evaluators collaborate in developing evaluation designs and data collection procedures. When an appropriate measure for a given goal does not exist within the organization, the evaluator can help staff find a valid and reliable measure or help them develop one. If it does not exist already, the evaluators also assist the organization to develop the capacity to analyze and interpret the data that staff members collect. The goal of this training is to help program managers and staff members develop the skills to detect problems and make midcourse corrections. As program staff master these new skills, they become more comfortable taking the risks that come with innovation (Usher, 1995). The objective is to create a "community of practice" that integrates research and practice to enhance the efficiency and effectiveness of programs (Phillips, 2005).

Table 14.3 illustrates the basic structure of self-evaluation teams developed in the Family to Family child welfare reform initiative sponsored by the Annie E. Casey Foundation. At the center of these teams is a triumvirate of stakeholders within the child welfare agency who bring unique perspectives to the evaluation process but who often do not have a history of productive relationships. These three stakeholders include data managers, analysts, and program staff, positions usually found in child welfare agencies in large communities. Data managers are staff members who oversee the operation and maintenance of information systems that support program operations and from which information about client characteristics and outcomes can be obtained. Analysts are staff members who are responsible for meeting state and federal reporting requirements. These responsibilities often are so demanding that they constrain analysts' capacity to respond to the information needs of managers, policymakers, and community stakeholders.

The role of program staff is specifically and pragmatically defined in self-evaluation. The team should include one frontline supervisor or mid-level manager who will have 15 percent of his or her time dedicated to self-evaluation activities. Preferably, that person will have demonstrated the ability to step back from the intensity of day-to-day, case-to-case activities and discern patterns in those activities.

The people in each of these roles bring unique perspectives. Direct-practice program staff self-select to work with families and children rather than pursuing roles that require more impersonal involvement with computer equipment and data. Although their sensitivity to and regard for individual families and children are essential to the agency's effectiveness, it can be difficult for some to look beyond each client and to see what all the clients have in common. Just the opposite, however, can be true of data managers and analysts, who may ignore the uniqueness of individuals in their attempts to identify patterns across those individuals. Bringing them together, therefore, can help create a richer understanding of agency operations and impact.

CLUSTER EVALUATIONS. Cluster evaluations are a new form of participatory evaluation developed by the Kellogg Foundation to promote self-evaluation capacity across the programs it funds (Greene, 1997; W. K. Kellogg Foundation, 1998). Representatives from each project gather semiannually for networking sessions. Cluster evaluations are founded on the idea of "open borders" in which the evaluation does not have to be protected from program activities to be considered valid. The purpose of these meetings is to aid and support member projects in their evaluations and program development activities and to promote the expression of "democratic pluralism." The foundation's intent is to ensure that the programs and evaluations that it funds take into account the interests of the least-enfranchised citizens. Kellogg staff help staff and evaluators of individual projects analyze their programs and evaluation implementation and give them feedback. Cluster evaluation feedback focuses on the degree to which the evaluations systematically include multiple interests. The foundation has used cluster evaluations extensively with many kinds of programs that it has funded, including child welfare reform initiatives (Walter R. McDonald & Associates, 2003) and university–neighborhood partnerships to improve family and community development practices (Insites, 1998).

The advantage of cluster evaluations is that they enable programs and evaluators to learn from each other about how to resolve common problems, such as how to engage stakeholders in the self-evaluation process or balance programmatic and materials development efforts. Cluster evaluators explicitly advocate empowerment values but avoid the charge of partisanship by promoting program staff and evaluator inquiries. Cluster evaluation discussions cover such topics as the role of expertise in evaluations, the appropriate balance of content and process, and definitions of the programs' and evaluations' stakeholders (Greene, 1997). Cluster evaluators also may help conference participants understand the range of their options within each dimension of an evaluation by developing typologies. The typology itself then is used as the basis of further discussion among participants.

The advantages of this approach also are potential limitations. Sponsors, evaluators, and participants must be willing to think beyond their individual sites. Sponsors must value democratic pluralism and be interested in promoting and supporting organizational learning across projects. The sponsors must have supported several projects similar enough to enable reasonable comparisons. Cluster evaluators are necessarily distant from the ultimate consumers of program services. They must be informed enough about potentially disenfranchised groups and the conditions that contribute to disempowerment to be able to ask appropriate questions. In addition, program administrators must be willing to allow staff to take time out from their primary responsibilities to attend such conferences. Finally, program staff must be able to connect the rather abstract level of discussions about program evaluation to their own work as caregivers.

Empowerment Evaluations

Empowerment evaluation aims to engage a wide range of stakeholders in the analysis of the role of programs within the larger social structure. Although empowerment evaluations seek to determine whether a program is effective, other goals also are considered important. These evaluations promote the learning that participants acquire in the process as much as the specific outcomes of the study. Stakeholders are taught to think critically in identifying key issues and different perspectives about how well a program addresses local needs. The goals of empowerment evaluations are ambitious: "to promote community-level collaboration, improve community climate, strengthen networks, promote positive identity, and increase community assets" (Weiss & Greene, 1992, p. 141). Such analyses can be used to lay the groundwork for future community mobilizations.

Ideally, empowerment evaluations increase the likelihood of precipitating institutional and policy changes. By participating on the evaluation team, members who historically have had little power establish relationships with others who are more powerful and influential. The evaluation team's decision-making process is intended to model standards of parity, justice, and caring. By collaborating in a joint effort with others who have historically been disempowered, stakeholders with power acquire insight from the historical perspective about social problems and are more motivated to support community activism (Greene, 1997).

ACTION RESEARCH. Action research represents an empowerment-oriented equivalent to formative evaluation in more formal research projects. Where formative evaluations limit their focus to specific programs, action research methods may be used to study a wider range of issues, including a program's outcomes and its impact on the surrounding community (Patton, 1990). Expert evaluators usually are called on to conduct formative evaluations, but action research is often conducted by people who are directly affected by the problems being studied. Community activists may use action research methods as a form of "rapid reconnaissance" to collect information quickly about a problem (Patton, 1990). This may involve content analysis of communication media, focus groups with stakeholders, interviews with key informants, and systematic observations.

The major limitations of this methodology are twofold. First, action researchers may not be skilled in data collection methods needed to ensure the validity of their findings. If they are not professional researchers, they may have a vested interest in one outcome over another. As a result, they may not collect the range of information needed to present a balanced view of the situation. Second, if researchers are strongly partisan and their positions on community issues are well known, opponents may obstruct their efforts to gain access to certain types of information. Lacking such information, community activists may not reach accurate conclusions about problem conditions or the full range of possible solutions.

EMPOWERMENT EVALUATIONS IN PROGRAMS. Where professional evaluators are involved in empowerment-oriented program evaluations, they primarily serve as teachers and facilitators. Their role is to help stakeholders acquire the skills they need to carry out an evaluation that produces valid and useful results. In essence, the evaluators teach stakeholders to use the rational decision-making model by following four basic procedures. First, the evaluator works with community members to establish a baseline against which future progress can be measured. Participants "take stock" by informally rating programs and their activities and learn about data collection by collecting information that would support their assessments of their programs. Second, participants engage in goal-setting exercises to develop a shared vision of what the program should be doing. Third, participants work to develop program models that specify clear causal connections among starting points, intermediate goals that are linked to routine program activities, and their global desired outcomes. In the process, participants learn how to use critical review and consensus-building processes to reduce and refine their goals to those that are most significant to the program's operation. In the final step, participants learn how to document program progress toward their goals. They identify the data that they need; review existing data collection methods to see what data are already being collected; and, where necessary, develop new forms and methods for monitoring data collection (Fetterman, 1996).

Professional evaluators often take charge of the data analysis because program staff do not have the skills or the time to do this work. However, the results of such analyses are always given back to the participants, who are responsible for interpreting them and determining how this new information is used.

Although empowerment evaluation has the potential for revitalizing programs and communities, it also is more vulnerable to breakdown than more conventional forms of evaluation. They are more time consuming because they involve not only the evaluation but also a high degree of organizational and community learning. Differences in the individual skills and capacities of participants may cause some of them to feel frustrated and others intimidated. Because empowerment evaluations have explicitly political goals, they may break down if conflicts between stakeholders cause some to become alienated. Because empowerment evaluations compete for staff time and other program resources, the support of program leaders is essential. The evaluation also can break down if the leaders do not support the process and withhold resources or are unwilling to make the changes endorsed by the evaluation participants.

APPRECIATIVE INQUIRY. Participatory and empowerment evaluation approaches can provide opportunities to identify program strengths, but more often they focus on deficits. By contrast, *Appreciative Inquiry* (AI) combines continuous quality improvement, empowerment, and asset-based approaches. In the other participatory evaluation approaches described earlier, stakeholders engage in strategic planning or develop theories of change. First developed in the 1980s as a system for organizational development, there is now an active online community called Appreciative Inquiry Commons (see Appendix 14.1 for more information) in which practitioners and students from around the world discuss how to best to apply the principles of this system to promote system change. AI also has been used in program evaluations of school curriculum reforms (McNamee, 2003) and youth development programs (Smart & Mann, 2003).

AI combines participant-developed theories of change development with an explicit constructionist theory of change. The latter is founded on European postmodernist assumptions that there are multiple realities and that people's conceptions of reality are socially coconstructed, with language and words serving the building blocks of social reality. All organizations are, therefore, arbitrary social constructions, and people's ability to create new and better organizations is limited only by their imagination and collective will. As participants change the stories they tell each other about their organization and the images they hold of it, they can begin to reshape it. AI proponents call this the heliotropic principle. They reason that, as "what you look for you will find," stakeholders who focus first on problems in their evaluations are most likely to find aspects of the organization that are "broken," or sources of frustration. AI promotes a theory of change that focuses on "what works well, on individual peak experiences and noblest aspirations" so that "the organization moves toward its most desired future while along the way addressing things that need to change so that the image of the future can be realized" (Watkins & Kelly, n.d., p. 39). Rather than seeking to identify organizational deficits that need to be remedied, evaluation using AI frame their evaluation questions affirmatively. Participants are asked to talk about what "gives life" to the organization and the individuals who work in it.

All AIs involve a five-phase, participatory process, "the 5-D cycle." In Phase 1, participants work in small groups and come to consensus in defining the area of their inquiry (e.g., service excellence, leadership). In Phase 2, they use in-depth peer interviews to discover what is happening when the organization is at its best in relation to this topic and develop a list of positive themes or attributes that characterize the organization's history. In Phase 3, participants shift their temporal focus from past to future. Facilitators lead them through "dreaming" exercises in which they coconstruct preferred futures. During these group sessions, participants draw on their lists of positive personal and organizational attributes to develop "provocative propositions" that depict in detail how the organization as a whole would look, feel, and function when all of the positive conditions are present.

In the later phases of the 5-D cycle, participants begin to use the data they have collected to operationalize their change goals. In Phase 4, they embark on the design phase to align the organization's social architecture with its core values and preferred future. They develop "macro provocative propositions" about the organization's processes, policies, systems, roles and relationships, and structures that support their dreams for their individual and collective futures. Each participant is then asked to think about the parts of the dream that he or she personally wants to help bring to life. At this point, each person is given an opportunity to make a simple commitment, make an offer to provide needed resources, or articulate a request about something he or she needs from another person or group. In Phase 5, participants initiate an ongoing process of cocreating and delivering their preferred futures. During this phase, they begin to implement the innovative ideas and propositions they developed in earlier phases and to build in structures and processes that sustain the momentum and create an appreciative organizational learning culture.

Because AI represents a significant shift in perspectives, consultants who are experts in AI are brought in to run workshops in which participants are oriented to assumptions underlying AI using experiential exercises. Participants are then trained in the skills they will need to develop and conduct their in-depth interviews with coworkers and to construct the "provocative propositions" that they will use to motivate and guide organizational innovations.

In their review of a series of studies that used of AI in evaluations, Patricia Rogers and Dugan Fraser (2003) concluded that AI is

> Most useful in longstanding programs that have become depleted or exhausted and require an infusion of positive energy and recognition in order to be revived and that also have completed more usual evaluations to identify problems that exist. Appreciative Inquiry is particularly valuable in programs that are highly complex, where the technique can serve to restate and reframe what is valuable, useful, and important. (p. 80)

They have cautioned, however, that AI is a good choice only if the facilitators have the requisite skills to guide the process, the multidisciplinary teams to carry out the AI tasks that are composed of members with the affirming types of skills to apply the technique properly, and the leadership willing to support this kind of exploration and a change process that is sustained over time. Without these conditions, organizations run the risk avoiding hard issues and coming up with only self-congratulatory findings or providing cynical participants with opportunities for voicing destructive opinions about the differences between present realities and collective aspirations.

LIMITATIONS OF EMPOWERMENT APPROACHES TO EVALUATION. As described earlier, empowerment-oriented evaluations have the potential for revitalizing programs and communities. However, they also are clearly more vulnerable to breakdown than are more conventional forms of evaluation. They are more time consuming because they involve not only the evaluation but also a high degree of organizational and community learning. Differences in the individual skills and capacities of participants may cause some of them to feel frustrated and others to feel intimidated. Because empowerment evaluations have explicitly political goals, they may break down if conflicts between stakeholders cause some to become alienated. Because empowerment evaluations compete for staff time and other program resources, the support of program leaders is essential.

The evaluation also can break down if the leaders do not support the process by withholding resources or being unwilling to make the changes endorsed by the evaluation participants.

CONCLUSION

Managers of nonprofits and public agencies and their staffs are more often the subjects (or victims) of evaluations than they are participants in the evaluation process (Terry, 1997). Conventional evaluations call for a clear separation of the roles of manager and evaluator, often making them adversaries. However, two factors are causing these roles to blur: (1) managers' greater discretion in implementing policy and (2) increased demands for accountability by policy makers and the public. Anticipating policymakers' concerns, more managers are trying to develop the capacity to provide answers before questions are asked. In addition, more managers recognize that they are managing learning organizations whose work entails a series of midcourse corrections that bring them ever closer to the outcomes they seek.

These newer formulations of evaluation are gaining grudging acceptance among professional evaluators who traditionally adhered to a role more akin to that of the scientist than a vital participant in the public policy process. The changes in approach entail changes in context and method as well as attitude. The new context is one in which policymakers and the public understand evaluation to be more than auditing and evaluators understand that it is more than detached, "objective" research. The changes also involve the enrichment of evaluation to encompass a wider range of methods and designs that collectively capture a more valid and reliable composite of what works in programs and how.

Regardless of the type of nonprofit organization in which they work, the most effective managers have probably always understood the importance of evaluation and have incorporated it into their work. Recent political changes and emerging changes in the practice of program evaluation lend legitimacy to this dimension of human services management. By taking advantage of this opportunity, managers who develop their personal skills in evaluation and their organizations' capacity to conduct evaluations and use their findings are likely to see substantial benefits as a result of the insights that they acquire about their efficiency and effectiveness. Simply being able to produce valid and reliable information about program operations and impact helps build positive relationships with a wide range of organization stakeholders.

SKILLS APPLICATION EXERCISE

Programs can be difficult to evaluate because their designs are underspecified (Connell, Kubisch, Shorr, & Weiss, 1997). Often, client problems, precipitating conditions, and desired outcomes are known. However, the specific ways that program activities help consumers move from the problems that lead them to seek program services—or have them mandated—to improved states may not have been explicitly thought through. Table 14.2 diagrams the relationship between program logic models and program theories of change. Table 14.3 lists the questions that need to be answered to develop a working theory of change. Managers and staff need to decide what kind of data needs to be collected to determine whether program outcomes are being achieved at various time scales (e.g., long term, penultimate, intermediate, earlier outcomes); whether these data are currently available; and, if not, what data collection methods can be used to fill in the information gaps.

This exercise is designed to help you articulate the theory that underlies and intervention, starting from its ultimate objects and working backward. Each step is linked to a set of evaluation design questions to help you understand how you know what you know.

1. Think about the program for which you work or for which you have management responsibility. Review the questions in Table 14.3, and write brief answers to as many as you can.
   - Which are easy to answer? Why?
   - Which are hard to answer? Why?
   - For the questions that are difficult to answer, is there information available to answer those questions? Why or why not?
   - Who can provide this missing information?
2. After you have answered the questions, construct a diagram with a theory of change model showing how you believe the program works.
   - Identify any logical gaps.
   - Identify situations in which program activities conflict with each other (e.g., in their objectives, sequencing, scheduling).
3. How does your organization analyze and use the information that is available to help staff improve their performance and improve the program's overall functioning?

REFERENCES

Alexander, J. (1999). The impact of devolution on nonprofits. *Nonprofit Management & Leadership, 10*, 57–70.

Bandura, A. (1977). *Social learning theory*. Englewood Cliffs, NJ: Prentice Hall.

Bandura, A. (1986). *Social foundations of thought and action*. Englewood Cliffs, NJ: Prentice-Hall.

Campbell, D. T., & Stanley, J. C. (1963). *Experiential and quasi-experimental designs for research*. Boston: Houghton-Mifflin.

Center for the Study of Social Policy. (1996). *Toward new forms of local governance: A progress report from the field*. Washington, DC: Author.

Chawla, S., & Renesch, J. (Eds.). (1995). *Learning organizations: Developing cultures for tomorrow's workplace*. Portland, OR: Productivity Press.

Connell, J., & Kubisch, A. (1997, January). *Applying a theory of change approach to the evaluation of comprehensive community initiatives: Progress, prospects, and problems*. Paper presented at the Aspen Institute Roundtable on Comprehensive Community Initiatives for Children and Families, Aspen, CO.

Connell, J., Kubisch, A., Shorr, L., & Weiss, C. (Eds.). (1997). *New approaches to evaluating community initiatives* (Vol. 2). Washington, DC: Aspen Institute.

Dugan, M. A. (1996). Participatory and empowerment evaluation: Lessons learned in training and technical assistance. In D. M. Fetterman, S. J. Kaftarian, & A. Wandersman (Eds.), *Empowerment evaluation: Knowledge and tools for self-assessment and accountability* (pp. 277–301). Newbury Park, CA: Sage.

Durning, D. (1993). Participatory policy analysis in a social service agency: A case study. *Journal of Policy Analysis and Management, 12*, 297–322.

Edwards, R. L., Cooke, P. W., & Reid, P. N. (1996). Social work management in an era of diminishing federal responsibility. *Social Work, 41*, 468–479.

Eikenberry, A. M., & Kluver, J. D. (2004). The marketization of the nonprofit sector: Civil society at risk? *Public Administration Review, 64*, 132–142.

Fetterman, D. M. (1996). Empowerment evaluation: An introduction to theory and practice. In D. M. Fetterman, S. J. Kaftarian, & A. Wandersman (Eds.), *Empowerment evaluation: Knowledge and tools for self-assessment and accountability* (pp. 3–46). Newbury Park, CA: Sage.

Fetterman, D. M., Kaftarian, S. J., & Wandersman, A. (Eds.). (1996). *Empowerment evaluation: Knowledge and tools for self-assessment and accountability*. Newbury Park, CA: Sage.

Fine, A., H., Thayer, C., E., & Coghlan, A. T. (1998). *Program evaluation practice in the nonprofit sector*. Washington, DC: Aspen Institute Nonprofit Sector Research Fund & Robert Wood Johnson Foundation.

Frankfort-Nachmias, C., & Nachmias, D. (1992). *Research methods in the social sciences* (4th ed.). Harrisburg, PA: St. Martin's Press.

Freire, P. (1971). *Pedagogy of the oppressed* (M. B. Ramos, Trans.). New York: HarperCollins.

Gitlow, H. S., & Gitlow, S. J. (1987). *The Deming guide to quality and competitive position*. Englewood Cliffs, NJ: Prentice Hall.

Greene, J. C. (1997). Evaluation as advocacy. *Evaluation Practice, 18*(1), 25–36.

Greene, J. C., & Caracelli, V. J. (Eds.). (1997). *Advances in mixed-method evaluation: The challenges and benefits of integrating diverse paradigms* (Special Issue, Vol. 74). San Francisco: Jossey-Bass.

Hall, R. H. (1991). *Organizations: Structures, processes, and outcomes.* Englewood Cliffs, NJ: Prentice Hall.

Harding, S. (1993). Rethinking standpoint epistemology: What is strong objectivity? In L. Alcoff & E. Potter (Eds.), *Feminist epistemologies* (pp. 49–82). Boston: Routledge & Kegan Paul.

Insites. (1998). *Partnerships: A powerful tool for improving well-being of families and neighborhoods.* Battle Creek, MI: W. K. Kellogg Foundation.

Kaplan, R. S., & Norton, D. P. (1996, January/February). Using the "balanced scorecard" as a strategic management system. *Harvard Business Review,* pp. 75–85.

Langton, P. A., & Taylor, E. G. (1992). Applying a participatory research model to alcohol prevention research in ethnic communities. In P. A. Langton (Ed.), *The challenge of participatory research: Preventing alcohol-related problems in ethnic communities* (CSAP Pub. 95-3042, pp. 1–20). Washington, DC: U.S. Department of Health and Human Services.

Levitan, S. (1992). *Evaluation of federal social programs: An uncertain impact* (Occasional Paper 1992-2). Washington, DC: George Washington University, Center for Social Policy Studies.

Lipsey, M. W. (1990). *Design sensitivity: Statistical power for experimental research.* Newbury Park, CA: Sage Publications.

Lowi, T. J. (1993). Legitimizing public administration: A disturbed dissent. *Public Administration Review, 53,* 261–264.

Loyacono, L. L. (1995). The arts: Singing the blues. *State Legislatures, 21,* 24–27.

McCarthy, K., Brooks, A., Lowell, J., & Zakaras, L. (2001). *The performing arts in a new era.* Retrieved December 1, 2004, from http://www.pewtrusts.com/pdf/cul_rand.pdf

McNamee, S. (2003, Winter). Appreciative evaluation within a conflicted educational context. *New Directions for Evaluation,* pp. 23–40.

Mulroy, E. A. (1997). Building a neighborhood network: Interorganizational collaboration to prevent child abuse and neglect. *Social Work, 42,* 255–264.

Nelson, D. (1994, September). *Keynote address.* Paper presented at the "Reforming Systems, Reforming Evaluation," a conference sponsored by the Annie E. Casey Foundation, Baltimore.

Patton, M. Q. (Ed.). (1990). *Qualitative evaluation and research methods.* Newbury Park CA: Sage.

Phillips, S. D. (2005). *The National Child Traumatic Stress Network: In context, theory, and practice.* Unpublished doctoral dissertation, University of North Carolina, Chapel Hill.

Quade, E. S. (1979). *Analysis for public decision.* New York: Elsevier.

Quinn, R. E. (1988). *Beyond rational management: Mastering the paradoxes and competing demands of high performance*. San Francisco: Jossey-Bass.

Rogers, P., & Fraser, D. (2003, Winter). Appreciating appreciative inquiry. *New Directions for Evaluation*, pp. 75–84.

Sayer, A. (1992). *Method in social science: A realist approach* (2nd ed.). Boston: Routledge & Kegan Paul.

Schorr, L. B. (1997). *Common purpose: Strengthening families and neighborhoods to rebuild America*. Garden City, NJ: Doubleday.

Smart, D. H., & Mann, M. (2003, Winter). Incorporating appreciative inquiry methods to evaluate a youth the development program. *New Directions for Evaluation*, pp. 63–72.

Terry, L. D. (1997). Public administration and the theater metaphor: The public administrator as villain, hero, and innocent victim. *Public Administration Review, 57,* 53–59.

Usher, C. L. (1995). Improving evaluability through self-evaluation. *Evaluation Practice, 16*(1), 59–68.

Usher, C. L. (1998). Managing care across systems to improve outcomes for families and communities. *Journal of Behavioral Health Service Research, 25,* 217–229.

Usher, C. L., Gibbs, D., Wildfire, J., & Gogan, H. (1996). *Measuring outcomes in child welfare: Lessons from family to family*. Baltimore: Annie E. Casey Foundation.

Usher, C. L., & Wildfire, J. B. (2003). Evidence-based practice in community-based child welfare systems. *Child Welfare, 82,* 597–614.

Walter R. McDonald & Associates. (2003). *Families for kids: Final cluster evaluation report*. Battle Creek, MI: W. K. Kellogg Foundation.

Walters, J. (1994, September). TQM: Surviving the cynics. *Governing*, pp. 40–45.

Watkins, J. M., & Kelly, R. (n.d.). *Appreciative inquiry for organizational change: Theory, practice, and application*. Unpublished manuscript.

Wedel, K. R. (1991). Designing and implementing performance contracting. In R. L. Edwards & J. A. Yankey (Eds.), *Skills for effective human services management* (pp. 335–351). Washington, DC: NASW Press.

Weiss, H. B., & Greene, J. C. (1992). An empowerment partnership for family support and education programs and evaluations. *Family Science Review, 5,* 131–148.

Wildavsky, A. (1979). *Speaking truth to power: The art and craft of policy analysis*. Boston: Little, Brown.

W. K. Kellogg Foundation. (1998). *Evaluation handbook*. Battle Creek, MI: Author.

W. K. Kellogg Foundation. (2003). *Logic model development guide: Using logic models to bring together planning, evaluation, and action*. Battle Creek, MI: Author.

FOUNDATIONS SUPPORTING INNOVATIVE APPROACHES TO EVALUATION IN HUMAN SERVICES

Annie E. Casey Foundation	http://www.aecf.org
California Wellness Foundation	http://www.tcwf.org
W. K. Kellogg Foundation	http://www.wkkf.org
World Bank	http://www.worldbank.org

OTHER IMPORTANT WEB SITES

Appreciative Inquiry Commons   http://appreciativeinquiry.cwru.edu/
The "AI Commons" is a worldwide portal devoted to the fullest sharing of academic resources and practical tools on Appreciative Inquiry and the rapidly growing discipline of positive change. The site provides links to training in AI, names of facilitators who conduct AI, examples of research, and access listservs for communicating with others who share an interest in AI.

American Educational Research Association   http://www.aera.net
AERA is the most prominent international professional organization with the primary goal of advancing educational research and its practical application. Its 20,000 members are educators; administrators; directors of research, testing, or evaluation in federal, state, and local agencies; counselors; evaluators; graduate students; and behavioral scientists.

American Evaluation Association   http://www.eval.org/
The American Evaluation Association is an international professional association of evaluators devoted to the application and exploration of program evaluation, personnel evaluation, technology, and many other forms of evaluation. Evaluation involves assessing the strengths and weaknesses of programs, policies, personnel, products, and organizations to improve their effectiveness.

Evaluation Center @ HSRI   http://www.tecathsri.org
The Evaluation Center is a national technical assistance center for the evaluation of adult mental health systems change. The mission is to provide technical assistance in the area of evaluation to states and nonprofit public entities within states for improving the planning, development, and operation of adult mental health services carried out as part of the Community Mental Health Services Block Grant program.

Harvard Family Research Project   http://www.gse.harvard.edu/~hfrp/
HFRP strives to increase the effectiveness of public and private organizations

and communities as they promote child development, student achievement, healthy family functioning, and community development. In its relationships with national, state, and local partners, HFRP fosters a sustainable learning process—one that relies on the collection, analysis, synthesis, and application of information to guide problem solving and decision making.

National Academy of Public Administration   http://www.napawash.org/
The National Academy of Public Administration is an independent, nonpartisan organization chartered by Congress to assist federal, state, and local governments in improving their effectiveness, efficiency, and accountability. For more than 35 years, the academy has met the challenge of cultivating excellence in the management and administration of government agencies.

ELECTRONIC DISCUSSION GROUPS
ON NEW APPROACHES TO EVALUATION

Action Research List

Arlist-L is a medium-volume, multidisciplinary electronic mailing list. It is a moderated forum for the discussion of the theory and practice of action research and related methods. To subscribe, e-mail listproc@scu.edu.au with the following message:

> subscribe ARLIST-L Your Name
> (for example, subscribe ARLIST-L Margaret Thatcher)

American Evaluation Association

The AEA Web site (http://www.eval.org/) hosts many free online topical interest groups on a wide variety of evaluation-related topics, including the Collaborative, Participatory, and Empowerment Evaluation. To subscribe, e-mail majordomo@lists.stanford.edu with the following message: subscribe empowerment-evaluation97@lists.stanford.edu (username@hostname) Do not add anything to the message (including thanks); it is an automated system.

Appreciative Inquiry Discussion Forum

AIList is a forum for individuals interested in learning more about the practice of Appreciative Inquiry. The list has more than 1,000 subscribers from all over the world. Questions are welcome, as are case postings, observations, and other experiences that can help subscribers improve their organization change prac-tice. This is a moderated list, and all members must be approved for membership by the moderator before they are able to receive or post messages or access list archives. The online application form to subscribe can be found at http://mailman.business.utah.edu:8080/mailman/listinfo/ailist.

15

Assessing, Planning, and Managing Information Technology

Laura I. Zimmerman and Andrew Broughton

Nonprofit managers work in a difficult environment in which they are simultaneously pulled in many different directions (see Chapter 1). Pressures often include shrinking resources, growing service responsibilities, and increasing demands for accountability. In response to this set of circumstances, many organizations have increased their use of automation and technology. Unfortunately, technology has been changing at an increasingly fast pace, which causes many problems for nonprofit organizations. As Heath (1991) has pointed out, "Information technologies are changing the way people communicate with each other, where they work, how they earn a living, and how they entertain themselves" (p. 238). This is statement is as true today as it was when written 15 years ago.

To say that several significant developments have taken place over the past 40 years in availability and uses of computers and information technology in nonprofit organizations is a gross understatement. Initially, as mainframe computers became more available, many larger nonprofit organizations began to use them for such administrative tasks as payroll and accounting. Next, as personal computers (PCs) became more available, they began to be used to fill in the gaps in mainframe applications and for office tasks such as word processing. (All computer terms are defined in the glossary at the end of this chapter.)

Subsequently, local area networks (LANs) began to be used to connect computers together. With LANs people could easily work together on the same tasks and share equipment, such as printers, and software. Currently, nonprofit managers and organizations are confronted with challenges and opportunities presented by the growing presence of the Internet and the World Wide Web.

Throughout this period, nonprofit managers have had to make many decisions. In the area of technology alone, managers have had to find ways to fund it; manage it; anticipate the changes caused by it; and, often most daunting, try to anticipate the direction of the next technological advances. This environment requires managers to make many difficult choices.

This chapter reviews some of the most recent advances in computer technology, including networks and the Internet. These developments are likely to have profound effects on how nonprofit organizations function and how their staff and clients or patrons interact. In addition, it discusses specific management steps for planning for technology in these organizations.

CHANGES IN TECHNOLOGY

Since 2000, computers have continued to undergo innovations and improvements. PCs have become more powerful, easier to use, and more interconnected than ever before. They also have become less expensive. Word-processing programs now have the capacity to do what only desktop-publishing programs could do a few years earlier. Desktop-publishing programs now allow for the creation of even more sophisticated products. Databases are more powerful, and computer users with average skills can make good use of them. Electronic spreadsheets make it possible to do more sophisticated analyses, and they have the charting functionality that only a dedicated graphics program had a few years ago.

Even with these improvements, many of the new versions of software do not require more powerful hardware to be effective. We have reached the point where any computer built in the last few years should handle the work that is needed in most nonprofit organizations for the next few years. This section lays out some basic computing needs and changes with which managers should be familiar to make good use of technology.

Hardware

Recent changes in hardware now allow people to process information faster, view an increased amount of information more clearly on the screen, and use new ways to enter information into the computer. All of these functions require changes in the hardware; some also require software additions and changes. We begin the discussion with what are currently considered standards for hardware and then consider some of the changes that are on the horizon.

The central processing unit (CPU) of the computer is the "box" that comes with the monitor and keyboard. This box usually includes a motherboard and random-access memory (RAM), hard disk drives, compact disc (CD-ROM and DVD) drives, and a power supply with fan. Additional accessories also can be obtained, such as a sound card for speakers and microphones, a video card (for processing video input) or a network interface card (wired or wireless—to connect the computer to a network); a modem (to connect to outside networks; or an external drive (to increase storage capacity or to move large amounts of data). Many of these accessories are now built in to current computers. Such characteristics as speed, hard-disk size, and RAM have changed the most over time. A typical computer today has a two-gigahertz Pentium processor, 512 or more megabytes of RAM, and an 80-gigabyte or larger hard disk. A few years ago these numbers were unthinkable for the average desktop computer. Most were less by a factor of ten.

Monitors have grown in size and capacity as well. Standard monitors have 17-inch screens and at least super VGA capability (and much larger screens using alternate technologies are available, as well). This means that monitors can display more information or display it in a larger format, and often on a flat screen (which is less stressful for the eyes).

Keyboards have undergone a few technical changes. Several companies have changed the size and shape of the keyboard for ergonomic reasons or to fit laptop size limitations. The mouse is often incorporated onto the keyboard, especially in laptops. Two main types of mouse are common: One type uses the thumb to move the mouse, and the other uses the pointer in the middle of the keyboard, with the buttons controlled by the thumb. The second type allows the user to keep the hands in place on the keyboard while using the mouse and is very efficient and practical. Many mice also have a third button or a scroll wheel, and many are wireless.

With miniaturization and mobility requirements on the increase the laptop now challenges the desktop computer for primacy in the work place. There is only a small premium to be paid for a laptop and it can make computing available for many workers while they are in many different locations. When they are back at their desks, through the use of docking stations and port multipliers, they can use a regular keyboard and monitor with their laptop.

Software

Although hardware is important, it is probably more important for managers to be aware of the potential uses of software. The appropriate use of the following software tools will help maintain an efficient and productive organization.

The most common way to buy software is through the purchase of office productivity suites that have come to be the preferred mode for marketing this software. These software packages typically include three or four basics: databases, word processors, spreadsheets, and presentation software. Today's word-processing software (for example, Microsoft Word, WordPro, Open Office Writer) is still useful for writing letters and memos, newsletters, and reports, and it also can produce much more sophisticated products. Spreadsheet software (for example, Lotus 1-2-3, Excel, Open Office Calc) works well for financial tracking, charting numerical data, and performing many basic statistical analyses. Database software (for example, Access, Paradox, Foxpro, Oracle) are useful for tracking client and transaction (service) information. Presentation software (for example, PowerPoint, Open Office Impress) can be used to make sophisticated video (and audio) presentations.

Some basic tasks that are performed in nonprofit organizations nearly every day can be done more efficiently using a computer and a good office software package or suite. Word processors can be used to do a mail merge for any type of mass mailing. (A mail merge allows the sender to personalize a single letter sent to several, or many people.) Setting up a mail merge involves writing the letter and setting up another file that contains each individual's unique information, such as mailing address and preferred form of salutation. This process has many advantages both for an organization and the clients or patrons who receive an organization's letters. Using the mail-merge capability can save significant time (depending, of course, on the number of mailings performed). This also may save wear and tear on photocopy machines.

Modern word-processing software can produce sophisticated newsletters. Most allow the inclusion of digitized images to make the newsletter more attractive. The most difficult part of producing a newsletter may be getting the articles written, not putting it together. When the articles are keyed in and edited, basic formatting takes just a little time. Of course, newsletters that are laden with graphics take longer to produce. Some software also can put a newsletter into hypertext markup language (HTML), which is the format for the Web, thus making it much easier to publish a newsletter on the Internet.

Many nonprofit managers give presentations or provide training to various groups. Often the presentations are for funders or funding prospects. Presentation software has many advantages for this purpose. Some software provides preset presentation packages; the user has only to tailor the "slides" for a particular topic. For instance, PowerPoint has an autocontent wizard that asks what type of presentation will be made and gives an attractive background for each slide and a standard outline from which to work. An attractive presentation can be made in little time and, with a color printer, handouts can include copies of the slides. Or, with a liquid crystal display (LCD) panel or projector, the presentation can be displayed directly from the computer (allowing last-minute changes, if necessary).

Budgeting is much more efficiently done with the help of a computer and a spreadsheet program. This type of software can be used for simple or complex budgeting processes. Some software packages allow the exploration of the ramifications of different scenarios with regard to income and expenses. Many non-profit organizations use spreadsheet applications to track simple data on clients, patrons, or consumers. Spreadsheets also provide an excellent vehicle for the graphic display of data. Chart wizards allow the display of data visually for reports and presentations. Some spreadsheet packages can be used to perform sophisticated statistical analyses.

Perhaps the most sweeping change in information technology has come about in the area of communication. Initially, LANs connected computers within offices. Then the networks were connected to each other sometimes to form intranets that are all connected within a single organization. Finally, these became connected to the Internet, that network of networks, which connects computers around the world. This makes the communication possibilities almost limitless.

Whereas the most popular function performed on a PC used to be word processing, now it is electronic mail (e-mail). Through the use of this application, managers can communicate with other managers, staff, clients or patrons, board members, funders, or other stakeholders. Managers can send and receive many kinds of files as attachments to an e-mail. However, e-mail is not plausible or possible in an organizational setting unless PCs are interconnected.

There is also software to help people create Web sites, type short messages to each other (via chat), talk on the "phone" to one or many (using Voice Over Internet Protocol), and collaborate (for example, WebEx or Marratech) or video conference with each other (using H.323). The Web is all about communication and managers can use this in many ways.

Groupware

Groupware is a software category made possible by the increasing use of LANs and the Internet. These networks make it possible for computers to be interconnected and to share resources within an office or organizational environment. As a result, office groups can use software that allows them to share files. Such software includes group scheduling packages (for example, Schedule+, Ontime) and workflow applications (for example, Lotus Notes). E-mail, collaboration software (e.g. WebEx, Marratech) and personal information managers (PIMs; for example, Groupwise, Outlook) are usually included in this category.

This class of software, used in a network environment, allows information to be shared, processed, and communicated to large and small groups instead of to a single individual. These software applications are used interactively by all computer users in the organization. Although potentially extremely useful to an organization, these packages require more time to manage the network and the software on the network. Thus, resources need to be allocated to provide the necessary staffing, and time needs to be allowed for this administration so that all users can take advantage of the tools and work more efficiently. Consequently, although this type of software can be very useful, all nonprofit organizations may not have the staff resources to be able to use it.

Group scheduling has many advantages over individual calendars, especially for managers. While we were writing this chapter, people called to make appointments with us. Our administrative assistant could schedule appointments for either of us through any computer. When we go to our computerized calendars, each of us is notified about these new appointments. We can accept or reject the appointment. If one of us needs to schedule a meeting with a few people, we can set the time, and the scheduling software tells us whether it conflicts with other people's schedules. If it does, we can either schedule the appointment anyway or change to another time. It is possible to add the meeting to several calendars at one time instead of going to each individual's calendar separately.

Groupware packages may include scheduling, mail, and contact management all in one package. This can work well for an organization that has a LAN. Some packages can synchronize the calendar on a desktop computer with that kept on a portable PIM (for example, Pilot, Newton) or a laptop with its own scheduling software. This corrects an earlier problem in which people could not schedule meetings in a timely way because they frequently did not have their schedules with them because they were away from their desktop computers.

Networks and the Internet

Perhaps the most profound change in computer technology in recent years is in the ability to interconnect them. Today, the majority of PCs sold for office use come with their network interface as part of the motherboard. When these computers are placed in an office, they can be immediately connected to the building network. This permits the sharing of files and peripheral devices such as printers and also makes possible the use of groupware software. People can now consult others' schedules and work on shared reports without leaving their desks. As networks and Internet connections become more widespread, groupware using the Web also is becoming readily available. Managers who use this kind of software can use an Internet connection to check e-mail or the schedule no matter where they are.

This is possible because more and more networks are in turn connected to the Internet. An Internet connection is important for several reasons. First, it makes statewide, nationwide, and even international communication possible. Second, it makes sending and receiving information, be it numeric data, case information (properly treated for privacy regulations and related concerns), or policies and procedures, a simple task. Organization members can seek and send information almost anywhere in the world, and they can see their own information from anywhere in the world.

In a relatively short time, vital statistics, program participation information, and even images of documents and pictures are readily available to qualified users over the Internet. In about the same amount of time, sound and video are easily transmitted on the Internet. This makes many kinds of training, client services, and meetings possible at a worker's desktop (Holden, Rosenberg, & Weissman, 1996).

Connections to the Internet also make it possible for workers to share expertise and questions with their peers, or even with a distant expert. A popular method for achieving this is to set up a listserv or discussion forum. Through the use of a listserv, people with e-mail can hold an "electronic discussion" about a topic of common interest to them. Thus, a group of people might start a listserv on a topic such as family protective services or funding possibilities for arts programs. People can write e-mail messages about problems and solutions in this area, and everyone on the list would receive each message. With discussion forums, the conversations can be stored and read on a Web page or an electronic bulletin board at anytime. Each member of the listserv can read and respond to the posting. Either can be an effective vehicle for organizations in rural or geographically isolated areas.

With the advent of video and sound on the Internet and the use of broadband connections to the Internet, many other uses for an Internet connection are possible. Staff training can be performed using the Internet as the transmission medium for online continuing education courses. "Phone calls" can be made over the Internet to coworkers or outside experts. Clients can be interviewed at a distance. Paper-and-pencil diagnostic measures can be administered and scored immediately over the Internet. In short, the Internet offers many new opportunities.

Challenges

How do these changes affect organizations, and how can organizations plan for them? How can they be sure to have the money and staffing to keep the technology at the most beneficial level possible for them? Managers must have an understanding of these new technologies and be able to assess their viability for their particular organizations. Among the things to consider are the extent to which new technologies result in increased worker efficiency and organizational effectiveness. How do managers educate themselves and their staff about these changes while maintaining workflow? What barriers exist that limit technology in organizations?

Recent years have been financially challenging both for nonprofit and public or governmental organizations and agencies. The need for greater program efficiencies has required many leaders to plunge into technology. The second part of this chapter presents an approach to doing this.

MANAGING TECHNOLOGY

Managers need to consider six basic components to planning and managing technology. First, assess the current state-of-technology in the organization. A strategic planning process to define goals and to gain a technological vision should follow this. The third and fourth components are personnel and training, which are often overlooked by managers when implementing technology. The fifth component is the place of hardware and software in the technology plan. The last component entails the budgeting strategies and changes to support the technology.

Assessment

To prepare to make some strategic decisions about information technology, managers must first assess the organization's current situation. Depending on the organization's goals and objectives, the assessment can take many forms and can be basic or comprehensive. Minimally, the assessment should include an evaluation (inventory) of the current hardware and software in the organization. A machine description should include dimensions of hardware components (for example, storage capacity, amount of RAM memory, CPU speed, number of accessory cards in each) and the installed software components with their respective versions (for example, Office XP).

Another important part of the assessment phase is to define goals for automation. Goals can be developed for different levels of the organization, and this should be done with input from all levels. Typically, the executive director's goals include a vision of technology for the organization. Direct service providers and supervisors typically focus more on computer tools and training to improve their skills. Both sets of technological needs are important and must be balanced by budget constraints and the efficient use of resources.

A comprehensive assessment should measure the computer skills of employees in relation to the goals of the organization. This information also can be used to determine training needs. For example, a comprehensive assessment of health worker's computer skills (Zimmerman & Broughton, 1996b) helped in the development of a computer training curriculum for the State of North Carolina (Zimmerman & Broughton, 1996a). This assessment found that three levels of training were needed: (1) basic skills, (2) a core curriculum, and (3) advanced skills. Not all employees needed advanced-skills training, and many had already completed basic skills. The core skills included computer skills that all employees needed to perform their jobs.

Strategic Plan

Too often, nonprofit organizations introduce computer technology in an unplanned, haphazard, incremental manner. This can be costly in the long run. Instead, it is advisable to take some time to engage in a strategic planning effort that relates to the organization's technology needs. When this is done, the strategic plan guides the implementation of technology in the organization and should be based on the goals of the organization, the results of the technology skills assessment, and the current technological environment. The technology strategic plan should be reviewed at least yearly and adjusted for changes in technology and business practices. The following sections are designed to help managers consider important issues to implement better computer technology, including such items as personnel, computing inventories, training, and the budget.

Personnel

Technology support personnel are probably the most important commodity necessary for increasing the use of computer technology in an organization. A single computer used by one person may never need much technical support. As more computers are introduced into an organization, the need for support increases, not so much for the computers as for the computer users. Initially, more sophisticated computer users in an organization may provide the support for technology. However, with the addition of more computers and users, this role can become a job in itself. The number of people needed to support computers and users depends on the size of the organization, its goals, the software on the computers, and the computer skills of the staff.

When planning for a LAN, consider budgeting for at least one staff person to support the network. Whether this responsibility can be handled on a part- or full-time basis depends on several factors, including the size of the organization and the magnitude of the planned network. If a vendor installs the LAN for only a few computers, a savvy computer user on staff may be able to support it, whereas a larger network requires more staff time and more specialized knowledge and skills. As a rule, generally figure that at least a half-time position, or one-half the workload of a full-time staff person, for every 20 to 25 computers in a LAN environment.

The staff person who provides technological support should have some experience with the type of network installed in the organization and most of the software applications used by staff. For a smaller group, a generalist who knows something about application software and networks is generally the best choice for this type of position. For larger organizations, in which two support people are needed, one should administer the network while the other handles the application software. Both should share information for emergency coverage.

Ideally, the network administrator will have prior experience working with the type of network installed in the organization. Although many formal training and certification programs are available, experience is the most important qualification. If the person is not certified (and in most cases, nonprofit organizations cannot afford certified network engineers), funds should be put aside for training and for outside support for emergencies. Such support can be by telephone, dialing in to desktop computers or servers to observe and fix problems, or onsite. Of these, telephone support is usually the least expensive.

The support person for applications should know how to use different software applications, assess the work that needs to be done, and recommend appropriate software. This person should know database and spreadsheet programming and other applications used by the organization. Frequently, if the organization has a presence on the World Wide Web, this person is expected to build and maintain Web sites. If this person does not know how to program, he or she should obtain some formal training at a local community college or other training facility.

Training

Training is an important component that is often overlooked or intentionally excluded in the development of an organizational plan for technology. This may be in part a result of the expense of training staff and the time it takes for them to develop computer skills. We also have found on several occasions that, without training, the costs of doing work the less-efficient, less-productive way can be just as high as or higher than the cost of training. However, some steps can be taken to reduce the cost of training without reducing the benefits. In our experience, people can learn only so much in a session. We find that short, hands-on experiences are more fruitful than all-day intensive cram sessions. We also find that most people learn best in small classrooms with each learner at a computer. An isolated environment allows close interaction among the learner or trainee, the computer, and the instructor with minimal disturbances. Time for practice also is needed. Because most computer skills are best acquired through hands-on computer training, we recommend the following:

- *Train in small groups.* Hands-on computer training needs to be more intensive than most other types of training. In general, the lower the trainee-to-instructor ratio, the more effective the training.

- *Train for short periods of time.* Usually a two- to four-hour training session with a break gives users time to learn and practice new skills without being overloaded with information.
- *Make sure that workers have access to computers and software at their work site before training.* Training should not occur until workers have ready access to computers (preferably on their desks). If employees cannot immediately use what they have learned during a training session, the usefulness of the training may be lost.
- *Make sure that workers train on the same software they have on their work computers.* Training workers on the software they use at their office is optimal. This includes training on the same version of the software. It often is difficult to learn how to use software in training that does not apply directly to the work environment.
- *Do not interrupt training with other work.* The training environment should be away from a worker's desk, where the worker is not distracted by other problems and concerns. The best training environment is away from a person's office, and an off-site location is often preferable.
- *Have workers take classes appropriate for their level of competence.* Beginning users are lost in an advanced class. It is better to have workers begin with introductory classes and review techniques rather than have them enter a class that is beyond their current skill level. Often, even in basic classes, the workers with slightly more advanced skills can learn a new or different way to use the software.
- *Give new computer users time to practice their new skills.* New computer skills take time to master. Becoming comfortable using a mouse may take some practice. Workers also must apply their new skills in practical situations before they completely commit them to memory. At first, using the computer may take longer than processing items by hand, but with practice, users pick up skill and speed, and the automated system eventually becomes a timesaver. Workers need time to process, practice, and implement what they have learned outside the training environment.
- *Use the buddy system for training.* Workers who learn together often help each other outside the training environment. Sometimes two workers pick up two different pieces of information in training that can be shared while they are practicing in the office later.

Having an onsite expert in the organization has some benefits. One method of training that managers may find helpful is to send one person to intensive training and then have that person train or help the less-skilled computer users. Another strategy is to send a few people for basic training and then send individuals from this group to more advanced or concentrated training programs that focus on different areas (for example, one to word-processing training and another to spreadsheet training). These individuals can then train their colleagues.

Computing

Software and hardware make the computer useful. Hardware includes the things that one touches and sees: monitor, keyboard, mouse, and CPU. Software is what makes the computer perform. It is important to understand the difference and the need for both parts. Many managers make the mistake of allocating money for computers without also allocating money for software and training. As a result, many organizations make little use of these brand new pieces of equipment, which tend to become expensive paperweights. It is better for the organization to have fewer computers, with more software and training, than more computers that are not being used efficiently.

When purchasing computers, select a brand and model that can run all of the software that the staff need to use. Ideally, a computer with power (for example, fast CPU, large amount of RAM) is able to handle future changes in software and should be useful for a long time. It is important for decisions about purchasing computers to be made on the basis of a fair amount of research. Compare features and prices. The best computer for the organization may not necessarily be the least expensive, but it may not be the most expensive either.

Budget

Support personnel, hardware, software, and training all require resources. Budgeting for technology resources can be as difficult as learning some of the technical jargon associated with the technology. In most nonprofit organizations, lump-sum budgeting tends to be the norm for computer technology. Lump-sum budgeting is useful to initiate the purchase of computers, software, and training, but it does not help cover the required year-to-year personnel, maintenance, and upgrades for the information technology used in the organization. One organization with which we are familiar obtained a $36,000 grant "for technology." The organization's managers wanted to purchase 12 computers (for $3,000 each). If they had followed this initial plan, they likely would have had 12 expensive paperweights taking up valuable space on small desktops. However, after further discussion with technology support personnel and some careful planning, the organization purchased a LAN and connected five computers to it, purchased some software for the workers and a database system for collecting client data, trained a staff member to become the LAN administrator, and trained workers to use the software. In the final plan for the original $36,000 grant, half of the budget went to purchase computers, a portion to software, and a portion to training personnel. Seven years later, this organization, with more than 150 staff, is almost fully automated.

An efficient approach to budgeting for a technology project involves allocating funds among four major categories: (1) software, (2) support personnel, (3) hardware, and (4) training. The first budget item (which is usually left for last) should be software which, although it may not be the most expensive budget item, is nonetheless the most important. Software determines what an organization can do. As part of the strategic plan for technology, managers should have defined goals (such as what the organization want to do), so the initial phase of the budget planning should consider those goals. Estimate the cost of the software that best allows the organization to perform the functions that it needs to perform. Look for a combination of software, such as an office suite, that is easy to learn and provides these functions. Then take steps to standardize this software application throughout the organization. Otherwise, you may have different individuals and staff groups using different word-processing programs or spreadsheet packages, and this greatly complicates network administration and technical support needs. Standardizing creates a simpler work environment that is much more cost efficient and effective.

Most software companies give discounts for multiple copies of software (site licenses), so also consider in budget projections whether to secure a license per computer or simultaneous usage licenses, if the latter are available. Simultaneous usage licenses allow an organization to purchase only the number of licenses needed for the number of people who are using the application at any one time (on a network). Therefore, a large organization that has only three people use a software package at any one time will need only three licenses, even if more people use the software at different times. For very large organizations, some software companies sell site licenses that further reduce the price of software.

The second item to include in the budget plan is technology support personnel. Computers are intricate tools. Just as pencils need sharpening, computers need care and maintenance. When something goes wrong with a computer, it takes time for technology support personnel to figure out what is wrong and whether they can repair it or if they need to send the computer out for repair. The less knowledge that computer users have about their computers, the more technology support personnel time is needed per machine and user. In smaller organizations, technology support personnel often emerge from within the organization, often with little or no time dedicated to these tasks.

The more computers, linkages, software, and so on that an organization has, the more personnel time needed to dedicate to the tasks of supporting computer users and their machines. Generally, an organization should consider at least one full-time technology support staff person for about every 30 to 40 machines and users. The primary role of this staff person should be the support, maintenance, and upgrading of the machines, the software, and the LAN. If computer programming is needed, this should be considered a separate task from that of supporting the computer users. Often, database development is needed for specialized applications. Do not assume that a person trained in database programming also can support users and the LAN on anything but the database software program itself.

The third component of the technology budget plan is hardware. Computer hardware and software (and related technology) change rapidly. Ideally, computers have an effective life of at least four years, but some may need to be replaced more frequently, depending on particular software applications. Thus, hardware purchases need to be made with thought about the software to be used, capacity, the likelihood that the machines can be used for several years, hardware standards for the organization, and what comes with the hardware. It is a good idea to develop hardware standards, just as it is important to have software standards. As new, more powerful computers come out, an organization can continue to buy the same type or, in some instances, the same brand of machine, making sure that the new machines are fully compatible with existing hardware and software. This helps maintain software licenses with little or no extra cost for software. Depending on which users need new machines, the used machines can be circulated to staff for whom these machines represent an upgrade.

Of course, budget ultimately defines the types and numbers of machines purchased. Managers may find that they can save money by purchasing equipment through mail order or on state contract, rather than from local vendors. Nonetheless, it is important to try to adhere to the organization's hardware and software standards as much as possible. This minimizes personnel support time for different machines and older machine upgrades. It also makes it easier to use old parts to keep older machines running and upgraded.

Some drawbacks to the mail-order approach are worth noting. An organization just beginning to become involved with information technology may need to work with a local vendor to obtain onsite support or technical assistance. Another drawback is that new computers come with newer versions of software. It can be very difficult, if not impossible, for an organization to keep one version of software on multiple machines, let alone have everyone learn every new version. The choice, then, is between spending more time setting up new computers using a single, older version of software or requiring all support personnel to know each new version and the various combinations. Some prefer the latter approach because of the useful tools in newer versions of software, but it is not for the faint of heart.

The fourth budget category is personnel training, which should be viewed as an ongoing event to accommodate organizational changes. For example, if an organization is planning for a LAN or already has one, the people supporting this LAN need to keep up with the latest changes to the network software. End-users, that is, those personnel who use the computers on their desks, only help the organization by expanding their knowledge of desktop software. Turnover also affects an organization's training needs, because employees often need training on the standard software used in the organization.

Staff training often is more important for nonprofit organizations than for other types of organizations because many nonprofits, particularly smaller ones, cannot afford to pay the salaries of network administrators. In isolated areas, this can be a particular problem. It may be far less costly to train an existing staff member who is an astute computer user and who is committed to the organization and geographical area than it is to try to hire someone with the necessary skills. This approach has worked successfully in several organizations, especially smaller nonprofits in rural areas. A great deal of network support can occur through telephone consultation once the network support staff has had some training. For midsize and larger organizations, having two people trained in this capacity is helpful.

Maintaining and Upgrading the Technology

Whether an organization's technology infrastructure is started through donated computers, computers purchased for the organization for a specific task, or large donations of money for this purpose, the technology obtained eventually becomes old and unreliable. A good computer should be expected to last at least four years; some last longer. Many companies now provide three- or four-year warranties on their computers. Issues of warranty and service availability should be considered when planning to purchase new computers or upgrade existing ones. With present-day computers, it is generally not necessary to purchase maintenance agreements. Almost all hardware problems occur during the warranty period; most of the problems tend to be related to software, not to the machines. Upgrading software, installing new software on the computer, and turning off the computer without correctly closing programs tend to be the major causes of problems. Support personnel should be able to help when these problems occur. Training end users also helps reduce these problems.

When an organization starts building its computer infrastructure, two areas require attention. One is continuing to build and upgrade the infrastructure; the other is maintaining the current level. Both need to be considered but often pose some difficulties for nonprofit managers. A three- or four-year maintenance budget is necessary to maintain a base level of service. If old equipment is replaced with brand new equipment, then a software upgrade for office productivity software should be included.

Finally, an organization must decide how much of its total budget should focus on information technology. This is up to the manager and should be related to the four-year replacement cycle. Many for-profit companies that use high levels of technology spend up to 10 percent of their annual budgets on information technology; nonprofit organizations tend to average less than 5 percent. As a rule, to have a technology infrastructure that works, aim for at least the 5-percent level.

CONCLUSION

Technology is changing at an increasingly rapid rate. Among the roles that managers must perform are those of monitor and coordinator. Clearly, modern computing and information technology provide managers with tools that can greatly aid them in performing these roles. At the same time, managers must engage in thoughtful planning; acquire resources necessary to accomplish their organizations' missions; and ensure that they have an adequately trained, competent workforce. Thus, as pointed out in Chapter 1, managers must function in an atmosphere of competing values, which often requires that they make some hard choices.

To use technology effectively, managers must engage in careful assessment, planning, budgeting, and managerial oversight. Sufficient resources must be allocated for hardware, software, training, and technical support. When these resources are made available, nonprofit organizations and managers can realize the benefits of technology.

GLOSSARY

CD-ROM   Compact Disc-Read Only Memory; used to store large programs and great amounts of data.

CPU   Central processing unit (the "computer" part of the computer); the chip where the computations are done.

database   Software used to store, sort, select, and track information of all kinds. These applications are often used to track and report data on clients. Some popular PC-based databases include Access, Foxpro, and Oracle.

desktop publishing   Software used to prepare publications from brochures to books. Some popular PC-based desktop-publishing software includes PageMaker and QuarkXPress.

discussion forum   Software that allows people to communicate about a topic. People must post messages to the discussion forum. The software documents the discussion and participants can interact with any posting. See also *listserv.*

e-mail   Electronic mail; allows computer users to send, receive, and store messages.

HTML   Hypertext markup language; used to present information of all kinds on the World Wide Web.

Internet   Millions of computers around the world linked together through the use of the Internet Protocol (IP) for communication. Each computer on the Internet must have an IP address (in the form nnn.nnn.nnn.nnn) to communicate with other computers on the Internet.

intranet   An internal Internet system that is limited to the confines of a single organization.

LAN   Local area network; computers in the same locale linked together for communications and sharing of software and hardware.

LCD   Liquid crystal display; a method for displaying computer images used mostly in laptops and for projectors.

listserv   A computer program that manages e-mail communications to a list of e-mail recipients. By sending a single message to the list address, each member of the list receives the message. See also *discussion forum*.

mainframe   Large computer usually shared by many users running different programs. Mainframe computers are more massive than PC computers. The PC computers today are more powerful than many older mainframes.

modem   Modulator–demodulator; allows computers to communicate over circuits such as telephone lines or cable TV lines. A computer connects to a modem that communicates with another modem connected to another computer, allowing the two computers to communicate with each other. Software is needed to allow the computers to communicate with the modem.

PC   Personal computer.

PIM   Personal information manager; software that helps organize schedules, telephone numbers, and personal contact information. Some popular PIMs are Outlook, Organizer, Sidekick, and Up-to-Date. Some software can be used in a handheld device to synchronize with information on the computer (for example, Newton, Pilot).

RAM   Random access memory; memory used by the computer chip while doing computations. This memory is used only when the computer is turned on. Any information in RAM is deleted when the computer is turned off.

spreadsheet   Electronic version of an accountant's pad of columns and rows that may contain text, formulas, or numbers. Many software packages allow the user to make charts from data.

super VGA   Super video graphics array; a video display standard for color monitors.

World Wide Web   A method for organizing information of all kinds located on the Internet.

zip drive   A drive that holds a removable disk that can store up to 100 megabytes of data.

SKILLS APPLICATION EXERCISES

- Obtain a budget for a nonprofit organization and determine the percentage of the total budget that the organization currently expends on information technology.
- Draft a proposal for developing a strategic information technology plan for your organization or another with which you are familiar. Indicate what issues are addressed in the strategic planning effort, who is involved, and how the process must proceed.
- Assess the current state of information technology in your organization or another with which you are familiar, then develop a proposed four-year budget for upgrading computers and computing skills.

REFERENCES

Heath, P. P. (1991). Managing information technology. In R. L. Edwards & J. A. Yankey (Eds.), *Skills for effective human services management* (pp. 238–250). Washington, DC: NASW Press.

Holden, G., Rosenberg, G., & Weissman, A. (1996). World Wide Web accessible resources related to research on social work practice. *Research on Social Work Practice, 6*, 236–262.

Zimmerman, L. I., & Broughton, A. (1996a). *Education plan for local health workers in North Carolina*. Chapel Hill: University of North Carolina, Human Services Smart Agency.

Zimmerman, L. I., & Broughton, A. (1996b). *A survey of staff computer knowledge in local health departments*. Chapel Hill: University of North Carolina, Human Services Smart Agency.

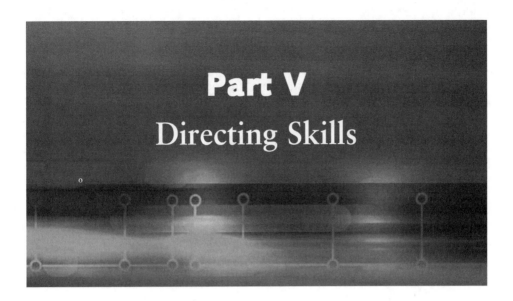

Part V
Directing Skills

Managerial directing skills encompass the roles of producer and director. Competencies for the producer role include personal productivity and motivation of others. Competencies for the director role include taking initiative, goal setting, assigning and guiding the work of others, and effective delegating.

Thomas P. Holland, in Chapter 16, stresses the importance of the manager's role in strengthening the performance of the organization's board. He suggests that creating, nurturing, and renewing the board is basic to an organization's survival and effectiveness. Holland considers the basic functions of nonprofit board, suggests criteria for selecting board members, and identifies characteristics of effective boards. He also discusses the role of the chief executive in relation to the board and suggests several steps that managers can take to enhance the performance of their boards.

In Chapter 17, Douglas C. Eadie discusses the field of strategic planning and management, suggesting that the central issue for nonprofit organizations is maintaining a dynamic balance between their internal and external environments. He argues that managers need to engage in strategic issue management and delineates specific steps in the process. Eadie believes that the enhancement of the relative position of an organization to its external environment is a key function of nonprofit managers.

In Chapter 18, David Campbell, Barbara Jacobus, and John A. Yankey point out that mergers and other types of alliances among nonprofit organizations have become an increasingly important response to a multiplicity of internal and external forces. The authors use six theoretical frameworks—Resource Interdependence, Environmental Validity, Operational Efficiency, Domain Influence, Strategic Enhancement, and Social Responsibility—to examine why nonprofit organizations are increasingly exploring the formation of all types of strategic partnerships. For each theoretical framework, Campbell, Jacobus, and Yankey suggest a series of questions to guide such exploration.

In Chapter 19, Yankey and Carol K. Willen explore the increased demand for consultation services by nonprofit organizations. They identify reasons why consultants are engaged, as well as provide guidelines that nonprofit leaders can use to help them select and contract with consultants. Yankey and Willen present an overview of the consulting process, as well as define the array of roles that consultants assume. They offer a series of "tips" to make consultative engagements more productive. The authors conclude the chapter by noting some of the changes occurring in the current consulting landscape.

Strengthening
Board Performance

Thomas P. Holland

The competing-values framework suggests that managers must be adept at performing many roles simultaneously (see Chapter 1). Some of these roles involve attending to the organization's external environment and providing appropriate structure. Given that nonprofit organizations are established to accomplish societal objectives, managers must be aware of environmental trends affecting the organization and its users, patrons, or clients. Managers must be concerned about the process of establishing organizational goals, ensuring organizational continuity and goodwill, and stimulating the individual and collective achievement of staff and volunteers. The governing board is a nonprofit organization's most important volunteer entity. Having an effective, supportive, and involved governing board is essential for an organization's long-term success.

The governing board carries out a range of vital functions for any nonprofit organization. Its members—sometimes called *trustees, overseers,* or *directors*—are people in whom power is entrusted by the community to act as fiduciaries and to guide their organizations with care, skill, and integrity. They represent the voice of society and are expected to act on behalf of the interests of the community, constituents, and sponsors. Creating, nurturing, and renewing this core group of leaders are basic requisites for an organization's survival and effectiveness.

BASIC FUNCTIONS OF THE BOARD

The board has a wide range of functions and responsibilities. As summarized by Houle (1989) and others (Scott, 2000; Widmer & Houchin, 2000), these include

- Formulating and sustaining the mission of the organization, making sure that every component of the organization is consistent with the mission and is focused on accomplishing the collective goals;
- Representing the interests of those sponsors whose resources allow the organization to pursue its mission, while balancing those interests with the needs of the intended beneficiaries of the services;
- Translating values into policies that guide the operations of the organization providing the top-level manager (hereinafter referred to as the chief executive officer, or CEO) and staff with rules to govern operations and clarifying the latitude allowable for action;
- Selecting, guiding, overseeing, and evaluating the organization's CEO; obtaining, allocating, and monitoring the use of the organization's resources;
- Working with the CEO to develop long-range plans and to revise them periodically;
- Ensuring that all legal and ethical responsibilities of the organization are being fulfilled; and
- Ensuring that the organization's goals and objectives are being achieved as efficiently and effectively as possible; setting aside time at regular intervals to assess its own performance and composition.

In summary, the board is the focus of power and legitimacy of the organization. It brings together representatives of the major stakeholders in the organization and seeks to synthesize their values and concerns into guiding principles for mobilizing and using resources. The board is the arena within which all the competing values, interests, and perspectives are articulated, examined, and resolved into a single direction for the future of the organization. The responsibility of implementing the policy directives of the board falls on the CEO (Carver, 2002b).

Boards have multiple responsibilities—so many in fact, that they usually create a variety of committees to which specific tasks are delegated (e.g., financial planning, nominating, evaluating the executive, fundraising, personnel, services). These work groups develop specific plans and recommendations for consideration by the full board at its regular meetings, and they may be charged with responsibilities for overseeing the CEO's implementation of recommendations approved by the board.

In addition to regular committees, some boards also create special ancillary structures or advisory groups to provide the board and CEO with particular resources or forms of assistance. For example, a need for specialized expertise in some program or service area (e.g., accessibility by people with special needs, analysis of legislative bills) may prompt the board to establish an advisory group composed of leading experts in the relevant area that may also include some of the organization's senior staff. Such groups may work closely with the board's own committees and assist with their efforts to provide recommendations to the full board, or they may link with the CEO or other management staff, who in turn present the group's recommendations to the board.

Fundraising is another responsibility of the board in which it may involve others selectively. Some boards create an honorary trusteeship status for people whose major role is limited to making financial contributions or providing access to others who can make such contributions. Through its capital campaign committee or its fundraising committee, the board can link with these individuals and draw on their specialized resources to advance its overall plans. (See Chapter 4 for a more complete discussion of fundraising.)

CRITERIA FOR SELECTING MEMBERS

The board is composed of leaders who are committed to carrying out their responsibilities so that the organization thrives. For most nonprofit organizations, selecting these members is the responsibility of the board itself, carried out by its committee on nominations. The goal is to have a cohesive group of hard-working, resourceful, creative, and dedicated trustees who work together effectively to mobilize concerted action across the community or region on behalf of the constituencies that the organization intends to serve. The board should be large enough to allow it to carry out its duties, yet small enough to be a cohesive working group. It should contain that blend of diverse characteristics and skills required to carry out the organization's mission.

Numerous criteria should be considered in identifying potential board candidates. The following are some of the most important attributes of a good board candidate:

- An interest in learning about and working on the issues of primary concern to the organization. The person should be interested in and committed to the organization's specific programs or services. Boards also have found it helpful to include among their membership people with related areas of interest such as public policy, legislative processes, financial management, law, fundraising, and community relations.
- A reputation as an opinion leader, having prestige and esteem in the broader community or region. This should include the ability and willingness to open doors to others needed by the organization.
- The ability to contribute money to the organization or to afford access to others who can provide funds, including key individuals, corporations, and foundations.

- The ability to identify the major issues facing the organization, to focus clearly on the tasks facing the board, and to work effectively with the group to achieve its goals.
- The interpersonal skills and sensitivities necessary to develop, nurture, and sustain communications within the board and between the board and various outside groups.
- A leadership role with a specific constituency that is important to the organization, defined perhaps in terms of age, geographic area, gender, race, profession, or other relevant characteristics.
- Willingness to make one's skills, talents, and time available to the organization. Without this quality, any other characteristics are of limited value to the organization.

CHARACTERISTICS OF EFFECTIVE BOARDS

In addition to being composed of individuals with desirable characteristics, strong boards also have several distinguishing features relating to the whole group. Researchers (Chait, Holland, & Taylor, 1993; Holland, Chait, & Taylor, 1989) found that effective boards differ from ineffective ones in the following ways.

The Contextual Dimension

Effective boards understand and take into account the culture and norms of the organizations they govern. They adapt to the distinctive characteristics and culture of the organization and its staff. Relying on the organization's mission statement, values, and traditions to guide their decisions, they act so as to exemplify and reinforce its core values and commitments. They cultivate this competence in various ways:

- Orientations include explicit introduction to the organization's values, norms, and traditions.
- Former members, administrators, and "living legends" are invited to convey the organization's history.
- Current leaders discuss the concepts of shared governance, collegiality, and consensus.
- Leaders review the organization's hallmark characteristics and basic values that set it apart from competitors.
- They resocialize members to the board's role and the organization's values through readings, stories, pledges, and other practices.
- They are explicitly conscious of their actions and decisions as statements of values.

The Educational Dimension

Effective boards take the necessary steps to ensure that their members are knowledgeable about the organization; the profession; and the board's own roles, responsibilities, and performance. They consciously create opportunities for board education and development. They regularly seek information and feedback on the board's performance. They pause periodically to self-reflect, assess strengths and limitations, and examine and learn from the board's experiences, including its mistakes.

Board members learn how to improve their performance through educational programs and retreats where matters of substance and process are examined. They use introspection on the board's internal operations and the ways that it carries out business. They reflect on the lessons that can be learned from their own experiences and mistakes. Other ways that effective boards strengthen this educational competency include the following:

- Setting aside some time at each meeting for a seminar or workshop to learn about an important matter of substance or process or to discuss a common reading;
- Conducting extended retreats every year or two for similar purposes and or analyzing the board's operations and its mistakes;
- Asking members and senior staff to report briefly on the best ideas they heard at a recent conference or meeting;
- Meeting periodically with "role counterparts" from comparable organizations;
- Rotating committee assignments so that members come to know many aspects of the organization; and
- Establishing internal feedback mechanisms such as evaluative comments from members at the end of each meeting, seeking feedback from senior staff and outside observers, and conducting annual surveys of members on individual and collective performance.

The Interpersonal Dimension

Effective boards nurture the development of their members as a working group, attend to the board's collective welfare, and foster a sense of cohesiveness. They create a sense of inclusiveness among all members, with equal access to information and equal opportunity to participate and influence decisions. They develop goals for the group, and they recognize group achievements. They identify and cultivate leadership within the board. Board members develop this competence in many ways:

- They create a sense of inclusiveness through events that enable members to become better acquainted with one another, distributing annual note-books with up-to-date biographical sketches of each member, building some "slack time" into the schedule for informal interaction, and shar-ing information widely and communicating regularly.
- They communicate group norms and standards by pairing newcomers with a mentor or coach and by being sure that everyone understands the informal "rules of the game."
- They cultivate the notion of the board as a group by establishing and publicizing group goals for the board itself.
- They ensure that the board has strong leadership by systematically groom-ing its future leaders and encouraging individual growth in skills and contributions to the group.

The Analytical Dimension

Effective boards recognize the complexities and subtleties of issues and accept ambiguity and uncertainty as healthy preconditions for critical discussions. They approach matters from a broad institutional outlook, and they critically dissect and examine all aspects of multifaceted issues. They raise doubts, explore tradeoffs, and encourage expressions of differences of opinion. This competence is cultivated by:

- Fostering cognitive complexity by using multiple frames of reference toanalyze issues and events;
- Seeking concrete and even contradictory information on ambiguous matters;
- Asking a few members to be critical evaluators or "devil's advocates," exploring the downside of recommendations and worst-case scenarios;
- Developing contingency and crisis plans;
- Asking members to assume the perspective of key constituencies by role-playing;
- Brainstorming alternative views of issues;
- Consulting outsiders and seeking different viewpoints; and
- Reinforcing and rewarding constructive criticism.

The Political Dimension

Effective boards accept as a primary responsibility the need to develop and maintain healthy relationships among major constituencies. They respect the integrity of the governance process and the legitimate roles and responsibilities of other stakeholders. They consult often and communicate directly with key constituencies, and they attempt to minimize conflict and win–lose situations. Board members nurture this competence by:

- Broadening channels of communication by distributing profiles of board members and annual board reports, inviting staff and consumers to serve on board committees, inviting outside leaders to address the board periodically, visiting with staff, and establishing multiconstituency task forces;
- Working closely with the CEO to develop and maintain processes that enable board members to communicate directly with stakeholders;
- Monitoring the health of relationships and morale in the organization;
- Keeping options open and avoiding win–lose polarizations;
- Being sensitive to the legitimate roles and responsibilities of all stakeholders; and
- Protecting the integrity of the governance process.

The Strategic Dimension

Effective boards help the organization envision a direction and shape a strategy for the future. They cultivate and concentrate on processes that sharpen organizational priorities. They organize themselves and conduct their business in light of the organization's strategic priorities. They anticipate potential problems and act before issues become crises. They cultivate this competence in the following ways:

- They focus attention on strategic issues by asking the CEO to present an annual update on organizational priorities and strategy, establishing board priorities and work plans, and developing an annual agenda for the board and its committees.
- They structure their meetings to concentrate on strategic priorities by prioritizing items on the agenda, providing overviews of the major topics and linkages among committee agendas, and providing a preface to each major policy issue to place it in a larger context.
- They reinforce attention on priorities by providing key questions for discussion in advance of meetings, displaying prominently the annual or continuous agenda, reserving time at each meeting for the CEO to discuss future issues, and making use of a "consent agenda."
- They develop a board information system that is strategic, normative, selective, and graphic.
- They monitor the use of board time and attention.

Such behaviors enable a board to add value to the organization by taking actions and reaching decisions that enhance the organization's long-term vitality and quality. Effective boards intentionally cultivate these skills and apply them in several ways.

HOW BOARDS ADD VALUE TO ORGANIZATIONS

The skills and practices of high-performing boards serve as examples for other boards to consider. Although not every practice may be transferable, boards that want to improve their effectiveness can draw selectively on the lessons offered by their high-performing counterparts and adapt them locally (Carver, 2002a; Holland, Ritvo, & Kovner, 1997; Taylor, Chait, & Holland, 1996).

One basic way that effective boards add value to their organizations is by helping the CEO determine what matters most. Working closely with the CEO, a board identifies and examines the most significant issues facing the organization and influencing its future. Not every matter is equally important, and not all issues can be addressed, so relative priorities must be set. The board concentrates its attention on identifying and addressing such matters.

Boards also add value by creating opportunities for CEOs to think aloud about questions and concerns well before it is necessary to come to conclusions or make recommendations. However, boards do not add much value through listening passively to voluminous reports. If they are to help as sounding boards for executives, time must be available for candid discussion of embryonic ideas, ambiguous issues, and unclear challenges in the road ahead. Through such unstructured discussions, boards can help CEOs frame the issues and reflect on the values, alternative directions, and tradeoffs that may eventually lead to a recommendation. Such exploratory discussions allow members' wisdom and counsel to contribute to the definition of issues the organization must face in the future.

Effective boards encourage experimentation, trying out new approaches and alternative ways of dealing with issues. The seeds of change can come from insightful questions that help others "get outside the box" of old assumptions and patterns. Raising critical questions and challenging assumptions can stimulate new ideas and creative alternatives for the future of the organization (Pound, 1993; Schein, 1993).

Another way that effective boards apply their skills and add value to organizations is by actively monitoring their own progress and assessing their performance. Most boards are given reams of data on inputs, numbers of clients or patrons served, and costs of various programs. Less attention is given to the effects or results of those activities. Part of the problem is lack of agreement on what would serve as appropriate indicators of effectiveness. Many trustees are unsure how to go about measuring performance or results of the organization's activities.

Strong boards have developed sets of specific performance indicators that enable them to monitor performance. These "dashboards" of indicators of key aspects of performance include periodic information on such areas as number of clients completing recommended services, costs per contact and per program, staff assessments of outcomes, and client satisfaction.

Such indicators are especially important as a component of the organization's strategic plan. Each goal in that plan should have accompanying indicators that allow the board to monitor progress toward its accomplishment. For example, if the plan calls for improvements in the quality of services or staff morale, the board and staff should work together to identify appropriate ways to measure the results of efforts intended to achieve those goals. These indicators should provide the board with means to assess progress, to see whether midcourse corrections are needed, and to draw conclusions about the effects of changes.

Most importantly, effective boards model the behaviors they desire in others (Holland, 1997a, 2002). Boards are appropriately seen as the leaders of the organization, and their decisions are subjected to critical scrutiny by all constituencies. Boards appropriately are concerned about the quality, costs, productivity, and innovation of staff; however, many boards are hesitant to apply the same expectations to themselves. Boards that call for accountability of staff have far greater credibility if they "walk the talk" and show by example how quality improvements are made.

Board members cannot be both leaders of change for the organization and followers of the status quo. If they want staff to identify and implement changes that reduce costs and increase productivity, then they should demonstrate that they have defined their own productivity, measured it carefully, and made changes that increase the value they add to the organization. Such efforts put the boards own actions in line with its policies for the whole organization and demonstrate commitment to them for others to observe and follow.

CONDITIONS FOR SUCCESSFUL BOARD DEVELOPMENT

In considering efforts to improve board performance, many obstacles should be anticipated and faced, including ambiguous expectations of boards, weak accountability, unclear returns on the investments of time for development, and members' discomfort over giving up familiar patterns and practicing new ones. Overcoming these barriers requires the concerted and sustained attention of the board. For these efforts to be successful, several conditions must be met.

For improvement to take place, a board must be ready for change and accept the importance of attending to and improving its own performance. Board development cannot be imposed on members or the top-level management. The CEO, the chairperson, and a substantial number of board leaders must have concerns about the board's performance and want to work on improving it. These leaders must initiate the process with enthusiasm and clear commitment to working with the board to bring about changes. Many of the members must come to share these concerns in the context of loyalty to the organization and its mission.

Development of improved performance must be carried out as the board works on its business items rather that doing the business and then doing "development."

Distinguishing board development from the "real" work of the board is a false dichotomy. The processes of learning how to work together more effectively should be embedded within the efforts to carry out the instrumental expectations of the board. Learning involves looking at tasks the board carries out and identifying ways that enable the group to work better and produce more useful results.

Next, the focus of development efforts should be on changing a board's behavior rather than changing attitudes or personalities. Exhortations and prescriptions do not work nearly as well as changes in routines, procedures, or structures for doing work together. Members begin to think differently and act differently as a result of such practical steps as bringing thoughtful questions to the board, providing relevant and focused information on the issue, dividing members into small groups to brainstorm alternative solutions and formulate recommendations, and encouraging critical and analytical thinking about issues before the group.

Development activities should be individually tailored to the specific needs and concerns of the board. Although a retreat approach is often useful in getting started, development activities should be built into the board's ongoing agenda and ways of doing business rather than being treated as a separate activity. This is due to the instrumental expectation of many members who tend to see the board's effectiveness primarily as a means to advance the organization's performance rather than seeing board development as an end in itself.

The best approaches link process and substance. For example, asking the board to set goals for itself or to formulate indicators to monitor its performance sets in motion a process that builds cohesion and educates participants while also generating substantive products.

Board development is an extensive, long-term process, not a quick fix. To sustain the process, some of the board members must be "product champions" for the board and its performance, just as some advocate balanced budgets or client satisfaction. The pressures of business as usual are strong, and without continuing attention to how well the board is performing, it settles back into comfortable ways of working that may not match the needs of a changing organization or environment.

Initiating Attention to the Board's Performance

Boards can make productive use of recent successes or problems as occasions to reflect on what happened and how the board contributed to the results. Both positive and negative situations provide opportunities for the board to consider how it has performed during the time leading up to this point and to think about how it wants to perform in dealing with similar situations in the future. Such reflection invites members to look beyond mere reaction to external events and to consider ways that the board might carry out its business more intentionally in the future so as to provide more effective leadership. Whatever the issue, the board can ask itself how it has contributed to the successes and problems in the area and what lessons it should take from the experiences to become more effective in the future.

Even when it is not facing critical turning points, the board can periodically ask its CEO to talk about some of the major challenges on the horizon or to describe the organizational issues that keep him or her awake at night. The group can then discuss how it has contributed to the organization's readiness to deal with these matters and how it could prepare itself to provide stronger leadership in the future.

The board should include in its agenda some time at each meeting for candid, off-the-record talk with the CEO about the most complex or troublesome issues coming in the months or years ahead. Then it should explore ways that the board could become a stronger partner with the CEO in working on those issues. Thus, the board uses work on substantive challenges to the organization as opportunities to learn how to improve its own performance.

Another opportunity for examination of the board's own performance is in discussions of how the organization deals with accountability for its use of resources. Most boards expect the CEO to report on how staff are being held accountable, and many boards specify expectations of the executive and criteria for assessing that person's performance. Fewer boards, however, apply the same principles to themselves and have clear evidence of how the board itself is being accountable for its use of time and resources.

Developing means for demonstrating the board's own accountability is crucial for modeling the behaviors it expects of others in the organization. Initiating such a process begins with recognizing that the board has a duty of accountability for its responsibilities and then engaging in candid discussions of how well it is carrying out this obligation (Holland, 2002). Useful questions for group discussion include the following:

- How is this board adding value to the organization, beyond the contributions of staff and administration?
- What steps should the board take to improve its performance and increase the value it adds to the organization?
- What criteria or indicators are appropriate for monitoring and demonstrating the board's improving performance?

Rather than approaching this matter in terms of forced compliance with external rules or avoidance of public embarrassment, it is more productive to approach accountability as a matter of mutual expectations and shared commitments among members. Conversations about goals and promises to one another about steps the board will take together to attain them serves to build a climate of responsibility and mutual commitment to one another. Such commitments guide behavior more powerfully than external rules or threats (Fry, 1995). Intentional examination of the board's commitments and the ways that it ensures that they are carried out sets the stage for further steps to strengthen individual and group performance.

Boards can take advantage of a wide variety of opportunities to look at their own performance and the value that they have been adding to the organization. Efforts to look at this area are prompted by participants' desires to increase the value the board adds to the organization and to maximize its contributions to the organization's accomplishment of its mission. However they are expressed, members' concerns provide vital signals that it is time to begin involving others in reflections on the group's work together. As one experienced board leader advised, "Don't hesitate to ask yourself and others, 'Is this board truly adding as much value to this organization as it could? Could we do better?'" Raising such questions may seem like small beginnings, but numerous boards have found that they are vital first steps toward important changes.

Although every member of the board should be concerned about how well the group is doing its job, it is important that these concerns move from individuals and come to be shared and owned by the full group. The board's leaders are vital to this step, and it usually falls to them to initiate open attention to the board's performance. Anyone can propose a discussion of how the board is working, but the positive response and commitment of the CEO and board chair are essential to the success of efforts to bring issues before the whole group.

The best orchestra or sports team steps back from each performance and reviews how well it did and where changes could be made to improve future work. High-performing groups take time for practice and for reviewing their performance, thus learning and growing together as a team (Senge, 1994). Boards can learn from such examples. As the leader of one strong board noted, "After we've finished working a particularly difficult problem, we try to take some time to reflect together on what we can learn from what we've just come through." Boards that take time to examine and reflect together on their own performance can identify useful lessons that will guide them into increased effectiveness as leaders.

Using Assessments to Identify Targets for Change

Initial discussions about board performance can be carried to an important next step by getting more extensive information from all participants regarding their views of the board's work, areas warranting attention, and suggestions for change. It is useful to broaden the inquiry so that participants can find out if their concerns are things that more than just a few want to work on. An assessment of the full board supports this step. As one experienced member emphasized,

> Any board interested in improving should get going with an evaluation of its strengths and weaknesses. It should ask a whole series of tough questions about what's working well and what isn't. You can't just depend on a few insiders to run things. You're ALL the owners of the institution and all responsible for finding ways that enable you to help it work better.

In addition to gathering information for everyone to examine, a crucial function of board assessment is that it serves to spread responsibility for findings and conclusions across the whole group, thus building shared ownership of conclusions and consensus for taking steps of change. In the words of one board chairperson,

> The most important result of starting to evaluate our work as a board was that the group began to think about itself purposively and to ask questions about how we could do our work better in the future. It got all of us going with taking responsibility for improving the quality of our own work.

Approaches to board assessment may be divided into two areas of focus: (1) group performance and (2) individual performance. A few approaches link these domains. Many boards have used one or more assessment methods to identify aspects of board performance that members see as needing improvement. They can choose from numerous resources and approaches in such efforts, and many national associations have developed board assessment tools. The various approaches include self-evaluations, constituency surveys, third-party reviews, internal reviews by an ad hoc or standing committee on trusteeship, reflective discussion of critical incidents, and feedback at the conclusion of meetings.

One comprehensive board self-assessment package is offered by BoardSource (Slesinger, 1991); another approach is based on the six competencies of effective boards (Jackson & Holland, 1998). Other approaches range from brief evaluations at the end of meetings to bringing in outside evaluators to interview and summarize the views of board members, staff, consumers, and sponsors.

Each approach to board assessment has strengths and limitations. They vary in time and resources required and in vulnerability to bias. A board should begin by experimenting with whatever approach to assessment seems comfortable and appropriate and then evaluating the usefulness of the results. It should revise and expand the steps in ways that the group finds helpful and comprehensible. At some point, the group should invite in some outsiders who bring objectivity and experience with other boards for comparisons and for innovative ideas.

Retreats as a Means to Work on Board Performance

Many boards have found that retreats are powerful tools for stimulating and extending board growth. A retreat is typically a one- or two-day special meeting, held off site and away from wherever the group usually meets. Retreats allow a group to devote extended time to working on a major issue, such as developing or updating its strategic plan, gaining a better understanding of the external environment, clarifying its mission, evaluating a possible new market, or solving some problem. In this section, we consider their use specifically for working on improvements in the board's own performance.

A board development retreat is an investment in the future of the board and the organization it governs. It provides an opportunity to step back from routine business agendas for an in-depth look at the future and the board's role in it. A retreat can be a major boost to the board's efforts to make more effective and efficient use of the time that it gives to the organization (Holland, 1997b; Savage, 1995; Scott, 2000).

Boards have found that their retreats served several important purposes, such as

- Strengthening performance through a review of governance processes and the board's roles and responsibilities;
- Assessing the board's contributions to the organization and identifying ways that it can add greater value;
- Establishing priorities for the board and identifying strategies and actions to achieve them;
- Enhancing collegiality and working relationships among board members and between board and staff;
- Determining the next steps in board development and in the implementation of overall action plans.

A board may use numerous resources in planning and conducting its retreat. BoardSource (http://www.boardsource.org) publishes useful resource materials on board development and maintains lists of consultants and facilitators in many regions of the country. Similar resources are available through the national associations of many other organizations.

A retreat can generate a great deal of enthusiasm among participants. However, a board can lose momentum when it returns to its regular meeting schedule and reverts to familiar old patterns. Likewise, turnover in membership introduces newcomers who are unacquainted with the board's efforts to change behavior and improve performance. Agenda items that are scheduled almost automatically demand attention, and promises made at a retreat may be forgotten like New Year's resolutions. Therefore, it is essential to have explicit methods for reminding everyone of the agreements and changes identified at the retreat and regular evidence of how those resolutions are being implemented. The underlying goal is to build habits of reflection and learning into the group's culture, so that both newcomers and old-timers are socialized into effective patterns of behavior.

Ongoing Board Education

Incorporating educational activities into board meetings is a vital practice for making ongoing improvements in the board's performance. Boards should be models of "learning organizations" (Senge, 1994). The assembled intellectual abilities of members are extended by acquiring new knowledge and skills as a group and by identifying and developing improved ways to carry out their work.

Rather than simply relying on past knowledge and skill as sufficient, effective boards acknowledge their need to learn and take responsibility for continuing to expand their competencies. They identify topics and issues to examine, develop appropriate programs and resources, and encourage all members to participate in ongoing educational sessions. Effective boards encourage ongoing education among their members by bringing in special speakers, holding mini-seminars and study groups, visiting other boards, attending conferences on governance, and rotating committee assignments (Scott, 2000; Taylor, et al., 1996).

It is especially important to have thorough orientation programs for incoming members. New members should be enabled to get off to a good start by means of receiving clear expectations for board membership, extensive orientation to the board's roles and responsibilities, and information about the organization. Assigning an experienced member as a mentor for a newcomer is another useful practice that provides both with a greater awareness of board performance.

Outside speakers and mentors from other boards also are useful resources to help a board learn. Many national and regional associations can recommend knowledgeable leaders to serve in such educational or consultative roles, and some boards also recruit resource people from similar organizations in their region. Any board can occasionally use outside consultants, mentors, or evaluators to help the group gain independent perspectives on its performance, identify issues needing its attention, and learn about best practices of other boards.

Better boards enlarge this process of education by helping every member develop learning plans that enable him or her to make greater contributions to the group in the following year. This process may be as simple as rotating committee assignments or as extensive as sending members to conferences on governance and bringing in speakers on topics of interest to members. Some boards establish procedures for all their members to set individual performance goals and to obtain feedback on their progress. They use feedback to coach members in improving their contributions to the group's overall effectiveness. They use coaching sessions and mentors for underperformers and term limits to ease out chronic poor performers. In these ways, boards can use individual and group goals as well as monitoring and feedback to sustain attention on improved performance.

Restructuring Meeting Time and Committee Work

An important approach to improving performance is to restructure the board's use of committees and meeting time to emphasize its strategic priorities (Carver, 1990). Careful use of the scarce resource of meeting time is a concern of many members, and many sense that agendas pack too many issues into limited meeting time. Meeting agendas should be designed so that they sustain focus on the few, most important issues of strategy and policy. Preparation for making changes in the agenda may begin with having a member simply monitor the amount of time that the board spends on each issue in a meeting and rate its relevance to the board's priorities. The board can discuss the feedback and consider the relationship between its priorities and its actual use of time.

Better use of meeting time can result from setting clear priorities for the board's attention and leaving nonessential items for individual review. Strong boards limit the agenda of meetings to a few, top-priority matters rather than trying to cover the waterfront. They cluster routine reports and unexceptional motions that require board approval into a "consent agenda" to be voted on in one action rather than separately. Any member can request that an item be separated out for discussion, thus protecting the board's ultimate right to examine any issue. However, the practice allows the board to concentrate most of its attention on those matters of highest priority to the organization and avoid getting bogged down in operational details.

Restructuring how the board organizes and charges its committees is another way to improve performance. Instead of committees that mirror management divisions (e.g., personnel, programs, finances), boards should let form follow function. The strategic priorities provide the point of departure, from which work group assignments and meeting agendas are derived. Board committees should be constructed to focus members' efforts on each of the board's goals, and each committee should be dissolved when a goal is attained.

Rather than using board meeting time to hear routine reports from every committee, the board can structure its meetings to focus on one or two goals or priorities at each meeting, with discussions led by those groups that have carried out the background preparation. Leaders should make sure that every report begins with a clear statement of the question being presented to the board and how the issue is linked with a goal or priority of the board.

For changes to outlast individuals and become embedded in the board's culture, there must be some "champions" for the group's performance, in the same manner that a finance committee or buildings and grounds committee carries its portfolio. To build in advocacy for the board itself, members can assign to a group the task of keeping the board reminded of its commitments, monitoring its performance, and periodically recommending actions that will strengthen meeting processes. Strong boards have their committee on nominations or some other permanent group take the responsibilities for developing and implementing steps for monitoring board meetings, soliciting participants' assessments and recommendations for improvement, and arranging for periodic board education sessions and retreats on issues of interest.

Many of these boards expand the duties of the nominating committee to include carrying out periodic assessments of individual and group performance. This group uses findings to coach members in expanding their leadership contributions to the board, to identify people to nominate for additional terms, to identify skills needed in new members, and to plan regular educational sessions in areas in which the board needed improvement.

The committee's experience in carrying out these tasks is applicable in its nominations of future members. It broadens the scope of characteristics sought in new members to include skills in working with groups, linkages to key constituencies, ability to contribute new perspectives to examining issues, and a track record of making positive contributions to group communication and learning.

Boards that restructure their meeting agendas and committees can then monitor the usefulness of those changes by evaluating their meetings, including plenary sessions as well as committee meetings, and getting feedback and suggestions to improve future meetings. Brief assessment forms, followed by discussion of participants' concerns and recommendations, can lead to more productive and satisfying meetings.

Building Group Cohesion and Teamwork

The instrumental orientation of many members makes structural changes more attractive than efforts directed explicitly at relationships, processes, or communications. However, the most effective boards take careful steps to transform an assembly of talented individuals into a well-integrated group.

Many board members are comfortable providing individual expertise or advice to the CEO, whereas others see their service taking place on a committee related to their area of interest. The most effective boards go beyond these efforts and also emphasize the whole group as the decision-making unit. A cohesive board makes better decisions than individuals do, yet it draws on members' multiple perspectives to avoid the traps of "groupthink."

Transforming an assembly of skilled individuals into a well integrated team is a long and difficult process. It requires taking critical issues to the group for deliberation and taking the time necessary to hear the views of each participant rather than relying on a few leaders to predigest issues and present foregone conclusions. It requires that the issues taken to the board are vital to the future of the organization and not merely window dressing. It requires making sure that everyone has equal access to information about the issues and the organization. It requires taking time for members to get to know one another beyond the formal setting of the boardroom. Strong boards pay careful attention to communications among members, to nurturing and sustaining inclusive relationships, and developing a sense of mutual responsibility for the board's success. They are aware that silent members may have some important concerns that the board needs to hear. Social events and informal time for conversations are important means to build trusting relationships.

The most effective steps for building group cohesion are ones that closely link instrumental and relational components and allow members to deal with the latter by means of overt attention to the former. For example, working to formulate goals for the board itself is a good means for building group cohesion while also serving to focus the board's use of time and energy. Goals for the board should be distinct from—but lead to—the overall goals it has for the organization. They identify specifically what the board will do to maximize its contributions to the attainment of the organizations strategic goals.

The board identifies its goals, which should be kept in everyone's awareness by posting them in conspicuous places and by repeating them in meetings and at the beginning of reports. Keeping the boards own goals paramount in meetings by means of the agenda plan and the focus of each report or discussion keeps everyone clear about the purpose and direction of each step. It also allows the board to monitor and evaluate its own progress toward its goals.

Formulating specific goals for the board also helps the process of clarifying expectations of the board as a group and of individual members, officers, committees, and senior staff. It is important to make sure that each participant understands what is expected of him or her and how those expectations contribute to achieving the overall goals. Setting goals for the board as a whole and periodically reviewing progress toward them serve to maintain the board's attention to its own performance and how it adds value to the organization. The board should monitor indicators of its performance regularly and make sure that each member has this information. Sharing this information with outsiders and inviting their assessments of progress further sharpens accountability for performance.

Throughout these steps, an underlying concern is to develop a stronger sense of inclusiveness and cohesiveness among board members as a group. This requires paying careful attention to communications among members and intentionally nurturing and sustaining inclusive relationships. These processes should begin at recruitment and orientation, be carried forward by all leaders, and be reinforced at social times and retreats. Strong boards are careful to schedule social time and informal interaction for their members. They celebrate members' accomplishments, have meals together before or after meetings, take breaks for refreshments, regularly use name tags, and participate as a group in social events sponsored by the organization.

ROLE OF THE CEO

The CEO plays a central role in creating and sustaining an effective board. He or she most often initiates attention to the board's performance and advocates for improvements. No longer content with the cynical old advice to "keep them in the dark so they'll leave you alone," good executives realize that their boards can be their best partners in creating a strong organization. They invest time in examining the group's performance and educating members in leadership skills.

If boards are to improve, CEOs must be committed to leading efforts to learn better ways of working together and take the initiative in raising members' sights and expectations of themselves. Working closely with the chairperson of the board, the CEO raises performance questions with the group and helps members consider new approaches to its work. The CEO describes approaches to governance that raise aspirations and prepare the group for making changes in its own patterns. He or she helps the group focus its attention on those aspects that warrant attention and then identify specific steps for change. The CEO raises group expectations and aspirations by initiating questions about group performance, suggesting alternative approaches to dealing with issues, and offering new possibilities for improving group effectiveness.

By opening up discussion about the board's performance, the CEO demonstrates that it is appropriate to direct attention to the board's own work and to explore ways of improving it. Rather than avoiding discontents or treating problems as occasions for blaming someone, effective CEOs turn problems into occasions for the group to learn more effective ways of carrying out its work. Discontents are moved from back channels to the forefront of everyone's attention, and the group is invited to take on responsibilities for identifying solutions to problems and better ways to deal with issues. The CEO models the desired behavior of respectful listening and constructive use of feedback to improve the quality of work, inviting others to join in similar steps. In so doing, he or she confirms that everyone in the leadership group is committed to doing their jobs more effectively, not just avoiding criticisms, blaming others, or settling for business as usual.

Effective CEOs expect and tolerate some anxiety that comes with questioning old assumptions and relinquishing familiar practices for the unknown. Their persistence in seeking improvements, even when solutions may not yet be apparent, encourages experimentation with new approaches to dealing with tasks and invites others to try out alternatives without fear of being blamed for mistakes along the way. Reflecting on experiences together, identifying areas to change, and trying out new approaches are difficult but crucial steps in learning for anyone in the organization, including the board. CEOs recognize and celebrate incremental steps toward goals of improved board performance, thus establishing it as a model for others in the organization.

CONCLUSION

By working intentionally on its own performance, a board makes some fundamental changes in the ways that it uses its time and energy, not just engaging in a temporary quick fix that solves immediate problems. Attention to how it is carrying out its work becomes part of the agenda rather than something separate from and independent of ongoing tasks and responsibilities (Holland, Leslie, & Holzhalb, 1993). The board makes fundamental changes in its culture, reinventing and rejuvenating itself. It incorporates into its basic sense of responsibility a continuing concern with improving the quality of its performance rather than seeing it as something separate or occasional. Leaders can reinforce this understanding by pausing occasionally during discussions or at the conclusion of a major agenda item to invite reflection on how the group dealt with the issue and what could be done to improve the process next time. Such reflective practices become part of the group's culture.

Time and intentional work are essential for changes to become integrated into the board's culture. To ensure that lessons are learned and used, boards have found that they must allow enough time to fully address their concerns and explore alternatives. This cannot be accomplished at one meeting; rather, some attention should be devoted to regular reflection on the group's work performance. The group should build into its expectations that time is allocated to discuss how it dealt with key agenda items as well as to work on the tasks themselves. Even a few minutes per meeting on such reflections can lead to greater board efficiency and effectiveness. It also can ensure that minor irritants do not mushroom into major problems.

Taking time to reflect on how the board has used its time and attention, particularly after dealing with a difficult issue, enhances the group's ownership of its own processes and performance. Such discussions should take place at the conclusion of each meeting and allow members to share perceptions of performance and consider ways to improve future meetings.

Effective boards attend to how they work together as well as to what they do. Members take responsibility for initiating discussions of ways the group carries out its work and seek ways to improve performance. They take advantage of breaks or turning points in the organization's experience to draw attention to the board's role in leadership and change. They test their perceptions with others and identify shared concerns of the group. They move ahead by means of assessments of group performance to identify specific issues and goals for change. They lay the foundation for ongoing work by means of retreats and mindful follow-up. They reinforce and institutionalize changes by means of in-meeting discussions of feedback on performance and educational sessions that contribute to strengthening the board's effectiveness. These efforts bridge the gap between learning and doing, integrating reflection with work. They help the group develop a culture of active responsibility for making ongoing, self-directed improvements in its own performance.

By taking consistent initiatives to improve their work together, boards set the example for others and show how to add greater value to their organizations. However, boards rarely are able to initiate such activities by themselves; they generally require strong leadership and direction from their CEO. The payoff can be substantial. As one senior chairperson summarized his group's experience,

> Our board members' sense of the importance of working on our own performance went from zero to extremely high. I've had a lot of experience as a member of several national corporate boards and initially was impatient with more time spent on this area. But now it has become a basic part of the way this board works. . . . To come through all the changes this organization faced, you really have to become a team with many skilled players. . . . We started off with some retreats and had some speakers who really opened my eyes. . . . Now board development is fully owned by this board, and one of our members arranges for us to work together on some topic for about an hour at every meeting. We're all committed to moving ahead with our own education as a board so we will be more effective leaders of this organization in the future.

SKILLS APPLICATION EXERCISES

Metropolitan Family Services Board

Beth Jefferson, CEO of the Metropolitan Family Services Center, and Frank Watson, chair of its board, were talking over lunch about how the board was performing and possible ways that it might be improved. "I think we're going to face increased pressure from managed care and from other service providers coming into our area," Beth reflected. "I think we should get the board to work on doing a better job so we can survive in the years ahead."

"But we already have a fine board," Frank responded. "Our members have their hands full with overseeing all we do now. All the committees are working hard, and most of our members have many years of experience in their roles. They've all done good work, so I don't see why you think we need to change."

"Well, perhaps we're victims of our own past success," said Beth. "There's no doubt that our committee structure and our membership have served us well in the past, and I don't mean to be critical, it's just that things are changing from how they were even a few years ago. The population we serve is getting younger, poorer, and more troubled. I doubt that many on our board know much about our current clients. If we're going to understand our community and the people we're supposed to be serving, we need some new blood."

"But we'd be losing a lot of wisdom and experience by changing membership just for the sake of change," replied Frank. "After all, these folks have come through many years with the center and know it inside and out. They trust you and each other, and they work together well. I just don't see how changing the people will accomplish what you seem to want. It certainly will cause a lot of disruption. There's lots to lose and little to gain, as I see it."

"It's certainly true that our board members have been helpful," Beth acknowledged. "But they seldom dig in and help improve recommendations that I bring to the table. They're willing to listen and raise a few questions, but the weight is all on me to come up with the ideas and the plans. They're passive reactors, not real leaders. I don't think most of them are actively in touch with much of the community. As a matter of fact, I fear that this group really has no clear goals or criteria for evaluating the quality of anything, other than how comfortable they feel about where I'm taking them. That may have been acceptable in the past, but I want some bright and capable partners who can really contribute to our understanding of trends and political issues, people who can actively chart a course into the future. Maybe we could start by suggesting term limits and then talk about what characteristics we'd like to see in new nominees. Perhaps we could plan some new education sessions for the board on changes in the community."

SKILLS APPLICATION EXERCISES (continued)

"I'm afraid many of our members would view your efforts to change the board as a power grab," Frank replied. "A few may be willing to retire, but most are just pleased with the way things are going and would resist change. I doubt they'd understand what you're trying to do. You know the old saying, 'If it ain't broke, then don't fix it.' Why not just leave well enough alone?"

Discussion Questions

- What are some of this board's strengths, and what are some of its weaknesses? How would you rate it on each of the characteristics of effective boards presented in this chapter?
- What opportunities and constraints confront Beth in moving toward on her goals for the board? How could she take advantage of the opportunities, build on strengths, and overcome weaknesses?
- What should be Beth's short-range and long-range objectives? What resources could she draw on for each?
- How would you describe the relationship between Beth and Frank? What important steps should each take to work together more effectively?
- Develop an action plan for Beth, identifying important steps and resources.
- What criteria should she use to monitor progress toward her objectives?

Westside Community Center

The slow-moving traffic drew little attention from Wilma Jefferson this afternoon. She was headed for Westside's quarterly board meeting and was decidedly uncomfortable about what lay ahead. "Why do I keep on doing this when it's so frustrating?" Wilma grumbled to herself.

Four years earlier, Wilma had been nattered by Executive Director Don Carlisle's call asking her to serve on the board. She was sure that the request had been linked to her family's ownership of one of the largest manufacturing corporations in the city, but the prospect of helping improve the quality of what was already a top-notch community center had caught her interest.

She'd like to feel that she was a part of such an effort to "ratchet up Westside," as Don had put it, so she had agreed to this venture onto a nonprofit board. Over her first year on the Westside board, Wilma had kept a low profile as she watched how this group conducted its business. The organization's budget had been balanced every year, membership and participation were growing, and programs were of good quality.

SKILLS APPLICATION EXERCISES (continued)

Everyone on the board and the management team seemed quite contented with how things were going for the organization. Although fund accounting still struck her as a curious way of financial management, Wilma really enjoyed the occasional talks by senior members of the staff at board meetings.

The four meetings a year were efficient, usually starting with committee meetings in the afternoon, followed by a social dinner sometimes including a staff "show and tell," after which the board met as a whole from 7 p.m. until about 10 p.m. to hear and discuss committee reports. Some of the committee reports were thorough; others seemed vague and pointless. Neither sort evoked much response from anyone in the meetings, and Wilma wondered if others found these sessions as tedious and boring as she did. Only occasionally were there recommended actions that were not routine and, for all intents and purposes, predetermined. "Surely," Wilma mused to herself, "there's more to being a board member than approving contracts with suppliers, building renovation projects, and joint activities with other organizations in the city. The only real discussion each year was about setting membership fees and staff salaries."

When Wilma joined the board, she had acquiesced to the request that she serve on the fund-raising campaign committee. Soon, however, she became dismayed at the confusion in signals from the CEO and the committee chairman. She made several calls to friends and opened some doors that led to other contributions. However, the campaign ended far short of its goal, and it seemed to have concluded with a whimper, not a bang. Even more curiously, from Wilma's perspective, the board had never addressed the lingering dissatisfactions from that experience. Two years later, Don was pushing hard for the board to start yet another campaign, this time with an even higher goal.

One evening after the end of that last campaign, Wilma and several other members of the board had talked in the parking lot after a board meeting about what might have gone wrong. Part of the problem seemed to have been that there was no clear strategic plan for the organization, a point brought up at the next board meeting by another member. Don had really gone to work on that challenge and had done a fine job with it. Over the next nine months, a series of planning meetings included many of the board members and several staff and community leaders. The plan that emerged was saluted by everyone—staff as well as the board—as excellent, distinctive, and comprehensive. There was a sense that the document, although ambitious and a bit ambiguous in places, had instilled in Westside a new sense of purpose and overall direction.

Why, then, Wilma wondered, was she still uncomfortable? The strategic plan was unquestionably good, just what the organization needed. However, the subsequent board meetings seemed to have continued with business as usual, with only occasional references to the plan. It didn't appear to have had any evident effect on either the substance or the processes of meetings. At the most recent meeting, Don had pushed

---

SKILLS APPLICATION EXERCISES (continued)

---

hard for the board to authorize the new campaign. Backed by the board chair, Don called for volunteers to form a campaign committee. However, few members had responded. The "usual suspects" had raised their hands but with little evident enthusiasm. The spark just did not seem to be there for anyone in the room.

During a break in the meeting, Arnold Moore, the chair of the committee on programs and services, had commented to Wilma and a few others gathered around the coffee urn that there seemed to be a lethargy in the room. Everyone, including Wilma, had nodded in agreement, but no one raised the issue once the meeting resumed. Apparently nobody wanted to seem like a wet blanket, Wilma surmised, especially without some specific reason or recommendation about how to improve things.

After that meeting, Wilma had tried to engage Don in some conversation about her unease, but somehow the response seemed to miss the point. "I'm not sure that our board members see how we fit into the plan," she said to him. "Isn't the board itself one of the organization's strategic assets that should be included in our thinking somehow? Shouldn't life on the board be different now that we actually have a strategic plan?"

"Certainly the board is central to the plan," insisted Don. "Its job now is just to roll up its sleeves and get to work raising the money so Westside can achieve the goals detailed in the plan. We're all counting on the board this time, Wilma, to make sure that we reach our target. And frankly, I see you as a key player."

"Get on board or get out of the way," Wilma thought as she drove to the next board meeting. That was a motto that Wilma had often heard among her own company's senior staff when a new venture was getting started, and now she was hearing it at Westside. Why did it seem so irritating now? "Maybe it's just me," Wilma mused as she pulled into the parking lot. "Am I just getting too old for all this? Should I just get out of the way, resign this volunteer position, and take that long overdue vacation?"

The meeting was just getting under way when Wilma walked into the conference room. "Welcome, ladies and gentlemen," boomed the chairman. "We have a full agenda this evening, so I hope you are prepared to work a little later than usual. In addition to all our usual committee reports, we have two bids for renovations to review, a proposal for some changes in programs and in membership regulations, plus several budgetary adjustments. Then I'd like for us to get back to preparations for the campaign and see what we need to do to get that project launched. Any questions before we dig in?"

By the time the meeting ended, Wilma was exasperated by what she regarded to be an endless stream of trivia and minutiae. On her way out to the parking lot, she walked with Freddie Ackerman, assistant director of Westside, and said, "Freddie you know this organization and this board better than I do. Am I crazy to think that the board should be dealing regularly with crucial issues like strengthening our competitive advantage,

SKILLS APPLICATION EXERCISES (continued)

monitoring the quality of our programs, improving our market share, and controlling costs? It seems like our leaders steer clear of issues like that in favor of discussions of program regulations and rehabbing the physical plant. Those things may be important to somebody, but frankly they just sap my energy. Furthermore, I just don't think the board's heart will be in another campaign now. So, I have two questions for you: First, am I correct in my perceptions about what a board should be and what this one is? And second, if I am correct, what should be done to change things? I really hope you can help me out, because frankly I've about had it."

Discussion Questions

- Why do board members sometimes raise questions and offer comments outside the board room that they wouldn't make inside the board room? What, if anything, should a CEO or a board chairperson do about this?
- If you were Freddie, how would you answer Wilma's two questions?
- Why do some boards have difficulty in keeping focused on strategy instead of operations?
- What, if anything, should this board do differently? What should the executive director do? What should Freddie do? What should the board chairperson do? What should Wilma do?
- What goals should this board set for itself (as distinct from goals it has for the organization)? How should it go about that process?
- How could this board know if and when it was improving its performance? What would be some useful indicators for it to monitor?
- What are the implications for such issues for the development of effective trustees and volunteers for a nonprofit organization?

Group Discussion

Executive Director Don Carlisle has called together the executive committee of the Westside board and made the following request: "Please help me come up with a plan that will significantly improve the value added to this organization from our board members. I am particularly concerned that we make effective use of these folks in our upcoming campaign. Our plan should include specific objectives, a credible approach, assignable tasks, observable outcomes, and minimal expenses." Your assignment is to develop and present the key features of such a plan, including your recommendations and the reasoning that supports each of them.

REFERENCES

Carver, J. (1990). *Boards that make a difference*. San Francisco: Jossey-Bass.

Carver, J. (2002a). *Corporate boards that add value*. San Francisco: Jossey-Bass.

Carver, J. (2002b). *John Carver on board leadership*. San Francisco: Jossey-Bass.

Chait, R. P., Holland, T. P., & Taylor, B. E. (1993). *The effective board of trustees*. Phoenix, AZ: Oryx Press.

Fry, R. E. (1995). Accountability in organizational life: Problem or opportunity for nonprofits? *Nonprofit Management and Leadership, 6,* 181–195.

Holland, T. P. (1997a). Board self-assessment: A model of accountability. *Not-for-Profit CEO Monthly Letter, 4*(1), 5–9.

Holland, T. P. (1997b). Setting the stage: Planning board retreats. *Board Member, 6*(4), 10–11.

Holland, T. P. (2002). Board accountability: Some lessons from the field. *Nonprofit Management and Leadership, 12,* 409–428.

Holland, T. P., Chait, R. P., & Taylor, B. E. (1989). Board effectiveness: Identifying and measuring trustee competencies. *Journal of Research in Higher Education, 30,* 451–469.

Holland, T. P., Leslie, D., & Holzhalb, C. (1993). Culture and change in nonprofit boards. *Nonprofit Management and Leadership, 4,* 141–155.

Holland, T. P., Ritvo, R. A., & Kovner, A. R. (1997). *Improving board effectiveness: Practical lessons for nonprofit healthcare organizations*. Chicago: American Hospital Association.

Houle, C. O. (1989). *Governing boards: Their nature and nurture*. San Francisco: Jossey-Bass.

Jackson, D. K., & Holland, T. P. (1998). Measuring the effectiveness of nonprofit boards. *Nonprofit and Voluntary Sector Quarterly, 27,* 159–182.

Pound, J. (1993, March–April). The promise of the governed corporation. *Harvard Business Review,* pp. 89–98.

Savage, T. J. (1995). *Seven steps to a more effective board*. Rockville, MD: Cheswick Center.

Schein, E. H. (1993). How can organizations learn faster? The challenge of entering the green room. *Sloan Management Review, 34,* 85–92.

Scott, K. T. (2000). Creating caring and capable boards. San Francisco: Jossey-Bass.

Senge, P. (1994). *The fifth discipline: The art and practice of the learning organization*. New York: Doubleday.

Slesinger, L. H. (1991). *Self-assessment for nonprofit boards*. Washington, DC: National Center for Nonprofit Boards.

Taylor, B. E., Chait, R. P., & Holland, T. P. (1996). The new work of the nonprofit board. *Harvard Business Review, 74*(5), 36–46.

Widmer, C., & Houchin, S. (2000). *The art of trusteeship*. San Francisco: Jossey-Bass.

ADDITIONAL READING

Association for Governing Boards of Universities and Colleges. (1986). *Self-study criteria for governing boards of independent colleges and universities*. Washington, DC: Author.

Bowen, W. G. (1994). *Inside the boardroom*. New York: John Wiley & Sons.

Brudney, J., & Nobbie, P. D. (2002). Training policy governance in nonprofit boards of directors. *Nonprofit Management and Leadership, 12*, 387–408.

Chait, R. P. (1994). *The new activism of corporate boards and the implications for campus governance*. Washington, DC: Association of Governing Boards of Universities and Colleges.

Chait, R. P., Holland, T. P., & Taylor, B. E. (1996). *Improving the performance of governing boards*. Phoenix, AZ: Oryx Press.

Drucker, P. F. (1990). Lessons for successful nonprofit governance. *Nonprofit Management and Leadership, 1*, 7–14.

Eadie, D. C. (1994). *Boards that work: A practical guide for building effective association boards*. Washington, DC: American Society of Association Executives.

Eadie, D. C. (1997). *Changing by design: A practical approach to leading innovation in nonprofit organizations*. San Francisco: Jossey-Bass.

Eadie, D. C., & Edwards, R. L. (1993). Board leadership by design. *Nonprofit World, 11*(2), 12–15.

Herman, R. D, & Van Til, J. (1989). *Nonprofit boards of directors: Analyses and applications*. New Brunswick, NJ: Transaction.

Holland, T. P. (1991). Self-assessment by nonprofit boards. *Nonprofit Management and Leadership, 2*, 25–36.

Holland, T. P. (1996). *How to build a more effective board*. Washington, DC: National Center for Nonprofit Boards.

Iecovich, E. (2004). Responsibilities and roles of boards: The Israeli case. *Nonprofit Management and Leadership, 15*, 5–24.

Smith, D. H. (1995). *Entrusted: The moral responsibilities of trusteeship*. Bloomington: Indiana University Press.

Zander, A. (1993). *Making boards effective: The dynamics of governing boards*. San Francisco: Jossey-Bass.

Planning and
Managing Strategically

Douglas C. Eadie

Strategic planning and management processes have been widely used in the for-profit sector for the past quarter-century, and their application is now spreading rapidly in the nonprofit arena. Sound reasons support the growing use of these processes in nonprofit organizations:

- Nonprofit managers work in a complex, rapidly changing environment that places a premium on flexibility, adaptability, and the conscious management of change—in missions, strategic directions, plans, and programs.
- Strategic planning and management processes focus on the management of change, whereas traditional long-range planning approaches basically have projected current activities into the future, on the assumption of continuing environmental stability.
- Competition among nonprofit, public, and for-profit organizations is increasing in many fields—from education and training to health and human services—and organizations that can plan and manage strategically are far better equipped to survive and flourish.

Strategic planning and management techniques are quickly becoming staples in the nonprofit manager's cupboard. However, discussing them is far easier than putting them to practical use in the near term, with concrete results and at an affordable cost. The popular adage "no pain, no gain" is all too true in applying strategic techniques. Not only are these technically demanding, but their application inevitably involves significant costs, most notably in the time of board

*"The strategic plan says we facilitate the timely flow of interdepartmental and exter-
nal communications. So try not to think of yourself as 'just a mailroom clerk.'"*

members and managers. No simple cookbook can be followed to plan and manage strategically. Rather, a broad logic and methodology must be adapted to the specific needs, circumstances, capabilities, and personnel of particular organizations.

The history of planning in nonprofit and public organizations is replete with tales of woe, as elaborate, ambitious planning processes have not achieved the expected results or have even broken down midstream. This chapter prepares managers to venture confidently onto the complex, shifting, and occasionally even treacherous terrain of strategic management, to recognize certain guide posts, to spot and avoid certain pitfalls, and to ultimately find a path that leads to successful application.

This chapter begins with a description of the rapidly changing field of strategic planning and management, with special attention to a variation on the theme that is proving especially useful in the nonprofit sector: the strategic change portfolio process. I describe the process of designing applications to fit particular organizations and then address two special issues: (1) the role of the nonprofit board in strategic planning and management and (2) the tie between strategic management and the annual operational planning and budget preparation process. Finally, practical exercises provide an opportunity to try some of the techniques.

LOGIC AND METHODOLOGY

Strategic management is a balancing act among competing values; its primary purpose is to maintain a dynamic balance between an organization (its mission, goals, plans, resources) and its external environment. The balance is maintained by ensuring that the organization's scarce resources are invested to take maximum feasible advantage of opportunities (e.g., for new or additional revenues, new patrons or clients, new products or services) and to deal effectively with challenges (e.g., the decline or disappearance of a major source of revenue, the appearance of a significant competitor) (Eadie, 1996, 1997a).

Strategic planning and management is a relatively new and rapidly developing field, especially in the nonprofit sector, where its presence is just now being felt (Bryson, 1989; Eadie, 1996, 1997a). One important innovation in the field in recent years has been the rejection of the notion that the primary product of this process is a weighty, comprehensive plan that encompasses all of an organization's activities. It is now widely accepted that the real product is a portfolio of strategic change initiatives (projects) that are intended to deal with environmental change, not the elaborate codification and projection into the future of current programs and functions. Indeed, experience has shown that, in a time of often dizzying environmental change, the production of massive documents may be a harmful waste of time.

The term *strategic management,* which is now used far more widely than *strategic planning,* developed in response to the early overemphasis on the production of documents at the expense of attention to actual change. Strategic management encompasses both the formulation and implementation of strategies and is best seen as an ongoing process (Bryson, 1989; Eadie, 1996, 1997a; Edwards & Eadie, 1994).

Another major current in the field is the attention paid to the collective involvement of people in fashioning and implementing strategies (Eadie, 1996, 1997a). Strategies are implemented by people, not computers, forms, procedures, or six-pound documents. Now that people are recognized as being important for the formulation of successful strategies, developing the human resource and building strong teams are rightly seen as critical to the success of strategic management (Gluck, 1985; Nutt & Backoff, 1987).

There are strategies, and there are strategies. A community may stage participatory meetings that result in a vision and a set of broad directions for development—a kind of global strategy far removed from detailed action planning. A nonprofit organization may develop such a global strategy as well. However, the community or the nonprofit organization also may formulate detailed action strategies (i.e., specific change targets, or initiatives, along with implementation plans) to address particular issues that have been identified.

To narrow the focus even further, a particular division or department in a nonprofit organization may produce its own strategies, including both a global strategy and detailed action strategies. The point is that saying that an organization is engaging in strategic management means nothing until the kind of strategy being produced is known. As is explored later, until an organization knows the kind of strategy it wants to produce, it cannot determine the specifics of the process required to produce it.

STRATEGIC CHANGE PORTFOLIO PROCESS

Strategic change portfolio is increasingly used to describe a process that begins with the clarification of an organization's strategic framework (its values and vision) and ends with a portfolio of strategic change initiatives that are intended to deal with strategic issues (in the form of opportunities and challenges). As is demonstrated, the focus on strategic issues safeguards against using the process merely to describe and codify what an organization is already doing. Therefore, the strategic change portfolio process has sometimes been called "management by selection" (Eadie, 1996, 1997a, 2001b, 2004).

The principal elements in the process are

- The clarification of values and vision,
- The external and internal environmental scanning,
- The identification and selection of strategic issues, and
- The formulation and implementation of strategic change initiatives to address the selected issues.

The following discussion addresses both the content involved in each element and the process used to generate it, drawing on real-life examples.

Clarification of Values and Vision

Values are the most cherished principles—the "golden rules"—that guide an organization's planning and management activities. A vision is a word picture of an organization's desired impact on or contribution to its community or service area and of the organization's role in the community (O'Toole, 1995).

The clarification of values and vision provides the strategic issue management process with a kind of "natural law": a strategic backdrop for scanning the environment, selecting the issues, and gaining information about the strategies. Without this backdrop, the strategic management process would be like an automobile engine without a driver or a steering wheel: undirected motion and energy.

Meeting with the executive director and members of the management team, the board of the Glen Retirement System (GRS) in Shreveport, Louisiana, fashioned a statement of values (Eadie, 1997b) that included the following points:

- We believe in the value of elderly people as contributors, using their gifts to enrich the lives of the people around them.
- We believe in the independence, dignity, and security of elderly people.
- We believe in health care of the highest quality.
- We believe in meeting individual needs and in personal growth.
- We believe in professionalism, competence, attention to detail, and accountability.
- We believe in responding promptly and positively to complaints.

At a two-day retreat, the board and executive team of the Maryland School for the Blind (MSB) in Baltimore envisioned the following effects of its efforts in the community (Eadie, 2003b):

- MSB is recognized as the premier statewide resource for people with visual impairments.
- Every student with a visual impairment in Maryland knows of the MSB's work.
- MSB meets or exceeds all regulatory oversight requirements and legal expectations.
- Students are fully prepared for life in terms of living skills and employment.
- The community is prepared to fully accept MSB's graduates.

Statements of values and vision are often fashioned in intensive, facilitated work sessions involving board members and top managers. Certainly, something this important to the long-term success of an organization should not merely be delegated to staff and then passively reviewed by a board. The board and staff of the National Parks and Conservation Association (NPCA; Eadie, 1995), for example, developed detailed impact and role statements as part of a vision statement, which was refined by staff and the board's planning committee and eventually adopted by the full board.

External Environmental Scanning

In light of its vision and mission, what information must a nonprofit organization have about the world in which it works to spot issues and formulate effective strategies? The environmental scan answers this question. The vision and mission provide the boundaries that keep the scan from being an overwhelming task.

Developing the Content. Whether the scan is prepared by a staff task force and then reviewed in an intensive board–staff work session or is developed in a work session, it is necessary to identify the national, state, regional, and local trends and conditions that must be understood to fashion a strategy. The board and management team of the Kentucky School Boards Association (KSBA; Eadie, 2005) were interested in the following:

- The increasing polarization of U.S. society
- The aging population
- Unfunded federal government educational mandates (particularly the No Child Left Behind Act)
- The growth in single-parent households
- New educational options such as home schooling and charter schools
- State educational funding
- Weak gubernatorial support for education
- Resistance to change in school districts.

ANALYSIS OF STAKEHOLDERS. In the quest for statistics, it is all too easy to forget that an organization's environment also consists of other entities that significantly influence or have the potential to influence its vision, mission, and strategies. These influential organizations are often loosely known as *stakeholders*, and understanding them is a critical part of the external environmental scan.

Stakeholders may be understood both in terms of organizational characteristics and actual and potential relationships with the organization. Organizational characteristics include vision, mission, priorities, plans, resources, style of operating, track record, and (perhaps most important) perceptions of the organization. Vis-à-vis the organization, a stakeholder may be a cooperator, a partner in a joint venture, a provider of resources, a provider of legitimacy (blessing the organization's endeavors), a wielder of authority, a competitor, a paying customer, or a client.

For example, the board and staff of the GRS identified as key stakeholders the Louisiana Nursing Home Association, local hospitals, the local Council on Aging, and higher education institutions, among others (Eadie, 1997b). Each stakeholder relationship was assessed. To take the Council on Aging as an example, the GRS hoped to obtain client referrals, information on trends, and networking opportunities. In return, it expected to "pay" the council with political support, transportation, food service, and communication on its activities. The relationship was assessed as "generally positive."

CUSTOMERS AND CLIENTS. When analyzing stakeholders, nonprofit organizations must distinguish between paying customers and clients, because the two groups involve different relationships that require special management. Clients of a battered women's shelter or rape crisis center, for example, do not directly buy the services they receive (although, indirectly, they may pay through taxes), but funders, such as the state's Department of Welfare, the county commissioners, and the local United Way, are direct customers with considerable power over the mission, plans, and programs of the organization. The point is that the service delivered to the client is only one kind of product; other kinds may be delivered to the paying customers.

Internal Environmental Scanning

The foundation for identifying strategic issues is fully in place when an organization leaves its external environment and looks inward. The internal environmental scan basically involves assessing organizational strengths and weaknesses in terms of human, financial, technological, and political resources, and organizational performance in its major programs and businesses. For example, during their two-day work session, the GRS board and staff assessed the performance of each major site and then identified strengths and weaknesses in board leadership, management, finances, and organizational image and clout (Eadie, 1997b). With regard to the board's leadership, they identified strengths as "talent, level of involvement, commitment and enthusiasm, teamwork, strong staff support, being manageable in size, and successful fund-raising" (Eadie, 1997b, p. 38). The weaknesses they saw included "lack of diversity in membership,; too little contact with staff, limited use of standing committees, lack of a strong board role in strategic planning, and the absence of a systematic approach to board member capacity building" (Eadie 1997b, p. 40).

Identification and Selection of Strategic Issues

WHAT ARE STRATEGIC ISSUES? Strategic issues may be thought of as major "change challenges"—opportunities and problems that appear to demand an organizational response, so a successful balance can be maintained between the organization's internal and external environments. Opportunities are principally avenues to organizational growth—delivery of new services or products—through tapping new sources of revenue and through addressing new needs (these avenues of growth, or levers, are intertwined and are never mutually exclusive). Problems are conditions, events, or trends that threaten to reduce an organization's resources and its program's competitive position (including its reputation and political clout).

No scientific test can determine whether an issue is truly strategic or merely operational. Certainly, in the course of an organization's annual operational planning and budget preparation process, many issues arise that relate to refining and adjusting operating programs, and they can involve major expenditures (e.g., instituting a new computer registration system in a recreational department). However, some issues always rise above others in terms of the stakes involved (both benefits and costs) and their complexity.

It is worth noting that, because strategic issues often cut across organizational functions and departments, they require organization-wide attention; similarly, because they sometimes transcend organizations, they require that different organizations cooperate in addressing them. Moreover, issues may relate to administrative or managerial concerns and to the content of programs and services.

SOME EXAMPLES. In their two-day work session, the board and staff of the NPCA identified the following strategic issues:

- The need to tap more fully the tremendous resources brought to the organization by its board members,
- The absence of an ongoing strategic management capability that provides for a proactive leadership role for the board,
- The need to strengthen image and public relations, the need to provide opportunities for member involvement,
- The need to strengthen retention of younger members, and
- The reality of a Congress that is more hostile to environmental concerns (Eadie, 1995).

The members of the Organizational Structure Task Force of the American Health Information Management Association (AHIMA) met for two days in Chicago and identified the following as key issues facing the association:

An organizational structure "that is baroque in its complexity, that is too vaguely defined, that is tremendously time-intensive. . . and that too often leads to adversarial interaction"; "uncertainty about who the primary customer is: members at the local level or highly active members climbing the volunteer 'career ladder'"; a House of Delegates that "tends to operate as a quasi-legislative body that is competitive with the AHIMA Board of Directors, causing considerable tension and confusion among AHIMA members"; and various task forces and committees that mix operating and governing responsibilities that are "only vaguely tied into mainstream AHIMA planning and management processes," and that "chew up far too much volunteer time." (Eadie, 1997c, pp. 5–6)

SELECTION OF ISSUES. As a preface to the selection of strategic issues, keep in mind that any nonprofit organization's resources in time, energy, dollars, political capital, and so forth are not only finite, they also are usually stretched to the limit. Therefore, it is highly unlikely that many strategic issues can be addressed effectively at any one time. Selectivity is thus more than a virtue; it is a necessity.

One cannot choose in a simple or scientific way which issues to address in the short term through the formulation of strategies. Some believe that a highly effective approach is to analyze issues in two ways:

1. Evaluate the potential cost that the organization might bear if it does not move forward now in addressing a particular issue, considering both direct costs (e.g., dollars, lost credibility, human pain and suffering) and lost benefits (e.g., lost revenue from a grant not obtained).

2. Assess the organization's ability to have a positive impact on an issue within the resource constraints.

For example, a school district may think more than twice about taking the lead in addressing the drug dependence of students because of the complexity of the issue and the substantial costs involved in addressing it comprehensively. The ultimate decision on which issues to tackle in the short term will depend, then, on a rough cost–benefit analysis. The objective is a set of issues that promises the most potential benefit (and avoided costs) for the price in time, dollars, and political capital (Eadie 2003a).

FORMULATION AND IMPLEMENTATION OF STRATEGIES. When the strategic issues to be addressed have been selected, task forces often are appointed to fashion action strategies to address them. A staff steering committee, comprising senior managers, may be used to review the work of the strategy formulation task forces, and the board ultimately reviews and approves the task force's recommendations. The steps involved in formulating strategies are as follows:

- Get a firm grasp on an issue by breaking it into its various subissues. This step inevitably involves the task force doing a more detailed, second-stage scan of an issue than was possible when it identified and selected the issues.
- Determine which subissue to tackle.
- Brainstorm action initiatives to address each of the subissues and to select the initiatives that appear to yield the most benefit for the cost, within acceptable resource limits.
- Fashion detailed implementation plans that set forth a schedule of events, specify who is accountable for what action, and detail the costs involved. Implementation involves three key issues: (1) the organization's commitment, (2) the allocation of resources, and (3) the implementation structure and process. Commitment means that, at the very least, the policy body, the chief executive officer (CEO), and senior managers are committed to the results anticipated from implementing proposed strategies, to the roles that must be played to implement these strategies, and to the costs that must be incurred.

The wider the ownership is felt for an organization's strategy, the more likely the strategy is to be fully implemented. This fact argues for widespread participation in strategy formulation task forces as a vehicle for building ownership; another vehicle is effective internal communication.

Financial resources can be explicitly allocated to implement strategies through the annual operational planning and budget preparation process by ensuring that the work of the task forces feeds into the budgetary decision-making process in a timely fashion. Another approach is to allocate dollars from a contingency fund established to finance innovation and change.

Finally, a structure and managerial process is required to ensure the full and timely implementation of the strategy. This process may include a steering committee of senior managers that meets once a month, a technical coordinating committee that provides detailed guidance, implementation task forces that provide hands-on management of the implementation process, a high-level staff person to coordinate the whole effort, and a system for regularly reporting progress and resolving problems (Eadie, 2001b, 2004; Kanter, 1989).

DESIGN APPLICATIONS

Experience with unsuccessful planning processes has at best made many managers of nonprofit organizations skeptical of planning initiatives: at worst, it has bred cynicism. Processes have collapsed midstream because organizations have lacked either the capability or the commitment required to implement them. Some organizations have faithfully gone through all the steps in their planning processes, only to find that the results were not worth the effort (witness the many shelves groaning under the weight of never-consulted, dust-covered tomes).

The purpose of design is to ensure that an organization achieves precisely what it wants through its planning process and at a cost that it can afford. Through design, the outcomes or products to be generated are identified, the process and structure required to produce the outcomes are developed, and the resources required to implement the process are specified. Armed with a sound design, an organization can move forward with confidence to implement the techniques of strategic issue management, knowing that it can implement a process to produce the outcomes that it wants.

The design process is a prelude to applying the strategic change portfolio process that is typically initiated by the CEO and preferably involves both board members and senior staff. In one or more intensive work sessions, process outcomes are identified, and the process and structure of strategic issue management are worked out. The resources (e.g., time, consulting fees) that are required to implement the process also should be spelled out. The design should be described in a document that is formally reviewed and accepted by the board, the CEO, and senior managers.

A Word on Outcomes

There are two primary categories of outcomes in the strategic change portfolio process: (1) Those that relate directly to the kinds of strategies that are generated and (2) Those that are process-related spinoffs.

For example, an organization that is facing a fiscal crisis may decide in the design process to deal during the first cycle of the strategic change portfolio process with only one issue—the enhancement of revenue—and to make the primary outcome of the first-year planning effort a detailed action strategy to deal with that overriding issue. Another organization may determine that during its first cycle, its whole focus is the generation—in a concentrated work session of the board and top management staff—of a vision for the organization and a set of broad strategic directions. A third organization may decide to engage in the full process, from environmental scanning through the identification of issues to the selection of issues to the formulation of strategic change initiatives.

The foregoing are direct, content-related outcomes. In addition, organizations can identify some less direct—but not necessarily less important—outcomes. For example, building a team of managers may be an important outcome of the process, as may strengthening the leadership role of the board. Another outcome may be to increase the staff's morale or to strengthen the public's understanding of the organization's mission and goals. All these outcomes—direct and indirect—drive the development of the process and structure of strategic issue management.

Also driving this development are what may be called "rules of the game." For example, an organization may specify in its design that any strategies that its task forces recommend during the first cycle must be achievable within current resource limits or specify precisely how the additional required resources are to be obtained. An organization may specify in its design that a highly controversial matter not be raised during the process (e.g., the distribution of syringes to addicts as a tactic to prevent AIDS). The point is to ensure through these rules that the strategic ship does not hit an iceberg that could have been avoided through forethought.

A Word on Process and Structure

Designing the process and structure to achieve the identified outcomes involves determining what should be done, when it should be done, and by whom it should be done. This determination will be driven by the identified outcomes, the rules of the game, and the organization's capability. It is important not to underestimate the potential for any process to collapse midstream if it is not carefully designed. The strategic management effort, no matter how modest or elaborate, will not be an established organizational routine during the first one or two cycles; it will always be threatened by the press of day-to-day events and loyalties to established organizational units (in contrast to ad hoc task forces).

Examples of structure are a board task force to formulate a statement of vision; a staff task force on environmental scanning; a two-day work session of the board and staff to review and confirm the statement of vision, discuss the environmental scan, and identify strategic issues; and the use of task forces to formulate strategies.

The Organization's Capability

Whether an organization is able to carry out a design successfully depends on its capability. Although organizational capability is a nebulous concept, practical experience suggests that the following factors should be explicitly considered.

1. The commitment of the board and CEO to the process is central, in terms both of the outcomes to be generated and the costs that are incurred in going through it. The board's and CEO's participation in developing the design and reviewing and approving it help ensure this commitment. The commitment of the organization's senior managers also is critical to the success of the design.
2. People make or break strategic management processes, so understanding the human resources dimension is critical to developing a sound design. Obviously, skills and experience deserve consideration. A staff that has never participated in strategic planning and management activities is less capable than one that has. Also important is the organization's internal climate. Skepticism of planning on the basis of negative experiences or a general malaise related to working conditions definitely lessens the staff's capability to engage in strategic management activities.
3. Time and attention also are important aspects of organizational capability. An organization that is severely understaffed is hard pressed to devote time to strategic management. Similarly, one that is grappling with one or more crises, such as a looming budget deficit or an audit uncovering irregularities, is less able to devote attention to strategic issue management.
4. Money is always an important aspect of capability. Carrying out the strategic change portfolio process costs money—for work session space, the production of materials, and external technical assistance.

Following the inexorable rule that the strategic management process and the organization's capability must match, an organization can always reduce its expectations of outcomes and the demands of the process or spread a process out over a longer period. Keep in mind, however, that systematically strengthening capability may be part of the strategic management design. For example, funding from foundations may supplement the organization's budget. Orientation and training sessions may enhance skills while reducing skepticism. Participation in shaping the design may counter low morale.

BOARDS AND BUDGETS

Board Leadership

The boards of many nonprofit organizations are highly frustrated at what they rightly consider to be their vaguely defined, often obviously unimportant roles

(Eadie, 1994, 2001a, 2001b, 2004). It is common to see the "illusion of control" that comes from two equally unimportant and unproductive kinds of board work: (1) paying inordinate attention to the review of trivial details, such as detailed reports of payments to vendors, and (2) thumbing through finished documents, such as a completed, bound budget, and asking random questions.

The strategic change portfolio process provides ample opportunity for a board to be fully engaged in carrying out important leadership responsibilities: in defining outcomes of the process and confirming the design, in formulating statements of vision and mission, in reviewing the environmental scans and identifying strategic issues, in selecting the issues to be addressed, and in reviewing the strategic change initiatives that are recommended to address the selected issues.

A particularly effective device is to stage an intensive one and a half- to two-day work session involving the board, staff, and key "outside" stakeholders. The KSBA, GRS, and AHIMA, for example, all held sessions that focused during the first day on organizational strategy. Using breakout groups, they clarified values, vision, and mission; assessed the external and internal environments; identified strategic issues; and brainstormed possible change initiatives to address the issues. The second day was devoted to assessing the performance of the governing board and discussing possible enhancements in board role, structure, and processes. In every case, the staff comprising the management team in follow-up sessions analyzed the issues and possible initiatives and recommended action to the board's planning committee.

Such board–staff work sessions are likely to be successful if the outcome agenda is agreed to in advance, a comfortable off-site location is used, preparation is meticulous, and adequate time is allowed. Professional facilitation also can help, particularly when highly complex and possibly emotional or controversial issues are being addressed.

Budget Connection

An explicit connection is needed between any strategic change portfolio effort and the annual operational planning and budget preparation process. Two obvious connections are these:

1. Scheduling the formulation of statements of vision and mission, the environmental scan, and identification of issues so they can be factored into the budgets of operating units (strategic input helps guide preparations of the budget at the operating-unit level, where trends, conditions, and issues are, indeed, pertinent in shaping budgets)
2. Ensuring that the recommendations of strategy formulation task forces include detailed cost estimates and that the cost estimates are considered part of the decision-making process on the budget.

CONCLUSION

This chapter has traced the rapid development of strategic management in the nonprofit sector, from the original notion of heavily documented comprehensive planning to the more action-oriented strategic change portfolio process. Strategic management enables an organization to respond effectively to challenges—significant opportunities and major constraints or problems—in its environment. The key elements of the process are the clarification of vision and values, an external and internal scanning, the identification and selection of issues, and the formulation and implementation of strategic change initiatives.

The chapter examined the design process, through which an organization ensures that it achieves what it wants from the application of strategic management at a cost that it can afford. The design spells out the outcomes or products that the strategic management application generates and details the structure and process required to achieve the outcomes. As part of the design process, an organization explicitly determines that it has the capability to implement the process or it builds the requisite capability.

SKILLS APPLICATION EXERCISES

- If the organization you work in has a vision and a mission, describe them. If not, create a statement of vision and mission for your organization.
- What is your personal vision, in terms of career aspirations and personal lifestyle? Scan your environment externally and internally, and identify any strategic issues that you face in light of your vision. Formulate broad strategies to address those issues.
- Make a list of stakeholders of the immediate organizational unit in which you work and of the organization in which your unit fits. Analyze each stakeholder's characteristics and the relationships (actual and potential) that your unit and organization may have or build with each stakeholder.
- You also have stakeholders with whom you must deal in your career and personally. Name a few of the most important, and analyze their characteristics and the nature of your relationships with each. Fashion stakeholder management strategies to ensure that the working relationships are effective.
- Scan the external and internal environments of your organization to identify major trends and conditions and assess the organization's resources and strengths and weaknesses.
- On the basis of this scan, identify some strategic issues that your organization may need to address, and evaluate the potential costs (direct or in lost benefits) of not addressing each issue.
- Select one or two of what appear to be the most critical issues and brainstorm possible strategic change initiatives to address them. Identify for each initiative the anticipated impact on the issue and the costs (e.g., time, money, political capital) that may be anticipated in implementing it.
- Your organization is considering carrying out a strategic change portfolio process. Assess your organization's capability to undertake such an ambitious project, paying special attention to the barriers that may be faced.

REFERENCES

Bryson, J. M. (1989). *Strategic planning for public and nonprofit organizations.* San Francisco: Jossey-Bass.

Eadie, D. C. (1994). *Boards that work: A practical guide for building effective association boards.* Washington, DC: American Society of Association Executives.

Eadie, D. C. (1995). *Report to the National Parks and Conservation Association.* Cleveland, OH: Strategic Development Consulting.

Eadie, D. C. (1996). *Meeting the change challenge: The executive's guide to leading change in the nonprofit world.* Washington, DC: American Society of Association Executives.

Eadie, D. C. (1997a). *Changing by design: A practical approach to leading innovation in nonprofit organizations.* San Francisco: Jossey-Bass.

Eadie, D. C. (1997b). *Report to the Glen Retirement System.* Cleveland, OH: Strategic Development Consulting.

Eadie, D. C. (1997c). *Report to the Organizational Structure Task Force, American Health Information Management Association.* Cleveland, OH: Strategic Development Consulting.

Eadie, D. C. (2001a). *The board-savvy CEO: How to build a strong, positive relationship with your board.* Washington, DC: BoardSource.

Eadie, D. C. (2001b). *Extraordinary board leadership: The seven keys to high-impact governance.* Sudbury, MA: Jones & Bartlett.

Eadie, D. C. (2003a). *Eight keys to an extraordinary board–superintendent partnership.* Lanham, MD: Roman & Littlefield.

Eadie, D. C. (2003b). *Report to the board and CEO of the Maryland School for the blind.* Palm Harbor, FL: Doug Eadie & Company.

Eadie, D. C. (2004). *High-impact governing in a nutshell: 17 questions that board members and CEOs frequently ask.* Washington, DC: American Society of Association Executives.

Eadie, D. C. (2005). *Report to the board and CEO of the Kentucky School Boards Association.* Palm Harbor, FL: Doug Eadie & Company.

Edwards, R. L., & Eadie, D. C. (1994). Meeting the change challenge: Managing growth in the nonprofit and public human services sectors. *Administration in Social Work, 18,* 107–123.

Gluck, F. W. (1985). A fresh look at strategic management. *Journal of Business Strategy, 6,* 4–21.

Kanter, R. M. (1989). *When giants learn to dance.* New York: Simon & Schuster.

Nutt, P. C., & Backoff, R. W. (1987). A strategic management process for public sector organizations. *Journal of the American Planning Association, 53,* 44–57.

O'Toole, J. (1995). *Leading change: Overcoming the ideology of comfort and tyranny of custom.* San Francisco: Jossey-Bass.

18

Creating and Managing Strategic Alliances

David Campbell, Barbara Jacobus,
and John A. Yankey

Historically, the merger of organizations has occurred primarily in the business sector. However, recently there has been a proliferation of merger activity in the nonprofit community. Merger, as a restructuring strategy, has become an increasingly important means by which nonprofit organizations are addressing a cross section of critical management and leadership challenges. The proliferation of nonprofit mergers has led several academics and practitioners to research and write about this phenomenon. Their work has considered the many forms through which nonprofit organizations come together, the reasons why organizations merge, and the process by which organizations make the decision to merge (Arsenault, 1998; Bailey & Koney, 2000; Campbell, 2000a; Campbell, 2000b; Kohm, LaPiana, & Gowdy 2001; LaPiana, 1997; McCambridge & Weis, 1997; McLaughlin, 1998; Singer & Yankey, 1991; Yankey, Jacobus, & Koney, 2001).

This chapter explores *why* nonprofit organizations merge. We consider that question through the lens of six theories adapted from organizational behavior literature. However, for theories to have life, people need to be able to apply them to "real-world" situations, so we do that, providing an overview of steps that a nonprofit organization would take to take to determine whether merger (or some other form of strategic alliance) is an advisable management strategy. Finally, following each theory we offer a set of critical questions (and exercises at the end of the chapter) for readers to determine whether the theory is applicable to conditions within their own organizations. As such, we hope to bring together theory and practice in a way that is valuable.

DEFINITION OF MERGER

What is a merger? *Merger* is a form of restructuring in which one or more organizations is completely absorbed by another organization whose corporate existence is preserved. The body being absorbed dissolves and loses its corporate existence (Singer & Yankey, 1991, p. 352). The American Hospital Association (1989, p. 4) defined merger as a statutorily defined corporate transaction in which two similar corporations come together permanently, leaving a single survivor corporation and the other extinguished. Assets do not have to be transferred, as this happens by operation of law, with the surviving corporation owning all the assets and liabilities of both parties.

CONDITIONS LEADING TO NONPROFITS COMING TOGETHER: SIX PERSPECTIVES

Nonprofit mergers are different from those that happen between for-profit organizations. Nonprofit sector scholars' understanding about why nonprofit organizations merge has been adapted from research about *collaboration* between organizations within and across all sectors (e.g., nonprofit, for-profit, government). In that preliminary work, researchers have argued that both conditions in the business environment and operational problems organizations experience on their own lead them to pursue collaborative strategies (e.g., Emery & Trist, 1965; Gray, 1985; Wood & Gray, 1991). Because the environmental conditions or organizational problems that they face are difficult, if not impossible, for them to address on their own, they look to organizational partners to solve them through collaboration. Wood and Gray (1991) identified six theoretical perspectives as collaborative strategies that lead organizations to come together in this way.

Bailey and Koney (2000) conducted a ground-breaking analysis that adapted Wood and Gray's work to the nonprofit sector. Their analysis considered how the theories identified by Wood and Gray could be used to explain a wide range of collaborative activity in the nonprofit sector, from simple referral relationships to the much more complicated merger. In this chapter, we borrow from that adaptation, discussing nonprofit mergers as a form of collaboration explained by these theories.

In the following section we use the term *framework* to describe each of the collaboration theories. We define each framework, identify how it can be adapted to explain nonprofit mergers, and identify the key planning questions that each implies. The six frameworks, as defined by Bailey and Koney (2000), are

- Resource interdependence,
- Environmental validity,
- Operational efficiency,

- Domain influence,
- Strategic enhancement, and
- Social responsibility.

It should be noted again that Bailey and Koney (2000) adapted these frameworks to explain nonprofit sector collaboration in general. In applying them to mergers in this chapter, we acknowledge that some frameworks (e.g., social responsibility) are more likely to explain other forms of collaboration, such as coalition-building or network development, than merger. Readers should be mindful that the conditions we identify as leading to merger in the pages ahead may also, more appropriately in some circumstances, lead to other, less intense forms of collaboration.

Resource Interdependence

The *resource interdependence* perspective suggests that organizations need resources such as infrastructure (administrative capacity), funding stability, or technology (e.g., management information or financial management systems) to accomplish goals, if not simply to survive. Organizations unable to access resources on their own look to other organizations for the resources that they need to ensure their survival (Galaskiewicz, 1985).

Funding stability is critical to an organization's survival; if stability cannot be secured by the organization on its own, it will look to secure it from other organizations. Organizations pursue mergers because they are interdependent; each needs the resources of the other. If one organization is approached by another about the possibility of merger, it will respond affirmatively only if it needs or is dependent on resources available from the other.

What would a merger look like that came about because each partner needed resources that could be provided by the other? This situation is not uncommon, particularly because the number of nonprofit organizations is growing and the competition for resources is becoming more intense. Consider the example of the founder of a 10-year-old organization with a mission to provide advocacy training for parents of children with special needs. Following a significant cut in its state contract and a similar reduction in United Way support, the director faced a difficult management challenge. She needed replacement resources to operate her organization and had few options. Neither the United Way nor the state was willing to reconsider the funding cuts, and her organization lacked the fundraising expertise and history of success needed to generate support from other sources.

The director was committed to the organization that she founded and its mission. Yet, she had few options to generate the resources that she needed on her own. If she did nothing, the loss of state and private dollars would dramatically affect her organization's capacity to achieve its mission. She needed to consider other resource acquisition strategies. She chose merger because she feared that her organization was too small to develop sufficient and effective resource development strategies in house (e.g., social enterprise, a more traditional fundraising campaign). Merger was clearly a more radical strategy, but the organization was dependent on resources that she could secure only from another friendly competitor. She had been impressed with another local organization with a similar mission that had greater resources and capacity. Merger with that organization, she thought, was likely to provide the resources needed to secure the advocacy training services that were at the core of her agency's mission. That organization appeared to share a commitment to these services and had the capacity to generate the funds needed to support them (through private fundraising and advocacy with government—its primary funder).

The merger partner in this case also faced management challenges that reflected its interdependence with the other organization—it needed resources that the other organization had. It was a provider of services to children with special needs that received much of its revenue from service fees, state contracts, an annual fundraiser, and the United Way. The state—the organization's largest source of support—had expressed concern about a lack of service breadth and indicated as well that the organization's limited infrastructure impeded its ability to generate the statistical and service reports that the state required. The organization knew that if it wanted to continue to receive state funding for its services, it needed to increase service capacity and enhance infrastructure. Merger with the smaller organization provided the perfect opportunity to accomplish both goals. In that way, it also was a more efficient means of securing those resources than other available, less reliable strategies, such as new program development, grant writing and fundraising.

Conditions of resource need and interdependence defined the coming together of these two agencies. Merger worked as a strategy because the partners were interdependent; each had a resource that the other needed. The parent advocacy training organization brought valuable service enhancements and the potential for greater infrastructure when combined with the other organization. The special-needs agency brought administrative support, stable finances, and the potential for greater fundraising needed by the parent advocacy training agency. The resolution of each agency's resource needs through merger responds to resource challenges neither was able to address on its own and positions the new combined agency for future growth.

An organization considering its future in terms of its dependence on resources might ask these questions:

- What are the critical resources that the organization needs to survive?
- How critical are these resources? Today? Over the long term?

- Is there an organization from which the organization can acquire those resources without sacrificing those things that are most important (e.g., mission, values, strategic direction)?
- What is the range of places from which the organization can acquire resources?
- Is there another organization with which the organization is obviously interdependent?

Environmental Validity

The *environmental validity* framework identifies the role that institutional legitimacy plays in defining organizational success and, consequently, organizational behavior. That is, the greater an organization's perceived legitimacy in its community, the greater the organization's success. As such, if "legitimacy is the primary resource sought or at risk" (Wood & Gray, p. 157), an organization will pursue strategies that bolster its institutional legitimacy. Such strategies could include merger (or other kinds of collaboration). Wood and Gray (1991) have used the term *negotiated order* to refer to this framework, which suggests that the process by which institutional legitimacy is accomplished is through a negotiated strategy involving community partners.

In what ways is legitimacy critical to the success of nonprofit organizations? Legitimacy or perceived credibility among key stakeholders in a community can be a major factor in an organization's ability to accomplish its mission. For example, when seeking resources to address a critical problem, public and private funders will consider the organization's reputation before making a decision to invest. Is the executive director acknowledged as a community leader? Are the organization's trustees well known, respected members of the community? What clues has the organization provided that the investment of private or public dollars would be money well spent? Or, that the organization would accomplish what it claims it would accomplish with those resources? Absent that legitimacy, a nonprofit organization may be seriously limited in its ability to achieve its mission.

Sometimes an organization's legitimacy changes because of changes in the external environment. For example, following the September 11 terrorist attacks, some organizations in New York worried that they would not be considered credible if they did not play some role in the relief effort established following that event. Organizations that were stable and credible actors in the local community on September 10 were uncertain of their status at the end of the next day. At other times, an organization's credibility is affected by its entry into a new area of activity. If that field is dominated by a different set of stakeholders than that to which the organization currently relates, then it is faced with a legitimacy challenge. Finally, another, less dramatic example of evolving legitimacy occurs when funders change expectations for funded agencies.

In each case, the "delegitimized" organizations need to determine how to reacquire their legitimacy, and as such, their competitiveness. In the first case, it may have been possible without too much effort to become a provider of disaster relief services (no merger or other form of collaboration required). In the second situation, cultivating relationships with leaders in the new area of interest through the hiring of new staff, selection of new board members, or other outreach efforts may provide the credibility needed to ensure legitimacy—again, no need for merger.

The third scenario is the one most likely to lead to merger, largely because of the inability of the organization to create the capacity it needs to be competitive on its own. Organizations look outside themselves for solutions that enable them to establish (or re-establish) their legitimacy because they may be unable—it may not be feasible, in fact—to develop successful strategies that make them legitimate on their own. Mergers may result from a realization that institutional legitimacy is a requirement for survival and may not be accomplished without merger. The merger creates a new order that responds to the environment. That new order is a negotiated one.

What would a merger look like that came about because of each partner's need for greater legitimacy? Let us consider the third scenario in a little more detail. In this case, a public funder of mental health services changes the administrative reporting requirements for funded agencies (one could imagine such a case involving any number of publicly funded social services, including child welfare, substance abuse treatment, or job training). The changes involve adding new administrative functions that provide information analyzing and describing the service provided by funded agencies. The new administrative services require infrastructure that many of the small, currently funded agencies lack. However, without the capacity to meet the new administrative requirements, funded agencies will lose the legitimacy they have established with the funder.

What options do small agencies have in this case? One option might be for two or more of the smaller agencies to consider merger. How would merger increase institutional legitimacy? The combining of two (or more) similar agencies could accomplish economies of scale (efficiencies) that could be reallocated to create the administrative capacities needed to be competitive. With increased administrative capacity, the new organizations formed from the merger would be able to maintain the reputation each agency held with the funder previously and enhance institutional legitimacy through the demonstration of new capacity to meet the funders' administrative requirements.

An organization considering its future in terms of its legitimacy might ask these questions:

- What are the institutional requirements for long-term success (as defined by key funders or other stakeholders)?
- Can the organization acquire what it needs to be legitimate on its own, or would it more effective to look outside the organization?
- What are the other sources in the community from which the organization can acquire those institutional requirements?
- Do those other organizations share the organization's mission and values?
- What organizations are perceived favorably by institutional forces?
- Are funders directing the organization to another organization or particular kind of organization?

Operational Efficiency

The *operational efficiency* framework emphasizes that organizations come together in merger to operate more efficiently, in particular to accomplish economies of scale that may not be accomplished by one organization on its own. This perspective is prevalent in settings in which funders are relentlessly concerned about the cost of service or settings in which service activity has proliferated, usually among many providers. In such situations, funders or other key stakeholders encourage (or sometimes impose themselves on) the development of strategies to reduce the cost of doing business. In particular, funders will emphasize the importance of reductions in the cost per unit of service.

A primary strategy for reducing unit costs is increasing service volume without increasing infrastructure or fixed costs. Yet, increases in service volume often require a minimum level of infrastructure, which often is lacking in smaller organizations. As such, a small organization would view its lack of infrastructure as inhibiting and would look to merger with another organization as a strategy to increase service volume, reduce service cost, and make management more efficient. For a larger organization, merger may be the best way to increase service volume, particularly if the service is not market based, but government funded, and no new service contracts are available.

What would a merger look like that came about because of a need for efficiency? Consider the previous case. This time, the same funder of mental health services adjusted its provider expectations so that greater volume was expected at a lower reimbursement rate. How would local agencies respond?

It is not hard to imagine merger as a primary strategy among the agencies funded by the government to provide mental health services. Larger agencies might look to merge with smaller agencies. In this case, the problems with which the agencies grapple is inefficiency; its solution requires the ability to operate a balanced budget and provide service at a lower reimbursement rate. How would the necessary efficiency be accomplished? To operate a balanced budget and provide more for less requires significant increases in service volume. Merger is an important, and perhaps the only, strategy that would accomplish those goals. The small agency, with its limited base, could not compete without a dramatic increase in volume. A large agency, with a significant base on which to build, could accomplish the needed volume by adding the service provided by the smaller agency. Merger would force administrative efficiencies within the two agencies (shared functions would be eliminated in the merger) and would provide the capacity to increase volume to remain competitive with the new reimbursement rates. In effect, merger solves the problem created by the funder when it expressed concern about the high cost of service and the perception of inefficiency.

An organization faced with concerns about inefficiency and the need for economies of scale (either self-generated or identified by funders) might ask these questions in determining whether to pursue merger (or some other form of alliance):

- Where are the functional areas in which the operation is least efficient? Administration, direct service, support, fundraising?
- What are the inefficient areas that have been identified by funders or other key community stakeholders?
- Can the organization create greater sufficient efficiency within itself on its own?
- Are there other organizations that share the organization's mission from which to gain needed efficiencies?
- Are those other organizations weak in places that the organization is strong?

Domain Influence

The *domain influence* framework emphasizes the acquisition and maintenance of power as a reason organizations come together. Power, or influencing the domain within which organizations operate, is a means by which they can secure resources or affect the larger environment in which they operate with competitors. Organizations can increase their power through combining resources through partnerships and the withholding of needed resources from other organizations. The domain influence perspective describes the relationship between organizations, explaining both how and why they come together.

A setting in which the political framework explains merger activity is one in which many active interests (represented by individuals or nonprofit organizations, government entities, and other key stakeholders) vie for predominance. Those interests with sufficient power will dominate discussions about resource use and establish rules that enable the accomplishment of goals they support. As policymakers identify new needs or change expectations, previous certainties are made uncertain, and organizational futures become unclear. In such situations, organizations that share a common interest in a particular outcome may pursue various forms of working together, including merger, to respond to these new needs or expectations. Mergers might occur to guarantee an outcome that saves the interest of the merging organizations at the expense of other organizations in the sector.

What would a merger born under such circumstances look like? Consider a situation in which a local government chooses to devote a significant amount of new resources to address a newly prominent social problem, such as low literacy rates among a certain group of elementary school students. The government appoints a commission to determine the kinds of programs in which to invest. The commission includes representatives of local schools, literacy service providers, academics, elected officials, and business leaders. Of the seven literacy program models currently in use in the community, the commission decides to invest significant new resources in expanding only three of them.

How does that decision affect local literacy services providers? Most view this infusion of resources as unique; it is unlikely that other significant resources will be made similarly available any time soon. Considered from the perspective of the need for power, providers may seek to acquire sufficient power to be more effective advocates for literacy services or position themselves better to receive some of the new resources. For example, two smaller organizations, each of which delivers services using the same literacy model, one of the three in which the commission is investing resources, might seek merger as a means to create a single, larger organization, with greater capacity, that is more competitive in the changing environment. As single-purpose organizations, they might fend off competition from other providers of the same service model that also perform a multiplicity of other services. Their singular focus could make them appear the most expert and best positioned to do a good job with the new dollars. The merger also would increase their power as advocates for literacy services.

A second option might involve a large multiservice organization that delivers literacy services using one of the models in which the commission chose *not* to invest. That organization is very concerned because it faces the prospect of being shut out of the new funding. It has a decided interest in providing literacy services and shaping the larger policy debate about the best way to do so. As a large organization, with significant infrastructure, a solid reputation, and well-known board, it has considerable power in the community. If the organization were a provider of one of the three models in which the commission is investing, it would be a likely recipient of some of the new resources. Yet, its power and position is at risk.

In contrast, a grassroots organization that is a provider of one of three funded literacy models should be well positioned to receive some of the new government money. Yet, its lack of capacity, the absence of any association with high profile community leaders, and its relative unfamiliarity in the community make investing in it an unsure thing. The organization lacks the power needed to position it for new grant money.

The grassroots organization's need for power and the power of the multiservice organization and its long-term interest in providing literacy services could lead the two organizations to pursue merger. Combined, the two would create a more powerful organization, with community standing, capacity, and expertise that would strengthen their overall position and potentially weaken the position of competitors.

An organization considering its future in terms of maximizing power might ask these questions:

- Does the organization lack the power it needs to accomplish its goals?
- If yes, from what kinds of other organizations can the organization acquire the power it needs?
- What other like-minded organizations can benefit from linkage with the organization (and increase its power and standing in the community)?
- What organizations are well positioned to have power in the future?
- What will determine the power of organizations in the near and longer-term future?
- How will that power be acquired?

Strategic Enhancement

The *strategic enhancement* framework emphasizes collaborative action as a means "to support the positive gains of competitive advantage" (Wood & Gray, 1991, p. 156) not only providing access to resources but also strengthening the collaborating organizations in the marketplace.

A setting in which the strategic enhancement perspective explains merger activity is one in which organizations must respond to the requirements of the environment in which they operate to increase their competitive advantage. For example, funders may move from funding stand-alone services to integrated services or continuum of care. Such a demand also could be driven by the market and customer demands for "one-stop shopping." These changes dramatically alter the status quo and affect how organizations within that environment envision their future. The challenges created by funder or market changes create problems for organizations that they are unlikely to be able to solve on their own. A long-term strategy would be to achieve competitive advantage through a merger that is responsive to evolving market or funder demands (in this case, the development of a continuum of care).

What would a merger look like that took place to gain competitive advantage? Let us revisit the example of agencies funded to provide mental health services. If the changes required by the funder are modified to include not only increased administrative capacity but also a broader range of services, then it becomes easier to see how the strategic management perspective provides an explanation for merger between the provider organizations.

Strategic enhancement emphasizes maximizing strategic advantage. In an environment shaken up by changing funder requirements, the best way to achieve strategic advantage would be to pursue a strategy that enables an agency to meet both the additional administrative requirements and provide a broad range of services, that is, to create an advantage that is responsive to the funder. Two medium-sized agencies would merge for strategic advantage if together they could meet these requirements. A merger would be a reasonable course of action if it accomplished both the broad range of service and the administrative capacity required by the funder.

It would not be difficult to consider the same scenario shaped by changing market demands. If satisfaction or other trend data suggested that the mental health organization was unresponsive to client needs because of the limitations of its service offerings, then it would risk losing clients to other, more comprehensive providers. Merger with a partner that provided a different type of service and also was frustrated by its limitations could strategically enhance the market position of both and create a stronger new organization.

Strategic enhancement suggests that organizations see and seize advantage when the realities within an environment are shaken up. The advantage to organizations is accomplished through merger.

An organization considering its future in terms of strategic advantage may ask these questions:

- What are the requirements of the competitive organization of the future?
- Does the organization have the capacity to achieve competitive advantage on its own, as presently configured?
- If not, what other mission-compatible organization can most enhance the organization's competitive advantage?

Social Responsibility

The *social responsibility* framework emphasizes an organization's role and responsibility in solving social problems. It describes how responsibility and risk are shared among the various players who have a stake in the issue or problem.

The kind of setting in which this framework would explain merger (or more likely other collaborative activity) would be one in which some new phenomenon or social problem emerges. In such situations, the community (e.g., government, local leaders, business community, others) looks to and works with the nonprofit sector to develop a response to the problem. Well known recent examples include the emergence of new forms of drug use, the influx of immigrants needing resettlement assistance, and the HIV/AIDS crisis in the 1980s. Addressing such problems often requires the coming together of service providers that have expertise in areas related to the new social problem. Successful development of a solution to an emergent problem may best be accomplished through the merger of the related organizations.

What would a merger look like that was attributable to the social responsibility framework? The best example again may be the establishment of services to people affected by HIV/AIDS. In the early 1980s, when HIV/AIDS was first identified and diagnosed, an HIV/AIDS-specific service infrastructure did not exist. The community looked to the nonprofit sector to develop a response to the social services needs of those affected by the illness. One immediate response was the proliferation of grassroots organizations that addressed different aspects of the social services needs presented: prevention, housing, counseling, nursing care, and so forth.

The service infrastructure that developed was fragmented, and HIV/AIDS services were provided for different purposes in different organizations throughout the community. However, there was concern that a fragmented delivery system was inefficient and not sufficiently responsive. Some community leaders argued that a social service delivery system was needed to offer a cross section of services. In that way, community pressure and a reconsideration of the best way for the sector to respond to HIV/AIDS as a social problem led different providers of HIV/AIDS services to consider merger as a means to accomplish that goal.

An organization considering its future in terms of better solving a community problem may ask these questions:

- What services or activities does the community need to solve a problem?
- How can the organization add value in solving a new community problem?

WHY DO ORGANIZATIONS PURSUE MERGERS?

The six frameworks described earlier each seek to explain why organizations come together in merger. As noted, each was developed initially to explain collaborations between organizations across all sectors (e.g., government, for-profit, nonprofit). Indeed, it is important to acknowledge that these frameworks also explain less formal alliances between nonprofit organizations. For example, organizations can create back-office arrangements to create capacity and enhance efficiency; they can develop coalitions to increase their political

*"It isn't your 'desire' to buy Park Place or Boardwalk that concerns me. . . .
It's your 'motivation.'"*

power; they can create many forms of alliances to address environmental and organizational challenges.

However, these frameworks are applicable to nonprofit mergers as well. Two caveats are important to keep in mind in applying these six frameworks to mergers. First, it is unlikely that any one framework on its own (with a possible exception of resource interdependence) is likely to explain completely why organizations come together in merger. Recent research has suggested that organizations are most likely to merge to address a variety of concerns that cut across the different theoretical frameworks (Campbell, 2000b). For example, future success may require an organization to be more efficient, to have enhanced power and legitimacy, or to resolve some other combination of problems addressed by the frameworks. Second, the rationale for merger usually grows out of some kind of assessment of an organization's short- to medium-term challenges (often through strategic planning or similar planning activity). It is important to note that such assessments often identify some combination of changes in the external environment and internal organizational challenges. In response to those challenges, the organization must ask what strategies would best address them. Can the organization respond sufficiently to these challenges on its own, or does it require capacity that can be acquired only through merger with another organization? The right answer to that question is not always merger or collaboration.

Finally, this overview speaks only to the reasons why nonprofit organizations pursue merger. It does not address whether, ultimately, merger is an advisable action for an organization. The decision to merge is a difficult one that involves a wide range of considerations, including whether at least one of the partner organizations is willing to give up its independent decision-making authority and whether an executive director is willing to give up his or her role. Our purpose here is not to assess those and the other key questions that must be determined before organizations decide to merge. However, they cannot be completely ignored when identifying the reasons why organizations pursue merger.

CONCLUSION

Many of the environmental and organizational challenges identified in these six frameworks are raised in strategic planning and other organizational planning activities. For organizations that encounter any of these challenges, the descriptions in this chapter and the accompanying assessment questions can be useful tools in determining whether merger (or some other form of alliance) would be an advisable strategy.

Should an organization see merger in its future, that decision is only the beginning. In their study of mergers and consolidations, Singer and Yankey (1991) concluded that two years is the average time required for exploring, deciding, planning, and implementing a merger or consolidation.

SKILLS APPLICATION EXERCISE

Identify a nonprofit organization with which you have involvement. and develop answers to the following questions:

- What impact would increased power have on your organization? What are your options for increasing your power? If merger is an option, what characteristics in a merger partner should you identify to increase power in the community?
- What resources is your organization lacking? How important are these resources to your long-term survival? What is the possible range of places from which you can acquire these needed resources?
- What is required of your organization to be competitive in the future? Can the organization meet those requirements on its own? Do you have a defined strategy? Is it cost effective? What are your strategic options?
- How do its key funders and other stakeholders view your organization? Are you perceived as having credibility? What do they require for the long-term success of the organization? What characteristics in a merger partner should you identify to increase credibility and legitimacy with funders and stakeholders?
- What potential changes in community values may affect your organization? What might the community ask of your organization to meet these changes in values?
- In what functional areas is your organization least efficient? What are the inefficient areas that have been identified by funders or other stakeholders? What characteristics in a merger partner should you identify to increase your organization's efficiency?

REFERENCES

American Hospital Association. (1989). *Merger guidelines/checklist*. Chicago: Author.

Arsenault, J. (1998). *Forging nonprofit alliances: A comprehensive guide to enhancing your mission through joint ventures, partnerships, management service organizations, parent corporations, and mergers*. San Francisco: Jossey-Bass

Bailey, D. & Koney, K. (2000). *Strategic alliances among health and human service organizations*. Thousand Oaks, CA: Sage.

Campbell, D. (2000a). High-end alliances as fund-raising opportunities. In Weisman, C., (Ed.), In *Secrets of successful fundraising* (pp. 297–321). St. Louis, MO: F. E. Robbins & Sons Press.

Campbell, D. (2000b). *Interorganizational restructuring in nonprofit human service organizations*. Unpublished dissertation, Case Western Reserve University, Cleveland.

Emery, F., & Trist, E. (1965). The causal texture of organizational environments. *Human Relations, 18*, 21–32.

Galaskiewicz, J. (1985). Interorganizational relations. *Annual Review of Sociology, 11*, 281–304.

Gray, B. (1985). Conditions facilitating interorganizational collaboration. *Human Relations, 38*, 911–936.

Kohm, A., LaPiana, D., & Gowdy, H. (2000). *Strategic restructuring: A study of integrations and alliances among nonprofit social service and cultural organizations in the United States*. Chicago: Chapin Hall Center for Children.

LaPiana, D. (1997). *Beyond collaboration: Strategic restructuring of nonprofit organizations*. Washington, DC: National Center for Nonprofit Boards.

McCambridge, R., & Weis, M. (1997). *The rush to merger*. Boston: Management Consulting Services.

McLaughlin, T. (1998). *Nonprofit mergers and alliances: A strategic planning guide*. New York: Wiley.

Singer, M., & Yankey, J. (1991). Organizational metamorphosis: A study of eighteen nonprofit mergers, acquisitions, and consolidations. *Non-profit Management and Leadership, 1*, 357–369.

Wood, D., & Gray, B. (1991). Toward a comprehensive theory of collaboration. *Journal of Applied Behavioral Science, 27*, 139–162.

Yankey, J., Jacobus, B., & Koney, K., (2001). *Merging nonprofit organizations: The art and science of the deal*. Cleveland, OH: Mandel Center for Nonprofit Organizations.

Consulting With Nonprofit Organizations
Roles, Processes, and Effectiveness

John A. Yankey and Carol K. Willen

The past decade has seen a dramatic expansion in the field of nonprofit management consulting. Although the magnitude of this phenomenon is difficult to document empirically, both anecdotal evidence and objective indicators confirm that the need for and the use of consultants are on the rise. A 2004 membership survey by the Alliance for Nonprofit Management revealed substantial increases in the demand for capacity-building assistance from 2002 to 2003, most notably in the areas of fundraising and income generation; board development and governance; strategic and business planning; and leadership, mentoring, and coaching (Panepento, 2004). The trend toward greater use of consultants' expertise has been fueled not only by the explosive growth of the nonprofit sector but also by the increasingly complex and ever-changing environment in which nonprofit organizations function.

NONPROFIT CONSULTING FIELD TODAY

The factors underlying the more prevalent use of consulting services are varied. Due to leaner budgets resulting from reduced fundraising and cutbacks in external support, nonprofits may find it to be more cost effective to engage consultants than to hire new staff, particularly if the need is expected to be of short duration. Additionally, the intensified demand for demonstrable outcomes and enhanced performance leads some organizations to seek consultant expertise to achieve greater effectiveness and increased efficiency. The recent emphasis on collaborative endeavors and strategic alliance formation as ways of advancing organizational mission and achieving economies of scale is yet another driver of the quest for external assistance.

The increased demand for consulting services in the nonprofit sector has been paralleled by heightened competition for clients. Indeed, a scan of the nonprofit consulting field reveals the emergence of service providers from many new sources. Downsized and retired nonprofit managers, particularly executive directors and others who have held positions of major responsibility, may turn to consulting as a new career. The same is true for retired business executives and corporate consultants. Also swelling the ranks are graduates of nonprofit management, organizational behavior, and organizational development programs, many of whom view independent consulting as a potential career direction.

The management service infrastructure is expanding, as well. For example, some nonprofit academic centers offer pro bono consulting (often in conjunction with student practicums) as a community service, while others may furnish consulting services or technical assistance on a fee basis as a means of generating revenue. Many management support organizations (MSOs) make expertise available though customized consulting. Similar in both appearance and function to MSOs are groups of independent nonprofit management consultants who affiliate for marketing purposes. Additionally, local, regional, and national associations of nonprofits often maintain registries of consultants by area of specialization and list consultants and other resources on their Web sites. Finally, the philanthropic community itself may be a source of consulting help and management support, not only through the advice of program staff but also by way of grants to underwrite research, resource materials, technical assistance, and consulting projects and processes.

One noteworthy development in the consulting field in recent years is the extent to which the nonprofit community has come to be regarded by those in the for-profit world as a "land of consulting opportunity." Paul Light, in his 2000 Aspen Institute report on nonprofit management reform, cited a growing interest in the third sector as a national consulting market. Firms ranging from McKinsey, Accenture, and the Boston Consulting Group to KPMG and PricewaterhouseCoopers have established nonprofit practices—special divisions in which they seek to apply knowledge and expertise drawn from their considerable experience in all disciplines of corporate management consulting. While for-profit consultants often can be of great help to their nonprofit clients and while much managerial knowledge is transferable, consulting with nonprofits is decidedly different from consulting with for-profit and public entities (Lukas, 1998). Consequently, nonprofit organizations should be aware that such consultancies may be strongly influenced by corporate notions of efficiency and effectiveness, which could be in conflict with the mission and philosophy of many nonprofits.

No overview of the current state of the nonprofit consulting field would be complete without a formal acknowledgment of the themes that are increasingly associated with the consulting process and its goals. One such theme, the connection between consulting and change, appears to cut across all three sectors—nonprofit, for-profit, and public. Kubr (1993) identified planning and implementing change as a common purpose of many consulting assignments, while Cope (2000) articulated this relationship even more forcefully. Noting that "consulting is fundamentally about change, ... [be it] physical, cognitive, emotional, structural, technological, or organizational" (p. xii), he defined a *consulting engagement* as "the delivery of value through sustained change by an objective agent" (p. 6).

Within the nonprofit realm, Kibbe and Setterberg articulated the importance of effecting change as early as 1992 in their Foundation Center publication *Succeeding With Consultants: Self-Assessment for the Changing Nonprofit*, wherein the six assessment instruments that they offered are referred to as "tools for change." More recently, Lukas (1998) stressed the need for nonprofit consultants to understand the dynamics of change, foster an openness to organizational learning, build ownership for the change effort, and support the client during the transition.

Another clearly discernable theme in the recent literature on nonprofit consulting is the role of consulting in building nonprofit capacity and enhancing organizational effectiveness. *Capacity building,* as defined by Third Sector New England (2004), is "the process of developing and strengthening the skills, abilities, processes, and resources that organizations and communities need to survive, adapt, and thrive in a fast-changing world." MSOs have themselves benefited from consulting initiatives aimed at "building the capacity of capacity builders" (Connolly & York, 2003, p. 1). By pursuing the kinds of "promising practices" identified by Connolly and York, MSOs and other capacity-building organizations can become more knowledgeable and skilled in their own consulting efforts and can, in turn, be of greater assistance to nonprofit clients striving for maximum organizational effectiveness.

Related to the themes of effecting change and building capacity is the notion of sustainability. For Cope (2000), a key step in the consulting process is to ensure that the changes created through the efforts of the consultant and the client will continue once the consultation itself is complete. Indeed, the notion of "sustained change" is central to his definition of a consulting engagement. On a macro level, the organization's potential for sustainability will be enhanced to the extent that it is able to maintain the changes proposed during the consulting process and implement the knowledge and insights gleaned during that experience. Ekstrom (1997) viewed the enhanced viability of the client organization—its "long-term capacity to self-sustain and grow" (p. 243)—as the hallmark of a successful capacity-building consultation.

DEFINITIONS OF CONSULTING AND CONSULTANTS

The *Random House Dictionary* (Flexner, 1988) defined *consulting* as being "employed in giving professional advice, either to the public or to those practicing the profession" and a *consultant* as "a person who consults someone or something . . .a person who gives professional or expert advice" (p. 289) According to Shulman (1995), *consulting* is "an interaction between two or more people in which the consultant's special competence in a particular area is used to help the consultee with a current work problem" (p. 2377).

In the literature, a distinction is sometimes made between the *expert model* and the *process model* (Kubr, 1993), between *expertise-based* consulting and *capacity-based* consulting (Ekstrom, 1997), between consultants who extend staff capabilities and those who lead a change process (Lukas, 1998). The title given to the consultant may reflect such differences. For example, one who helps the organization by extending staff capabilities in an area such as government relations may be referred to as a *specialist,* while one who develops its Web site is a *vendor* or an *outside service provider* (Smith, Bucklin, & Associates, 2000). On the other hand, a consultant who guides or coaches the organization through a set of steps so that it may learn, grow, or change—thus helping the organization to build internal capacity—is a *facilitator* (Howe, 1997; Smith, Bucklin, & Associates, 2000; Stern, 1999), a *change agent,* or *manager of a change process* (Cope, 2000). The consultation itself is characterized as "collaborative" (Block, 2000) and is defined by Lukas (1998) as both "a process and a relationship."

While the themes mentioned earlier in this chapter—the connection between consulting and change, the role of consulting in building capacity and enhancing organizational effectiveness, and the concept of sustainability—relate more specifically to the process model of consulting than to the expertise-based model, it goes without saying that in either case the consultant must meet high standards of knowledge, experience, and skill. Otherwise, he or she would be ineffective as a capacity builder and coach.

The notions of content expert and process facilitator are useful ways to portray the opposite ends of a spectrum of consulting possibilities, but content work and process work are not mutually exclusive. Exploring this dichotomy in a paper entitled "Expert or Facilitator?" Turner (1982) quoted the following statement by Sloane (1982): "I have never seen an issue of any significance that is entirely substance or entirely process" (as cited in Schaffer, 2002, p. 47). For the management specialist Schaffer, "high-impact consulting offers a results-oriented framework for blending substance and process" (p. 47).

Given this inextricable connection, a certain agility may be necessary on the part of the consultant. Referring to Goodstein's 1978 work on consulting in the human services field, Fletcher (1995) cited his observation that "organizations in the third sector often hire consultants as content specialists to help with a specific issue. If more generic issues emerge over time, the consultants must attempt to change their role from content to process consultation" (p. 79). Fletcher's assessment of consultant roles in fund-raising interventions confirms Goodstein's point that successful consultants may shift from content to process consulting during the course of an engagement.

WHY HIRE A CONSULTANT?

On an immediate and practical level, nonprofits may engage a consultant as "an extra pair-of-hands" (Block, 2000) in situations in which they have sufficient expertise to do what the consultants are being engaged to do but cannot afford the disruption that would occur were employees with the relevant expertise deployed to do the required work. In other instances, the urgency of the task requires the use of a consultant. Some nonprofits view it as both productive and cost effective to engage consultants on a time-limited basis for "contract services" rather than establishing a permanent position and hiring new staff. Finally, some consultants are engaged to do the "dirty work" of effecting changes (as opposed to leading a change *process*) when leaders in the organization cannot or do not want to undertake the necessary steps to achieve such change. Illustrative examples could include organizational turnarounds, staff reorganizations, and fiscal house cleaning. Although serious questions may be raised about the appropriateness of using a consultant as a "hatchet person" (Davis, 1983; Turner, 1982), no list of reasons would be complete without the inclusion of this purpose.

Beyond the notion of engaging an outside person to supplement current staff or to perform duties that could otherwise be accomplished internally (time and circumstances permitting), there are many sound reasons to hire consultants. Such reasons tend to reflect the distinction between expertise-based consulting and process-focused consulting. The following fall under the rubric of *expertise-based* consulting:

- Conducting research and analysis;
- Furnishing information about new trends and practices or about similar situations or efforts elsewhere;
- Providing expertise not currently possessed;
- Offering technical assistance or training, teach new skills, or foster new behaviors;
- Conducting evaluation and assessment;
- Identifying, diagnosing, and defining organizational problems;
- Offering expert recommendations that will aid the organization in solving its problems;

- Providing an independent perspective that is regarded by the individuals and organizations involved as legitimate, objective, and credible; and
- Offering services cutting across multiple professional disciplines.

Among the *process-related* roles that a consultant can play are the following:

- Serving as a catalyst or facilitator;
- Mediating, or conducting interventions aimed at resolving conflicts or overcoming communication problems;
- Assisting in effecting organizational change;
- Developing the organization's capacity to sustain the change or the new behavior or to resolve similar issues in the future; and
- Serving as a mentor or coach to volunteer leaders or professional managers.

Nonprofit leaders must be very clear, not only about the reasons for engaging the consultant but also about the nature of the assignment, for the array of potential functions is vast. While the demand for consultant assistance continues to be strong in such traditional domains as fund-raising, board development, strategic planning, and financial management, nonprofits increasingly seek support and capacity-building services in the areas of organizational assessment and development; evaluation and outcomes measurement; operational efficiency; collaboration and strategic alliances; leadership, mentoring, and coaching; and executive transition and succession planning. So profound are the changes in the nonprofit field that there is now considerable demand for consultants who can serve as interim executive directors (Panepento, 2004). The greater the degree of clarity as to the reasons for the consultation and the tasks or functions for which the consultant is responsible, the greater the likelihood of satisfaction for all parties.

IDENTIFYING AND SELECTING A CONSULTANT

After nonprofit leaders have clearly identified the reasons for a consultation engagement and the nature of the service to be provided, they are confronted with the significant challenge of identifying and selecting the appropriate consultant. In many communities, no common repository of information about individual consultants or consulting firms is available to nonprofit organizations. Frequently, identification of consultants results from lay and professional leadership's personal relationships with or knowledge of particular individuals or firms. Such personal relationships and knowledge are not inappropriate, but neither are they usually sufficient to provide organizations with a range of consulting options. Consequently, many nonprofits use a request-for-proposal (RFP) approach to increase their options. The RFP details the work to be done, required or preferred qualifications and experiences of the consultant being sought, procedures for submitting a proposal, and the approximate amount of funding available for the consultation. This approach usually generates a list of interested consultants from which nonprofit organizations can make an appropriate selection.

Traditionally, these two approaches—personal relationships with consultants and issuance of an RFP—have been the most frequently used methods of identifying consultants. Additional approaches include the following:

- Asking other area nonprofits to identify consultants with whom they have had satisfactory consultations;
- Seeking recommendations from foundation staff or from federated planning and funding bodies, which often have broad local or national networks;
- Contacting local management, organizational development, social work, or public administration programs for referrals to faculty, staff and, in some instances, graduate and professional students;
- Checking regional consultant directories maintained by professional associations and management support centers or calling the association or management assistance program directly;
- Visiting Internet sites that provide information on consultancy services, including those of national organizations offering consulting services on a local basis; and
- Exploring nonprofit services provided by major national or international consulting firms whose primary activity is management consulting in the for-profit sector.

Once potential consultants have been identified, the task of selecting the individual or group most appropriate to an organization's needs becomes pivotal. Bruner (1993) pointed out that whether nonprofit organizations simply employ the consultant without competitive bidding or use a formal review and selection process, each prospective consultant should be asked to submit a brief written proposal outlining plans, approaches, and projected costs. Organizational leadership should study these documents, giving careful consideration to the experience and qualifications of the consultant and (if a firm) the qualifications of the personnel who actually will be working on the project. Before making any commitments, the client should conduct probing interviews and in-depth reference checks.

Among the points to be considered when checking references and making a final selection are the following:

- Nature and scope of the consultant's previous work;
- Professional competence, objectivity, and integrity;
- Understanding of, and appreciation for, the various disciplines or professions within the organization;

- Ability to communicate effectively and work constructively with the organization's personnel, including adhering to time lines and completing assignments at the anticipated level of quality;
- Quality, practicality, and appropriateness of the consultant's recommendations; and
- Overall assessment of the value of prior consulting engagements and willingness of past clients to engage the consultant again.

Interviews with consultants being considered should be structured not only to address the points of discussion listed earlier but also to obtain a sense of the candidate's

- Honesty about his or her capabilities,
- Compatibility with the organization,
- Beliefs and values regarding organizational development,
- Personality fit,
- Motivations,
- Ethics, and
- Appreciation for confidentiality.

ESTABLISHING FEES AND PAYING FOR CONSULTING ENGAGEMENT

Both the consultant and the nonprofit organization have several decisions to make in establishing fee arrangements. From the consultant's standpoint, a major determinant of the fee structure is the type of project to be undertaken. If highly specific financial, legal, or technological expertise is required, the consultant's fees will be reflective of the prevailing wage in that industry. In determining fees, consultants must also consider the

1. Length and complexity of the project;
2. Need, if any, to engage additional help;
3. Expenses entailed by the project;
4. Stability of the organization; and
5. Likelihood that this assignment will lead to other consulting engagements.

From the nonprofit's perspective, the key decisions pertain to the basis and method of payment. Before signing the consultation agreement or contract, the hiring manager of the client organization must select the basis and method for compensation from among four options:

1. Venture marketing,
2. Hourly rate,
3. Retainer, and
4. Fixed rate.

In the venture-marketing approach, payment is structured in direct relation to goal achievement, while in the hourly-rate method, the consultant is paid according to hours clocked (or fractions thereof). The retainer arrangement, which involves the payment of fixed amounts according to a mutually agreed-on schedule, places the consultant "on call." The fixed-price arrangement, according to which the consultant conducts the engagement for a specified amount, is the preferred method among most nonprofit organizations. Because each approach offers advantages as well as disadvantages, the choice of a payment arrangement is not a decision that can be taken lightly.

Regardless of the type of fee arrangement chosen, if the cost of the consultation is to be borne by a funder—whether directly or through a grant (or portion of a grant) to the nonprofit organization—then the funder may become a third party to the negotiation. In situations in which a consultation has been mandated by a funder, it is the funder who pays the consultant and receives progress reports as well as any deliverables. Alternatively, if the funder authorizes a grant to the nonprofit for the purpose of underwriting a consulting project, the organization becomes the client. "For the nonprofit to be fully engaged in [its] own development," writes Lukas (1998), "it is important for the organization, funder, and consultant to be clear about [whom] the consultant is working for and how information is to be shared" (p. 156). While consultants are typically compensated by receiving payment from either the organization or its funder, an alternative system has recently emerged—barter, a new twist on one of the oldest forms of transaction. Writing in the *Nonprofit Consulting Review*, Feldman (2004) explained how a barter or trade exchange can benefit consultants and nonprofits alike.

Once the fee structure and payment arrangements have been established, it is to the benefit of all parties to put into writing their expectations of the engagement. Both agreements and contracts are used to capture and formalize these expectations. Because in practice they share the same goal, the choice of one over the other often relates to the mandates and policies of the organization. As Tepper (1993) stated, "The cardinal rule is to be as specific as possible" (p. 125).

Although agreements and contracts have the same objective of ensuring specificity in the consultation engagement, nonprofits tend to use the agreement approach when offered a choice. This approach seems to be less intimidating to nonprofit managers and suggests creating an environment for a cooperative or collaborative working relationship rather than one governed by more formal, legalistic stipulations.

While agreements and contracts typically include such items of common interest as fee structures, projected costs, and payment schedules, other, more detailed considerations cannot be overlooked if potential misunderstandings are to be prevented. For example, if the agreement is based on cost estimates, the contract should indicate what is to be done in the event that actual costs are higher than anticipated. If the consulting engagement involves the development of print or electronic materials, the topic of intellectual property should be addressed. In all cases, the agreement should specify how and when progress will be monitored and evaluated.

Whatever its form, the agreement should be constructed so as to show that the consultant is an independent contractor, as opposed to an employee. If the Internal Revenue Service construes the "service provider" to be an employee, the organization may find itself liable for back taxes and penalties. Thus, it is in the best interest of the nonprofit to make it clear that the consultant is not functioning as a manager and to allow this individual considerable discretion in determining how, when, and where the work will be done (McNamara, 1999).

CONSULTATION PROCESS AND CONSULTANT ROLES

The levels and stages of the consultation process are portrayed differently in various sources, as are the many possible roles played by the consultant during the course of a single engagement. Although most descriptions of consulting processes tend to obscure the distinction between levels, it is important to understand that, in any engagement, two types of activity are taking place concurrently.

At the macro level, one can trace the evolution of the relationship between the client and the consultant. A map of this progression would begin with the initial point of contact and proceed to securing the engagement and developing the agreement, followed by the planning, implementation, and evaluation of the project and concluding with the termination of consultation services. The second level of mapping is the diagnostic level, at which the consultant and the client are tackling the real work of the project. On this plane of activity, one could speak of problem identification, data gathering and analysis, formulation of proposed solutions, implementation of recommended action steps, evaluation of actions taken, and plans for follow-up.

In the literature, various models of the consultation process reflect both structural and semantic differences in their representation of stages or phases (Kubr, 1993). In his "client's guide" to the selection and use of consultants, Kubr outlined a five-phase model of the consulting process. This model, drawn from the International Labour Organization's guide to the management consulting profession, encompasses (1) entry, (2) diagnosis, (3) action planning, (4) implementation, and (5) termination. A similar model is presented by Lukas (1998) in her "practitioner's guide" to consulting with nonprofits. Her six-stage view includes (1) contracting, (2) gathering and analyzing data, (3) planning the work, (4) implementing and monitoring, (5) sustaining change and evaluating impact, and (6) terminating the consulting project.

The "Seven Cs" framework developed by Cope (2000) is "constructed around a number of dynamic stages, each of which emphasizes a different aspect within the consultancy life cycle" (p. 15). These stages include

- Understanding the _client,_
- _Clarifying_ the nature of the problem,
- _Creating_ a plan for the change process,
- Effecting the _change,_
- _Confirming_ that the change has taken place,
- _Continuing_ the change by ensuring its sustainability, and
- _Closing_ the engagement.

Regardless of the model to which one subscribes, it is essential to recognize that the number of stages is arbitrary and that the consulting process is not necessarily a linear sequence of well-ordered events. "It can be very fluid or elastic," wrote Lukas (1998), whose six stages are simply "a way to provide some structure to what is really a more organic discovery process for both the client and the consultant" (p. 103). The iterative and at times nonlinear nature of the process is underscored by Cope (2000) as well. He, too, emphasized that the stages are "symbolic rather than prescriptive" (p. 18) and that "each of the stages can be undertaken independently, jointly, or in parallel with each other" (p. 15). On a practical level, Ekstrom (1997) pointed out that the stages of the consulting process may call for a series of sequential contracts.

As the consulting process unfolds, the consultant may assume various roles. These roles may change according to client circumstances and the phase of the client–consultant relationship (Lippitt & Lippitt, 1986, as cited in Fletcher, 1995). Among the most commonly cited roles are those of

- The learner who attempts to understand and appreciate the organization,
- The instructor who provides the client with new insights,
- The investigator who seeks to discover the reasons for the client's problems,
- The monitor who observes the client system from multiple levels or vantage points, and
- The change agent who advocates for action to address the identified problems.

Lists of consultant roles found in the literature demonstrate both overlap and originality. Lippitt and Lippitt (as cited in Fletcher, 1995) posited eight distinct roles. Their 1986 compendium, ranging from the roles that are most consultant centered to those that are most client centered, includes the following: (1) advocate, (2) information specialist, (3) trainer-educator, (4) joint problem solver, (5) identifier of alternatives and link to resources, (6) fact finder, (7) process counselor, and (8) objective observer. Lukas (1998) identified the roles of the nonprofit consultant as advocate, expert, trainer or educator, catalyst, and re-flector—with the final role being that of the empathetic supporter who actively listens, helps clarify issues and explore alternatives, and helps the client address feelings or conflicts that are a source of difficulty.

Steele's 1975 list (as cited in Fletcher, 1995) included—in addition to the conventional roles of teacher, student, monitor, and advocate—a series of even more creative entries: the consultant as (1) a detective who pieces together evidence to create an accurate picture of the client organization; (2) a barbarian who violates comfortable norms and challenges accepted ways of thinking; (3) a "clock" that reminds the client to complete each assignment in anticipation of the next consultant visit; (4) a talisman that provides a sense of security and legitimizes experimentation; and finally, (5) a ritual pig who must be sacrificed so that the client will feel sufficiently empowered to engage in self-examination and initiate change.

As indicated, consultants assume these roles with varying frequency and intensity as dictated by the circumstances of a given consulting engagement. Establishing appropriate role relationships is essential for success. Indeed, Fletcher (1995) cited Goodstein's 1978 observation that "it is critically important for both the client and the consultant to be aware of what role the consultant is playing at any given moment in time" (p. 79). Consultants and nonprofit organizations share responsibility for developing role relationships and, usually, both must assume some portion of blame when consulting engagements go off course.

MAKING CONSULTATION MORE PRODUCTIVE

While there is no magical formula that will guarantee a successful outcome, the literature provides many recommendations for enhancing the consulting relationship and maximizing the productivity and potential benefits of the engagement. Insights can be gleaned not only from texts written specifically for a nonprofit audience by authors such as Lant (1997), Bruner (1993), and Lukas (1998), but also from the work of for-profit management consultants such as Schaffer (2002).

On an immediate and practical level, nonprofits and consultants can take several measures to maximize the benefits of a consultation engagement.

Assess Organizational Readiness

The likelihood of a successful consulting engagement is greater when the organization is truly ready—ready to acknowledge the need for external assistance, to participate in the consultation process, and to follow the advice that is provided. Reflecting on the work of Lippitt and Lippitt (1986), Fletcher (1995) observed that "an essential part of the consultant's job is to explore the readiness of the

"Terry is our so-called motivation consultant."

client system to devote time, energy, and the committed involvement of appropriate people to the process of change" (p. 71).

Seek the Right Fit Between Organization and Consultant, Between Consultant and Assignment

Organizations bear responsibility for choosing consultants wisely. This includes screening applicants carefully, checking references thoroughly, and determining objectively whether the prospective consultant, however well regarded he or she may be, has the appropriate background and qualifications for the task at hand. Consultants, for their part, have an ethical obligation to present their professional expertise and qualifications accurately, to promise only what they can deliver, and to decline assignments that are beyond their capabilities.

Get Agreement on Problems Within the Organization

Before seeking assistance from a consultant, the organization should identify and articulate as clearly as possible the problems for which it needs help. In so doing, the client determines the type of consultant it requires, defines the consultation focus, avoids unrealistic expectations about consultancy outcomes, and reduces the potential for dissatisfaction. Furthermore, if there is agreement as to the nature of the problem or problems, the organization will be better prepared to listen to the consultant's recommendations. At the same time, it is important to emphasize that the consultant must not take the client's diagnosis as a given and has a professional obligation to independently assess the situation before accepting the assignment. All parties must agree on the definition of the problem, at least in broad terms, before the work begins.

Get Agreement on Objectives and Methods of the Consultation and the Manner in Which it Will Be Evaluated

The organization and the consultant should agree on the outcomes sought and the methods for achieving them. As noted earlier, the agreement should be in writing, as either a formal or informal contract. The process of developing this document provides an opportunity to review alternatives, determine precisely which tasks will be done by the consultant and which will be undertaken by the organization, and assign responsibilities accordingly. By describing the anticipated outcomes and chosen methodology, detailing the required resources, and delineating the time frame within which the consultation will occur, the agreement will help clarify expectations. It also will provide a comprehensive framework for the organization to use in evaluating the consultant's performance throughout the process.

Manage Consultant and Maintain Control Over Process and Product

While the consultant must be held accountable, it is the client's responsibility to manage the consultant and maintain control over the both the process and the product. Therefore, the agreement should specify the type and frequency of progress reports to be furnished by the consultant. Overmanaging the consultant, however, will impede progress and result in a less-than-optimal use of everyone's time.

Establish Explicit Expectations for the Consulting Process to Be Interactive

If the client organization is to benefit from the engagement, then the process must be "participative" (Kubr, 1993). For Schaffer (2002), "a high-impact consulting project is a collaborative process. . . . The partnership relationship also makes each project a learning experience for both the client and the consultant" (p. 44). Those representing the nonprofit client can help the consultant gain a running start by educating him or her about the organization and its mission, history, and culture. This includes informing the consultant about the motivations for, and anticipated resistances to, the consultation, as well as any human or financial resource limitations that may make certain types of solutions impractical.

As a partnership, the client–consultant relationship will be enhanced by periodic, but not necessarily time-consuming, communication (Smith, Bucklin, & Associates, 2000). While exchanges between the parties can, in some instances, be done through telephone contact and written reports, most consulting relationships are made more productive as a result of regularly held and thoughtfully structured meetings. An interactive consulting process affords multiple opportunities for effective consultants to present findings, ideas, and issues that may be unpalatable to organizational leadership.

Establish a Relationship Based on Honesty, Openness, and Mutual Respect

Dissimulation and dishonesty—destructive forces in any relationship—can spell disaster for a consultancy. Both parties must learn to be direct and at the same time diplomatic. Readers of the *Connecticut Nonprofit Consultant Directory* are advised that, if the client organization is dissatisfied with the work or unclear as to what the consultant is doing, its representatives should request a meeting to address the situation. Once the immediate issues are resolved, the client and the consultant should reach consensus as to how to proceed (Connecticut Nonprofit Consultant Directory, 2005).

For nonprofits to achieve the best possible return on their investment, organizational leaders should encourage both employees and volunteer leaders to be candid and should encourage consultants to tell the unvarnished truth. Truly ethical consultants who care more about being effective than being popular welcome such encouragement, and all parties will consider the engagement more productive. While the truth may not be pleasant for the organization to hear, anything less than an honest professional assessment would diminish the value of the consulting engagement.

Trust, like honesty, is an indispensable ingredient for a successful relationship. The absence of trust between the parties can spell doom for a consulting engagement. As Bellman (2002) noted, the usual role of the consultant is to effect change, and "change requires risk taking. Risk taking requires trust" (p. 74). He further observed that trust and risk are interdependent, and that while "building trust can make risk more acceptable, . . . it will not make risk go away" (p. 77). A climate that is conducive to the building of trust will not only make the relationship a more pleasant one but will also help increase the likelihood of a successful consultation.

Commit the Organization to Work with the Consultant

Many consultancies are not as productive as they could be because clients did not adequately inform all employees and lay leaders about the goals and objectives of the engagement, the methods and timelines of the process, or the roles that the consultants are likely to assume. If such preparation has not taken place, consultants may encounter needless resistance as they begin to interact at different levels of the organization.

It also is an ongoing responsibility of the organization's lay and professional leadership to encourage and support open and energetic involvement of employees in the consultancy process. This includes allowing consultants access to needed information. Full participation should not only lead to a better set of recommendations by the consultant but also should contribute to a greater willingness by employees to adopt and implement those plans.

Do Not Become Overly Dependent on Consultants

As helpful as consultants may be, organizations must learn to use them in a leveraged rather than a labor-intensive way (Schaffer, 2002). This is particularly true for organizations that employ consultants because they lack the resident knowledge and skills to carry out required tasks. Schaffer has characterized this overreliance on consultants as a "fatal flaw."

An interactive consulting process should help organizations develop the capacity *not* to hire consultants for similar purposes in the future unless having an external consultant is viewed as essential (e.g., in strategic planning). When a consultant has been engaged to carry out tasks that are likely to be required again, it behooves the client organization—if at all feasible—to build some additional time into the engagement to allow selected staff to learn the knowledge and skills necessary to carry out those tasks. Many consultants greatly enjoy teaching and mentoring. Not only can this be a rewarding experience for all parties, but the organization gains longer-term returns on its investment in the consulting engagement. The more a consultancy does to build organizational capacity, the more productive it can be considered to be and the greater the likelihood of sustainability.

While there are benefits to long-term relationships, total reliance on a single consultant or consulting firm is not the wisest course of action (Kubr, 1993). Indeed, organizations should strive to reach the stage where no consultant is deemed indispensable. Those that have diversified their sources of expertise, as Kubr recommended, are likely to find themselves in a stronger position.

Evaluate Consulting Relationship to Find Out
What Went Right—and Wrong

As noted earlier, evaluation should be integrated into the ongoing consulting process and should not be delayed until the consultation is concluding. The client organization should not only give itself an out in the event of a worst-case scenario but also should ensure that it can bring the project to closure on its own terms (TechSoup, 2000).

At the end of a consultancy, it is important to conduct a formal evaluation that focuses on both the things that went well and those that did not. This process should include input from a variety of people affected by the engagement and should focus on ascertaining why certain aspects of the consulting relationship worked while others did not. Answers to the "why" questions enable organizations to strengthen their future consulting relationships. If this evaluation is to be maximally helpful, consultants should be engaged in an honest discussion of the organization's attitudes and behaviors in carrying out its responsibilities in the consulting relationship. Although this may entail some highly subjective exchanges, the consultant's views and opinions are a part of what the organization has paid for and deserve to receive.

Avoid Fatal Flaws of Conventional Consulting

Less-than-satisfactory outcomes can result when the consultant and the client organization behave according to what Schaffer (2002) termed a "nearly universal pattern" (p. 22) that virtually guarantees the failure of the project. He identified the "five intrinsic characteristics" of this pattern as "the five fatal flaws of conventional consulting" (p. 22). These include

- Defining consulting projects "in terms of the 'products' the consultant will deliver, but not in terms of specific client results to be achieved" (p. 22).
- Allowing the scope of the project to be "determined mainly by the subject to be studied or the problem to be solved, with little regard for the client's readiness for change" (p. 24).
- Undertaking projects that "aim for one big solution rather than incremental successes" (p. 26).
- Creating "a sharp division of responsibility between client and consultant" with "little sense of partnership between them" (p. 27).
- Making "labor-intensive use of consultants, instead of leveraged use" (p. 29).

If organizations give serious attention to the foregoing considerations, they can enhance the consulting relationship for all parties. Noting that consultants who are truly professional "enjoy working with well-informed and highly demanding clients," Kubr (1993, p. 2) provided sage advice to organizations that wish to become more competent users of consulting services:

- Understand what consulting is about;
- Choose the best consultant—and the consultant best suited—for the particular assignment;

- Become the consultant's active partner;
- Pursue clear objectives;
- Learn from every assignment;
- Aim at the highest professional standards;
- Cultivate and diversify the organization's sources of expertise; and
- Define an organizational policy for choosing and using consultants.

Consultants, when selected and used wisely, can be a great asset to nonprofit organizations.

CHANGES IN THE CONSULTING LANDSCAPE

While much of the information contained in this chapter has stood the test of time, it is clear that several new developments are taking place in the consulting field. Because many nonprofit organizations will need to consider engaging a consultant at some point in their existence, it may be useful to enumerate some of the ways in which the field is changing:

- The list of areas of nonprofit management in which consultants are being sought continues to grow. In addition to the relatively new areas of transition planning and succession planning, there now seems to be mounting interest in consultants who can help with leadership issues and serve as mentors and management coaches (Panepento, 2004).
- The number and variety of providers of nonprofit consulting services are growing.
- The ease with which prospective consultants can enter the field—and the absence of a body whose mission is to establish credentials and regulate entry—mean that nonprofit organizations have little protection from unqualified would-be experts. The Alliance for Nonprofit Management has researched this area and may one day create an accreditation system (Panepento, 2004).
- For-profit consulting firms can be expected to continue their pursuit of nonprofit clients, but the issue of their proper role in this arena will most likely be a topic of ongoing debate.
- The increased number of individual consultants and consulting firms targeting the nonprofit sector may lead to more focused, and possibly more aggressive, marketing efforts. Advice on promotional strategies and techniques for "reputation-building" and "relationship-building" can be readily found in the current nonprofit literature. Lukas (1998), for example, has suggested that those targeting the nonprofit market publish products, articles, and books; contribute to nonprofit newsletters and publications as well as professional publications; develop promotional materials; offer to do conference presentations; establish referral networks;

serve on nonprofit boards; and "network fiercely" at workshops and conferences (pp. 142–143). Other authors have advised consultants interested in breaking into the nonprofit market to offer discounted fees to nonprofit organizations; volunteer their services—in other words, do pro bono work—particularly when there is a public relations benefit to be gained; join nonprofit boards and use relationships with fellow trustees as a way of gaining entrée into the *other* organizations on whose boards those trustees serve; and parlay one's own voluntary service into publicity in the local media. Although some of these tactics may seem less than altruistic, they are not at all uncommon. It is a wise nonprofit organization that recognizes when it is the object of such a strategy.

- Some independent consultants have begun to form group practices. Moreover, some consultants have adopted a team approach to service delivery and capacity building whereby each member agrees to address a different aspect of the organization's presenting problem.

- Membership organizations, including some that would appear to be trade associations, are emerging. Nonprofits seeking assistance from organizations of this type may find that after undergoing a diagnostic assessment, they will be referred to or matched with either an individual consultant or a consulting team.

- With the proliferation of group practices and membership organizations, the use of standards of professional conduct may spread. A recent development in this area is the creation of codes of ethics by voluntary associations of consultants. Two such examples are the code of ethics developed by the Consultants Network for Excellence in Nonprofits, a forum for independent consulting practitioners in Boston, and the code of professional standards of the Association of Consultants to Nonprofits, a membership group in the Chicago metropolitan area.

- Although it may be premature to call this development a trend, nonprofit organizations may find that the consultants whom they are interviewing promote themselves as adherents to a set of professional standards or best practices or a code of ethics. It is conceivable that, in the coming years, affiliations of this type could become a factor in the selection process. Regardless of whether a consultant belongs to a membership organization or subscribes to a formal standard of professional conduct, the prospective client should never hesitate to raise questions about how the consultant would handle specific ethical dilemmas.

- The field of nonprofit consulting may further professionalize, possibly becoming a subspecialty of nonprofit management. The development of codes of professional standards is one such sign. Another manifestation of the trend toward professionalization is the creation of educational programs designed specifically for consultants. For example, for several years, the San Francisco-based organization CompassPoint has mounted a three-day Institute for Nonprofit Consulting. INC, as it is known, presents a conceptual framework for consulting and provides both new and experienced consultants in the Bay Area with theoretical as well as practical knowledge.

- Consulting online has already become a reality, which suggests that technically adept consultants may increasingly exploit technology in the future, not only for communication but also for training, education, and other purposes (Panepento, 2004).

- As a growing number of foundations come to understand the role that excellent consulting can play in building nonprofit capacity and improving the effectiveness of their grantees, support for consulting-related activities and initiatives may become a more significant portion of the grant-making budget.

It is fascinating to contemplate where these developments may lead, but for now nonprofit consulting is primarily a local industry. The insights offered by Light in the year 2000 remain, for the most part, true today. He wrote,

> Even as one can applaud the decision of high-end private consulting firms . . . to provide pro bono or low-cost services to nonprofits, even as one can find occasional examples of for-profit firms . . . that specialize in the nonprofit sector, and even as one can celebrate national . . . and regional foundations . . . for providing the dollars to purchase technical assistance, the reality is that most small- to medium-sized nonprofits rely on local capacity. (pp. 40–41)

Regardless of how the field may change in the future, the goal of clients and consultants alike will continue to be the same: to ensure that consulting engagements are win–win situations. As Lant (1997) stated,

> Clients should get the result they bargained for, consultants should not only get paid but should get a constant stream of referrals from satisfied clients. If both clients and consultants insist upon and follow these simple steps, they will both get what they want out of the relationship. Which is just the way it should be. (p. 36)

CONCLUSION

Selecting and using consultants effectively is like most other aspects of nonprofit management and leadership. It is a matter of identifying and examining relevant issues and applying common sense. It is hoped that the foregoing points and considerations will help make consultative engagements more productive and satisfying for nonprofit clients and consultants alike.

SKILLS APPLICATION EXERCISE

You are the chief executive officer of Arts 'R Us, an arts organization that has an important social services component related to teaching art appreciation to inner-city children. The organization has been in existence for 35 years but has never had a business plan or a strategic plan to guide it. During each of the past three years, Arts 'R Us has ended with a financial deficit. Two funders—one corporate and the other a community foundation—have determined that they can no longer make grants to Arts 'R Us unless they are shown business and strategic plans. The two funders have each committed $10,000 to Arts 'R Us to engage a consultant to develop these plans.

The organization has never used a consultant previously. The board of trustees requested that you develop and present to them a plan to identify and select a consultant. Please develop a proposed plan (maximum of five pages) for board consideration. The plan should address, at a minimum, the following areas:

- Consultant's qualifications (required and preferred),
- Methods for identifying potential consultants,
- Ingredients for an RFP,
- Process for selecting the consultant,
- Fee amount and payment arrangements, and
- Deliverables and timelines.

REFERENCES

Association of Consultants to Nonprofits. (n.d.) *ACN consultants' code of professional standards.* Retrieved November 27, 2005, from http://www.acnconsult.org/consindx/code.html

Bellman, G. (2002). *The consultant's calling: Bringing who you are to what you do.* San Francisco: Jossey-Bass.

Block, P. (2000). *Flawless consulting* (2nd ed.). San Francisco: Jossey-Bass.

Bruner, C. (1993). *So you think you need some help? Making effective use of technical assistance.* New York: Columbia University, National Center for Service Integration.

Connecticut Nonprofit Consultant Directory. (2005). *How to manage a consultant.* Retrieved April 2, 2005, from http://206.128.27.141/cdb/manage_consult.htm

Connolly, P., & York, P. (2003). *Building the capacity of capacity builders: A study of management support and field-building organizations in the nonprofit sector.* Retrieved April 2, 2005, from http://www.tccgrp.com/pdfs/buildingthecapacityofcapacity builders.pdf

Consultants Network for Excellence in Nonprofits. (n.d.). *Code of ethics.* Retrieved November 27, 2005, from http://www.consultantsnetwork.org/codeofethics.html

Cope, M. (2000). *The seven Cs of consulting: Your complete blueprint for any consultancy assignment.* London: Prentice-Hall.

Davis, B. (1983, March–April). How and why to hire a consultant. *Grantsmanship Center News*, p. 27–34.

Ekstrom, H. (1997). Fund raising and nonprofit management consulting. In E. Scanlan (Ed.), *Corporate and foundation fund raising: A complete guide from the inside* (pp. 241–248). Gaithersburg, MD: Aspen.

Feldman, K. (2004, February 27). Charities and trade exchanges: How consultants and nonprofits can benefit from bartering, Part 1. *Nonprofit Consulting Review*. Retrieved December 23, 2004, from http://charitychannel.com/publish/templates/?a+962&z=17

Fletcher, K. (1995). Roles consultants play in successful fundraising interventions. *Nonprofit Management and Leadership*, 6(1), 67–83.

Flexner, S. B. (Ed.). (1988). *The Random House collegiate dictionary* (rev. ed.). New York: Random House.

Howe, F. (1997). *The board member's guide to strategic planning: A practical approach to strengthening nonprofit organizations*. San Francisco: Jossey-Bass.

Kibbe, B., & Setterberg, F. (1992). *Succeeding with consultants: Self-assessment for the changing nonprofit*. New York: Foundation Center.

Kubr, M. (1993). *How to select and use consultants: A client's guide*. Geneva, Switzerland: International Labour Office.

Lant, J. (1997). Why consulting relationships fail. *Contributions*, 11(2), 32–36.

Light, P. (2000). *Making nonprofits work: A report on the tides of nonprofit management reform*. Washington, DC: Brookings Institution Press.

Lukas, C. (1998). *Consulting with nonprofits: A practitioner's guide*. St. Paul, MN: Wilder Foundation.

McNamara, C. (1999). All about using consultants. Retrieved November 14, 2004, from http://www.mapnp.org/library/misc/cnsltng.htm

Panepento, P. (2004, March 18). Clamoring for consultants. *Chronicle of Philanthropy*. Retrieved December 23, 2004, from http://philanthropy.com

Schaffer, R. (2002). *High-impact consulting: How clients and consultants can work together to achieve extraordinary results*. San Francisco: Jossey-Bass.

Shulman, L. (1995). Supervision and consultation. In R. L. Edwards (Ed.-in-Chief), *Encyclopedia of social work* (19th ed., Vol. 3, pp. 2373–2379). Washington, DC: NASW Press.

Smith, Bucklin, & Associates. (2000). *The complete guide to nonprofit management* (2nd ed.). New York: Wiley.

Stern, G. J. (1999). *The Drucker Foundation Self-Assessment Tool: Process guide*. New York: Drucker Foundation.

TechSoup (2000). Managing a consultant: Don't just fade away when a consultant comes in. Retrieved December 5, 2004, from http://www.techsoup.org/howto/articles/consultants/page2735.cfm

Tepper, R. (1993). *The consultant's proposal, fee, and contract problem-solver*. New York: Wiley.

Third Sector New England. (2004). *Consulting: FAQ's*. Retrieved December 23, 2004, from http://www.tsne.org/section/21.html

Turner, A. N. (1982, September–October). Consulting is more than giving advice. *Harvard Business Review*, pp. 120–129.

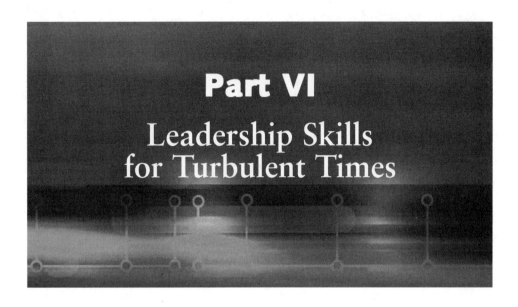

Part VI

Leadership Skills
for Turbulent Times

As discussed in Chapter 1 and elsewhere throughout this book, managers must function in an atmosphere of competing values in which change is virtually constant. In this context, managers must use various sets of skills and perform many different roles, often more or less simultaneously. In the day-to-day world of nonprofit managers, it is easy to get bogged down with the work at hand and lose sight of the reason for it all. Periodically, it may be important for managers to pause and ask themselves, and to engage other members of their organizations in discuss on, questions such as "Why?," "So What?," and "What difference does it make?" The answers to these questions should have something to do with the organization's mission and with the people served.

Daniel A. Lebold and Richard L. Edwards, in Chapter 20, discuss the impact of financial uncertainty on the management of nonprofit organizations. They consider the causes of organizational decline and the impact of major budgetary reductions or increases on nonprofit managers and staff. Lebold and Edwards also identify specific strategies that managers can use to effectively manage under conditions of declining funding. They include examples from two nonprofit organizations that successfully addressed severe funding crises.

In Chapter 21, the final chapter, Brook Manville presents a case study of how a major national organization, the United Way, has been undergoing a significant transformational change. He considers the reasons why the organization has been losing its relevance and the implications for its leadership. Manville presents an overview of a new competency model that is emerging for the United Way executives of the future, identifying the key dimensions and skills sets that such managers will need to be effective leaders of a transformed organization.

Managing Financial Uncertainty

Daniel A. Lebold and Richard L. Edwards

Rapid and unexpected shifts in funding—whether up or down—frequently have strong negative effects on the delivery of services provided by nonprofit organizations and on the clients or patrons who are served. Sizable increases or decreases in annual revenues also can impact an organization's mission and the types and frequency of services offered, or cause significant shifts in staffing. What is less obvious is the impact of budget changes on the lives of the people who work in nonprofit organizations. This chapter addresses the potential causes of organizational decline, the impact of budgetary reductions (or increases) on managers and staff in nonprofit organizations, and strategies that nonprofit managers can use when facing budgetary crises. The chapter reviews the literature on downsizing, rightsizing, cutback management, and retrenchment and draws on the personal experiences of upper-level managers in organizations that have experienced major funding cuts necessitating significant reductions in programs or workforce.

A NEW ERA OF FISCAL AUSTERITY

For most of the 20th century, government policies regarding funding for social welfare, community development, and the arts and humanities evolved from an "activist ideology" (Firstenberg, 1996). From President Franklin D. Roosevelt's Works Progress Administration initiatives in the 1930s to President Lyndon B. Johnson's War on Poverty in the mid-1960s, it was popularly accepted that government had both a role and a responsibility for providing solutions to chronic social and economic problems (Firstenberg, 1996; Newland, 1996). This period, which peaked in the 1960s and early 1970s, represented nearly 50 years of almost uninterrupted growth in government support of social programs (Cooke, Reid, & Edwards 1997).

During that era of federal expansion, many nonprofit organizations came to depend heavily on the widely available federal funds for their services, leading some nonprofit managers and board members to assume, falsely, that those dollars would always be available. However, public sentiment toward the federal government began to sour in the 1970s due to American involvement in the Vietnam War, the Watergate scandals during President Richard M. Nixon's administration, and the economic recession triggered by an international oil embargo. By the time Ronald Reagan assumed the presidency in 1980, antigovernment rhetoric was at an all-time high. Government was no longer viewed as a problem solver but as the cause of many economic and social problems (Firstenberg, 1996; Newland, 1996).

During the mid-1990s, the rapid growth of the U.S. stock market—powered by low oil prices, new home construction, the broad-base commercialization of the Internet, and a surge in health and technology sector profits—created new wealth that fueled an unprecedented expansion in the nonprofit sector; several hundreds of thousands of new nonprofit organizations were established in the United States during this period.

By 2002, however, this rapid expansion began to level off as a new economic recession set in, and public attention and funding priorities shifted to national and global crises: the attacks on the Pentagon and World Trade Center on September 11, 2001; the "war on terror"; the AIDS pandemic; and worldwide reaction to scores of natural disasters. This post-9/11 era has been characterized by a sluggish economy, federal tax cuts, flat wages, and relative low-asset growth for many of the nation's largest foundations. These conditions have led to significant decreases in available funding for nonprofits from nearly all sources—government, corporations, foundations, and to a lesser degree, individuals. Nonprofits face additional challenges. The avalanche of corporate accounting frauds beginning in 2001 with Enron and WorldCom added to a growing public mistrust of nonprofits that erupted 10 years earlier with the 1992 firing of William Aramony, president of United Way, who was convicted of 25 counts of embezzlement. Nearly 14 years later, the Aramony scandal continues to plague United Way campaigns across the United States and contributes to continued donor cynicism (See Chapter 21). In 2002, the U.S. Congress passed the American Competitiveness and Corporate Accountability Act, or Sarbanes–Oxley Act (P.L. 107-204, 116 Stat. 745) to ensure financial accountability and rebuild public trust in the corporate community. As more states begin to enact specific legislation aimed at nonprofit organizations, this climate of increased fiscal oversight will have implications for nonprofit organizations as well.

The dilemma for nonprofit managers is that they are entering into an era of increased uncertainty when funding patterns are in decline or fragmented and demand both for services and accountability is on the rise. While increased accountability may improve the overall quality of nonprofit operations and services, it will certainly drive up administrative costs related to program administration and oversight, financial accounting, and data collection activities required to measure and substantiate service outcomes.

Nonprofit managers will be required to develop new skills to deal with this rapidly changing environment. Funding streams are increasingly complex and difficult to predict, and competition for scarce resources has reached an all-time high, causing many nonprofits to close. Those that are surviving—or thriving—are organizations with leaders who have acquired the necessary skills to effectively navigate these turbulent fiscal times. All signs indicate that this period of fiscal austerity is likely to persist for many years. To prepare for this future, managers must learn from the earlier rounds of cutbacks.

OVERVIEW OF ORGANIZATIONAL DECLINE

According to Menefee (1997), the primary administrative responsibilities of a nonprofit manager are to identify emerging trends and anticipate their impact, create vision and purpose, and introduce and sustain innovation. The capacity to ensure that adequate funding is available to support an organization's core mission and staff is directly tied to a manager's capacity to understand and respond effectively to environmental changes.

At some point in the life of most organizations, budget shortfalls will occur requiring managers to make hard choices, sometimes involving cutting services or staff. It is important that nonprofit managers recognize the organizational and individual responses that accompany shifting financial resources. Regrettably, many nonprofit managers, like their counterparts in other fields, tend to be inadequately prepared to manage effectively under conditions of rapid change or decline. This tendency is not surprising given that most managers have more experience in—and receive more training for—responding to conditions of growth.

Growth has been viewed as consistent with the ideology and values of American culture, which considers growth and expansion to be primary indicators of effectiveness (Cameron, Sutton, & Whetten, 1988). Most organizations must increase their budgets annually just to keep up with inflation (Firstenberg, 1996). The idea that "bigger" or "more" is better has long been an internalized assumption held by many nonprofit managers and their staffs, particularly those working in the human services arena. Whetten (1980) noted that U.S. culture views "bigness" as a highly desirable characteristic. The enhancement of economies of scale, the ability to absorb shocks that accompany environmental changes, and increased productive capacity are among the presumed benefits of largeness.

Managers tend to be regarded as successful if they produce more, obtain larger budgets, and expand their organizations and are regarded as ineffective if they do the reverse. The question is, How big is too big? Most agree that growth is desirable, but there is less agreement on the merits of growth once it has been achieved (Cameron et al., 1988).

Sudden windfalls in funding can have potentially destabilizing effects on nonprofit organizations as well. According to Young (2000), sudden windfalls and shortfalls are in many ways "conceptual twins"; either can disrupt the ability of an organization to plan effectively or lead to significant adjustments in the organization's activities and priorities. For example, if an unanticipated large gift is received that significantly increases the relative size or scope of what had previously been considered a peripheral or "low-priority" activity, incorporating the windfall into the budget may divert critical resources away from higher priorities that could yield bigger results, financially or in terms of mission, or both. Making long-term adjustments to the organization's mission or core programs in response to a one-time funding windfall could lead to a dramatic fluctuation in activities and staffing or create a situation in which the organization cannot sustain the new initiative once the windfall has run out. It is always important to carefully consider how a new and sizeable funding source may, in the long run, alter the organization's focus on its overall mission.

Much has been written about organizational decline in recent years as a direct result of the many rounds of cutbacks that were experienced in both the nonprofit and corporate sectors (Cameron et al., 1988; Edwards, Cooke, & Reid, 1996; Edwards, Lebold, & Yankey, 1998). Throughout the past 30 years, fashionable topics in the literature regarding cutback management included downsizing, deregulation, and devolution. The literature in the 1990s focused on retrenchment, rightsizing, reinvention, and re-engineering (DuBran, 1996; Newland, 1996). Even so, management training programs in this new millennium rarely focus on developing skills related to managing under conditions of decline. Most current organizational theory is based on assumptions of growth. Decline tends to be either ignored or treated as an aberration.

CAUSES OF ORGANIZATIONAL DECLINE

The most common causes of organizational decline include economic shifts in the external environment, mismanagement or overexpansion of program activities or staff, overreliance on a single funding source that ends, or loss of a competitive edge on a particular niche service (Banning, 1990; Cameron et al., 1988). In some cases, shortfalls may be the result of a single event, such as a factory closing that displaces hundreds or thousands of workers who were the primary supporters of a local United Way campaign. Scandals also can inflict enormous damage to an organization's credibility and cause substantial losses of financial support. Mismanagement or uncontrolled growth in services beyond available resources can lead to budget shortfalls.

Whetten (1988) suggested that organizational decline may be a natural process associated with the stages described by life-cycle models of organizational behavior. He pointed out that the four most common stages defined in life-cycle models are (1) entrepreneurial (early innovation, niche formation, high creativity), (2) collectivity (high cohesion, commitment), (3) formalization and control (emphasis on stability and institutionalization), and (4) elaboration and structure (domain expansion and decentralization). These four stages roughly mirror the four skills sets—boundary spanning, human relations, coordinating, and directing—identified in the competing-values framework discussed in Chapter 1.

Although biological models frequently are used to describe organizational behavior, they generally fail to include research about the later stages of decline and death. Whetten (1988) pointed out that

> This reluctance to concentrate on the stages of decline and death ignores important finds in the life cycle literature. Research on the effective management of declining organizations has shown that the problems associated with shrinking economic resources and moral support are qualitatively different from problems associated with growth. (p. 29)

Determining the life cycle stage of an organization is important in responding to an organizational crisis.

Typically, a combination of factors ultimately leads to organizational retrenchment or requires cutbacks in programs or staff. Whatever the situation, it is imperative that a manager carefully identify and fully understand the specific cause or causes of the crisis to develop strategies that will ensure the organization's ultimate survival.

PRELUDE TO DISASTER: TWO AGENCIES FACING DECLINE

Directions for Youth and Families, Columbus, Ohio (Part I)

Directions for Youth and Families (DFY) was established in 1968 to provide support and delinquency prevention services for at-risk youth who were becoming involved in the juvenile court system. Its core programs encompass an array of services that include family counseling, court diversion, pregnancy prevention, youth self-esteem promotion and mentoring, and violence prevention.

Shortly after assuming the position of CEO in the mid-1990s, Steve Votaw faced the unexpected loss of $500,000 from the agency's primary funder, Franklin County Children's Services (FCCS). At the time of the cut, the agency's annual budget was $1.4 million. DFY was almost entirely dependent on grants and produced very little earned income. The agency had not developed a strong fundraising program, and private donations were not a significant source of revenue.

"We were completely dependent on FCCS for over 67 percent of our budget," Votaw explained. "Cash reserves were low, the agency had deplorable facilities, we didn't have a fundraising track record, and the administrative layer was top heavy. The loss of funding just about closed us down."

Further complicating matters, DFY was not well known in the community outside its major funding and referral partners. Those who were aware of the agency generally thought of it as a volunteer organization with limited professional services. In addition to across-the-board cuts from local, state, and federal sources, the local United Way was in financial decline due to the Aramony scandal. To top it off, Votaw was new to Columbus and had not yet established a professional network.

"I was forced to begin reducing the workforce immediately," Votaw said. "We had to eliminate programs, cut staff, and totally rebuild the organization from the ground up."

Triangle Family Services, Raleigh, North Carolina (Part I)

Triangle Family Services (TFS) is a United Way agency serving the Raleigh–Durham metro region. Established in 1937, the agency's core programs include family violence intervention, emergency-housing assistance, consumer credit counseling, mental health, and supervised visitation and exchange services.

When the agency hired its first senior development director in fall of 2000, the anticipated goal was to build an annual giving campaign that would raise $100,000 in unrestricted support primarily from individuals. The yearly budget was $2.2 million, and the agency had just experienced a 10-year growth period, spawned by sizeable increases in its annual United Way allocations and "voluntary contributions" from creditors through its consumer credit counseling program. The agency also was receiving an increasing portion of its revenue from earned income (reaching 36 percent) through third-party insurance payments and client fees.

Following the attacks of September 11, TFS experienced a rapid decline in its core funding. Individual contributions to the agency dropped off sharply as many donors shifted their giving to the 9/11 relief effort. The economic recession forced many of the region's largest corporations to downsize, causing the local United Way to fall short of its fundraising goals. As the area's largest United Way recipient, TFS lost over $350,000 annually from its allocation and nearly half of its funding from government sources. Combined, the agency lost more than $600,000 of its annual operating budget from what it thought were its most stable funding sources.

Cutting staff only exacerbated the problem. Because client fees and insurance reimbursements comprised 36 percent of the agency's budget, reducing professional staff only triggered additional revenue losses. "We couldn't simply cut our way out of the deficit, or the whole agency would have died," observed Wayne Freeman, the agency's vice president of finance. "We knew that, to survive, we had to increase revenues."

GENERAL RESPONSES TO DECLINE

No matter how effective a nonprofit manager is, he or she will likely face financial challenges that necessitate serious cutbacks in either programs or staff. Unfortunately, most managers find that their knowledge and skills are inadequate for the challenges presented by decline. This inexperience often contributes to the following conditions that organizations undergo during cutbacks in funding (Cameron, 1983):

- High levels of manager and staff stress;
- Low trust, secretiveness, and centralization;
- Increased conflict and decreased morale;
- Conservatism and aversion to risk; and
- Staff turnover and a self-protection orientation.

Under conditions of growth, the availability of slack resources makes it easier to overcome most of these problems. That is, when sufficient resources are available, people are more likely to be able to get what they want from the organization and staff tend to feel more valued and secure. Slack resources create conditions in which experimentation and innovation are possible. In addition, slack resources create buffers for the staff and organization. When there are no slack resources, or the budget begins to head into a deficit situation, a manager's personal skills become more critical for the effective management of the organization.

In organizations that are experiencing cutbacks, there is often a mood of anger and hostility. Employees feel insecure or threatened. Scapegoating is common, managers are blamed, and employees believe that management should have foreseen the problem and taken action earlier to lessen the impact. Because slack resources are no longer available, managers are less able to neutralize conflicting interest groups or "buy" internal consensus. Adaptation by addition is no longer possible, and managers must contend with their own high levels of stress as well as the stress of their employees. This stress often results in a restriction of the flow of communication in the organization, both from the top down and from the bottom up.

Concern for human relationships tends to be substantially reduced during times of retrenchment, and relationships among managers and their staffs tend to become more formalized. Decision making becomes more centralized as managers begin to feel a need to maintain control.

A sense of impending crisis often pervades the organization as individuals fear that they may lose their jobs. Staff turnover begins to rise as those who can leave, do. Employees who are unable to leave may become embittered and feel trapped. For the organization, this atmosphere creates a major personnel problem because the staff who are able to leave and find new jobs are often the most capable. Managers who are aware of this possibility may attempt to guard against it by keeping bad news to themselves, intensifying their own stress and increasing the mistrust of their subordinates.

Impact on Staff

Studies on cutback management tend to focus more on the impact of cutbacks on managers and strategies for dealing with declining resources than on staff in lower ranks. However, all employees are affected by funding cuts, even when their particular jobs are not lost. Despite the best professional efforts of staff to avoid letting their concerns interfere with their relationships with volunteers, clients, or patrons, it is not reasonable to assume that these stakeholders are not adversely affected. Consequently, it is essential that, when an organization is experiencing declining resources, a manager must concern himself or herself with the range of reactions of employees at all levels.

According to DuBran (1996), when the worst does happen and layoffs are required, the consequences for employees and their families can be devastating:

> While still in shock, [downsized workers] hurriedly put together résumés and send blanket mailings to prospective employers. Stress-related disorders such as migraine headaches, colitis, dermatitis, and cardiac disease escalate. Abuse of family members skyrockets. The suicide rate for laid-off workers is 30 times the national average. In short, the layoffs associated with downsizing create enormous human suffering. (p. 263)

Austin (1984) suggested that employees in organizations that are experiencing declining resources often go through a five-step process that is similar to Kübler-Ross's (1969) stages of death and dying: (1) denial and isolation, (2) anger, (3) bargaining, (4) depression, and (5) acceptance. The first reaction of staff members to the possibility or reality of funding cuts is often denial and isolation or withdrawal. They express the belief that rumors of such cuts are exaggerated or that their particular organization, unit, or program will not be affected. They may justify this by pointing to the quality of services they provide. Many staff members may react by attempting to withdraw from any discussions of cuts, taking what may be called an "ostrich approach."

"After the layoffs, no one was left who knew how to fill out purchase requisitions, expense vouchers, or make coffee."

As employees become more aware of the reality of funding cuts, they will likely react with anger, frequently focused toward the organization's managers who are blamed for the situation. As their initial anger subsides, staff may begin to acknowledge the reality of the situation and attempt to bargain for the survival of their particular unit, program, or job. When such bargaining fails, depression often sets in. At this point, employees may feel helpless and hopeless, believing that the situation is beyond their control. If they are able to work through their depression, they are more likely to settle into a state of acceptance.

Unfortunately, not all staff members who are affected by cutbacks will be able to work through these stages to the point of acceptance. Many will leave the organization still angry or depressed. Managers involved in organizations that are facing a decline in resources must recognize that these stages are normal concomitants of the situation and find ways to help staff members navigate through them.

Impact on Managers

Studies on cutback management suggest that managers tend to deal with conditions of decline by focusing on internal organizational concerns to the relative exclusion of external concerns. While the tendency to focus on internal issues is natural, it can be dysfunctional. To be effective, managers must be able to traverse multiple dimensions of leadership concurrently (see Chapter 1), particularly when confronting significant organizational crises. Analyzing the organization's internal processes is critical—that is, revenue trends, expenses, monthly utilization reviews, service productivity—but it is just as important to understand the current crisis in the context of a broader external environment.

During retrenchment, middle managers will often distance themselves from upper management, choosing instead to align with their "team" to avoid being the target of anger and hostility should layoffs become necessary. Middle managers may suggest to their direct staff that "upper management" or the board is to blame for the funding shortfalls. They also may deal with their stress by diverting their attention away from bigger, more looming problems, focusing instead on day-to-day operations that feel safer and more familiar. This avoidance of the crisis, however, tends to diminish the amount of creativity and expertise that is available from "within the ranks," and it severely limits the number of ideas that may lead to practical solutions.

Organizations with multiple program units often experience fierce lines of division between programs driven by competing managers and staff who are struggling to protect their turf. On the other hand, if a crisis threatens the entire organization (as opposed to a single program unit), middle managers across programs may join forces in opposition to senior management. Similarly, senior executives may attempt to defer blame by telling middle managers that individual program units are responsible for maintaining the financial viability independently. Unfortunately, because middle managers have only limited control over their total budgets—particularly the indirect portion that supports the agency's overhead—program managers feel frustrated and trapped by deficit situations that they alone cannot solve.

As time wears on and problems multiply, friction between ranks and resistance to change can weaken the organization's ability to weather severe economic storms. These conditions can cloud a manager's judgment and cause the decision-making process to become muddled. At worst, existing problems become exacerbated, and new problems are created, causing the crisis to be prolonged indefinitely.

One of the first actions nonprofit managers typically take when confronted with declining resources is to institute an across-the-board freeze on hiring and order that positions that become vacant be left unfilled. They then develop revised budget projections that take into account the savings that are expected by not filling positions that became vacant through retirements or resignations. Turem and Born (1983) noted that

> Superficially, attrition seems a reasonable, conflict-avoiding response to newly imposed fiscal constraints. By combining attrition with hiring freezes, administrators may avoid the bureaucratic, union, and interpersonal hassles related to layoffs and quell the disruption of staff morale (and thus staff performance) that 'RIF' (reduction in force) rumors may have stirred up. (p. 207)

However, Turem and Born (1983) pointed out that attrition is not a good way to deal with budget cuts. At best, attrition represents personnel decision by default. At worst, it is a tactic to avoid confronting issues that should be addressed squarely regardless of their unpleasantness or difficulty. Attrition, like across-the-board reduction, does not require nonprofit managers and staff to undertake the arduous task of defining and setting priorities for specific goals for each service program. Both approaches ignore the possibility that the value of maintaining established staffing patterns in key areas may more than justify making disproportionate cuts in other areas.

When attrition and hiring freezes are instituted, staff may have to assume a greater workload. This change may be regarded as a move to make staff more productive and the organization more efficient. Over time, however, such a strategy may have an adverse affect on the cohesion and morale of the staff, whose higher levels of stress may lead to greater absenteeism, decreased individual efficiency, and greater staff turnover.

Another common response of managers to declining resources is to trim the "frills" from the budget by reducing or eliminating various support services, including janitorial, equipment and building maintenance, secretarial, or contract services. Benefits such as reimbursement for continuing education or professional development activities are curtailed or eliminated. Managers do so to protect or shield their professional staff members as long as possible and out of a desire to maintain direct services to clients or patrons.

Over time, these actions also can lead to increased stress in staff and may contribute to high turnover. The organization may find itself with a predominantly younger, less experienced staff that is not able to provide the same quality of services that more experienced staff who were with the organization might have been able to provide. The net result is that the organization may experience communication problems, the flow of information may be impeded by not having sufficient support staff, and operations will be increasingly less stable. These conditions may curtail productivity and the delivery of services, which may have a further adverse affect on funding.

Another common strategy that managers use to deal with declining resources is to institute across-the-board cuts. The rationale behind this strategy is that the organization will continue to do all it has been doing, albeit on a reduced level. This approach is intuitively appealing because it seems to be an equitable way to share the pain involved in cutting back and "no program, provider, or client constituency can claim to have been singled out to bear the brunt of retrenchment" (Turem & Born, 1983, p. 206).

Managers may find that the across-the-board approach to dealing with declining resources seems to be the most fair and least painful. And it may be effective when the reductions in resources are relatively small and likely to be short term. However, when reductions in resources are major and likely to persist for a long time, the across-the-board strategy will lessen the effectiveness of all aspects of an organization's programming. Reducing staff in revenue-producing programs, no matter how "fair" it may appear, is unwise. In the long run, it is far better for an organization to "right-size" and do fewer things strategically well rather than to adopt a "one-size-fits-all" approach.

Dealing With Staff

When confronted with the specter of declining resources, managers can take several actions that will help staff deal more effectively with the situation. Managers must first recognize that their own level of stress will likely increase and thus take steps to identify and handle their responses to this stress. Managers can attend to their own emotions through a variety of stress reduction techniques, from doing more physical exercise to creating and participating in support groups with other managers who are in a similar situation. In some cases, it may be helpful and entirely appropriate to consult with an "executive coach" who has expertise in dealing with cutback management.

Identifying and dealing with stress involves grappling with paradox. Managers who are stressed tend to react by withdrawing, keeping information to themselves, and becoming more autocratic in making decisions. Managers must resist these tendencies and make efforts to be *more* open about sharing information and decision making. Pay particular attention to those in the organization who will have the responsibility and burden of telling others that they are being laid off or that their jobs are eliminated. This is an extremely difficult task emotionally that usually falls on middle managers, and its impact should not be overlooked.

An important component of managerial activity in dealing with declining resources is the management of rumors (Hirschhorn, 1983). Decisions must be made about what to tell the staff and when to tell it. Rumors serve the purpose of helping staff structure and reduce their anxiety and offer a way to make sense of the situation. In other words, rumors often enable staff to gain a sense of control.

The members of the management team can counteract rumors by recognizing the purposes that rumors serve and by providing alternative mechanisms for staff to meet their needs for greater control. These mechanisms include helping staff members at all levels in the organization structure their anxiety by engaging them in planning activities as well as by providing them with opportunities to express the negative feelings they have.

Managers also should engage staff through planning groups that examine the organization's mission and goals to identify core activities and priorities. Managers can focus their teams on developing a range of best-case/worst-case scenarios with a set of alternative decisions for each scenario. Such identification can be helpful in subsequent development and structuring of a plan for handling decisions about retrenchment or layoffs. As Hirschhorn (1983) noted, managers often must confront the need to make trade-offs between the issues of fairness and strategy. When layoffs are contemplated, managers generally desire a fair process, yet they would like to be able to keep those staff members who are likely to prove most valuable to the agency in the future. A consideration of the organization's core programs helps identify those individuals within the organization who have the knowledge and skills that make them best able to further the core mission.

Of course, union contracts and civil service regulations may set limits on the ability to make staffing decisions under conditions of decline. When such contracts or regulations exist, it is incumbent on a manager to be well informed about their requirements and restrictions. When no such contracts or regulations exist, a manager may have more latitude in making decisions about retrenchment. In either case, decisions about whom to keep and whom to let go should be based on judgments about which staff members can contribute most to the organization's core programs and which will best enable the organization to be positioned to take advantage of environmental opportunities that arise in the future.

When decisions are made to lay off particular staff members, these individuals should be informed as early as possible to afford them the maximum chance to find other jobs. Managers should provide them with a range of supports or outplacement services. These supports may include assistance in preparing résumés, ensuring that they will be able to get reference letters that indicate the circumstances under which their employment was terminated and giving them opportunities to vent their feelings about the situation. In addition, managers may find it helpful to arrange for a representative of the local unemployment compensation office to meet with staff to explain how to apply for unemployment compensation, how long it will take for them to receive their first check, how much money they can expect to receive, and how long they may be eligible to collect benefits. This kind of information is essential to staff members who must plan how they will manage their lives in the period immediately after being laid off. Furthermore, every effort should be made to help staff learn about other employment opportunities.

The members of the management team should engage in planning activities aimed at defining the primary functions of the organization and developing strategies for the future. Friesen and Frey (1983) stated that cutbacks "may alter an organization's strategic position in the network, reduce its relative power, and increase its dependency on other organizations" (pp. 36–37). Thus, it is important to consider how the organization will relate to other organizations and whether it will enter coalitions, attempt to keep a monopoly on services, or look for new markets or opportunities for services.

Managers also must become actively involved in the development of *new* resources. These activities may range from writing grants, obtaining contracts, and instituting fee-for-service programs to devising strategies for using volunteers and paraprofessionals and building relationships with policymakers. Friesen and Frey (1983) observed that managers who are confronting declining resources "need to develop both technical skills (i.e., how to raise new funds) and interactional skills (i.e., how to build a constituency)" (p. 37).

STRATEGIC STEPS IN MANAGING ORGANIZATIONAL DECLINE

Determine the Scope of the Problem

When faced with severe shortfalls in funding, a range of strategies can be used depending on the nature of the specific crisis or crises. Cutback strategies may differ depending on the sector within which a nonprofit organization functions. For example, symphonies or art museums may elect to raise ticket prices for admission, whereas homeless shelters that depend solely on community donations may need to rally political support or face imminent staff layoffs. Strategies also will differ depending on how long the shortfall is anticipated to last. Across-the-board cost reductions may be effective for short-term crises but probably will weaken an organization further if implemented as a long-term solution. Therefore, when faced with a funding shortfall, managers must carefully evaluate the problem in all its complexity and develop a planned strategic response.

The first step is to determine the cause or causes of the decline. Behn (1988) argued that the understanding of a management problem is dependent upon how severe it is perceived to be. Questions that must be carefully considered include

- Is the problem likely to be short term or long term?
- Is the problem related to internal mismanagement or a lack of internal professional expertise?

- Is the problem related to inefficiencies caused by inadequate technology or a critical staffing position?
- Is the problem the result of a local or national trend in a particular industry?
- Is the crisis due to new competition from an alternative vendor or service provider?
- Is the problem the result of lost credibility due to scandal or fraud?
- Is the problem related to lack of visibility or marketing?
- How serious is the problem? That is, can the crisis be averted through short-term and limited cutbacks, or is the problem more serious, likely requiring a longer-term retrenchment?

Once it is determined that retrenchment is required, Behn (1988) suggested a two-stage process of (1) preparation and announcement and (2) implementation. Behn further stated that, throughout the process of retrenchment, a non-profit manager's primary responsibilities are to

- Decide what to cut;
- Maintain morale;
- Attract and keep quality people;
- Develop the support of key constituencies (and legislators);
- Create opportunities for innovation; and
- Avoid mistakes (pp. 350–351).

Selecting a Strategy

Deciding what or whom to cut is one of the most difficult decisions that non-profit managers will make, and the results of those decisions will likely affect many people throughout the organization. As managers consider the various options for retrenchment, it is essential that they conduct a strategic assessment of the organization. It may be helpful to establish a special task force composed of managers, staff, and board members to undergo a SWOT (*strengths, weaknesses, opportunities, threats*) analysis and then determine which strategies will be most effective and how to implement them. Managers must then evaluate the pros and cons of implementing various strategies, including cutting some programs or personnel. Managers may want to consider hiring an outside management consultant who can help develop a retrenchment plan as well as provide outplacement services for staff.

The most common strategies used in response to funding cutbacks are *cost reductions, political influence, cooperation and mergers, refinancing, commercialization and fund-raising, relocation,* and *downsizing* (DuBran, 1996; Palmer, 1997).

Cost Reductions

Cost reductions are most often used when the source of the cutback is temporary and when their impact will not likely affect the long-term performance of the organization. However, many nonprofit managers mistakenly use across-the-board cutbacks without fully addressing the real budget problems facing their organizations. Such overuse of cost reductions often leads to continued funding shortfalls and a further decline in the organization.

Political Influence

Political influence is used as an attempt to reverse externally imposed funding cuts, often when funding is received from government sources. According to Palmer (1997), the three most frequently used techniques of exerting political persuasion include (1) *reasoning*—rational presentation of the facts and an appeal to personal values; (2) *retribution*—the use of intimidation and coercion; and (3) *reciprocity*—creating exchanges or obligations between two organizations. This strategy usually involves board members, clients, patrons, local citizens, or other stakeholders who may be in positions of power to influence decision makers in the community. Although political leverage is usually a slow process and rarely leads to an immediate funding solution, it is an important strategy that often is overlooked.

Mergers and Cooperative Strategies

Cooperative strategies and mergers are frequently used when two or more organizations determine that cost savings can be made by combining elements of their programs or services. Also referred to as "survival sharing," these strategies move away from a stance of competition to one of cooperation. This may include sharing materials and supplies, office space, staff, printing, community networks and boards, fundraising, and joint marketing and distribution (Palmer, 1997). Cooperation strategies also can be used among program units within organizations that are particularly large or complex. An extreme form of cooperation is a merger between two independent organizations (see Chapter 18). Although mergers may save money in the long term, they are costly and extremely disruptive in the short term and can cause significant staff turnover or a change in leadership.

Refinancing

Refinancing is a strategy often used in the arts and humanities sectors. Many performing arts organizations will borrow money from a bank or lender against anticipated future growth in earned income through ticket sales (Palmer, 1997). Shortfalls result when proceeds are insufficient to cover costs, forcing organizations to then refinance to avoid defaulting on their loan. These types of strategies are used for short-term crises when shortfalls are deemed temporary.

Commercialization and Fundraising

Commercialization and fundraising involve a change in marketing strategy, usually through raising ticket prices, increasing fees for services, or expanding fundraising activities to raise additional funds for the organization. Fundraising activities, including special events, should be considered and may help attract attention to the needs of the organization, as well as increase the level of financial support from individuals, foundations, and corporations (see Chapter 4). Developing innovations or modifying existing programs also may increase revenues or efficiency. Each strategy should be pursued throughout the life of the organization, but they are especially important during periods of decline.

Relocation

Relocations are used when the cost of overhead for an existing facility becomes too expensive. Relocation may help reduce property taxes; involve a merger with another similar organization; or simply be a move to a smaller, less expensive facility. In some cases, relocation parallels a reduction in the overall scope of the services provided. However, many costs are associated with moving an organization, both in terms of real dollars needed to carry out the move and in the loss in productivity and potential loss of customers or clients who may not know where the new facility is located. In organizations that have multiple sites, it may be necessary to close one or more satellite locations to consolidate overhead expenditures. Further, long-term lease obligations may make relocation difficult, if not impossible.

Downsizing

Downsizing has been the focus of much concern since the mid-1970s because of the many organizations, both for-profit and nonprofit, that have experienced it. Downsizing typically is used either when organizations become too large or when substantial budget shortfalls necessitate immediate reductions in staff. According to Cascio (1993), *downsizing* is essentially "the planned elimination of positions or jobs" (p. 96). However, for many organizations, downsizing has been shown not to be a long-term cost-saving strategy. Many organizations that downsized during the 1980s discovered that low employee morale, decreased productivity, and the high cost of rehiring and retraining led to even further decline and retrenchment (Perry, 1988). Depending on the circumstances, an organization may have no choice but to downsize its workforce. When that is the case, it will probably be one of the most difficult and painful situations a nonprofit manager will have to encounter.

If it is determined that staff reductions are necessary, DuBran (1996) suggested the following four steps: (1) eliminate low-value and no-value activities, (2) keep future work requirements in mind, (3) identify the tasks that retained employees will perform, and (4) decide which workers will be let go. He further recommended that once it is determined who will be laid off, managers should make the cuts as quickly and completely as possible. In the long run, it will be far less disruptive to make a single round of cutbacks quickly than to make several rounds over a protracted time. Prolonging cutback decisions only increases staff insecurities and further demoralizes the workforce.

Determining the criteria to use when deciding whom to lay off is both complicated and controversial. Decisions often are based on seniority, employment status (part-time and temporary workers), voluntary resignations and early retirements, and performance. All of these options have advantages and disadvantages.

DuBran (1996) noted that basing layoff decisions on seniority may seem to be the most fair; however, managers lose control over which employees are maintained. On the other hand, letting go of senior staff may have serious negative effects on the staff who are left behind and who now fear that loyalty to the firm no longer ensures job security. Similarly, dismissing workers according to function may appear to benefit overall operations but may be interpreted as political on the part of management to get rid of staff whom they do not like.

Laying off temporary or part-time workers may have appeal because it protects job security for permanent employees. However, temporary employees are sometimes hired to carry out highly specialized tasks, and they are usually less expensive than permanent full-time employees. Hence, letting go of temporary workers may have a high negative impact on general operations but a relatively low impact on total budget.

Voluntary resignations and early-retirement incentive strategies often are used by organizations that have large workforces. Eligible employees are offered early retirement or severance packages that they can take now or risk being laid off later. The obvious disadvantage is that an organization may lose its most highly skilled workers because it is losing control of which employees it retains.

Basing layoff decisions on performance can be one of the most challenging, but more productive, methods of achieving a downsized workforce. Most authors agree that basing layoff decisions on performance both increases employee morale in the long run and minimizes productivity loss (DuBran, 1996; Perry, 1988). Essentially, program managers are asked to assess their staff and make recommendations for termination or dismissal based on individual performance measures. However, DuBran (1996) discouraged the practice of conducting performance appraisals strictly for the purpose of downsizing because they may appear too political.

Throughout the process of downsizing, it is essential that managers demonstrate compassion and understanding both for the workers who are laid off and for those who are left behind who may experience survivor guilt. Outplacement services should be provided for displaced workers. It also is important to recognize that, although downsizing may be necessary, it will undoubtedly cause a loss in productivity and may prove to be more costly in the long term than other retrenchment strategies.

EPILOGUE—EMERGING FROM THE ABYSS

Directions for Youth and Families, Columbus, Ohio (Part II)

Faced with a cataclysmic loss in funding, Steve Votaw had few options but to begin closing down programs and laying off staff immediately. He began by assembling his board of directors and management team to conduct an analysis of the agency's core mission and activities and to assess which programs had the capacity to produce the most income through fees or alternative funding. Because the agency was clearly top-heavy, Votaw initiated the first round of cuts himself, focusing primarily on upper- and middle-management positions. His goal was to move quickly to preserve programs and to keep those employees who could maintain services, produce income, and help carry out his vision for the organization.

"My challenge was to reduce the workforce, eliminate programs, strengthen overall financial operations, improve the agency's public image, and set a new vision for the organization," Votaw explained.

While cutbacks were necessary, a pivotal moment came when Votaw successfully negotiated a new service contract with Franklin County Children's Services, a move that helped reduce the size of the funding cut and extended the time frame he had to develop a new plan of action. While there was initial resentment expressed by staff in response to the layoffs, Votaw was successful in engaging the participation of those who remained in a strategic planning process that helped to chart the agency's future direction. Votaw emerged from this process with a new and clearly articulated vision for the organization that included several key elements. The first of these included the need to upgrade the credentials and professional expertise of core employees, particularly those who could generate revenues for the organization.

A second element of his vision involved the launching of a highly ambitious multimillion dollar capital campaign to construct a new building. This strategy was used to (1) upgrade and modernize the facilities for staff and services, (2) provide new incentives for corporate and individual contributions, and (3) significantly improve the organization's profile and credibility in the community. This second initiative was met with significant resistance after a fundraising consultant concluded that the agency did not have the necessary experience nor the depth of community support to launch a successful major fundraising campaign. However, the consultant provided a series of recommendations that Votaw's board of directors followed, including beginning to recruit board members and additional community volunteers who could help the organization raise money. This involved identifying leaders who were well known in the community and could help transform the culture and fundraising expertise of the board. When the organization actually began its fundraising campaign, a consulting firm suggested that it might be possible to raise $1.9 million. When the campaign was over, the organization had raised just more than $2.8 million.

A third element of his vision involved pursuing Ohio Department of Alcohol and Drug Addition Services Certification, which allowed the agency to begin billing Medicaid. Pursuing certification also provided a process and a structure to further professionalize the organization's core operations, including service delivery to consumers, quality improvement, and financial management.

With a more professional staff, DFY was now positioned to compete and qualify for a wide variety of new funding streams, including Medicaid and other federal funding through the U. S. Department of Health and Human Services. This enabled the agency to later merge with a local mental health and family-counseling center that also was experiencing financial shortfalls and that complimented DFY's mission. Licensed counselors and social workers were hired, which helped create new service initiatives and also opened up additional sources of funding.

Twelve years later, DFY has a budget of more than $7 million with no single revenue source making up more than 25 percent of the agency's budget. With a vision toward building a stronger, more dynamic and professional organization, DFY has emerged from its abyss with tremendous visibility, augmented by a new building and several satellite offices throughout the county. Further, the agency is both recognized and respected as the foremost provider of professional services to at-risk youth and their families throughout the Columbus region.

Triangle Family Services, Raleigh, North Carolina (Part II)

The growth experienced by TFS during the 1990s, to a great extent, masked many internal program and operational deficits that were later exposed during the post-9/11 economic downturn. Outwardly, the organization looked strong. Internally, however, several significant inefficiencies had been obscured by a profitable bottom line. These included delays in filing insurance claims resulting in a write-off of $45,000 in anticipated income; inconsistent documentation of direct-services activities by case managers, thus preventing the agency from billing those hours to county and federal grants; and obsolete DOS software and antiquated computer systems that made it impossible for consumer credit counselors to keep pace with a continuously changing banking industry. This latter issue resulted in a one-time write-off of more than $80,000 in "voluntary contributions" from creditors that the agency determined that it would never realize due to their lack of compliance with creditor regulations. When cutbacks began to hit, however, these problems could no longer be overlooked.

Further analysis of program operations exposed even deeper problems: a management team that was ill-equipped to handle the mounting challenges facing their programs. Efforts to engage middle managers in the process of modifying their programs or implementing system-wide changes led to greater staff resistance. In many respects, the agency had reached a state of internal stagnation and lacked the entrepreneurial spirit or expertise needed to effectively adapt to the changing environment. Attempting to correct this problem by holding managers more accountable, or by requiring additional training, ultimately led to a 300% turnover in management over a two-year period. Unfortunately, this slowed the agency's capacity to respond to the crisis.

"Our management team and staff were accustomed to focusing on the quality and delivery of services to our customers," explained George O'Neal, president and CEO. "But it became suddenly clear that their business skills were not on par with the new demands of the job."

Lack of public awareness also presented challenges. Although TFS had been operating in the community for nearly 67 years, the agency was still relatively unknown outside its primary service partners. In fact, the agency's programs were so little known that it was later discovered that City of Raleigh social workers were sending clients 20 miles away to Durham to receive individual housing counseling. Ironically, TFS was providing these services for free just four blocks away—and had been since the mid-1970s.

O'Neal dealt with the unfolding crisis by engaging the board of directors and management team in developing new strategies for increasing revenues and cutting costs. Together, they adopted the key principal of "going deeper, not broader." That is, the board and staff determined that the agency's current mission and core services were still relevant and needed in the community. Funding decisions would therefore be based on strengthening core activities, as opposed to chasing funding that would divert agency resources away from these activities.

In the short term, however, TFS was forced to open a line of credit and begin using operational reserves to maintain services. Described as a "rainy-day" fund, the agency had accumulated approximately $375,000 over a 16-year period to be used in the event of a financial downturn. These funds enabled the agency to continue its service mission while management undertook the arduous task of transforming internal operations to become more efficient and building external relationships that could help to leverage additional funding. In total, the agency was forced to spend more than $200,000 of its reserves in just 18 months.

In responding to funding shortfalls, a first priority was to maximize financial margins across programs. This was achieved by (1) increasing the productivity standards for income-producing positions (to 75%), (2) improving third-party billing procedures, (3) training case managers on what activities a "billable" hour could entail and increasing billing by capturing those hours through improved documentation, and (4) outsourcing the agency's consumer credit counseling accounting division to a firm that specialized in recouping creditor fair-share contributions on behalf of nonprofits.

The rapid turnover of managers eventually led to the hiring of new staff with more education and significantly more years of professional experience. This coincided with TFS's reaccreditation and the compulsory process of reviewing and revamping of all program policies and procedures. These steps helped bring programs throughout the agency to the same professional standards in terms of service delivery, internal documentation, and monitoring of program outcomes.

Another key event was the agency's participation in a unique collaboration formed to address a critical need for children who were victims of family violence. TFS was asked to be the lead agency to develop and establish a supervised visitation and exchange center for children in Wake County. This collaboration, which involved more than 15 organizations, was the first of many and served to strengthen the agency's core mission, invigorate the board, increase staff confidence in the development of new projects, and garner tremendous public attention and support. It also fostered a sense of innovation and creativity among the staff.

The management team was reorganized to shift away from program-level directors, and a vice president of programs was created. This position helped reduce the deep divisions between programs that were impeding the recovery process. It also helped upper management take a global view of operations and identify increased efficiencies and cost-sharing opportunities across programs.

The teaching of boundary spanning (described in Chapter 1) was critical to helping managers learn how to identify scores of new funding opportunities in multiple sectors of the community. These included building partnerships with local banks and corporations to support the delivery of financial education seminars; developing research projects to evaluate the success of specific program activities; and initiating partnerships with local foundations to launch multiyear collaborations with a variety of service providers, thereby leveraging new resources from local, state, and federal sources.

Eventually the board stepped up its role in helping stabilize the organization. For a time, the fundraising committee began meeting biweekly to accelerate the process of identifying and acquiring new supporters. A technology committee was established to help plan and fund a major upgrade of the agency's failing technology and computer systems, and a special-events committee was established to organize and host several evening cocktail parties and special events designed to introduce new potential supporters to the agency.

TFS emerged from its abyss as a leaner, more professional, and far more dynamic agency than it had been before the retrenchment. In three years, the agency's budget grew 35 percent to $3.4 million and its customer base grew from approximately 5,000 clients to more than 7,000 annually. This was accomplished, in part, through increased cooperation among program managers internally, pursuit of collaborations with multiple partners that enabled the agency to raise more than $2.5 million in *new* funding, and a commitment to deepening its focus and expertise in its core areas of service. Most importantly, the agency was able to grow—not diminish—during this time of retrenchment, thereby expanding its capacity to serve more consumers in the community.

CONCLUSION

Managers of nonprofit organizations are confronting a new era of fiscal austerity prompted by a profound philosophical shift in the perception of federal responsibility and a subsequent reduction in government funding for many community-based programs. It is clear that nonprofits will continue to experience increased demand for services in an environment of shrinking financial resources and increased competition for private dollars.

Effective nonprofit managers must be able to recognize their own reactions to stress and find ways to handle it effectively. Having done so, managers should involve staff in identifying the organization's core program and delineating the agency's mission, primary functions, and goals. At the same time, managers should pursue resource development strategies to increase revenues.

If layoffs are necessitated by dwindling resources, they should be handled in a straightforward, honest manner, and outplacement assistance should be provided to staff who are losing their jobs. It is evident that these varied responses to organizational decline will require both technical and interactional skills.

SKILLS APPLICATION EXERCISE

You are the director of large nonprofit shelter for runaway youths. Your programs include a 24-hour crisis hotline, a 24-hour runaway shelter (which provides meals, individual and group counseling, peer support, and crisis intervention), in-home family unification services, and services to prevent physical and sexual abuse (counseling and public education). Your funding sources include government grants (65 percent), small grants from foundations and corporations (20 percent), fees (10 percent), and individual donations (5 percent). You have been advised that your government funding will be reduced by 20 percent over the next two years.

The board of county commissioners has requested that you submit your plan for dealing with these budgetary cuts. What managerial actions or approaches would you take? Include in your design how you would respond to these questions:

- What activities can the agency stop performing?
- What activities can your agency get other agencies to do?
- What activities can be performed more effectively?
- How can you reduce the cost of labor?
- How can you increase the agency's revenues?

REFERENCES

Austin, M. J. (1984). Managing cutbacks in the 1980s. *Social Work, 29,* 428–434.

Banning, R. L. (1990, September). The dynamics of downsizing. *Personnel Journal,* pp. 68–75.

Behn, R. D. (1988). The fundamentals of cutback management. In K. S. Cameron, R. I. Sutton, & D. A. Whetton (Eds.), *Readings in organizational decline: Frameworks, research, and prescriptions* (pp. 347–356). Cambridge, MA: Ballinger.

Cameron, K. S. (1983). Strategic responses to conditions of decline: Higher education and the private sector. *Journal of Higher Education, 54,* 359–380.

Cameron, K. S., Sutton, R. I., & Whetten, D. A. (1988). *Readings in organizational decline: Frameworks, research, and prescriptions.* Cambridge, MA: Ballinger.

Cascio, W. E. (1993). Downsizing: What do we know? What have we learned? *Academy of Management Executive, 7,* 95–104.

Cooke, P. W., Reid, P. N., & Edwards, R. L. (1997). Management: New developments and directions. In R. L. Edwards (Ed.-in-Chief), *Encyclopedia of social work* (19th ed., 1997 Suppl., pp. 229–242). Washington, DC: NASW Press.

DuBran, A. J. (1996). *Reengineering survival guide: Managing and succeeding in the changing workplace*. Cincinnati, OH: Thomson Executive Press.

Edwards, R. L., Cooke, P. W., & Reid, P. N. (1996). Social work management in an era of diminishing federal responsibility. *Social Work, 41*, 468–479.

Edwards, R.. L., Lebold, D. A., & Yankey, J. A. (1998). Managing organizational decline. In R. L. Edwards, J. A. Yankey, & M. A. Altpeter. (Eds.). Skills for effective management of nonprofit organizations (pp. 279–300). Washington, DC: NASW Press

Firstenberg, P. B. (1996). *The 21st century nonprofit: Remaking the organization in the post-government era*. New York: Foundation Center.

Friesen, B., & Frey, G. (1983). Managing organizational decline: Emerging issues for administration. *Administration in Social Work, 7*(3/4), 33–41.

Hirschhorn, L. (Ed.). (1983). *Cutting back: Retrenchment and redevelopment in human and community services*. San Francisco: Jossey-Bass.

Kübler-Ross, E. (1969). *On death and dying*. New York: Macmillan.

Menefee, D. (1997). Strategic administration of nonprofit service organizations: A model for executive success in turbulent times. *Administration in Social Work, 21*(2), 1–19.

Newland, C. A. (1996). The national government in transition. In J. L. Perry (Ed.), *Handbook of public administration* (2nd ed., pp. 19–35). San Francisco: Jossey-Bass.

Palmer, I. (1997). Arts management cutback strategies: A cross-sector analysis. *Nonprofit Management and Leadership, 7*, 271–290.

Perry, T. P. (1988). Least-cost alternatives to layoffs in declining industries. In K. S. Cameron, R. I. Sutton, & D. A. Whetton (Eds.), *Readings in organizational decline: Frameworks, research, and prescriptions* (pp. 357–368). Cambridge, MA: Ballinger.

Sarbanes-Oxley Act of 2002 (P.L. 107-204, 116 Stat. 745).

Turem, J. S., & Born, C. E. (1983). Doing more with less. *Social Work, 28*, 206–210.

Whetten, D. A. (1980). Sources, responses, and effects of organizational decline. In J. Kimberly & R. Miles (Eds.), *The organizational life cycle* (pp. 342–374). San Francisco: Jossey-Bass.

Whetten, D. A. (1988). The organizational growth and decline process. In K. S. Cameron, R. I. Sutton, & D.A. Whetton (Eds.), *Readings in organizational decline: Frameworks, research, and prescriptions* (pp. 27–44). Cambridge, MA: Ballinger.

Young, D. R. (2000). Windfalls and sudden losses: How should nonprofits respond? *NonProfit Times* (Nov. 2, 2000), 16.

ADDITIONAL READING

Bielous, G. (1996, October). Stretch targets: The art of asking for miracles. *Supervision*, pp. 16–18.

Bombyk, M. J., & Chernesky, R. H. (1985). Conventional cutback leadership and the quality of the workplace: Is beta better? *Administration in Social Work, 9*(3), 47–56.

Boulding, K. (1975). The management of decline. *Change, 7*(5), 8–9, 64.

Brown, M. J. (1996, September). What can community organizers teach us? *Journal for Quality and Participation*, pp. 78–80.

Cameron, D. B. (1996). Do you need to rebuild your organization to survive the 3rd millennium? *Nonprofit World, 14*(3), 48–51.

Drucker, P. E. (1996, August). Nonprofit pioneers. *Executive Excellence,* p. 5.

Miller, J. R. (1997, March). Transforming for the 21st century. *Management Accounting,* pp. 15–16.

Pappas, A. T. (1996). *Reengineering your nonprofit organization: A guide to strategic transformation.* New York: John Wiley & Sons.

Tolchin, M. (1991, February 4). Cuts after decade of cuts: Governors grim at meeting. *New York Times,* p. A10.

21

Redefining Leadership in a Community-Impact Organization

A Case Study of Reframing CEO Skills Amid Transformational Change

Brook Manville

Over the past five years, the United Way has been in the process of a systemwide transformation: shifting from being primarily a fundraising charity to being a philanthropic leader of measurable "community impact" in hundreds of cities across America. In this chapter, the competing-values framework is used to describe the shift, particularly with regard to the new competencies required of the local United Way chief executive officer (CEO). This chapter relates, on the basis of discussions with United Way CEOs and research done on a new competency model, how the new leaders of the system must learn to confront the demands of each of the four quadrants of the competing values framework (See Figure 1.2 in Chapter 1) and redefining performance in terms of finding the balance among all of them, based on situation, needs, and community and organizational strategy.

For the past several years—especially since 2001, when Brian Gallagher became CEO of the United Way of America—the United Way system has been going through a process to transform itself (Aft & Aft, 2004; Brilliant, 1990; Brilliant & Young, 2004; United Way, 2006a). The transformation has been proceeding on multiple, interrelated levels: mission, "theory of change," business model, and operational processes. The core of the transformation is about changing a 120-year-old organization (or "movement," as United Way members like to say), from a network focused on fundraising to a more philanthropic leader of actual "community impact"—creating or catalyzing measurable improvement in people's lives in communities across America, through system change and the tackling of deeper, root causes of human welfare problems (Gallagher, 2001). A major driver of the transformation are the leaders of local

United Ways themselves—the staff CEOs of some 1,400 local affiliates supported by the volunteers of the communities they serve.

As the old saying goes, "To change those around you, you must first change yourself"—and not surprisingly, the progress of the United Way transformation rests heavily on the changes of leaders across the movement (see, for example, Beer & Nohria, 2000). In some cases, transformation moves ahead with the recruitment of a new CEO, more attuned to and skilled for the challenges of the new work; in other cases, the change evolves as existing CEOs develop new skills and mindsets required of "community impact" (Weil, 2005). In all cases, the transformation process has been enabled by the creation of a new competency model for the local United Way CEO, which makes more objective and concrete the skills and behaviors required of the new work. Led by the United Way's "Center for Community Leadership," the new CEO competency model reflects a simple and practical framework to assist local United Ways in the recruiting and development of CEOs suited to the mission of the future.

The development of the new competency model is a story unto itself; the final articulation of the model does not in itself reveal the iterative and highly collaborative problem-solving process that ultimately identified the key skills and behaviors. Nor does the model itself really capture the nuances and tensions among the skills and behaviors of successful "leaders in action," the ultimate benchmark of performance against the new mission. Although it did not actually inform the development of the new United Way CEO model, the "competing-values" framework that is the focus of this volume is a valuable tool to illuminate those nuances and tensions. The discussion that follows illustrates why and how the ongoing interplay of competing values lies at the heart of the new model for leadership in the "new" United Way. This essay is a case study of leadership change amid organizational change and a vivid example of why competing values, with all the necessary tensions and balancing required, is certainly the wave of the future at United Way and arguably most other major nonprofit organizations as well.

BACKGROUND AND CONTEXT

What is known today as the United Way began in the late 1800s in a few American cities, emerging as a series of social services exchanges, "community chests," and pooled charitable-donation programs to coordinate service provision in communities and achieve greater scale in fundraising efforts. The "movement" expanded, and such organizations proliferated through the 20th century, forming also regional and national associations. In the mid-1960s, building on the progress of earlier national membership efforts, several of the coordinating organizations came together to form the "United Way" as the first-ever national brand; the United Way of America (national office) was established to support the brand and increase the structure and formality of membership in the movement. Over time, more and more local organizations affiliated with the network, paying dues to the national office in exchange for use of the national brand, as well as for training, technical assistance, and other membership support. The local entities, however, maintained their status as separate legal entities and still today operate as a federation of largely autonomous organizations rather than a centralized hierarchy of "chapters" (Aft & Aft, 2004; Brilliant, 1990; Brilliant & Young, 2004; Green, 2004; United Way, 2006a).

Despite its federated culture (or some would say because of it), the United Way became one of the largest and most prominent nonprofit organizations in the United States; today, with its aggregate revenues of more than $4 billion, it remains the overall leader in terms of charitable contributions within the sector. The rise to that level of financial significance in the philanthropic sector did not happen overnight; rather, it is a story of progressive innovation and development of an overall network. A first major innovation was on the "demand side" for human welfare in communities, specifically the alignment of United Ways with community planning councils that analyzed and coordinated focus on key needs of local populations. In some cases these councils were funded by United Ways; in other cases, they operated independently. But in all events they helped focus the rationale and goals for United Way's fundraising.

The second major innovation was on the "supply side" and, specifically, achieving scale in the accumulation of funds for identified needs. In the first part of the 20th century, several local United Ways experimented with and later refined the process of "workplace giving," whereby employees of companies could make charitable contributions through payroll deductions. This fundraising tool spread rapidly and helped fuel the growth of the overall network as more and more member organizations duplicated the innovation. Besides enabling an enormous flow of donations, the workplace campaign strategy (both nationally and locally) helped United Way develop important strategic relationships with the private sector and especially large Fortune 500 companies; they similarly developed ongoing strategic relationships with national health and human services agencies, which were the standard recipients of United Way contributions. United Ways developed ties to both organized labor and corporate management, strengthened by electing labor and management representatives to the volunteer boards at both local and national levels. Not surprisingly, staff leaders of local United Ways increasingly succeeded with and were rewarded for skills primarily related to fundraising within the model of workplace giving and "account management" of leaders of workplace donor organizations and leaders of major social services agencies.

CHALLENGES, SCANDAL, AND LOSS OF RELEVANCE

The United Way fundraising powerhouse that grew through the 20th century was not invincible and faced serious challenges through the 1980s and 1990s. Its near-monopoly position caused problems, both direct and indirect, as changes in the charitable-giving market surpassed United Way's ability to adapt. One early sign of trouble was rising donor complaints in the early 1980s that United Way workplace efforts were coercive, as local United Ways and corporate partners were accused of forcing employees to give up more and more of their paychecks for the campaigns (Aft & Aft, 2004). Just as United Way had begun to get that under control (for example, with new codes of ethics), the movement was rocked by a major scandal that many say, in retrospect, was part of the same monopolistic mindset. In February 1992, the 20-year CEO of United Way of America and innovator of many aspects of the United Way system, William Aramony, was accused of financial mismanagement and use of his position for personal gain and later was convicted and sentenced to seven years in prison ("Ex-United Way Leader Gets 7 Years for Embezzlement," Arenson, 1995, as cited by Green, 2004).

As damaging as the Aramony scandal was, however, the deeper problems of the United Way were more significant in the long term. Simply stated, United Way had lost touch with the expectations and aspirations of its donors, operating as a transactional intermediary in a world increasingly wanting results and relationships. Taking the long view, the scandal of 1992 was more an accelerator than a primary cause of United Way's problems. The pressure for the United Way to change had been building for many years, reflecting a range of environmental pressures on the organization. First was a general increasing scrutiny of nonprofits and rising demands for accountability; in fact, the United Way scandal helped trigger accusations and problems discovered in other large nonprofits (for example, at the Nature Conservancy and the New Era organization, perceived mismanagement of funds by the Red Cross after September 11; personal communication with Brian Gallagher, CEO, United Way of America, June 28, 2005; Light, 2004, as cited by Green, 2004).

Second, during the same time, an increasing competitive marketplace for charitable giving began to arise, the result of an explosion of new (and often smaller, more entrepreneurial) nonprofits that began in the 1990s. Between 1993 and 2003, the number of 503(c)(3) registered organizations grew some 70 percent (United Way of America, Department of Research, 2004). Many of these organizations, led by a new generation of leaders, boasted of more nimble, customer-focused approaches, with an emphasis on measurable results—in step with the growing trend in society and the global economy of greater performance accountability. In parallel, the business model of the United Way was in itself challenged. The centerpiece "workplace campaign" was declining in relevance and effectiveness, as large corporations in some cases merged, in other cases became more decentralized, and in all cases began to adopt less hierarchical and more "worker-empowered" cultures. In aggregate, such changes were forcing the United Way to compete as never before, becoming more donor and relationship focused, emphasizing results and not just number of dollars raised and distributed, and generally operating more transparently and accountably to those investing their dollars and volunteer hours.

Finally, United Way's promise of "doing good" by raising money and donating to direct services for disadvantaged populations also was increasingly out of step with trends in the independent sector. As more theorists and practitioners began to focus not on just "helping the poor" but instead on creating "long-term sustainable change," the United Way's social work assumptions seemed increasingly out of date.

Buffeted by multiple challenges, the United Way suffered decline through the 1990s and early 2000s. The organization's share of market for charitable giving declined significantly, and the total number of donors to United Way also fell; growth in the sector outpaced that of United Way's overall growth (personal communication with Rick Belous, vice president of research, United Way of America, July 25, 2005; personal communication with Brian Gallagher, CEO, United Way of America, June 28, 2005; Green, 2004). The movement seemed adrift, characterized by a now infamous article in *Fortune* magazine, "Can Anybody Fix the United Way?" (Farchaver, 2000).

IMPERATIVE FOR CHANGE

In the years after the Aramony scandal, United Way executives, both locally and nationally, labored to find sources of renewal. Many actions were taken to improve accountability and financial management, but the deeper challenges to the fundamental business model were not really addressed until Brian Gallagher (then CEO of United Way of Columbus, Ohio) and other colleagues formed a task force to plot strategy for a new approach to renew the movement. Out of those deliberations emerged a new mission and strategy, focused on "improving lives by mobilizing the caring power of community," or in current United Way shorthand, becoming leaders of "community impact." Gallagher himself became CEO of the United Way of America in 2001 and has been leading the effort to transform the system ever since. Today, although he has described community impact as in many ways "returning to the roots of who we were" (i.e., as a community self-help organization), he also has been a tireless advocate of the critical new and much more relevant approaches to creating value for donors and investors (for example, focusing more on system-level and sustainable change, creating measurable results, and working collaboratively with a broader representation of the community to set an agenda for change), and developing the strategies to do so.

IMPLICATIONS FOR LEADERSHIP

In general, the new strategy of community impact has been well received by donors, volunteers, and staff. Fully 85 percent of the United Way system now voices commitment to community impact (vs. only about 50 percent in 2000), and overall revenue for the system has begun to rise again (outpacing inflation), much of it directly attributable to shifts to the new way of working. Also, the total number of donors has stabilized, and donated money designated for organizations other than United Way causes have dropped (signaling renewed trust in United Way; personal communication with Rick Belous, vice president of research, United Way of America, July 25, 2005; personal communication with Brian Gallagher, CEO, United Way of America, June 28, 2005; United Way of America, Department of Research, 2003–2004). The transformation, however, is still in its early stages, and members and knowledgeable observers all concede that there remains much to do to build the skills, knowledge, experience, and culture at the local level—and indeed across the entire system—to move from being a fundraising monopoly network to a more performance- and results-driven system of leaders of community change in the cities and towns of America.

A critical leverage point for the transformation rests with the leadership of the local United Ways—especially the staff CEOs. Most local United Ways are relatively small entities—only 95 of the 1,400 local United Ways have staff numbering more than 20, and of the $4.05 billion raised annually, about 65% comes from the largest 82 United Ways. The ability of local CEOs to demonstrate—and operate with the skills, knowledge, and behaviors of—leadership for community impact is thus arguably the most critical change needed to execute the new strategy. Without the right kind of leadership at the top of any local United Way, it is unlikely that the organization will be able to transition to the new strategy and build the kind of community relationships and strategies to really effect measurable improvement in lives.

To enable the necessary change in leadership, United Way of America has taken steps to define a new competency model for the "CEO of the future." Through the work of the Center for Community Leadership (established in 2001 to build knowledge, skills, and processes for transformation), United Way of America has constructed a competency model that is now being used both to recruit new CEOs into the system and to develop current CEOs through focused training, leadership development, and other approaches to behavioral change.

COMPETENCY MODEL FOR UNITED WAY "CEO OF THE FUTURE"

The new competency model was developed following a "star performer" kind of analysis—interviewing and assessing the knowledge, skills, and behaviors of the best CEOs in the system (that is, those who were doing the most to move their United Ways toward community impact and who were able to show results by doing so). As the model was constructed, drafts were iteratively reviewed and revised by other CEOS, leaders (including CEO Brian Gallagher) at the United Way of America, as well as volunteers and outside experts familiar with the United Way system. As consistent patterns started to emerge, the results were codified into what has now become a four-part model (See Figure 21.1). In aggregate, it represents the capabilities required of a leader who can change community in a visionary and collaborative way while also running a professional and increasingly knowledge-based operational organization, whose work is at the same time part of the community itself.

Each of the four components represents one collection of skills, knowledge, and behaviors essential to being a leader of community impact at the local level, addressing not only recent and existing demands of excellent United Way performance but also some strong consensus about emerging demands as the transformation shift continues to evolve. The first part of the model is "Community and Organizational Leadership," a complement of skills and behaviors related to the process of leading the community and the United Way organization in support of improving lives. Key dimensions of this part include

- Visioning and strategic thinking,
- Problem solving and decision making,
- Change leadership,
- Team leadership, and
- Talent development and management.

Although many of these sound relatively standard for any leader of the modern organization, what is special about the nature of this dimension of the competency model is the cross-cutting skills and behaviors required (i.e., visioning and strategic thinking or problem solving not just for one's own organization but also via partnerships and collaborations—for the broader community itself). The same goes for the talent dimension of this component—one needs to think not only about managing the talent of the United Way staff but also in some sense helping develop talent in partner agencies, associations, and across the broader community. Many progressive "community-impact United Ways," for example, run training programs and even provide leadership development opportunities for other community leaders.

FIGURE 21.1
LOCAL UNITED WAY CEO COMPETENCY MODEL

Local United Way CEO Competency Model

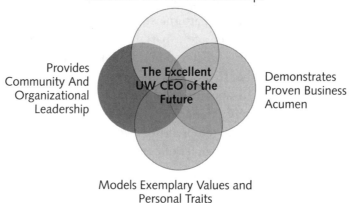

The second part of the model is "impact strategies, resources, relationships," including things such as

- Influence and impact,
- Strategy and product innovation,
- Coalition building,
- Development and investment of resources,
- Volunteer relationship management,
- Investor relationship management, and
- Political astuteness.

These skills and behaviors map heavily to the emerging new business model for the new United Way—which must not only raise funds, but also develop influence in the community, build coalitions and partnerships with multiple stake-holders, and create actual strategies for changing conditions at the community level. Strategies will, of course, require development of resources, but as opposed to simply raising money, the United Way leader must now develop both financial and knowledge resources and use those resources to operationalize actual approaches to making change. For example, leading United Way CEOs pursuing community impact serve on commissions chartered by local mayors; help create public–private partnerships to address causes such as increasing affordable housing units, enhancing early childhood literacy or ending domestic violence; and then also develop "products" to enable robust fundraising in support of such initiatives. The competencies for such leadership in the community derive seminally from the requirements of United Way's new "Standards of Excellence," which were developed in 2005 (United Way of America, 2006b), to articulate the specific business processes and performance objectives for operating as a community-impact United Way.

The third part of the new model is "business acumen," and includes knowledge—at a leadership and senior managerial level of

- Strategic and occupational planning,
- Financial management,
- Brand management,
- Human resources management, and
- Technology management.

All of these represent the kind of knowledge that a modern, well-schooled manager understands, but they are relatively new ideas for United Way CEOs who have not had to oversee such things with any degree of serious professionalism in the past.

The fourth part of the model is the underlying "values and personal traits," which, less substantive than the knowledge of the other components, nonetheless represent critical foundation for the United Way CEO of the future. Key elements of this part include

- Achievement orientation,
- Integrity,
- Flexibility,
- Continuous learning and self-mastery, and
- Inclusiveness.

The elements will again sound familiar to any observer of today's high-performing managers or leaders operating in a hypercompetitive global economy, with all the usual rationale for their being there. However, the last element, "inclusiveness," deserves some extra attention. By *inclusiveness,* United Way means to signify attitudes, behaviors, and processes that deliberately and consistently seek diversity in the people of both staff and community engaged in the new work and proactively aim to include all relevant stakeholders in the broad-based solutions of community impact. Whereas other organizations will often have a "diversity" value or set of initiatives to show its general support for America's increasingly multiracial and multiethnic demographics, for United Way "inclusiveness" is core to the strategy of the new business; the governing assumption is that change cannot be designed or effected at a community level without the active involvement of the increasingly wide diversity of population groups who have a stake in any kind of sustainable change.

CONTRASTING THE PAST AND FUTURE: COMPETING VALUES

At the risk of oversimplification, the new competency model represents a more complex, competitive, relational, knowledge-intensive, and politically dynamic leadership approach versus a simpler, transactional, and static requirement. New leaders are agents of change who innovate, partner, and entrepreneurially build coalitions for getting results; the former leaders raised money in an established way for a relatively unchanging list of priorities for "helping the disadvantaged." With a community-change mission, as opposed to a de facto monopolistic, fund-raising business model, the new United Way leader must constantly balance the short and longer term, the internal and external, the world of vision and solutions, and the world of operations.

The new leadership model of United Way can in fact be more richly understood with the framework of competing values, which is a central theme of this book. The notion that the new leader must find ways to balance a constantly shifting set of paradoxical roles, stepping in and out of "character" depending on the situation and pulled from one role to another depending on differing situations, is perfectly relevant to the more complex, and high-stakes world of community impact, as opposed to classic United Way fundraising work.

Whereas the traditional United Way leader focused on developing and cultivating donors in the community, the new leader has a much higher need for "boundary-spanning" skills, being creative, clever, and politically astute in defining strategies for change, as well as matching strategies to particular segments of interested "investors," and not just "donors." At the same time, he or she must periodically forsake the flexibility and boundary-spanning to ensure the "maximization of output"—keeping his or her organization task-focused and providing good structure and direction to execute on the strategies devised. Too many United Way CEOs, if challenged not just to be fund-raisers, swing to the other extreme and focus on the "world of social work"—but do so as dreamers and impractical thinkers and thus failing to find and deliver the necessary resources to build the momentum of change. Winning on the external side of the work requires "both/and"—managing the paradox of *both* flexibility and control *and* that of innovation and execution.

On the other side of the competing-values framework (looking at matters that are more internal) is the applicability of the complementary paradox between "managing human commitment" and "consolidation and continuity" of organization. Community-impact work is a fundamentally people-based business, calling on both head—the intellect of problem-solving and strategy development—and heart—the empathy and caring that fuels people who want to make a difference in their communities and with others who similarly care. The leader must constantly fan those flames of inspiration and "caring community," showing and modeling consideration for others and facilitating interaction to develop the organization and the values on which such work is founded. At the same time, the leader must be tough and analytically rigorous about the knowledge needed for community change; the people of the organization—and those with whom United Way must partner—must be technically proficient and structured and managed in such a way as to make the operations behind impact strategies high quality, transparent, and all aboveboard. Without such discipline, the "people commitment" can lapse into dangerous "touchy-feely" caring, and the concern for staff and volunteers can take away the necessary expertise and coordination needed for executing on mission. Here again, the flexibility of developing and caring for people must be balanced by the control and discipline of a well-run, continuous, and fact-oriented organization.

FINAL THOUGHTS AND LOOKING AHEAD

Like all transformations, the United Way's shift to community impact is not something to be finished quickly or by the stroke of one or two quick reforms—including a new leadership competency model. The process of evolution is just that—a steady move toward a future model whose outlines are only dimly understood and whose shape becomes clearer only through the experience and reflection on the progress of practice. One of the very biggest challenges is in fact transforming the leadership of the system while actually working with the leaders themselves to understand the challenges and needs for doing this important new work of the future. One of the surest guides as we do so will be to engage our leaders in real-time debate about the requirements of success, based on their actual experience, the results that follow, and the lessons learned that follow from intelligent reflection on what has happened here, there, or elsewhere in United Way communities and why. The richness of the debates—and the intensity of the learning—will be based on the capacity of leaders to confront the inevitable paradoxes of both managing an organization and inspiring a community, innovating for the future while also finding funding based on the present, and finding the balance between inspiring people to be the best that they can be while also disciplining them with just the same goal. The framework of competing values is a tool that can only enrich those discussions.

REFERENCES

Aft, R., & Aft, M. L. (2004). *Grassroots initiatives shape an international movement: United Ways since 1876.* Philadelphia: Philanthropic Press.

Arenson, K. W. (1995, June 23). Ex-United Way leader gets 7 years for embezzlement. *New York Times,* p. A14.

Beer, M., & Nohria, N. (Eds.). (2000). *Breaking the code of change.* Boston: Harvard Business School Press.

Brilliant, E. (1990). *The United Way.* New York: Columbia University Press.

Brilliant, E., & Young, D. R. (2004). The changing identity of federated community service organizations. *Administration in Social Work, 28*(3/4), 23–46.

Farchaver, N. (2000, November 27). Can anybody fix the United Way? *Fortune.* Available at http://money.cnn.com/magazines/fortune/fortune_archive/2000/11/27/292471/index.htm

Gallagher, B. (2001, September). *Reconnecting a national movement.* Unpublished essay. [Available from United Way of America, 701 North Fairfax, Alexandria, VA 22314]

Green, L. (2004). *United Way standards of excellence: Voluntary adoption, organizational learning, and system performance.* Unpublished master's thesis, John F. Kennedy School of Government, Harvard University, Boston.

Light, P. C. (2004). *Sustaining nonprofit performance: The case for capacity building and the evidence to support it.* Washington, DC: Brookings Institution Press.

United Way of America. (2006a). "Our History." Retrieved January 9, 2006, from http://national.unitedway.org/about/history

United Way of America. (2006b). Standards of Excellence. Retrieved January 9, 2005, from http://national.unitedway.org/soe/

United Way of America, Department of Research. (2003–2004). [Membership and other surveys]. Alexandria, VA: Author.

United Way of America, Department of Research. (2004). [Calculations based on IRS data]. Alexandria, VA: Author.

Weil, M. (2005). *The handbook of community practice.* Thousand Oaks, CA: Sage.

Thanks go to the editors of this volume; Brian Gallagher, CEO, United Way of America; and Rick Belous, vice president of research, United Way of America, for comments and suggestions on previous drafts of this chapter. Also, thanks go to William Mills, vice president of talent management, United Way of America; Cheryl Hubbard, director of talent management, United Way of America; and Dr. Karen McGraw, Cognitive Technologies for their work in developing and explicating the local United Way CEO competency model described herein.

Appendix

A Sampling of Web Sites
Related to Nonprofit Management

Compiled by Jeffrey A. Edwards
and Shannon Sellers-Harty

As a collection of computer networks that has been growing at an incredible rate, the Internet via the World Wide Web makes it possible for nonprofit managers to access up-to-date information about many topics, ranging from government policy to information about foundations and corporations. Numerous Web sites are of value to those involved in nonprofit management, and new sites are created every day.

A wealth of information can be obtained from a range of government, for-profit, and nonprofit organizations. Nonprofit managers often find that the Internet can help them locate possible funding sources and compile information that they need for funding proposals. Managers also may find that is useful to get current updates on legislation and governmental policy initiatives on the Web.

Given the new sites are rapidly being added to the Web, it is impossible to print an up-to-date, authoritative list of addresses. The following list is a starting point for nonprofit managers who want to access online resources.

ORGANIZATIONS

Alliance for Nonprofit Management
1899 L Street, NW, 6th Floor, Washington, DC 20036
202-955-8406
http://www.allianceonline.org
Professional association of organizations and individuals devoted to improving the management and governance capacities of nonprofit organizations.

American Association of Fund-Raising Counsel
4700 W. Lake Avenue, Glenview, IL 60025
800-462-2372
http://www.aafrc.org
Represents professional fundraising firms who help nonprofits plan and manage fundraising campaigns. Also publishes the annual *Giving USA*.

BoardSource
1828 L Street, NW, Suite 900, Washington, DC 20036-5104
202-452-6262
http://www.boardsource.org
Dedicated to improving the effectiveness of nonprofit organizations by strengthening their boards.

Center for Community Change
1000 Wisconsin Avenue, NW, Washington, DC 20007
202-342-0519
http://www.communitychange.org
Provides resources to nonprofits assisting low-income populations and helps racial and ethnic groups with planning, organizational, and fundraising issues.

Charity Channel
30021 Tomas, Suite 300, Rancho Santa Margarita, CA 92688-2128
949-589-5938
http://www.charitychannel.com
Goal is to create a place where nonprofit professionals can share information and learn from each other.

Council on Foundations
1828 L Street, NW, Washington, DC 20036
202-466-6512
http://www.cof.org
A nonprofit membership association of grant-making foundations and corporations, whose mission is to promote responsible and effective philanthropy. Members include nearly 1,500 independent, operating, family, community, public, and company-sponsored foundations; corporate giving programs; and foundations in other countries.

Donors Forum of Chicago
208 South LaSalle Street, Suite 740, Chicago, IL 60604
312-578-0090
http://www.donorsforum.org
Serves as a resource in leadership, education, research, and action on behalf of philanthropy and nonprofits.

The Foundation Center
79 Fifth Avenue, New York, NY 10003-3076
212-620-4230
http://www.fdncenter.org
Independent nonprofit information clearinghouse established to foster public understanding of the foundation field by collecting, organizing, analyzing, and disseminating information on foundations, corporate giving, and related subjects. Operates libraries at five locations, including national collections at its national office in New York City and at its field office in Washington, DC, and regional collections at its offices in Atlanta, Cleveland, and San Francisco. Center libraries provide access to a unique collection of materials on philanthropy and are open to the public free of charge.

The Grantsmanship Center
1125 W. Sixth Street, 5th Floor, PO Box 17220, Los Angeles, CA 90017
213-482-9860
http://www.tgci.com
A training organization that conducts workshops nationwide on grant writing, program management, fundraising, and other issues that affect the nonprofit sector.

GuideStar
4801 Courthouse Street, Suite 220, Williamsburg, VA 23188
757-229-4631
http://www.guidestar.org
Provides information on more than 600,000 American charities and nonprofit organizations, including up-to-date news on philanthropy and resources for donors and volunteers. Entire database is searchable by key word.

Harvard Business School, Initiative on Social Enterprise
http://www.hbs.edu/socialenterprise
Shares knowledge that helps individuals and organizations create and foster social value in the nonprofit, public, and private sectors.

Independent Sector
1200 18th Street, NW, Suite 200, Washington, DC 20036
202-467-6100
http://www.independentsector.org
A national coalition of nonprofit organizations, foundations, and corporate giving programs working to encourage philanthropy, volunteering, nonprofit initiatives, and citizen action that help better serve people and communities. Involved in advocacy, research, and leadership development activities.

Internet Nonprofit Center, Evergreen State Society
PO Box 20682, Seattle, WA 98102-0682
http://www.nonprofits.org
Internet resource about nonprofits and their work; information shared primarily through online discussions.

The Leader to Leader Institute
320 Park Avenue, Third Floor, New York, NY 10022
212-224-1174
Mission is to strengthen the leadership of the social sector by providing educational and leadership opportunities.

Mandel Center for Nonprofit Organizations, Case Western Reserve University
10900 Euclid Avenue, Cleveland, OH 44016
800-760-2275
http://www.cwru.edu/mandelcenter
An important resource for nonprofit managers and leaders, faculty members, researchers, and anyone who works in, supports, or studies the nonprofit/ nongovernmental sector.

National Committee for Responsive Philanthropy
2001 S Street, NW, Suite 620, Washington, DC 20009
202-387-9177
http://www.ncrp.org
Committed to making philanthropy more responsive to people who are socially, economically, and politically disadvantaged and to the dynamic needs of increasingly diverse communities nationwide. Programs aim to maximize the financial capacities of organizations that seek justice for these populations.

Nonprofit Resources Catalogue
http://www.informika.ru/text/intern/nonprof/Fundraising_and_Giving.html
Catalogs Internet sites that could benefit nonprofits and those interested in a wide variety of issues. Emphasis on metalinks to other catalogs in a particular subject area.

Nonprofit Sector Research Fund, The Aspen Institute
One Dupont Circle, NW, Suite 700, Washington, DC 20036
202-736-5838
http://www.nonprofitresearch.org
Awards grants and organizes conventions to expand knowledge of the nonprofit sector, philanthropy, nonprofit practices, and public policy related to nonprofits.

The Urban Institute
2100 M Street, NW, Washington, DC 20037
http://www.urban.org/index.htm
202-833-7200
Objectives are to sharpen thinking about society's social and economic problems and efforts to solve them, improve government decisions and their implementation, and increase citizens' awareness about important public choices. Provides up-to-date information on institute activities and research centers and also provides information about the National Center on Charitable Statistics, http://nccsdataweb.urban.org/FAQ/index.php?category=31

Volunteer Match
385 Grove Street, San Francisco, CA 94102
415-241-6868
http://www.volunteermatch.org
Uses the Internet to match volunteers with local nonprofit and public sector organizations.

PERIODICAL PUBLICATIONS

Chronicle of Philanthropy
1255 23rd Street, NW, Washington, DC 20037
800-842-7817
http://www.philanthropy.com
Published biweekly.

Connections
Association of Professional Researchers for Advancement
40 Shuman Boulevard, Suite 325, Naperville, IL 60563
630-717-8160
http://www.aprahome.org/publications/connections/connections.htm
Published quarterly, a journal of scholarly articles about advancement, management, and other fundraising issues.

Foundation News & Commentary
Council on Foundations
1828 L Street, NW, Washington, DC 20036
202-466-6512
http://www.cof.org
Published bimonthly.

Grassroots Fundraising Journal
3781 Broadway, Oakland, CA 94611
888-458-8588
http://www.grassrootsfundraising.org
Published bimonthly.

Nonprofit and Voluntary Sector Quarterly
http://www.spea.iupui.edu/nrsq/
Published quarterly by Sage Publications; sponsored by the Association for Research on Nonprofit Organizations and Voluntary Action.

Nonprofit Management and Leadership
http://www.josseybass.com/WileyCDA/WileyTitle/productCd-NML.html
Published quarterly by Jossey-Bass Publishers.

Nonprofit World
Society for Nonprofit Organizations
5820 Canton Center Road, Suite 165, Canton, MI 48187
734-451-3582
http://www.snpo.org/publications/nonprofitworld.php
Published bimonthly.

Index

About the Editors

Richard L. Edwards, PhD, ACSW, is dean and professor in the School of Social Work at Rutgers: The State University of New Jersey. Dr. Edwards was formerly dean of the School of Social Work and interim provost at the University of North Carolina at Chapel Hill and also dean of the Mandel School of Applied Social Sciences at Case Western Reserve University in Cleveland. He has worked in a variety of nonprofit and public organizations as a supervisor and manager and has served on the boards of directors of several nonprofits. In addition, he is a senior consultant with Doug Eadie and Company, a private consulting firm specializing in nonprofits. A frequent contributor to the management literature, he is coauthor of *Building a Strong Foundation: Fundraising for Nonprofits* and was editor-in-chief of *The Encyclopedia of Social Work—19th Edition*. He is a former president of the National Association of Social Workers.

John A. Yankey, PhD, is Leonard W. Mayo Professor Emeritus of Family and Child Welfare at the Mandel School of Applied Social Sciences at Case Western Reserve University in Cleveland. Dr. Yankey is a nationally recognized expert in the areas of strategic planning and developing strategic alliances. He continues to teach courses in both subjects at the Mandel School and at the Mandel Center for Nonprofit Organizations. He is an instructor in several state and national leadership development programs for public sector and nonprofit leaders, as well as a consultant to a wide range of organizations throughout the United States. He is coauthor of *Building a Strong Foundation: Fundraising for Nonprofits* and a frequent contributor to the nonprofit management literature.

About the Contributors

David M. Austin, PhD, is the Bert Kruger Smith Centennial Professor Emeritus in the School of Social Work at the University of Texas at Austin. Dr. Austin was a member of the Board of Directors of the Institute for the Advancement of Social Work Research and has many years of experience in community organization and social planning, as well as a distinguished career in university teaching and research. He has published extensively on issues related to management, evaluation, planning, and policy.

Darlyne Bailey, PhD, LISW, is vice president for academic affairs and dean of Teachers College, Columbia University. Dr. Bailey focuses her teaching, research, and service on leadership and organizational and interorganizational development. Previously, she served as dean of the Mandel School of Applied Social Sciences at Case Western Reserve University in Cleveland.

Richard E. Baznik, BA, is presidential fellow and director of the Institute for the Study of the University in Society at Case Western Reserve University in Cleveland. From 1987 to 2003, he served as vice president for public affairs and vice president for community and government relations at Case Western. Mr. Baznik was also special assistant to the president and director of communications. He has consulted on strategic planning and policy issues for several American universities and for the French National Ministry of Education. He completed the executive program in the Darden Graduate School of Business at the University of Virginia.

Elizabeth A. S. Benefield, MA, is president of Elizabeth Benefield Consulting, which helps nonprofits strategically develop effective and sustainable fundraising capacities. Ms. Benefield was formerly assistant dean for development and external affairs in the School of Social Work at the University of North Carolina at Chapel Hill. She is coauthor of *Building a Strong Foundation: Fundraising for Nonprofits*.

Andrew Broughton, PhD, is director of monitoring and evaluation at the National Center for Child Traumatic Stress, Duke University Medical Center. Previously, Dr. Broughton was senior research associate in the School of Social Work at the University of North Carolina at Chapel Hill, where he was responsible for designing and delivering training courses in technology and helping nonprofit organizations use computer technology.

David Campbell, PhD, is vice president of the Community Service Society of New York and adjunct faculty member in the Executive MPA Program at Columbia University. His doctoral research at Case Western Reserve University in Cleveland, focused on nonprofit mergers.

Todd Cohen, JD, is editor and publisher of the *Philanthropy Journal*, which he created in 2000 for the A. J. Fletcher Foundation in Raleigh, North Carolina. Mr. Cohen worked for weekly and daily newspapers in Massachusetts and North Carolina before joining *The News & Observer* in Raleigh, in 1981. During his tenure there, he reported on city and state government and politics and on education, insurance, and utilities, and also served as business editor.

S. Kay Dunlap, PhD, is assistant professor of education in the Department of Education and Allied Studies at John Carroll University in University Heights, Ohio. Dr. Dunlap's research interests include literacy and professional development. Among other academic activities, she is engaged in a research project related to cultural exchange programming. Before teaching at the university, Dr. Dunlap taught in the Shaker Heights, Ohio, school system.

Douglas C. Eadie, MS, is president of Doug Eadie and Company, a consulting firm that specializes in helping nonprofit and public organizations build higher impact board leadership and stronger board–CEO partnerships and take command of their own strategic change. Before founding his international consulting and speaking business, Mr. Eadie served in a variety of nonprofit and public executive positions, including community college vice president, state and city budget director, and chief operating officer of a large social services agency. As a Peace Corps volunteer, he taught for three years in Addis Ababa, Ethiopia.

Jeffrey A. Edwards, BA, is registered investment advisor with Lincoln Financial Advisors in Charlotte, North Carolina. Formerly, Mr. Edwards was prospect research analyst in the Office of Development at the University of North Carolina at Chapel Hill. He is coauthor of *Building a Strong Foundation: Fundraising for Nonprofits.*

M. Jennifer Ellison, BA, is a MSW student at the University of North Carolina at Chapel Hill. Her academic focus is in child and adolescent mental health. Before beginning her graduate studies, Ms. Ellison worked on issues of social justice, human rights, and marginalized populations for five years.

Jeff Griffiths, BS, is coordinator at Business Volunteers Unlimited (BVU), where he manages the organization's communitywide Volunteer Center, involving thousands of individuals, school groups, and senior citizens; he also assists businesses by involving employees in productive and rewarding volunteer activities and helps nonprofits engage volunteers from businesses and the community-at-large. Before joining BVU, Mr. Griffiths was project development coordinator for the Business Shares program at Chicago Cares, a nonprofit organization that provides opportunities for individuals and businesses to improve the Chicago community through participation in creative, structured-group volunteer programs designed to address Chicago's most pressing needs. He has customized, led, and managed the logistics of numerous group volunteer opportunities for corporations and nonprofits in the Greater Chicago area.

Christine E. Henry, MNO, is a consultant and certified coach who consults nonprofit organizations in the areas of program development, planning, communications, and fundraising. A former director of the William J. and Dorothy K. O'Neill Foundation in Cleveland, Ohio, Ms. Henry has served in various capacities in community education, hospital administration, and nonprofit public relations and volunteer management.

Thomas P. Holland, PhD, is professor and codirector of the Institute for Nonprofit Organizations in the School of Social Work at the University of Georgia, Athens. He has published extensively on nonprofit management and governance. Recent publications include *Improving Board Effectiveness: Practical Lessons for Nonprofit Health Care Organizations* and *How to Build a More Effective Board.* Dr. Holland teaches courses, conducts research, and consults internationally on issues in the management of nonprofit organizations. At the University of Georgia, Dr. Holland formerly served as director of the School of Social Work's Center for Social Services Research and Development and its doctoral program. He has also held the positions of associate dean and chairman of the

Doctoral Program at the Mandel School of Applied Social Sciences, Case Western Reserve University in Cleveland.

Barbara Jacobus, MNO, spent 10 years in new market development both domestically and in Southeast Asia for a for-profit corporation. Ms. Jacobus currently is president of Sententia Inc., a nonprofit management consulting firm in Cleveland.

Alice Korngold, MSEd, is an international consultant to corporations, foundations, and nonprofit organizations in the areas of corporate social responsibility, leadership development, and nonprofit governance. She is the author of *Leveraging Good Will: Strengthening Nonprofits By Engaging Businesses*. Ms. Korngold was the founding executive of Business Volunteers Unlimited, a national model organization that has placed more than 1,000 business executives on 275 nonprofit boards of directors. Her leadership training model has been recognized in *The Wall Street Journal*, the *New York Times*, and the *Chronicle of Philanthropy*.

Paul A. Kurzman, PhD, ACSW, is dean and professor in the Hunter College School of Social Work and the Graduate Center of the City University of New York. Dr. Kurzman specializes in organizational theory, risk management, and occupational social work practice. He has been administrator of public and nonprofit human services agencies and is author or editor of six books and numerous articles in professional journals. He contributed "Professional Liability and Malpractice" to the 19th edition of the *Encyclopedia of Social Work*.

Daniel A. Lebold, MSW, is director of development for the University Center for International Studies at the University of North Carolina at Chapel Hill. Before this appointment, Mr. Lebold served for five years as vice president of development at Triangle Family Services in Raleigh, North Carolina. He also served as assistant dean for administration and coordinator of the Nonprofit Leadership Certificate Program in the university's School of Social Work. He has more than 20 years of fund-raising and board experience in both public and nonprofit organizations.

Brook Manville, PhD, is executive vice president, United Way of America, and director of the Center for Community Leadership. Dr. Manville began his career on the faculty of Northwestern University and subsequently worked for media, technology, and consulting businesses. He has published widely in both academic and business publications. His academic training is in the classics and history.

Andrea Meier, PhD, is research assistant professor in the School of Social Work at the University of North Carolina at Chapel Hill. Her research focuses on multimethod intervention research methodologies and evaluation strategies. Other research interests include therapeutic applications of the Internet to social support groups.

Susan L. Parish, PhD, is assistant professor in the School of Social Work at the University of North Carolina at Chapel Hill. Her research addresses the impact of health and poverty policy on families affected by disability. Dr. Parish also has eight years of experience administering residential and family support programs for people with developmental disabilities and their families.

Janice K. Parish, BA, has 14 years of experience administering residential, recreation, and family support programs for people with developmental disabilities and their families.

Emily Pelton, MPA, has served and advised nonprofit organizations for ten years, including the humanitarian organization CARE, several U.S. colleges and universities, and small community service-delivery nonprofits. She also served as a budget examiner at the federal Office of Management and a member of the Office of the President's Science Advisor staff. She currently provides independent consulting services to nonprofit and nongovernmental organizations in organizational analysis, strategic planning, policy research, and fundraising.

Shannon Sellers-Harty, MTS, is enrolled in the MSW program in the School of Social Work at the University of North Carolina at Chapel Hill, where she has worked as a graduate research assistant. Her divinity degree is from Vanderbilt University.

Kimberly Strom-Gottfried, PhD, is professor in the School of Social Work at the University of North Carolina at Chapel Hill, where she teaches in the areas of direct practice, communities and organizations, and human resources management. Her scholarly interests involve ethics, managed care, and social work education. Dr. Strom-Gottfried has held leadership and administrative positions in the public and nonprofit sectors, as well as in academic institutions.

Marci S. Thomas, MHA, CPA, is clinical assistant professor in the Department of Health Policy and Administration at the University of North Carolina at Chapel Hill. Ms. Thomas writes and teaches continuing education for CPAs nationally on physician practice management, managed care, and various nonprofit topics. She also consults with nonprofits and health care organizations in the areas of financial management, process improvement, and governance, with an emphasis on Sarbanes–Oxley.

John E. Tropman, PhD, is professor in the School of Social Work and the School of Business at the University of Michigan in Ann Arbor, where he also teaches courses in the Program in Nonprofit Executive Leadership. Dr. Tropman has authored and edited several books, including *Meetings: How to Make Them Work for You* and *Making Meetings Work: Achieving High-Quality Decisions in Groups and Teams.* He frequently provides consultation and training to nonprofit organizations across the United States.

Charles L. Usher, PhD, is Wallace H. Kuralt Professor of Public Welfare Policy and Administration in the School of Social Work at the University of North Carolina at Chapel Hill. Dr. Usher formerly was director of the Center for Policy Studies at the Research Triangle Institute. He currently is directing evaluation activities in several systems change initiatives sponsored by national foundations. He also manages a program sponsored by the Annie E. Casey Foundation that seeks to identify and provide apprenticeship opportunities for consultants who can assist foundation grantees to develop their capacity for self-evaluation.

Elizabeth Hosler Voudouris, MA, is executive vice president, Business Volunteers Unlimited (BVU). In this role, Ms. Voudouris provides consulting, education, management assistance, and executive coaching services to strengthen the governance and management of nonprofit organizations, and she also is responsible for fund development and community outreach activities for BVU. In addition, she provides consulting services to businesses to establish and enhance strong community involvement and programs. She has provided national training and consulting services to assist other U.S. cities in replicating the BVU model and has coauthored a chapter in *Corporate Philanthropy at a Crossroads.*

Carol K. Willen, PhD, is manager of the Nonprofit and Public Service Center at Lakeland Community College in Kirtland, Ohio. Dr. Willen previously served as director of academic programs and student services at Case Western Reserve University's Mandel Center for Nonprofit Organizations and as senior program officer for education at The Cleveland Foundation.

Laura I. Zimmerman, PhD, is medical student in the University of North Carolina at Chapel Hill School of Medicine. Previously, Dr. Zimmerman was clinical associate professor at the School of Social Work at the University of North Carolina at Chapel Hill, where she directed the Computing and Information Technology Unit. She serves on nonprofit boards and has frequently consulted with nonprofits about computing and technology.